The ecology of natural resources

D1480220

I. G. SIMMONS

A Halsted Press book

John Wiley and Sons
New York

© I. G. Simmons 1974

First published 1974
by Edward Arnold (Publishers) Ltd
25 Hill Street, London W1X 8LL

Published in the U.S.A. by Halsted Press,
a Division of John Wiley & Sons, Inc.
New York

ISBN 0 470–79194–2
LC # 74–4812

Printed in Great Britain

Preface

There are now so many books dealing with man's relationships with his environment that yet another deserves some apologia for adding to them. My reasons for writing it spring from several years of teaching in this field, during which I found that many of the books I read and recommended to students were either too limited in scope or spatial coverage or too strident in their viewpoint for my taste. This book is the end-product of my reaction to that situation. I hope it will be primarily useful for students reading appropriate courses at second- and third-year levels in British universities, and for upper-division courses in North America; but I would stress that it is intended as an introduction and no more. Each component section has its own greater complexities, and I hope that some readers will use this book as a springboard for deeper studies. Beyond these people, other readers with an interest in the subjects discussed here may find in it some materials upon which to base their views as citizens.

To use the word 'ecology' in the title demands some further explanation, since it is a word whose meaning has latterly become not only elastic but stretched so far that it is unlikely to hold anything up. I take it to mean the study of the relationships of living organisms to each other and their inanimate environment, and I include man as one of those organisms. I have avoided the term 'human ecology' because I think that the local concept of ecology is a holistic viewpoint which is broken up a little more every time a qualifying adjective is attached, and I prefer to conceive of an 'ecology' in which, from time to time and place to place, one or other of the components may be dominant. In cities it is man, at the North Pole it is nature. But the admission of man means not only a particular species of tool- and material-using beast but a cultural animal also. If, as I believe and as will become apparent as the book progresses, ecology teaches us about the limits imposed by the dynamics and structure of natural systems, then we must also realize that all adjustments within this envelope must be made through the medium of culture. Thus economics, ethology and ethics all have a role to play in bringing about more harmonious interactions between man and nature. The special contribution, if any, of the geographer lies in his interest in (would that I could say understanding of) the points at which both natural and social systems meet.

Trying to cover such a wide field of knowledge and opinion brings two major problems. The first is that important material may be overlooked and, equally important, wrong interpretations may be made of published data and views. Oliver Goldsmith suggested that 'a book may be amusing with numerous errors, or it may be very dull without a single absurdity', and I would rather be classified in the first category: I shall be surprised if those thus offended do not make my mistakes clear to me. A second difficulty is the ageing of material between final draft and publication, especially in many of the areas covered in this book. As a partial attack on this problem, an Appendix written at the time of the submission of final proofs has been included: this sketches some of the more outstanding developments between the summer of 1973 and the early spring of 1974.

To acknowledge adequately all the help I have had would require a chapter in itself, but some debts are so great that they must be mentioned here. The basic idea of this type of book was conceived in that fertile womb, the Berkeley campus of the University of California. I am grateful to the American Council of Learned Societies for their award of an American Studies Program Fellowship, which made possible that year of study, fruitful also in fields other than resource studies, and to James Parsons, Chairman during 1964–5, who made me so welcome at Berkeley, then and since. During that year I first met Dan Luten, under whose genial but mind-stretching tutelage I have subsequently always regarded myself, even when the physical distance between us has been considerable. I have also benefited greatly from a Winston Churchill Memorial Trust Travelling Fellowship held in 1971 and 1972, which enabled me to visit North America and Japan to gather valuable information and meet interesting people. During the academic year 1972–3, I was Visiting Professor at York University, Toronto, and as well as paying a handsome salary, that lively institution provided time in which to prepare the final draft. Florence Davies, my secretary at York, typed furiously but accurately, checked references, packed parcels of manuscript and, most important of all, acted as intermediary between me and the Secretarial Services unit who actually produced the final typescript. The Chairman of the Department of Geography, Bill Found, who probably realized his Visiting Professor was more a visitor than a professor, bore this situation with a calm cheerfulness for which I am very grateful.

From my undergraduate days onwards, I have had the benefit of advice from and discussion with Palmer Newbould, currently of the New University of Ulster; much of this took place in contexts where that admirable material, ethyl alcohol, was consumed, and he can always claim that I thus misinterpreted totally what he told me. Since 1962 my membership of the Department of Geography at Durham has been a secure base from which to work and travel, and in particular its Head, Professor W. B. Fisher, has striven to provide conditions conducive to the production of academic work. Early drafts were typed by the grossly overladen secretarial staff of the Department, among whom Suzanne Eckford must be specially thanked. During 1969–70 a particularly lively group of students wrote essays along the themes of this book; none has been directly plagiarized, but some provided interest and stimulus, especially those by Cathy Goulder, Richard de Bastion, John Richardson, John Button, Alastair Steel, Jill Evered and Roger Weatherley.

My wife Carol deserves more than a paragraph to herself, for she has read, commented on, punctuated, corrected and re-read practically every word of this book, more than once while coping with domestic chores as well as this academic drudgery; only I know just how much she has helped.

Finally, this book is dedicated to my parents, Chris and Charles Simmons, as an inadequate, if sincere, expression of filial gratitude.

Contents

Names of organizations abbreviated in text and bibliography

AAAS	American Association for the Advancement of Science (Washington, DC)
AAG	Association of American Geographers (Washington, DC)
BTA	British Travel Association (London)
FAO	The Food and Agriculture Organization of the United Nations (Rome)
IBP	International Biological Programme (London)
IUCN	International Unions for the Conservation of Nature and Natural Resources (Morges, Switzerland)
NAS/NRC	National Academy of Sciences/National Research Council (Washington, DC)
OECD	Organization for Economic Co-operation and Development (Paris)
RFF	Resources for the Future Inc. (Washington, DC)
UNESCO	United Nations Educational, Social and Cultural Organization (Paris)

Part I
Introduction

1

Nature and resources

Man is a material-using animal. Everything he uses, from the food needed to keep him alive to the objects he fabricates, whether tools or sculptures, comes from the substances of the planet on which he lives. Wastes are then returned to the biological and abiotic systems of the earth. And because of his acquisition of culture, man desires to use these systems for non-utilitarian purposes of a recreational or spiritual kind.

If we look more closely at how man utilizes and processes materials from his surroundings, we see that a first group consists of resources which are used in the processes of the metabolism of his body, such as food and water (Table 1.1). These allow the growth and renewal of tissue and provide energy for chemical processes such as movement. The energy is consumed: it is transformed from chemical energy to heat and given off to the atmosphere, from whence it cannot be reclaimed. As a result of energy consumption and metabolic processes, excretory matter is produced. This often contains mineral substances which could be of value, for instance as plant food, and so use does not here necessarily mean consumption. The fact that in industrial societies these 'waste' materials are usually dumped in the nearest large body of water is not relevant to the basic chemistry of the processes. The substances which go to make up our bodies are theoretically available for re-use upon our death—as T. S. Eliot put it:

> . . . and ashes to the earth
> Which is already flesh, faeces
> Bone of man and beast, cornstalk and leaf.

The pattern of material use within the body is genetically and biologically determined, but the disposal of waste products and dead individuals is subject to considerable variation owing to different cultural practices among dissimilar groups of men.

The use of materials outside the human body, whether raw or chemically or biologically processed, is likewise subject to variations in practice. Many of these materials are non-renewable resources, like metals or stone; but some, such as wood and wood products, like paper, come from renewable resources. Re-use of the objects possessed is usually theoretically possible except where a transformation process is used to get rid of it, as in the disposal of waste paper by burning. That the opportunities to re-use materials may not be taken is again irrelevant to the basic characteristics of the resource.

A third group comprises resources used outside the body, the gathering of which leaves them unaltered. Such features of our surroundings as scenery, wildlife (if observed rather

TABLE 1.1   Daily human metabolic turnover

			Male of 154 lb (69·8 kg)				
		Input				*Output*	
Protein	80 g	Water	2,220 g		Water	2,542 g	
Fats	150 g	Food	523 g	BECOMES	Solids	61 g	
Carbohydrates	270 g				Carbon dioxide	928 g	
Solids and minerals	23 g	Oxygen	862 g		Other substances (CO, H_2, CH_4, H_2S, NH_3 plus organic compounds)	54 g	

Source: McHale 1972

than hunted) and water, for swimming or sailing, remain unchanged by our use of them for recreation and aesthetic satisfaction. Attrition of scenery may occur because there are too many users, or water may be fouled by the sailors and thus rendered unusable for the swimmers, but the potential exists for entirely non-consumptive and non-transformational use.

The total flow of a resource from its state in nature through its period of contact with man to its disposal (either consumptively or in a form available for re-use) can be termed a *resource process* (Firey 1960). Resource processes can be studied in a variety of ways. We can, for instance, see them as a set of interactions between living and non-living components of the biosphere in all their various solid, liquid and gaseous phases, and man may play a dominant role in these systems or may indeed have no part whatsoever. Such a viewpoint is generally termed ecological.

A second approach is to explore the manner in which the distribution of resources to people is achieved in various societies in attempts to match the demand and supply of a particular resource, i.e. the viewpoint of economics. Another method of study judges how man ought to use the biosphere and its resources, both for particular cultures and for the species as a whole: this is a particular branch of ethics. Yet again, the relationship between man's culture and his surroundings can be inspected in a behavioural context, thus studying the psychological activity leading up to the use of the earth's substances and habitats: this is clearly part of the field of ethology.

This book aims to emphasize the first of these four categories, the ecological point of view; but it recognizes that the objective, scientific study demanded by ecology does not portray the totality of man's interaction with the systems of this planet which comprises resource processes; it allows that many other factors, and in particular those usually designated as cultural, are of considerable importance. The next section of Part I expands upon the themes of nature and culture, especially the outgrowths of the latter such as economics and ethology.

Nature

The natural world may be studied in many ways, and the classification and cataloguing of phenomena have occupied many workers during human history. For our present purposes, studies which emphasize the connections between the various components, and especially the dependence of living organisms upon their abiotic environments, are most useful; hence the emphasis upon ecology, which can also encompass the impact of man upon natural systems. Since ecology is the study of living organisms and their relationship to each other and their surroundings, it is therefore mostly a study of the biosphere, which is influenced by the lithosphere, as in soil parent material, and the atmosphere, as in the incidence of climatic elements. The aggregate may appropriately be called the ecosphere. Since most of man's resources come from the ecosphere and since in gaining them he has greatly changed the ecology, the relevance of ecological study to our present theme cannot be gainsaid.

Within the subject of ecology various divisions have been made, generally focusing on one of the components of the biosphere and studying how all the other parts affect it. Thus plant ecology centres upon how plants and plant communities are affected by climate, soil, animals and other variables; animal ecology is concerned with their effect upon animals. Both may also study the reciprocal effects of the organisms upon their environment: how a growing forest affects microclimate, for example.

In every ecological system there are natural limits to the total amount of living matter that can be supported. These may be set by something as basic as the amount of solar radiation incident upon that part of the earth. Clearly, the polar regions receive insufficient of this to support the unaided growth of banana trees. On the other hand it may be spatial: a rocky islet may be filled to capacity at the nesting time of a particular bird and thus will determine the population level of those creatures, even if the sea around is teeming with fish waiting to give themselves up. Another important limitation is often the supply of a nutrient element: nitrogen and phosphorus frequently play this role. Ecology hence provides an envelope criterion for resource processes by telling us whether in the long run a particular process is possible or impossible. If it tells us that the maximum number of people that can be fed on the incident solar radiation trapped by photosynthesis is x billion, then this is an absolute limit. If it tells us that the continued practice of shifting agriculture or moor-burning will result in devastating soil erosion, then the presence of an absolute limit has been demonstrated and cultural adjustment must seek to work within it.

Ecosystems

A system is usually defined as a set of objects together with the relationships between the objects and their attributes: the ecology of an area can thus be categorized. The view of ecology encouraged by such a framework is obviously one which stresses interaction between parts and the mechanisms which control such connectivities. We can therefore designate a special class of systems dealing with ecological components, and call them *ecosystems*.

The term ecosystem was coined in 1935 by Tansley, but the concept has a much longer history, many attempts having been made to characterize the immense complexity and holistic character of the natural world. Thus the terms *microcosm, naturcomplex, holocoen* and *biosystem* have all been used from time to time for what is now generally called the ecosystem, with the major exception of the Soviet Union, where the term *biogeocoenose* is used with more or less the same meaning. As Tansley (1935) stressed, the term ecosystem includes not only the organisms, but

> also the whole complex of physical factors forming what we call the environment.

Terser and more rigorous definitions have been given by Lindemann (1942):

> a system composed of physical-chemical-biological processes active within a space-time unit of any magnitude

and E. P. Odum (1959):

> any area of nature that includes living organisms and non-living substances interacting to produce an exchange of materials between the living and non-living parts is an ecological system or ecosystem.

Two important characteristics stand out. Firstly the concept can be applied at any scale: a drop of water inhabited by protozoa is an ecosystem; so is the whole planet. This immediately introduces the problem of boundary definition: few ecosystems can satisfactorily be defined in space because one or more of their components overlaps with another system. A pond may appear to be a clearly bounded system, but the behaviour of wild ducks belies this simplicity.

A second feature is the reciprocity between living and non-living parts of the system. Not only does the 'environment' affect the organisms, but they in turn may change it. This has long been realized from studies of ecological succession, but in resource studies it becomes important to realize that use of the biotic member of an ecosystem as a resource may bring about changes in the non-living part too. The relationship between a forest and its soils is a very closely interconnected one, for example, and the replacement of deciduous trees by conifers in the temperate zone will often bring about a change in soil type from a Brown Earth to a Podzol.

The scientific study of ecosystems is clearly difficult: mere inventory of all the components will not tell us about the connectivity which has been so strongly stressed, and research has indicated that two of the most important pegs upon which to hang functional studies of ecosystems are the flows of energy and matter within a given (and often imperfectly bounded) ecosystem.

Energy in ecosystems

In all ecosystems, as indeed in all studies of resource processes, the role of energy is crucial. Without the input of energy from the sun, life could not exist; the movements of air and water in the atmosphere are driven by this source, and even non-renewable resources of a geological nature have been formed as the result of solar energy. Coal and limestone are obvious instances; sandstones derive from weathering processes that are themselves impelled by inputs of solar energy. Nothing more fundamental to the nature of the planet can be imagined (Woodwell 1970a, Gates 1971).

The total amount of solar energy that reaches the earth's surface is probably in the order of 3,400 kcal/m²/day. This is an average figure since the amount (flux density) is different from place to place. The maximum conversion of this energy by photosynthesis absorbs c. 170 kcal/m²/day (5 per cent); the average is inevitably lower (H. T. Odum 1971). The whole of organic life depends upon this small fraction, for the only way of fixing solar energy for use by living creatures is by green plants; our stores of energy from coal and petroleum are merely fixed solar energy in a compressed and fossilized form.

Photosynthesis is the process by which green plants trap energy and incorporate it in complex organic molecules which then form food for themselves and other organisms. In a very complex series of reactions, water and carbon dioxide combine to synthesize sugars which may then be metabolized to starches, or which by the addition of mineral nutrients will form the very complex molecules (amino-acids and proteins, for example) which are the basis of living matter. But not all the energy gained by photosynthesis appears as plant tissue, for some is used in the metabolism of the plant, e.g. in the process of respiration. Thus in the Silver Springs ecosystem in Florida studied by H. T. Odum (1957):

Insolation	1,700,000 kcal/m²/yr	
Absorbed by plants	410,000 kcal/m²/yr	
Photosynthesized	20,810 kcal/m²/yr	Gross primary productivity
Photosynthesis minus respiration	8,833 kcal/m²/yr	Net primary productivity

Of the original incident energy, therefore, only c. 0·5 per cent appears as plant material. The production of living matter by plants is clearly a vital element where biotic resources are concerned. The rate of production of organic material after respiration has taken its toll is called *net primary productivity*, and the study of production ecology is ideally part of the necessary knowledge about any biological resource.

Biological productivity

In natural ecosystems many of the plants are eaten by herbivorous animals. These in turn may be consumed by carnivores and thus is built up the idea of a simple food chain. The important feature, so far as energy is concerned, is that at each stage of the food chain energy is lost to the system. This is a direct consequence of the operation of the second law of thermodynamics, which states that all energy which undergoes a change of form will tend to be transformed into heat energy. Thus the 'concentrated' potential energy present in living tissue is 'dispersed' as heat by the metabolic processes of the organisms. In a simple food chain of the type described above, therefore, even if the herbivores were to eat all the plant material, the use of energy and hence dispersal of heat would ensure that a much smaller amount of energy became visible animal tissue. This quantity of organic matter is called secondary production. It follows that carnivores have even less energy available for their consumption, and should there be yet another carnivore then the amounts of energy available to it will be very small indeed. In the Silver Springs example quoted above:

Net primary productivity	8,833 kcal/m²/yr	First trophic level
Net secondary productivity (herbivores)	383 kcal/m²/yr	Second trophic level
Net secondary productivity (carnivores)	21 kcal/m²/yr	Third trophic level

The efficiency, therefore, with which each stage (called a trophic level) converts energy is very low. The implications for resource use are clear: the further away from the primary production stage that man takes his crop, the less energy per unit area will be available, and so, to be efficient, he must act as a herbivore.

Rarely is all the tissue at one trophic level cropped by the next: a terrestrial herbivore usually eats only the aerial parts of a plant; similarly many herbivores die without being eaten by a carnivore. At death, therefore, another type of food chain forms in which non-living organic material is the energy source. This second chain is usually called the detritus or decomposer chain and the organisms in it are taxonomically very diverse, but an especially important group are the fauna and flora of soils which break down dead organic matter into its components: fungi and bacteria are notable components of this group (Fig. 1.1).

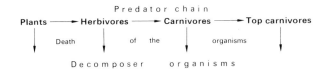

Fig. 1.1 A schematic diagram of trophic level structure of an ecosystem showing the basic energy paths through the organisms, beginning at the green plants. Not shown at each transfer stage is the loss of energy as heat

In addition, there are parasites on many organisms. These can be regarded either as a separate food chain or as components of the predator chain representing the next trophic level.

To summarize, energy enters the ecosystem as free, solar energy and leaves it as heat, having undergone changes from a 'concentrated' to a 'dispersed' state. Within the ecosystem is found energy-rich organic matter which upon the death of the organism, either plant, animal or fungus, undergoes decomposition. The complex organic materials are broken down to relatively simple inorganic compounds, with consequent dispersal of energy (Fig. 1.2).

Needless to say, the situation in nature and even in much modified ecosystems is more complicated. A herbivore may feed off many species of plants and in turn be eaten by several species of predators. A predator may have a preferred food source but shift to others in a time of scarcity. Omnivory is not uncommon, where an animal will eat plants, other animals and also be a scavenger on dead material: brown and black bears are examples of this and doubtless until affected by modern squeamishness our own species could rank thus. At any rate we are currently both herbivores and carnivores. Watt (1968) has diagrammed

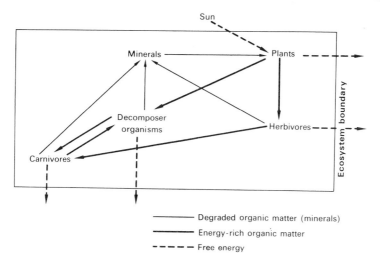

Fig. 1.2 The form in which energy and matter move through an ecosystem: the 'free energy' traversing the ecosystem boundaries outwards is the heat loss. Within the system, matter travels either as energy-rich organic matter or as mineral matter low in energy content.
Source: O'Connor 1964

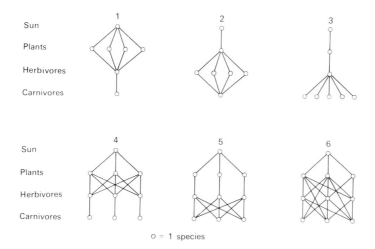

Fig. 1.3 Representations of trophic level relationships. In (1) a herbivore grazes several species of plants but has only one predator; in (2) a single species of plant is eaten by four herbivores which form the prey of only one carnivore; in (3) the single herbivorous species is the food of five species of carnivores. In (4) three herbivores range across three species of plant but are eaten by a prey-specific predator; (5) and (6) depict various states of omnivory and show a relatively high number of energy pathways. They would suffer a lower loss of stability if one species were to disappear.
Source: Watt 1968

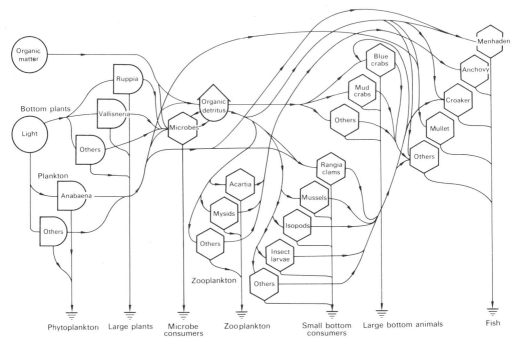

Fig. 1.4 An actual food web for an estuary in North America. The various trophic groups are labelled at the foot of the diagram. More detailed explanation of the compartment symbols is given by H. T. Odum (1971). The ☰ symbol represents heat loss.
Source: H. T. Odum 1971

some of the different types of relationship that can exist at different trophic levels in ecosystems (Fig. 1.3). At even more complicated levels, it is probably more realistic to talk about *food webs* rather than chains, since the points of contact (at which energy is transferred) are so many (Fig. 1.4). Even this concept is perhaps insufficiently close to reality, and Elton (1966) has expanded it into the idea of a *species network*, where not only food but other relationships, such as competition for space and other forms of competitive interference, are considered. These latter factors, he notes, do not necessarily cause any immediate transfer of energy or materials from one species to another; relationships within such a network do not imply simultaneous activity or existence.

The implication of such models for resource processes are quite simple: the multiple interactions within the networks mean that when man crops a species as a resource, accommodating shifts within the system will probably be made. Because of the complexity of the system, these are unlikely to be predictable (although increased knowledge and use of computers is improving this situation), and inevitably some of the consequences have been deleterious to further human activity and the continued viability of the ecosystem.

The loss of energy as heat at each trophic level in the ecosystem ensures that the amount of potential energy decreases through the species network. Thus the numbers of organisms and the amount of living tissue per unit area (usually measured as dry weight) usually

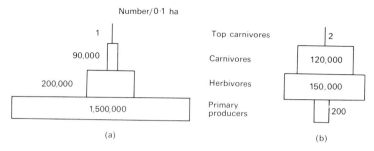

Fig. 1.5 Number pyramids of two ecosystems, exclusive of micro-organisms and soil animals. (a) is a grassland in summer, (b) a temperate forest in summer where the producers are trees which are large organisms and few in number.
Source: E. P. Odum 1971

diminish through the stages of secondary and tertiary productivity. A series of pyramids can be seen to exist which reflect this. The first is of numbers: in a measured area, the number of plants is many times the number of herbivores, which in turn greatly exceeds the quantity of carnivorous individuals. Carnivores and second carnivores are, therefore, relatively rare species (Fig. 1.5).

Such a relationship is made even clearer when biomass or standing crop is inspected (this is not the same as productivity, since biomass is a static measurement at one point in time whereas productivity is a rate). Again, the biomass of plants is much higher than any of the dependent organisms (Fig. 1.6). The calorific value of the tissues at various trophic levels

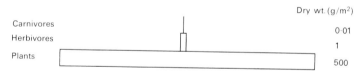

Fig. 1.6 A biomass pyramid (dry weight/unit area) for an 'old field', i.e. an abandoned agricultural field left to natural succession.
Source: E. P. Odum 1971

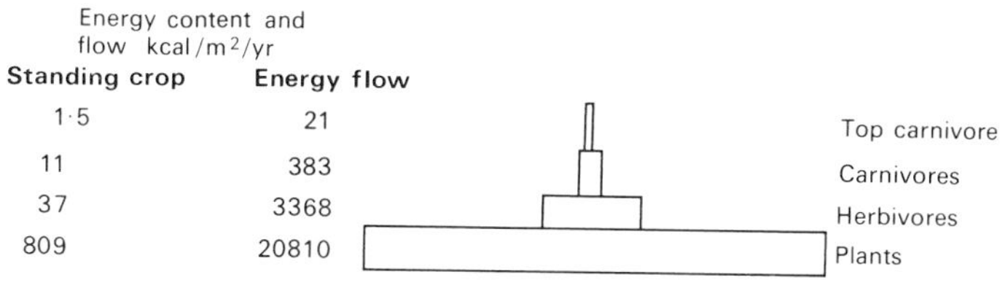

Fig. 1.7 An energy-content pyramid for Silver Springs, Florida. The pyramid represents the data for energy flow through the trophic levels in the course of a year. The standing crop biomass (left-hand column of figure; it is considerably less than the yearly flow in this instance, but in, for example, a grassland it might be almost equivalent to the annual productivity.
Source: E. P. Odum 1971

is perhaps the best guide to energy relations, and here the pyramidal form of the numbers is confirmed (Fig. 1.7). We may note that there is a tendency for the size of the animal components to get larger as the predator chain is followed: being bigger than your prey is an obvious advantage for a predacious species.

Inorganic substances

Living things require between 30–40 of the 90 chemical elements which occur in nature. Their supplies come from many elements and compounds which undergo constant cycling at a variety of scales: some have gaseous phases and hence involve the atmosphere in their ecosystems; others are either in a solid or dissolved state and remain in the terrestrial and aqueous parts of the biosphere. In the first category, CO_2 is an obvious fundamental substance since it is required by plants for photosynthesis. If this were not continually produced by respiration and by combustion of organic material, then the plant cover of the world would exhaust the atmospheric supplies in a year or so. Constant cycling of nitrogen, oxygen and water is also necessary for the support of life. Many mineral elements with sedimentary cycles, such as phosphorus, calcium and magnesium, are also essential for the growth of living tissue. These elements, along with many others, may impose checks upon the populations of a component of any ecosystem if they are in short supply.

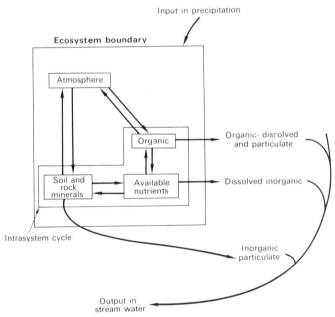

Fig. 1.8 A diagram of the flow and storage of essential elements through a terrestrial ecosystem. They cross the ecosystem boundary in an aqueous medium: in via precipitation and out via runoff. The atmosphere is regarded here as part of the system, i.e. that part of it performing gaseous exchange with the green plants. Within the system the lithosphere also acts as a *de novo* source of mineral elements in contrast to those which cycle between the organic matter and the pool of available nutrients.
Source: Bormann and Likens 1969

In nature, an ecosystem receives its inputs of inorganic materials from a number of sources. As with energy, the plant is the initial point of incorporation. The atmosphere contributes CO_2 to plants, also N_2 to species with nitrogen-fixing bacteria living symbiotically with them, and in turn the plants give off O_2 needed for the respiration of animals. The weathering of the rocks of the earth's crust further contributes basic minerals such as calcium, magnesium and phosphorus: they may also find their way into the atmosphere to be rained out (Fig. 1.8). Water makes its contribution both by assisting in weathering processes in the soil and sometimes, in the form of floods, by spreading nutrients around, as well as transporting them to the sea if they have been lost to the organic components of ecosystems. Its role in the transpiration stream is critical in the transfer of nutrients from the soil to the plant in terrestrial ecosystems.

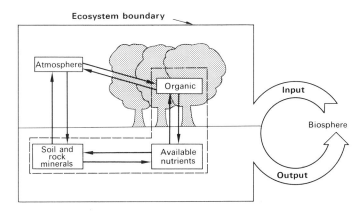

Fig. 1.9 A simplified and more graphic form of Fig. 1.8 showing the compartments for which nutrient levels can be measured.
Source: Bormann and Likens 1969

In the natural state, the flow of nutrients is conserved within an ecosystem. Input and loss are usually small (in terrestrial systems especially) compared with the volume which circulates within the system. In a forest, for example, minerals originating in the rocks enter the soil, become part of the tree, descend at leaf-fall, are mineralized by the soil fauna and flora and then are again available for uptake by the tree (Fig. 1.9). Litter fungi are especially important in forests, where they act as holding sinks for nutrients such as Ca, Fe, Cu, Na, P and Zn. Rhizomorphs may hold mineral concentrations of up to 85 times that of the leaves and have a 99·9 per cent efficiency in retaining them against leaching (Stark 1972). Animals have varying functions: in terrestrial decomposer chains they may perform a crucial role in physically commuting organic debris, and in the oceans the smallest zooplankton appear to be the key factor in the circulation of phosphorus and probably also of nitrogen; large terrestrial animals, however, appear to play a trivial role in nutrient circulation (Pomeroy 1970). Where climate seasonally inhibits many of the soil biota, as in boreal coniferous forests, unmineralized organic matter piles up on the forest floor and so fire may play a similar role. In natural terrestrial systems, the living organisms are very important in the retention of essential elements, and about 50 per cent of the total reserve appears to be incorporated in both living and dead organic matter. Succession appears to be a process by which enough nutrients are accumulated to make possible the rise of succeeding populations, and a climax community perpetuates its stability by conserving its essential elements (Pomeroy 1970). A stable system such as a forest retains most of its nutrients by circulating them within the soil-vegetation subsystem, and losses to runoff are balanced by inputs into the system, as shown by Bormann and Likens (1969) for calcium in a New Hampshire forest (Fig. 1.10). If the nutrient pathways are blocked by the destruction of one component of the organic material, such as the vegetation (for example, by clear-cutting or catastrophic fire), then there is a rapid loss of mineral elements and particulate material,

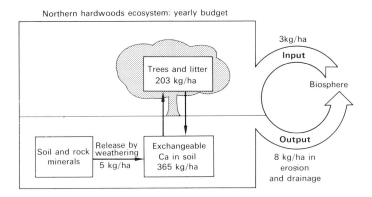

Fig. 1.10 The quantities of calcium present in a hardwood ecosystem in New Hampshire. The major feature of the diagram is the small quantities which cross the ecosystem boundary compared with the amounts cycling within the intrasystem cycle. The output equals the inputs from precipitation and the weathering of soil and rock.
Source: Bormann and Likens 1969

thus contributing to eutrophication and siltation downstream. After disturbances, successional species, such as shrubs and small trees, may play an important role in the rebuilding of the cycling and retention of nutrients. In New Hampshire studies, the pin cherry (*Prunus pennsylvanica*) had an annual uptake of nitrogen 50 per cent greater than that of undisturbed forest, and the rapid growth of such pioneer trees clearly acts to minimize nutrient losses from the ecosystem by the channelling of water from runoff to evapo-transpiration and so reducing losses by erosion and in solution; by producing shade and hence reducing rates of decomposition of organic matter so that the supply of soluble ions available for loss via runoff is lessened; and by incorporating into the vegetation any nutrients that happen to become available (Marks and Bormann 1972). Both successional and stable communities therefore appear to be geared to maximum retention and recycling of essential nutrients.

On a larger scale, the major flows in the world's nitrogen cycle have been modelled by Delwiche (1970) and the critical points can be identified. For example, the loss of N_2 to sediments is apparently balanced by the gain from volcanic action, and indeed the N_2 content of the air may have increased during geological time. The fixation of atmospheric nitrogen is limited to a few, but abundant, organisms like the free living bacteria *Azotobacter* and *Clostridium*, symbiotic nodule bacteria on leguminous plants like *Rhizobium*, and some blue-green Algae; these are the keys to the movement of N_2 from the air reservoir into the productivity cycle since no higher plants are able to fix nitrogen alone: legumes only do so with the help of their symbiotic bacteria.

Another element essential for living tissue is phosphorus, whose reservoir is the crust of the earth. Thus the release of P into ecosystems is very slow, whereas its loss can be very rapid, especially where soil erosion occurs. Such phosphorus is washed into the deep sea sediments and is for all practical purposes lost to ecosystems. Some, from the shallow sediments, is returned to the land via the guano of sea birds and some as fish, but of the 1–2 million tons of phosphate that are mined every year, most is lost to the sea, and of that only 60,000 tons/yr (60,420 mt/yr) is recovered. Compared with nitrogen, phosphorus is relatively rare (in the ratio of about 23 : 1 in natural waters), and so although crustal reserves are very large, some concern has been expressed about its future availability if a recycling interval shorter than that of major geological upheavals is not accomplished by human intervention (E. P. Odum 1971).

Man requires all 40 essential elements for his metabolism and most of the rest for extra-somatic cultural activities. The overall tendency of his use of these materials has been to speed up the natural cycles so that pulses occur: as an ironic counterpart to the possible phosphorus shortages mentioned above there is the eutrophication of many water bodies because of the output of phosphorus-enriched water from agricultural and urban areas (Hutchinson 1970). One of the results of the acceleration of natural cycles has been to speed up the movements of crustal elements into the oceans, from which their recovery, even if technically possible, is likely to be very expensive and ecologically disruptive. Resource processes which 'short-circuit' these flows seem therefore to be highly desirable.

Productivity and cropping

It will be apparent that biological productivity (the rate of appearance of energy and matter as living tissue) is the basis of all our biological resources, and it is involved with abiotic parts of the planet too. The metabolism of plants and animals is instrumental in maintaining the gaseous balance of the atmosphere, and the world's hydrological cycle interacts at several points with biological production. Again, 'fossil' matter sources appear in productivity considerations because of the limiting effects upon plants of inadequate mineral supplies, and in man-dominated ecosystems because of fuel-energy inputs into resource processes such as agriculture.

Although biological productivity is of considerable importance in human affairs, the study of production ecology is a recent one and subject still to wide margins of error. The measurement of rates of production, for example, is a difficult task involving sophisticated instrumentation in a field setting. Often the only practical way of proceeding is to measure standing crop biomass; this, however, may be very different from annual productivity since there are likely to be seasonal differences or, in the case of short-lived organisms, a turn-over rate several times higher than the biomass at any one point in time. In order to reduce some of the errors, and to standardize measurements internationally, the International

Plate 1 An estuary in west Wales. These habitats have a very high biological productivity and biotic diversity, and are often nurseries for offshore fisheries. In economic terms they are valued mostly as potentially reclaimable land for industry or for waste disposal. *(Aerofilms Ltd, London)*

Biological Programme for the study of Biological Productivity and its relation to Human Welfare was carried out during the mid-1960s–1970s. Research Programmes for each major biome have been aimed at providing comparable information on biological productivity.

Results of measurements of primary productivity from various ecosystems reveal, in general, the pattern expected from the visible biomass which is expressed in the physiognomy of the vegetation. Net primary productivities of major biomes (Table 1.2) clearly reflect the intuitive values suggested by the physiognomy of the vegetation type. The values for gross primary productivity given in Table 1.3 portray the same basic picture, using *per diem* data and including some man-manipulated ecosystems (Plates 1 and 2).

A very large proportion of the earth's surface therefore comes into the category of open oceans and arid/semi-arid lands, and thus has strongly constrained primary productivity (Fig. 1.11). In such comparisons we should be careful not to confuse productivity in its biological sense with yield to man or cropping, for even where productivity may be high, it may be of a biological product which for economic or cultural reasons does not form a vital resource.

Given the attention that cultivation brings, it is not surprising that during periods of maximum growth, such crops have very high productivities. On a year-round basis, however, the relatively simple nature of the ecosystem means that the amount of energy trapped is usually less than in a natural system; this is revealed by comparing the data in Tables 1.4 and 1.5. Such differences are emphasized by the data in Table 1.6, when all the measurements are made within the same region, and where the agricultural crops will

Plate 2 An arid steppe in California. Productivity and diversity are low, but owing to proximity to large urban centres, demands to convert such areas to recreational housing or to allow unrestricted access by cross-country vehicles are very high. The ecosystems easily break down under such pressures and regrowth is very slow. *(I. G. Simmons)*

Fig. 1.11 The worldwide production of organic matter during a single season, without complete adjustment for losses to consumers, decomposers and substrate. Thus net primary production may exceed the values shown here, but economically usable products may be much less. Values are g carbon/m²/yr.

Lands	g C/m²/yr
	Over 800
	600-800
	400-600
	200-400
	100-200
	0-100

Waters	
	0-50
	50-100
	100-200
	Over-200

TABLE 1.2   Estimated net primary productivity
(major biomes, c. 1950)

Vegetation unit	Mean NPP (g/m²/yr)	Total for area (10⁹ mt/yr)
Forests	1,290	64·5
Woodland	600	4·2
Tundra	140	1·1
Desert scrub	70	1·3
Grassland	600	15·0
Desert	3	n.a.
Cultivated land	650	9·1
Fresh water	1,250	5·0
Reefs and estuaries	2,000	4·0
Continental shelf	350	9·3
Open ocean	125	41·5
Upwelling zones	500	0·2
Total continental	669	100·2
Total oceanic	155	55·0
World	303	155·2

Source: Leith 1972

TABLE 1.3   Average gross primary productivity of world
biomes and land uses (g/m²/day)

Deserts and semi-arid grassland	0·5
Open oceans	1·0
Continental shelf waters, shallow lakes, forests, moist grasslands, agriculture	0·5–5·0
Coral reefs, estuaries, mineral springs, evergreen forests, intensive agriculture	5·0–20·0
Maximum rates for short periods in very productive ecosystems	60·0

Source: E. P. Odum 1959

have received an energy 'subsidy' from fossil fuels and added fertilizer. The reason for the greater dry-matter production by the trees is linked to the maintenance of a higher leaf-area index for the whole year by the pines compared with the low leaf area and short duration of the crops. The accuracy of measurement and the difficulties of comparing managed and unmanaged ecosystems are discussed by Newbould (1971a), who points out that the differences in seasonality of production and in the biochemical quality of the organic matter may render purely quantitative comparisons meaningless.

TABLE 1.4   Natural and semi-natural ecosystems

	Year-long net primary productivity (g/m²/day)
Giant ragweed, Oklahoma	3·95
Spartina saltmarsh, Georgia	9·0
Pine plantation 20–35 yrs old, England	6·0
Deciduous plantation 20–35 yrs old, England	3·0
Desert, Nevada	0·11
Seaweeds, Nova Scotia	1·98

Source: E. P. Odum 1959

TABLE 1.5   Cultivated ecosystems

	Year-long net primary productivity (g/m²/day)	Growing season only
Wheat, world average	0·94	2·3
Rice, world average	1·36	2·7
Potatoes, world average	1·10	2·6
Sugar cane, world average	4·73	4·7
Mass algal, culture outdoors	12·4	12·4

Source: E. P. Odum 1959

TABLE 1.6   Forestry and agriculture in the English Breckland

	Net above-ground primary production (mt/ha/yr)
Scots pine, maximum production	
23–31 yr age-class	22
mean production 0–55 yr span	13
Wheat	5·2
Barley	3·5
Sugar beet	9·0
Carrots	6·5
Mangolds	6·0
Grassland (hay)	7·5

Source: Ovington 1957

If there are difficulties in measuring primary productivity, then they are greatly compounded when secondary productivity is considered. At the simplest level of perplexity, animals move; and harvesting of them for biomass or calorific value measurements may produce problems, especially if the species is uncommon. Studies indicate that even in intensively managed ecosystems, only about 10 per cent of *gross* primary productivity appears as animal tissue. A measure often adopted is the ratio

$$\frac{\text{(calories of growth)}}{\text{(calories consumed)}} = \text{net growth efficiency}$$

which for beef cattle on grassland is about 4 per cent. The equivalent measurement for pigs, young beef animals and young chickens is of the order of 20 per cent, which is clearly used to advantage in modern intensive farming methods for 'baby beef' and broiler chickens.

The summarizing theme of all discussions of biological productivity is that of limits. These include the overall limit dictated by the quantity of solar radiation incident upon the earth, the efficiency of photosynthesis in fixing the energy, and the limits imposed by the ratio of gross to net primary productivity. Inorganic nutrients may also prescribe constraints by virtue of their short supply and the length of time they take to go through cycling processes. And since there is a loss of energy at each step through a food web, there are limitations imposed upon the productivity of the second and subsequent trophic levels.

Populations

In an ecosystem the flows of energy and matter in the form of organisms, and the adjustment of the individuals to the space dimension of their habitat, are expressed in terms of the dynamics of population of a given species. To understand the dynamics of the numbers of plants, animals and men is to be a good way down the road to the rational cropping of an ecosystem.

In the animal world as in man, the numbers of individuals of a species are determined by the relationship between natality and mortality. Usually these quantities are expressed in terms of time: thus a population increases when birth rate exceeds death rate. Conversely, if the death rate exceeds the birth rate then a population will dwindle and die out.

Three is an incremental rate of recruitment to a breeding population and the general form of the equation for such an expansion is (Boughey 1968):

$$N_t = N_0 e^{rt} \tag{1}$$

where N_t = numbers at time t

N_0 = number at time zero

e = base of natural logarithms

r = rate of population increase

t = time elapsed

which can be expressed logarithmically as

$$\log_e N_t = \log_e N_0 + rt \tag{2}$$

A growth curve derived from these equations is shown in Fig. 1.13. Such a rate of growth is called exponential, and its capacity for effecting rapid increases in numbers is very high. For example, the time taken to double a population can be tabulated thus:

Rate of increase % p.a.	Number of years to double population
0·5	139
1	70
2	35
3	23
4	18

From this we see that quite low percentage rates will produce high absolute numbers quite quickly, a fact not unfamiliar to people repaying mortgage loans at 11 per cent, for instance. As an extreme instance of the potential of the exponential curve we may quote the example of a bacterium which divides into two every 20 minutes. This could produce a colony 1 ft deep over the surface of the earth in 15 days; 1 hour later the layer would be 6 ft deep. That this does not happen is due to a number of factors which are generally termed *environmental resistance*, a term which subsumes a great many influences which affect animal populations (Figs. 1.12 and 1.13).

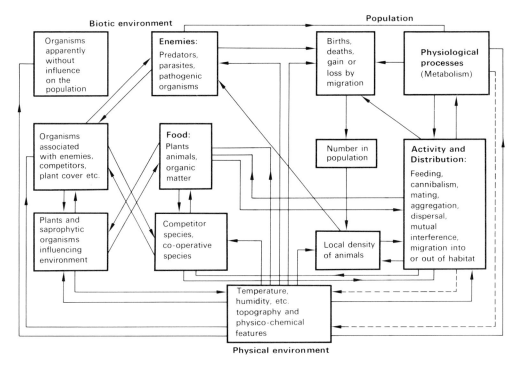

Fig. 1.12 A diagram of the major influences affecting animal populations. Apart from the virtual absence of predation and cannibalism, most of them apply to man too.
Source: Solomon 1969

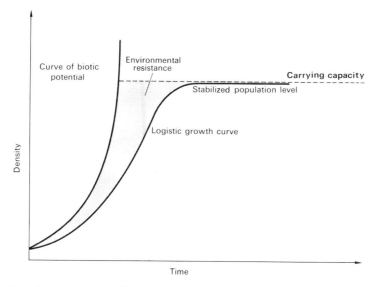

Fig. 1.13 The logistic growth curve flattens out at the carrying capacity, owing to increasing environmental resistance such as the factors in Fig. 1.12. If it were not for that factor, the curve of biotic potential would produce immense absolute numbers of any organism.
Source: Boughey 1968

Without such resistance, a population could fulfil its biotic potential to expand indefinitely. In reality, the exponential curve always levels off, at a value which is termed the carrying capacity of the habitat; it may approach this value gradually from below or it may overshoot and, by virtue of high mortality or low fertility, fall back (with the possibility of oscillations) to the carrying capacity level (Fig. 1.14). The concept of carrying capacity has been elaborated by Dasmann (1964b), who suggests that there is firstly a survival capacity where there is enough food for survival but not for vigour nor optimum growth, and where slight changes in ambient conditions can be disastrous. An optimum capacity appears superior since there is adequate nutrition and individual growth except perhaps for

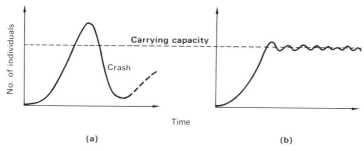

Fig. 1.14 Some populations rise rapidly, exceed the carrying capacity of their ecosystem and 'crash'; others level off near the carrying capacity, although oscillating around that level rather than maintaining it unvaryingly.

a few individuals. A third type is based largely on density, and is the tolerance capacity or the level at which territorial considerations at an intraspecific level force surplus individuals to migrate, or to be denied basic necessities like food, or the opportunity to reproduce. Populations at the survival level may also exhibit such characteristics. Some parallel with the human population may be seen if we equate the survival and tolerance capacity groups with the poorest nations and the optimum capacity with areas like North America and Western Europe; however, the density tolerance considerations might extend to the cities of the richer people too.

If we compare the dynamics of the human population with that of animals, some similarities emerge. The curve for the numbers of the species, upon which there seems a wide measure of agreement between authorities, resembles a J-curve, but so far without any tendencies to reach an upper level. This has given rise to fears that the human population may breed itself beyond the carrying capacity of the earth and has renewed interest in the mechanisms by which animal populations regulate their numbers, especially since many of them stabilize below the numbers which would be expected if all the energy and space resources of their ecosystems were used.

There is some disagreement among zoologists as to the causes of the phenomenon, some of which may be explained by their investigations in particular kinds of environments, and it is not clear which if any of the mechanisms apply to man. Andrewartha and Birch (1954) stress the importance of factors external to the study population, such as food supply at critical periods and sudden shifts in weather, and note the lack of stability of the numbers of any one species even when the whole ecosystem is apparently not prone to large-scale fluctuations. Much of this kind of pattern operates in unfavourable environments or concerns organisms with a short life-span, and by contrast workers in more benign areas such as Lack (1966) stress the importance of density-dependent factors such as intraspecific competition and territoriality, and the role of biological controls such as predation. The homeostatic mechanism, according to Wynne-Edwards (1962), operates via the social behaviour of many animals. Features such as territoriality (in birds especially), the emergence of a hierarchy of dominance (usually called a peck-order and often a male phenomenon), and male sexual displays which are usually designed to secure status among other males, not to woo the female, are all ways in which breeding can be confined to a selected group in the population; in times of low rates of natality there are presumably eugenic consequences with survival value also. The need for the inception of the limitation mechanisms seems to be established at mass displays of either the whole population (the aerobatics of starling flocks are a possible example) or of the males, as in displays at the beginning of the breeding season which involve a number of individuals, like the virtual tournaments of sage grouse or ruffs.

It is tempting to seek analogies of these instances in human populations. Recent trends in male fashion could perhaps be linked less with the desire to attract an already economically independent female and more with the need to establish status in a society which overtly prizes equality; mass synchronous social displays take place every morning and evening in large cities (often more or less coincidentally with the starlings) and are called 'rush hours': it is noteworthy that the display of social characteristics needed to gain admission to an American university fraternity or sorority is called 'rushing'. Further human displays occur on Saturday afternoons except in high summer: these are largely composed of males and bright plumage is not uncommon. It would be worth seeing if any foundation would finance a project to see if commuters and football fans tend to have fewer children than the rest of the population.

With more scientific logic, however, Wynne-Edwards (1962) concludes that *Homo sapiens* has lost its population regulation mechanisms. At the hunter-gatherer stage of culture this capacity was almost certainly present and contemporary 'primitive' groups provide evidence of population control, especially by infanticide. With the coming of the production of food surpluses by agriculture and the ability to store them against hard times, together possibly with growth in absolute numbers, the control of reproduction passed from society to individuals. It has remained there from the agricultural revolution to the present day; current controversy over 'the right to produce' centres fundamentally on whether society should reclaim that control and enforce it through cultural measures such as contraception and induced abortion. Writers such as Stott (1962) produce evidence that stress in animals is often induced by overcrowding in advance of food shortages, and it triggers off mechanisms which reduce fertility or the survival rate of the young; he adduces similar evidence for the human species, based on gynaecological studies, and concludes that a world population 'crash' by starvation will be forestalled by increased rates of the incidence of sterility, perinatal death and unhealthy children, together with malformed and mentally impaired people. Avoidance of such unpleasant conditions must come via the cultural alternatives which are open to us.

Culture

Man sees the world around him through the spectacles of culture, and nature is thus transformed into resources. The elements of behaviour and technology which are fused together to make up culture are very varied, and the mix is different for diverse times and places: for some the spectacles are rose-tinted whereas others seem to see their world through a very dark glass indeed. The sensory perception of the environment and the psychological translation and information of that knowledge into a decision to act, or not to act, upon the environment is a complex study, since between the perceptive input and the executive output lies a shadowy set of values conditioned by experience, imagination, fantasy, and other assorted intangibles derived from both rational and irrational sources. The ability to act is dependent largely upon the effective technology that a group or individual possesses, but behind the motivation lie the more elusive factors outlined above. There are, of course, cases where technology is used for its own sake: the alleged propensity of engineers to build dams whenever and wherever possible, irrespective of the need, is perhaps an example.

In general terms, the world exists not in absolute dimensions but in people's heads. The study of this state essentially consists of trying to understand the workings of the 'black box' of the human brain or group of brains, between the perceptive input and the output of action. The ways in which investigation may proceed vary according to the period of historical time involved. For the preliterate past, there is only inference from the data furnished by archaeology. From such sources it is difficult to make firm statements about the relationships between man and nature in the distant past; it is not, however, impossible to speculate usefully, particularly if ethnological parallels may be accepted. In the later chapter on the relations between unmanipulated ecosystems and hunting-gathering-fishing societies, some observations about this type of relationship will be found. In the case of the literate past, we have writings as a source of evidence for man's attitudes to nature. Some of these will deal explicitly with such a theme, others only implicitly, and there is in published work a great concentration upon the intellectual history of the West in this particular instance; other cultures have in general been little explored from this point of view. The use of written sources as a guide to themes in the relationship of man and nature carries over into the present, where many sources yield both clear-cut and covert clues about the ways in which men view their environment. But those who write about such phenomena may not be typical of those who act, and here the study of the environmental cognition or perception of resource managers of all kinds by means of the methods of psychological research has become of some interest and importance.

By such means the mental attitudes of man towards nature, and hence towards resources, can be studied in the same manner as his attitudes to other phenomena. At the present moment we shall concentrate heavily on the second and third of these sources of information, since both the numbers of men and the level of technology in the preliterate past have generally been such as to exert relatively little influence upon the development of the world's ecosystems.

Man and nature in the past

As hinted above, the evidence derived from written sources can sometimes be criticized as unrepresentative of the reality of its age: a partial sample of a social stratum far removed, perhaps, in values and motivations from those actually engaged in dirtying their hands with real resources. Yet such writers are the formers of images of the world, no less than the recorders of other people's images. They deserve consideration, for many people act according to the image of the world that they have in their heads rather than in the light of objective 'scientific' information, and in any case the whole intellectual climate of opinion of a given time may determine whether or not 'scientific' knowledge is used, or indeed, misused. Keynes said, 'a study of the history of opinion is a necessary preliminary to the emancipation of the mind', and to discern trends in man's view of nature, where externalized in communicable forms such as writing and art, is a necessary preliminary to any study of man–nature relationships, and the ecology of resources is no exception.

From the times of classical antiquity to the eighteenth century, as Glacken (1967) points out, certain themes have dominated man's view of nature in the West. The rest of the world has had its traits also, but they are more diverse and less practical than those of the West, and less widely exported. The idea of a designed earth, for example, is strong in the Judaic-Christian tradition. This essentially theological idea envisages the earth created for man or else for all life with man at the apex of a chain of being. Before the coming of evolutionary theory and ecology this was the West's great attempt to formulate a holistic concept of nature. In this way as many phenomena as possible were brought within the scope of the central theme, demonstrating a unity which was the achievement of a Creator. Although the seventeenth and eighteenth centuries saw criticism of this idea (not of the concept of design but of the relation of this order to the creative activity of the Deity), it could be extended to accommodate the theory of evolution when this began to emerge. At present indeed, the preoccupation with ecology, whose message is essentially that of seeing systems as wholes and of perceiving the order within them, is a logical heir to this tradition of thought. Part of it also is the concept of 'man's place in nature': the postulation of a division of man from the rest of nature was recognized very early and written about by Sophocles, for instance, and it appears most powerfully in Genesis (I, 28–9) where God says to men 'be fruitful and increase, fill the earth and subdue it, rule over the fish in the sea, the birds of heaven and every living thing that moves on the earth'. The persistence of this theme is symbolized by the papal encyclical of 1967, 'The development of peoples', which reasserts the idea of the creation of the earth by God for man. This book, while not aspiring to the authority of those two documents, also accepts that man and nature are different and must be reconciled.

A counter-argument to this theme finds it impossible to admit of a world being created especially for men when they themselves are often so wicked, and when the physical constitution of the world is obviously so imperfect as a habitation for them. In this tradition are the ideas of St Francis of Assisi, who asserted that, although man might be at the apex of creation, this did not mean that all life was for him and at his disposal. The same thoughts are exemplified in present-day protagonists of wildlife, who assert that plants and animals must exist in their own right rather than just by leave of, or for the use of, man.

A second major strand has been the study of environmental influence upon culture. This was one way of interpreting the endless array of human differences, and a powerful aid to the stereotyping of nations since men could be expected to behave as they did on account of the place where they lived. It carried with it the corollary of environmental limitations, and so we find Malthus's concern over the adequacy of food supplies falling within this theme. As is well known, he claimed that the growth of population would always outstrip the means of subsistence, and hence the potential perfectability of man being promulgated by some of his contemporaries was, for environmental reasons, an impossibility.

The Reverend Thomas also dilated upon the modification of the earth to accommodate the growing populations of men, thus participating in the long-lived philosophical theme of man as a modifier of nature, a third major strand of thought. In some forms this was an optimistic tradition: man's skill was to put the final touches to God's unfinished work, or he was to be a bringer of order to, and custodian of, nature. If Ray and Buffon were optimists, then Malthus and, later, George Perkins Marsh were pessimists, for they saw chaos instead of order and profligacy instead of stewardship. Malthus in particular did not believe that nature would improve or that institutional reform could alter his basic principle of population. Nature was niggardly and man was slothful (except, presumably, where the passion between sexes was concerned): optimism about the future of man had to be guarded and the possibility envisaged of only limited progress.

Marsh (1864) was mainly concerned with places rather than people. His writing about the changes wrought by man pointed out that not all these had been injurious to the environment, for soils had been improved and marshes drained so that civilized life might be enjoyed. He also pointed out that environmental change was a geological fact in many cases, but he is best known for his strictures on the misuse of nature that resulted in soil erosion, silting, fires and other downgrade processes. In many ways he is the intellectual forefather of the present all-pervasive concern with the disruptive effects of the technology made possible by our command of energy sources. His words might well adorn the portals of every resource agency in the world:

> man has too long forgotten that the earth was given to him for usufruct alone, not for consumption, still less for profligate waste.

Man and nature today

The themes of man's place in nature, of his subjugation of other components of the planet and his modification of its systems, cannot be said to be dead, although their context has been completely altered by the events of the nineteenth century. In practical terms the industrialization of the West was single-minded and inexorable; it produced the greatest alteration of nature, the greatest inroads on the world's resources and the greatest contamination then experienced. One effect seems to have been the heightening of confusion about man's place in nature. Omnipotence seemed to be manifest, yet the lot of many was so obviously unimproved. One twentieth-century reaction to drifting man, cut off from the earth by the advent of urbanism, has been labelled alienation. It appears to be partly due to the low quality of contemporary man–nature relationships and partly a result of the sheer numbers in our society: the old and the new are vividly portrayed by J. B. Priestley and Jacquetta Hawkes (1955), in their contrast of the Indians of New Mexico and the 'anglos' of South Texas. One literary expression of alienation comes in, for example, the plays of Samuel Beckett, for whose characters the world is unreal and cannot be related to themselves. Man no longer belongs in any natural setting and his externalities (including the environment) are alien and almost certainly hostile. It can thus be treated aggressively or at the very least be regarded as a storehouse whose depletion is of concern only to the owners. The inventiveness and applicability of nineteenth-century technology meant also that the resources of the world appeared to be infinite, for new means of making them accessible and new markets for material products went together. The generally cornucopian view of nature (provided that the proper social structure is present) promulgated by Marx and his later followers is an example of the attitudes to the relationship of man and nature which the nineteenth century produced. In the view that no environmental limits were apparent, Marx was a child of his time (if the bearded Colossus of Highgate may be so personified), but the attitudes live on. Colin Clark (1967), for example, values population growth because it forces innovation and social progress, and large populations enable economies of scale to be practised. He considers that it is possible to feed many more people than are at present alive but does not consider the environmental implications of doing so, and has been strongly criticized by Davis (1968) for being selective of only those aspects of population and economic growth which bring benefits. Deriving from a similar intellectual ancestry is much democratic socialist thinking, as of Crosland (1971) in the Labour Party of Britain. He contends that only continuing growth creates enough wealth to clear up the mess left by nineteenth-century industrialization, and that any diminution in the rate of economic growth results from the snobbery of the middle class in trying to prevent the workers from attaining what the wealthy already have. A slightly ameliorated version of the same document is taken by the committee of authors who wrote a British document (Verney 1972) in connection with the UN Stockholm Conference of 1972. The traditions of the mastery of man has become a central idea in, for example, contemporary Russian versions of Marxism and has led to various environmental disruptions (Goldman 1971). Traditional Chinese ideas about the harmony of man and nature have since 1949 been overthrown by the instilling of the necessity for man to dominate; but as Yi Fu Tuan (1968) has shown, the dichotomy between the philosophy and the actuality in ancient China regarding the treatment of nature was very wide, owing no doubt to the divorce between philosophers and peasants. The current emphasis in China on thrift and the avoidance of environmental contamination may well produce the least ecologically disruptive period for many centuries.

Alienation of a more intuitive character is expressed in the West in the 'dropout' or 'alternative society' concepts practised by some people, and it is significant that a return to older, land-based ways is advocated by many of them. (Their agricultural productivity is generally low, if the evidence of the Taos commune shown in the film *Easy Rider* is typical, so that a wholesale adoption of this philosophy would be nutritionally disastrous.) More conventionally, a scientific alienation is taking place. As a result of scientists' abandonment of control of their discoveries, various catastrophes could threaten, such as biological warfare, geophysical warfare and pesticide poisoning. Foreseers of doom have thus begun to emerge from science to postulate anew the 'dismal theorem' which Malthus first stated. The numbers of man and his treatment of the planet will, they aver, condemn *Homo sapiens* to speedy extinction: from starvation, from nuclear war, from poisonous compounds in all parts of the environment or from sheer breakdown caused by the impossibility of controlling and keeping healthy so many millions of people. A few more decades of present trends in resource use and population growth may, according to Ehrlich (1968), produce an 'ecocatastrophe' whose basic cause is the outstripping of the world's carrying capacity for people. The examination of this position is one of the purposes of this work.

The foregoing discussion has emphasized a dichotomy between man and nature. Whereas 'primitive' people seem to have enjoyed a close association with nature (probably too close for our present ideas of comfort), literate man has erected a dualism, in which 'progress' is linked with control over nature. For many commentators it becomes an increasingly unsatisfactory idea and to them the future would scarcely seem to permit the indifference to the natural world, our environment and provider of our resources, which this attitude allows and may even encourage: it appears healthier for man to regard the planet less as a set of commodities for use and more as a community of which he forms a part. They concede that such an attitude will mean the abandonment of the central theme of our intellectual heritage and especially of its religious accompaniment, its anthropocentricity. To do that requires a revolution in thought, involving essentially the realization that our survival as a species is dependent upon non-human processes; an idea antithetical to most of the traditions of thought discussed above. Too often they advocate, or are interpreted to advocate, a return to some pastoral idyll. There are already too many people for such a relapse and we cannot reverse the time-trajectory of our man-directed systems. In managing the earth for our survival there is no way in which technology can be abandoned: what appears to be essential is a deeper knowledge of the relations between man-made machine-dominated systems and the bioenvironmental systems, and ways in which a stable co-existence can be procured.

Economics

The practice of economics is today the single most important feature governing the relations between man and nature. Based simply on the premise that no substance is in unlimited supply for all individuals, it aims at bringing together supply and demand by the mechanism of price. The concept appears to be identical whether the currency be conch shells, gold or Eurodollars. As far as resources are concerned, economists suggest that they are very largely created by price. If a material becomes scarce, then its raised price will make economic its extraction from poorer quality sources or will enforce a substitution, the invention and production of which is one of the proper roles of science and technology.

In some ways, economics is not always totally suitable for regulating human resource needs at present. At the most elementary level, price cannot always be equated with value, or to put it the other way round, some things of value have no price. They may be thought to be beyond such considerations or there may be no accurate method of fixing a price. Nobody knows the true value of a large area of unspoilt land of outstanding scenic beauty, for all the methods normally used to fix prices fail in some respect or other. In this case, large numbers of people attach value to such an area simply because it is there; they may have no intention at all of using it. When a controversy arose over the construction of a dam in Upper Teesdale in NE England, the 'conservationist' party could not assess the 'value' of the rare arctic-alpine plants, some of which would be destroyed, whereas the Water Board could easily quantify the 'value' of the extra water to be gained from the impoundment.

This relates to another generality, namely that some resources, such as food uncontaminated by residual pesticides, or clean air, or indeed the whole complex of values usually called 'environmental quality', are not in the market, and hence are not subject to the choices normally experienced there. Unless we are very rich we cannot go into the resource supermarket and buy an absence of air pollution, for example, as we could iron ore or wood pulp. In connection with the side-effects of particular processes, we should note that the market mechanism frequently overlooks what are called 'external diseconomies'; the full social costs are not taken into account because they are paid for, usually by society at large, elsewhere in the economy (Mishan 1967). The increasing use of 'disposable' articles, and the whole industry of packaging, is an example in point: the price of disposable, wear-once, clothes for ladies does not include the costs of removing them from the household, converting them to ash and carbon dioxide, and taking the ash where it will not be deposited on the non-disposable clothes of the lady which are hanging out to dry. The external diseconomies of widespread private ownership of motor cars in relation to air pollution, noise and premature death are not reflected in the bargain price which the dealers seize every opportunity to acquaint us with.

Economics has long been concerned with a rational man who optimizes his spending in accordance with carefully chosen criteria. But Galbraith (1967) has argued that the manipulation of the market by large industrial corporations backed particularly by demand manipulation through advertising has made nonsense of the myth of 'consumer sovereignty'. Economics therefore is less and less concerned with the individual's basic needs and spontaneous demands: rather is it more and more determined that he shall buy what industry thinks he ought to have.

The outgrowth of these and other trends in values to which economics appears to have given rise is a series of priorities which have been unquestioned at least since the industrial revolution but which now are beginning to be examined more critically. Initially, attention has focused upon the high place given to the production and consumption of commodities, where a rapid rate of throughput (achieved where necessary by 'built-in obsolescence') is sought. To sustain and enhance this rate, indices like the GNP are watched as barometers of the nation's health, and if the GNP should fail to rise at a pre-ordained rate then dire consequences are forecast and everybody is exhorted to work harder (Boulding 1970). The world view adopted appears to regard the population as being a system with an infinite pool of resources from which to draw and with a sink of infinite size down which to flush unwanted by-products and other discarded materials. The thrust of industrial states, both capitalist and socialist, is towards increased production and throughput of materials, without any valuation of what biologists would call a dynamic equilibrium.

Although the views of established economists are still accorded prophetic status in most of the counsels of the world, challenges have come from radical thinkers such as K. E. Boulding (1962), whose contribution to the infusion of ecology into economics is discussed in the last part of the book; at present, however, the price of a material is usually what governs its pathway through a resource process. The ecological consequences of this movement are studied in more detail in this work since it is suggested that they deserve greater consideration.

Environmental perception

The role of the study of environmental perception or cognition has been briefly mentioned. The articulate expressions of attitudes may be seminal in determining long-term trends, but the majority of people make decisions at a more intuitive and less verbalized and rationalized level. Just as we have examined man–nature relationships viewed in terms of scientific and intellectual history, now we may turn to their study from within: how more ordinary individuals view the world about them and their use of it (Sewell and Burton 1971). Many aspects of the man–nature interaction result in patterns of resource use which are not 'rational'—rational in the eyes of Western science, that is, for we have a tendency to regard Western science as the answer to all problems, just as Western missionaries thought that putting primitive people into trousers might make them less 'savage'. The irrationalities which we detect in both industrial and non-industrial societies are plainly the result of conflict within the various elements of the resource process. In particular, the role of culture is very strong, and while we may study objectively the results of a particular cultural trait in terms of resource use, it is valuable to be able to penetrate the mind of the individual and see the way in which decisions come to be made (Saarinen 1969). The study of the environmentally orientated mental process of the individual 'resource manager' faced with the problem of what to do with his effluent may act as a key to the understanding of many of the irrationalities in resource management and use.

A number of processes are involved. There is firstly the sensory perception of the environment. At the 'primitive' level this is confined to the organs of the human body. Sight is clearly the most important of these as far as resources are concerned, but touch and smell may also be involved. Extra-somatic aids are generally simple: the domestic animals may be used, as for example with dogs flushing out deer or pigs sniffing for truffles. Using a dowsing-rod for water divining is the forerunner of the immense battery of electronic machines which is now used for the detection of materials where the capabilities of technologically advanced societies are available. In this respect, remote-sensing technology is becoming very important. Starting with conventional aerial photography, this has developed into a tool of immense precision using satellite photography, multi-spectral sensing, radar, and computer rectification of received images. In this way, photographs of infra-red reflection for example can be used to study variations in primary productivity, disease infestations of plants, or sources of thermal contamination of water. The United States currently has in orbit a satellite specifically designed for resources work and which transmits imagery from a number of optical-mechanical scanners and microwave bands. Radar imagery is of course independent of weather and diurnal conditions. Inventory and mapping of ecosystems and resources, quantification of ecosystem flows of matter and energy, and the monitoring of change are all facilitated by the application of this kind of technology (Badgley and Vest 1966, Colwell 1968, Johnson 1971). It may be noted, however, that for some substances, especially those in the earth's crust, the age-old methods of trial borings or diggings have to be adopted in the end. But the perception of resources is becoming ever more keen and the inventory of potential supplies more complete, although clearly we are a long way from knowledge of the entire stock of the world's potential resources.

The next stage is also very important. It is here that culture, in its myriad facets, plays a leading part, for the transformation of the perception of the source of a material into the cognition of a resource occurs at this stage. Here resources 'become'; the 'cultural appraisal' takes place. The values informing the cultural appraisal are many and varied. Knowledge, especially of an objective scientific kind like knowing the uses of a particular forest tree or the edibility of a fungus, is central; but so are various types of prejudice, experience and imagination. An item of knowledge may become ritualized into a prejudice, as may have happened with pork in the Middle East; religion and magic are often powerful at this stage, hence the selection of a settlement site may in some cultures be determined less by the environmental suitability than by the interpretation of the numinous qualities of the place by the practitioner of spiritual affairs. Numerous examples of apparently irrational cognition of the qualities of the environment can be discerned, and incomplete appreciation of the properties of a resource is termed cognitive dissonance.

Even in the most sophisticated societies, the completeness of the resource manager's cognition is imperfect. The constraints are many: the costs of obtaining additional information, the lack of technological knowledge, human fallibility and chance are all possibilities. The complexity of the ecology of environment and its social veneer means that the capacity of the human mind for formulating and solving complex problems (even when aided by the computer) is very small compared with the size of the problems whose solution is required for objectively rational behaviour in the real world. Resource managers then become, according to Kates (1962),

> men bounded by inherent computational disabilities, products of their time and place (who) seek to wrest from their environment those elements that make a more satisfactory life for them and their fellows.

In deciding between alternative resource processes, managers may elect to choose consciously, or may adopt more reflex attitudes such as habitual choice with its recourse to traditional or repetitive behaviour, or may engage in unconscious or trivial choice. The choice must then be implemented. Apart from institutional considerations, the primary factor here is the technology available to the manager: the extension, as it were, of his arm. Although physically and temporally separate from the cognition process, it is in reality also

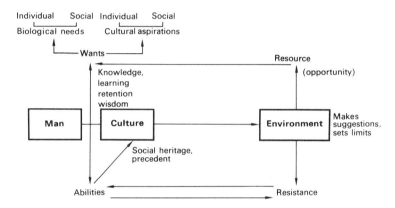

Fig. 1.15 A diagram of some of the factors involved in environmental perception. In reality there must be many more feedback loops than can be suggested in such a scheme, and culture appears to be very diverse.
Source: O'Riordan 1971b

part of the cognition process, for knowledge of technical capability is an important part of the decision-making process. The whole system can be approximately summed up in diagrammatic form (Fig. 1.15). The reality is much more complex, especially in the number and nature of feedback loops, but the diagram presents a useful summary model.

Whatever the complexity of the processes, the outcome in terms of cognition of, and adjustment to, the resources of the environment is of some importance. For sophisticated groups this result may mean the difference between comfort and discomfort, profit and loss; for subsistence cultures, life and death may be at stake. Nevertheless, before the advent of Western culture, some 'primitive' groups had been notably successful in adapting to extreme environments in which there appears to our eyes to be a paucity of resources. The Bushmen of the Kalahari Desert are an often-quoted example: to them the recognition of sources of moisture in their arid surroundings is the critical element. Thus all manner of plants and animals are used for food and some of these probably function largely as sources of moisture. The people become adept at spotting the traces of delicacies such as buried ostrich eggs, for example, which add a valuable element to their diet. The Eskimo groups of northern North America were also notably successful in adjusting to the food and material supplies of their unyielding environment. This success traditionally involved limitations of the population level of a group by means of infanticide and the exposure of non-productive old people. Contact with American culture has changed some of the Eskimo ways, and Sonnenfeld (1966) has suggested that landscape preferences among them may be related not only to their economy but to the degree of 'Westernization' which they have undergone.

Environmental cognition by more advanced people is often a very pragmatic consideration. It may often be important, for example, in the recognition of the probability of environmental hazards where these phenomena are not regular. This is particularly so in areas where such a hazard may make a great deal of economic difference to an individual or group. The role of drought in the farming of the Great Plains is an example, studied by Saarinen (1966). This unpredictable feature of the regional climate was perceived at varying levels. The nature of the hazard was best understood in the driest areas, not surprisingly, but the amount of experience of drought that a farmer had had was also significant in his recognition of the hazard, as was his particular personality. Although greatly variable, this latter generally resulted in an over-optimistic attitude; except in the driest areas almost all farmers underestimated the frequency of meteorological drought.

This somewhat unwarranted optimism is paralleled in work on the perception of storm-flood hazards on the urbanized eastern shoreline of the United States. Here, Burton, Kates and Snead (1969) found contrasts between the technical perception of the hazard by responsible public agencies, and that of the lay people who were the resource managers for much of the housing development along the coastline. They responded to the randomness of storms

> either by making the events knowable, finding order where none exists, identifying cycles on the basis of the sketchiest of knowledge of folk insight, and in general, striving to reduce the uncertainty of the hazard by making it certain. Or conversely, they deny all knowability, accept the uniqueness of natural phenomena, throw up their hands, and transfer their fates into the hands of a 'higher power'.

As one respondent remarked when asked to comment on the likelihood of future storms, 'God doesn't tell us things like that.'

The significance of environmental cognition and subsequent behaviour towards the local resources is not confined to instances of 'economic' activity such as agriculture, industry and settlement. Lucas (1965) has shown how the perception of the qualities of the Boundary Water Canoe Area (Minnesota-Ontario) varies with the type of user. Those who paddled their own canoe were willing to tolerate a lower level of obvious human use (i.e. logging) of the surrounding forest than those who used outboard motors. Clearly this has significance for the 'wilderness' type of recreationist for whom ecological virginity and the absence of fellow humans are paramount. Management of the resources of such an area can thus be directed at maintaining a certain mental condition through supplying the correct perceptive stimuli which assure the user that he is in a wilderness area. This may have considerable application in crowded countries where wild recreation areas are difficult to find.

The mind of the beholder is clearly of paramount importance. A landscape such as that of a British upland area like the Yorkshire Dales or Dartmoor may be perceived in different ways by different groups. One category of people may see the landscape as a set of concrete objects—farms, moorland, trees, roads—which can be preserved or altered. Landscape architects and planners perhaps fall into such a division. Another view is utilitarian: the land represents economic activity, the place where some people, such as farmers and quarrymen, make a living; all other features are subjugated to this central fact. Yet more people respond emotionally to the scenery, since for them it is a scene of beauty which stirs them and to which no change should come. For a last set of people the landscape is symbolic in that it represents freedom, a different place, 'the land beyond', or some other intangible. There is no need to have seen the landscape for it to have this significance. When all these groups are represented on a planning authority committee, the scope for disagreement over the future of the area is wide.

Different backgrounds can lead to differing opinions as to the significance of a given body of facts. This is very noticeable in the gap between some social scientists and most natural scientists over the 'population explosion' and its effects on resources and environment. The former tend (with notable exceptions) to be optimistic and to regard sustained population growth as an acceptable and even desirable phenomenon; the latter are often Malthusian in outlook and make gloomy prognoses. These divergent views of the relations of population and resources are clearly germane to the theme of this book and will be examined in more detail in Part III.

Ecology and economics

Of all the attitudes to the relationships of man and nature that have been discussed, ecology and economics have become most important, and of these two the latter is dominant. Its purpose, as Caldwell (1971) points out, is simple, direct and obvious: if material wealth is seen as the natural and proper goal of man's activities, then the mastery of man over nature (and the pre-eminence of economic thought over ecological thought) becomes a fulfilment of human destiny. The perspectives of ecology are different from those of economics, for they stress limits rather than continued growth, stability rather than continuous 'development', and they operate on a different time-scale, for the amortization period of capital is replaced by that of the evolution of ecosystems and of organisms. So some reconciliation of the two systems of thought might be held to be desirable, in which the findings of one science might be translated with some precision into its impact upon the other, and the values suggested by ecology might become the operational dicta of economics and *vice versa*.

Attempts to find isomorphic concepts and to transfer the language of economics into the realities of environment have been made for example by Boulding (1966b, 1971) when he compares vital flows in both systems, such as energy in one and money in the other. Economic accountings of 'production' of goods and services such as GNP are in fact mostly measurements of decay, since cars and clothes wear out and food and gasoline are oxidized. The bigger the economic system, therefore, the more materials that have to be destroyed to maintain it. Holling (1969) also draws parallels which rely on common features between ecological and economic systems, such as high diversity and complex interactive pathways, distinctive historical character and important spatial attributes, and important structural properties such as thresholds and limits. These led Holling to simulate the process of recreational land acquisition as a comparative process to that of predation in ecological systems. The possibility of energy as an intermediary between ecology and economics is fairly obvious, since it is important in ecosystems at all scales and can also be bought and sold; H. T. Odum (1971) attempts to provide energy flows for a set of marine bays in Texas which bring together all the flows of the ecosystem and man's industrial and recreational use of it, principally by allocating a dollar value to each kcal of energy expended in any activity, e.g. each visitor is assumed to expend 3,000 kcal/day in the area. Even more explicit is Deevey's (1971) statement that energy is the 'key to economic growth and the proximate cause of environmental pathologies', and he ranks the energy flows of the world in the following ratios:

Plant biosphere	Industry	Husbandry	Personal
300	25	2	1

noting that only the former is actually production, the others being consumption, and that the figure for industry represents a level of organization which he finds superior to pastoralism. He stresses, however, that if any of the 25 units is 'invested' in making the 300 non-renewable in a long-term perspective, then this is courting trouble; yet much of the use of energy by man in the cause of gaining economic wealth appears to be doing just that.

Energy appears to be a workable intermediary between ecology and economics in an empirical and descriptive context: we can say that so much energy has produced a particular degree of ecological change. But prediction is much more problematic, for some ecosystem energy-flows may be totally disrupted by the removal of one component, possibly by a very small input of man-manipulated energy, whereas others may require a gross perturbation before they are deflected from their stable state or their successional trajectory; without knowing most of the functional and structural characteristics of an ecosystem, the impact of economically directed energy flows is impossible to foretell except in the most general terms. The relations between order and diversity and the use of tools such as information theory may help to build a body of empirical and theoretical knowledge about this critical interaction, as may other scientific techniques; it is clearly a field in which the practical applications would be considerable.

Interactions

As has been stressed above, energy forms a medium of connection between man and his surroundings, no matter in what form it is used. The first and most obvious of the forms is manpower itself, which requires only social organization in addition to normal survival conditions for its effectiveness. Other forms of energy have to be harnessed and therefore at least to some extent understood before they can become useful ways of doing work.

Animal power was the first, made possible by the use of domesticated beasts in order to perform various tasks, particularly those associated with agriculture. Inanimate sources of power were for long dominated by wind and water, the latter being especially responsible for much industrial development before the nineteenth century; it persists in the importance to many societies of hydro-electric power. But the great surge of industrialization dating from the nineteenth century is linked to the elaboration of ways in which to exploit fossil fuels, dominated at first by coal and more recently by oil and natural gas. In the mid-twentieth century atomic power has been added, where the energy of the nucleus of the atom is released in a controlled fashion to provide immense quantities of energy, usually made available in the form of electricity.

It is possible therefore to divide the history of man–environment relationships into periods characterized by cultural stages in which man's access to sources of energy played a leading role.

The first level we can distinguish is that of the hunter-fisher-gatherer. Present in Europe during Palaeolithic and Mesolithic times, a few groups employing this mode of subsistence have persisted elsewhere to the present day. They have had access only to human energy for their environmental relations, which are dominated by the acquisition of food. The more advanced types have been able to channel this energy technologically: the blowpipe, bow and slingstick represent ways of concentrating the power conferred by human anatomy. Using these weapons, their access to environmental resources concentrated on the cropping of biotic organisms for food, with preferences for large mammals and fish being exhibited by many groups. Wood was used, and where a cutting edge or penetration power was required, then stone, especially in the form of flint and chert, was a common inorganic resource. Many other food sources such as small mammals, birds, berries and fruits were taken, but we may speculate that the expansion of human numbers took place up to the limits of a preferred food source rather than a total supply. Even so, such an economy required considerable space, and territoriality was probably well developed in the various biomes colonized by such people. Surprisingly, the extremes of both desert and tundra have been occupied at this level of technology, as well as the less hostile intermediate life zones. It seems likely that such groups altered their environment insubstantially, but access to a partly controllable energy use like fire was undoubtedly the most powerful way of altering the ecology of their territory. With it beasts might be run towards traps or over cliffs, and underbrush cleared for easier sighting of game. In forested terrain the regular use of fire would gradually produce a more open habitat, as is happening in regular burnt savannas today.

The emergence of *Homo sapiens* was an evolution; his learning of the techniques of domestication was a revolution. In particular, the early farms of the Neolithic of west Asia and Europe represent a tremendous change in the resource base of men. Now the food supply was under much more direct control and it was more concentrated; much less territory was required than for a purely hunting and gathering existence, although these activities persisted. Energy use at first was human-based only, via the hoe and digging stick, but the introduction of light ploughs made possible the use of draft animals. As metals like copper, bronze and iron came into use, so specialists in their fabrication emerged, and there is evidence from certain outcrops of rock in Britain that axe-factories with a far-flung trade network were established. The soil became a perceived resource, as did the forests, grass-lands and savannas which provided the background for much of the early agriculture of the shifting cultivation type. In Bronze Age Britain, for example, evidence of the differential clearance of lime (*Tilia* sp.) trees has been interpreted by Turner (1962) as indicating a knowledge that good agricultural soils would be found underneath such trees. Even relatively primitive forms of agriculture, such as that described by Rappaport (1971), show favourable energy relationships for the societies involved. Tono-yam gardens in New Guinea, for example, had a yield : input ratio (measured in kcal/ac) of 20 : 1 and sweet potatoes of 18 : 1, energy expenditures in weeding, harvesting and carrying the crop all being counted. As might be predicted from ecosystem energetics, the introduction of pigs reduces the ratio to 2 : 1 at best, and it is often < 1 : 1, the pigs being valued then for their protein rather than their calorific value, and for non-dietary purposes.

The success of agriculture, coupled with increased knowledge about the storage of sur-pluses, may well have led to the removal of the decisions about family size from the group, as in hunting societies, to the family, where it has subsequently remained; one result was usually a considerable increase in population levels whenever agriculture was introduced or evolved.

The uncertainties of crop failure from blight or drought are combated by more advanced agriculturalists of the types found in ancient Mesopotamia or medieval Europe. Their use of energy was greatly improved by the possession of the wheel, which made possible the more efficient use of the energy output of domestic beasts. Environmental resources already known assumed new degrees of importance: soil, for example, may be critical to success, and so the selection of the best soils for a particular crop, the draining of fields as by ridge and furrow ploughing, and the maintenance of soil fertility by replacing lost nutrients in the form of manure became subject to group decision and control, as in the manorial system of medieval Europe. Fossil sources of fertility like the calcareous Crag rock, which was used to add lime to the sandy fields of East Anglia, enter the resource nexus, and the uncultivated land or 'waste' beyond the fields was seen as a feeding ground for protein sources such as pigs as well as a source of raw materials and fuel. The overcoming of water shortages through irrigation is an aspect of environmental management and alteration. Its success in arid areas like the ancient Near East led to the accumulation of permanent surpluses which in turn permitted the development of urbanization. Large numbers of people were divorced from everyday contact with their natural environment, but at the same time they often became the rulers of societies characterized by a centralized authority. Ecological mistakes were sometimes made, as in Mesopotamia, where salinification of the irrigated fields and the choking of the irrigation canals with silt from overgrazed watersheds may have caused the downfall of great cities (Jacobsen and Adams 1958). By contrast, the agriculture of western Europe has been markedly stable in its environmental relations, although it is currently beginning to show some signs of breakdown in soil structure. Another effect of agricultural surpluses was the development of urban specialisms such as writing, which is crucial to centralized authority. In this manner, official attitudes to and uses of environment can be promulgated, and the archaeological evidence of the state religions of Egypt, for example, reveals a high degree of attunement to the hydrology and ecology of the Nile. In medieval Europe, authority might through the possession of literacy order an inventory of the resources of a kingdom: by no other means could Domesday Book have been compiled.

The age of the use of fossil fuels, which started in earnest in eighteenth- and nineteenth-century Europe and which flourishes unabated today, has marked a great difference of kind as well as degree in the environmental relations of man. Access to energy stored in coal and oil, with the later addition of hydro-electric power, has allowed the use of the earth's resources on a scale hitherto unimaginable. The steady improvement of technology has meant the recovery of progressively poorer deposits, so that scarcity, except on a regional basis, is practically unknown, thus encouraging moves towards energy-intensive economies (rather than labour-intensive ones) in industrial nations. A great environmental impact has been felt from the use of these energy sources in the mining, smelting and use of minerals and other materials of the earth's crust, so that every industrial region is marked with a million holes and heaps.

The environmental effects of this 'industrial revolution' have been massive and are well catalogued; in most Western countries they are still with us. Urbanization has been the most noticeable: in many ways quite unobjectionable but all the same providing concentrated sources of atmospheric pollutants, together with industrial and domestic effluents to affect the biota (and other men) far beyond the cities of their origin. There have been many other effects also, such as the devastation of forests to provide lumber for building and pulp for paper; more efficient hunting techniques have brought whales to the brink of extinction and some species of plants and animals have been exterminated due to habitat alteration or to increased accessibility allowing more thorough hunting: the passenger

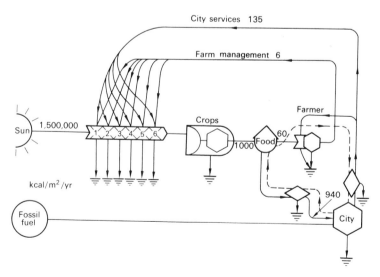

Fig. 1.16 An energy network diagram for modern agriculture. The chief feature is the application of fossil fuel (in this instance channelled via the city acting as an organizing centre rather than directly to the farmer) and the use of much of this energy in management and city-based services. The agricultural population can thus support 32 times its number in cities.
Source: H. T. Odum 1971

pigeon owes its demise to a combination of all these. Agriculture too has become industrialized, with energy from fossil fuels replacing the work formerly done by man. Planting and seeding have become mechanized and are preceded by commercial preparation of the materials; industrial fertilizers have replaced the virtually closed cycle of cropping and manuring; weeding is carried out by mechanical and chemical means, as is the preparation of the soil; and insecticide use further reflects the binding of agriculture to the industrial world. Thus, as H. T. Odum (1971) has calculated, an agricultural population living at 170 persons/km² can support 32 times that number in cities. A production yield of $60/ac ($24.30/ha) for grain in the USA, for example, is due to input worth $54/ac ($21.87/ha) for goods and services from the industrialized culture. The energy flows of an industrialized agriculture are summarized in Fig. 1.16.

Man has so far found he is able to remake the world according to his own plans, and his attitude to the natural world (at any rate the Western attitude, which at the height of European imperialism meant the attitude of much of the globe) has been by and large to maximize economic gain in the short run. The long-term consequences of actions have only rarely been considered and so there has been a build-up. In the past, further expansion of activity has often been seen as a cure for present problems, an attitude given much credibility by the explosive growth and impressive achievements of science and technology. Of late there has been a swing from the unbridled optimism of the nineteenth century, and concern over the protection of nature and scenery, moves towards pollution control and anxiety over the effects of population growth on the biosphere have all become fashionable in industrial nations; underdeveloped countries are as yet inclined to feel that these negative aspects of economic growth are bearable if they bring with them the enhanced prosperity enjoyed by industrialized countries.

The year 1945 was the beginning of the atomic age, with the release from the Los Alamos bottle of a genie of quite ferocious power, and one whose destructive powers have been subject to considerable augmentation since then. Energy from nuclear fission is used for power generation too but is also available for boats, mostly submarines. Nuclear fusion is currently difficult to control, but if it becomes more tractable, and available in small doses, we shall then have a virtually unlimited source of energy. We need to be reminded, of course, that whatever comes from planetary material is eventually finite, and that energy made to perform work is dissipated as heat. The rate of increase of the energy consumption of the USA, for instance, if projected for a few hundred years would make its land surface as hot as the sun.

The introduction of large-scale power is dominated by its cost in relation to the rising expense of the recovery of fossil fuels; and the true cost of nuclear power is not yet known, since at present its use is subsidized by fossil fuel utilization in the process of prospecting for nuclear fuel, for example, and in many other ways. The potential environmental effects of nuclear energy are immense. In an unlimited nuclear war, a great part of the surface phenomena of the earth would be devastated and the legacy of the explosions would live on physically during the lives of the radioactive fallout particles and genetically for innumerable generations of whatever organisms were left: imaginative playwrights and SF writers seem to favour either rats or insects as the ecological dominants. Extraordinary effects could be deliberately wrought. Edward Teller has suggested blowing huge holes deep in the earth's crust in which to store rubbish, and the possibilities of thus 'digging' a second and larger Panama Canal at sea level are under active exploration (Rubinoff 1968). Tables 1.7 and 1.8 help to summarize the role of energy as a crucial element in man's environmental relations. Table 1.7 shows in particular the relative productivities, in both dry matter and energy content, of different food-producing systems, in which the dramatic increase between non-fuel-subsidized systems and those with fossil fuel input can be seen and extrapolated to its extreme condition in algal culture.

TABLE 1.7   Food yield for man

	Edible portion of net primary production	
Level of agriculture	Dry matter (kg/ha/yr)	Energy (kcal/m²/yr)
Food-gathering culture	0·4–20	0·2–10
Agriculture without fuel subsidy	50–2,000	25–1,000
Energy-subsidized grain agriculture	2,000–20,000	1,000–10,000
Theoretical energy-subsidized algal culture	20,000–80,000	10,000–40,000

Source: E. P. Odum 1971

TABLE 1.8   Energy requirements for life support of one man

	Area/man (ac) (1 ac = 0·405 ha)	Organic matter (10⁶ kcal/ day/person)
Pygmies in deep forest	640	341
Monsoon agriculturalists	1	0·16
US man	12	
Fossil fuel base		0·6
Photosynthetic input		1·0
US city dweller	0·0064	0·1
Astronaut in capsule	0·001	2,740,000

Source: H. T. Odum 1971

Table 1.8 compares the living area needed to support one person at various economic levels with the quantity of energy needed to keep him alive. The non-agricultural pygmies must garner their supplies from a wide area of forest, whereas agriculturalists live off a smaller base both areally and energetically; industrial man in the USA receives energy from both photosynthetic and fossil sources in the order of 100–1,000 times the 3,000 kcal/day needed to maintain his metabolism. The quantity of energy support needed by lunar expeditions is astronomical.

Man and ecosystems

Abstraction about the crucial role of energy flows in man's relations with the natural world are not the only generalizations that can be made about his interactions with ecosystems. His effect upon other features of their metabolism, such as limiting levels and their self-regulating mechanisms, must also be briefly considered, as must the outcomes of the magnitudes of the manipulations which he exerts, i.e. the transformation of natural ecological systems into resource processes, whose landscape expression is often identified as land use.

Human effects upon ecosystem processes

There are a number of facets of the ecosystem concept which relate to resource processes, among which the notion of limiting factors occupies an important place. First enunciated by Liebig as a 'law of the minimum' with respect to the supply of chemical materials essential for plant growth, it has widened to include more factors. The idea of tolerance is now used, since it is realized that the continuing presence of an organism depends on the completeness of a set of complex conditions. The efficiency or indeed superabundance of any factor may mean that the limits of tolerance of the organism are exceeded. Tolerance, not only of 'environmental' factors but of intraspecific aggression and interspecific competition, varies with regard to each particular factor and may change synergistically in combination with other features of the organism's environment.

In any natural ecosystem the overall limiting factor must be the amount of solar energy incident upon it, but within this context many other boundaries may operate. The supply of a particular mineral nutrient may not only limit plant growth but because of its importance in animal metabolism may limit the number of animals too. Schultz (1964) has hypothesized that the short supply of phosphorus in the arctic tundra is basically responsible for the regular supply of lemmings: at the height of a lemming peak all the available supplies of that nutrient in the ecosystem are locked up in the small rodents, and only when they die and the element is mineralized, thus becoming available again in the lemmings' forage, can the population build up once more. The heavy grazing by large numbers of lemmings allows more solar radiation to reach the soil surface and speed the release of more phosphorus from the subsoil. The discovery of the importance of trace elements like boron in animal nutrition has highlighted the way in which a limiting factor may result from a quantitatively small component of an ecosystem. In his activities, man may alleviate a critical limit, as by using artificial fertilizers. Alternatively, he may introduce a new lower limit: the disposal of untreated sewage into coastal waters for instance, where its sheer physical presence may decrease the amount of light reaching the littoral and sub-littoral vegetation and hence limit productivity. Such an action also puts a limit on the recreational use of the system.

Another feature of ecosystems which can be relatively easily measured is its diversity, usually expressed as a species : number ratio or a species : area ratio. These ratios increase during the early and middle stages of succession but appear to decline slightly once a steady state or climax condition is reached. Diversity is taken to indicate a state of complexity where energy flux and transformational efficiency are at their highest. A species may have a wide variety of food sources and an equally diverse array of predators so that any accidental disturbance will be damped down. Thus has arisen the hypothesis that stability of ecosystems is a function of their diversity (MacArthur 1955). Such an idea is probably too simple to apply generally, and other research has indicated, for example, that stability at herbivore and carnivore trophic levels increases with the number of competitor species (Watt 1965); and in one study, greater diversity at one trophic level was accompanied by lower stability at the next higher level (Hurd *et al.* 1972). Again, in some systems a key component can determine the stability of the whole of the system, as suggested by Paine (1969) in the case of the Crown of Thorn starfish irruptions. In the case of ecosystems cropped to provide resources or into which wastes are disposed, the concept of overall stability is more important, i.e. the ability of the system to return to an original condition after a perturbation or even its ability to achieve a new level of stability under a permanent stress. Stability thresholds have been studied empirically, as in the case of trampling on alpine tundras (Willard and Marr 1970), and a good deal of research on computer modelling is designed to allow prediction of the changes that will follow a given natural or man-made input into the ecosystem (Woodwell and Smith 1969). The analysis of the resilience of ecosystems to human modification is nevertheless at an early stage and is a field in which considerable advances would be of great practical importance (Schultz 1967, Margalef 1968, Watt 1968, Hill 1972).

Ecosystems also have a multiplicity of homeostatic mechanisms, called feedback loops in cybernetic terms, which tend to maintain the system in a stable condition. By means of the growth, reproduction, mortality and immigration of the organisms, together with the process involving the abiotic components of the system, the quantities and rates of movement of matter and energy are controlled.

Instability in systems is a consequence of disorder and has been compared by Schultz (1967) to the thermodynamic concept of entropy: systems in which disorder is increasing are becoming highly entropic; those which are building up order are negentropic. Life itself would thus appear to be a massive and continuing accumulation of negative entropy. If it were possible to measure the rate of change of entropy or its real equivalent in ecosystems, then this parameter would possibly be a measure of the 'health' of systems from the human point of view. Its role in the manipulation of resource processes would be helpful, since man's main activities seem to be to remove the homeostatic mechanisms and promote instability, sometimes to the point of outright destruction: consider the example of an overgrazed range which first of all has rapidly declining plant productivity (and hence animal yields) and then undergoes soil erosion.

In ecological terms cropping means the removal of energy-rich matter from a particular ecosystem at a particular spatial scale. The products of the resource usage are then put back either into the same ecosystem or into another. Energy is irrecoverably being given off as heat, but the other products are not in fact lost to the world ecosystem, if we except astronauts' excreta. Man's cropping is at both herbivore and carnivore level but is less usual at top carnivore level because of the relative scarcity of the animals at this stage, unless they are gregarious organisms such as some species of fish. Solitary carnivores may often be utilized for culturally desirable products such as eagle's feathers and leopard skins. The detritus chain also supplies animal products: *moules marinières* are a crop from such a source.

The input of man consists of energy and matter in various forms. Much of the energy input into all resource processes is now from fossil fuels and some matter is also fossil, in the form of mined rock. The whole process of cropping is accomplished by the application of man-directed energy and matter. The mobility of man over the surface of the globe conferred by access to energy sources and the development of technology has also meant the transmission of species of plants and animals from their natural habitats to other places. Many of them are unable to survive in their new lands, but some have been spectacularly successful, as with the rapid spread of the starling into the urbanized eastern seaboard of the USA; the history of the rabbit in Australia is perhaps the best known. Success seems to occur either when there is a vacant niche that no native animal has succeeded in filling, or when the introduced species can outcompete the indigenous biota. Often too, the transplanted organism leaves behind its natural predators and may not have any in its new home. Highly manipulated ecosystems, such as cities, waste ground and agricultural land, frequently provide habitats for introduced species.

In the pursuit of crops, the removal of competitors becomes important because they represent energy and matter that man cannot or will not garner. Plants other than the chosen crop become weeds; animals that compete for forage at the herbivore level or predate upon the chosen crop species become pests. 'Weed' and 'pest', it must be emphasized, are cultural concepts since there are no such things in natural ecosystems. Such simplification reduces the energy flow through the system by reducing its diversity (Fig. 1.17). Inducing the food chains to converge upon man may well increase the net crop for man and make it more concentrated in protein, but the overall flux of energy in such systems is lower than in the natural state, since gathering and processing stages result in net losses of energy which are subsidized by fossil fuels in an industrial context (Fig. 1.18). Man very often thus puts the brake on succession (which represents the building up of diversity) and maintains systems at an early stage. Overcropping may well cause an ecosystem to revert to a very early stage of succession, one with much bare ground and hence susceptible to soil erosion for instance, and in some places this may mean a change to a more xeric kind of vegetation. Overgrazing on the semi-arid grasslands and the steppes of western North America or the Saharan fringes has enlarged the desert areas, and though this is not proven, the outbreaks of locusts could very well be a consequence of the years of overgrazing of the parts of the world in which they occur: removing any woodland or scrub that might harbour bird predators, for example, and providing suitable sites of oviposition in open sandy soils. The British grouse moor, reduced by management practices to a monoculture of heather (*Calluna vulgaris*) and grouse (*Lagopus scoticus*), with all other plant species burnt off and all other animal species shot off, is highly unstable. Heather bark beetle can spread very rapidly, as can grouse ringworm. They are in fact epidemics whose transmission is facilitated by the ready availability of more host organisms, and so they spread with the rapidity of hysteria in a women's college at examination time. Man's response to instability is usually to increase his inputs of matter and energy, thus producing an ever-increasing spiral of manipulation in which the inputs needed to promote temporary stability themselves require higher inputs to achieve equilibrium at a later stage.

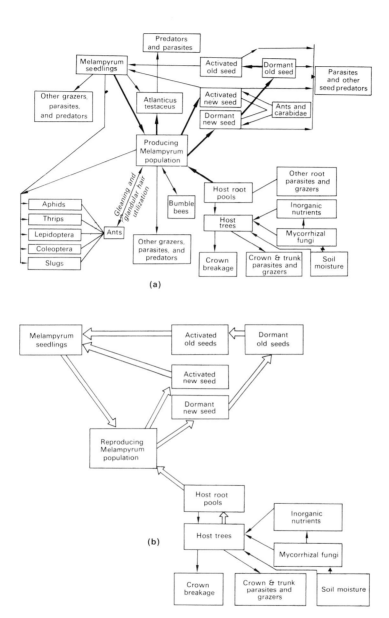

Fig. 1.17 An ecosystem centring around a plant parasitic on tree roots, *Melampyrum lineare*, in Michigan: (a) the natural system, showing biological relationships; (b) the system after the application of insecticides had eliminated certain components. The simplified nature of the ecosystem in (b) is apparent.
Source: Cantlon 1969

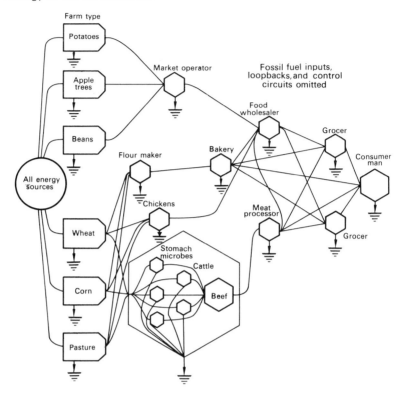

Fig. 1.18 An energy network diagram (unquantified) of the convergence of food chains necessary to develop high-quality (especially high in animal protein) nutrition in industrial countries. The network of 'middlemen' who perform the gathering-in are a source of numerous losses of energy from the system. 'All energy sources' refers to fossil fuels used in agriculture as well as solar energy; industrial power sources are also needed to enable the convergers to perform their functions.
Source: H. T. Odum 1971

One aspect of simplification is the extinction of biota. By various methods, from outright killing off for food or pleasure to the alteration of habitat, a wide variety of plant and animal species have been eliminated at local or regional and world scales. Where these groups were rare anyway and possibly towards the end of their evolutionary term, then man has perhaps merely accelerated a natural process. But it is difficult to imagine this to be true of the passenger pigeon, whose flocks were said to have darkened the sun at noon in the Mid-West of the nineteenth century but the last specimen of which died in a Cincinnati zoo in the 1920s. Neither is it likely to be so of the blue whale or the Javan rhinoceros or the oryx, to name but a few of the animals on IUCN's list of endangered species. Such devastation must be placed in perspective: the phenomenon of 'Pleistocene overkill' indicates a long history of man's effect upon animal population. Extinction of biota appears therefore to have been a long-term concomitant of man's status as an ecological dominant, although there are now powerful cultural currents, in the Western world at any rate, to try to halt this process. By definition, however, the loss of currently rare species is unlikely to produce unstable ecosystems: it is more probable that large uniform strands of very common species will produce that particular effect.

Man's manipulation of ecosystems

We turn now to providing an introduction to the major part of this book, the consideration of man's uses of the world's environments, considered in ecological perspective. Each of the themes briefly reviewed here is taken up at greater length in a section of its own.

At some stage in the last million or two years, all the ecosystems were unaffected by man: they were pristine or virgin. A few such places remain, but much of the rest of the terrestrial surface has been altered in some way. The nature, intensity and antiquity of his transformations enable us to compile a simple ranking of the land-use systems according to their degree of manipulation away from the pristine condition. At one end are ecosystems which are either left untouched or which it is desired to keep in as 'natural' a condition as possible; at the other man's structures obliterate entirely those of nature. Thus the lowest manipulation is typified by the sea or the high peaks of the Andes, the most alteration by Manhattan or Europoort.

At present, our knowledge does not enable us to compile all the data about these systems that we would like, such as their primary and secondary productivity, their response to increased demands for their components, and the history and type of man's alterations. Many of these features are known about at a quantitative level and the work being pursued under the aegis of the International Biological Programme (IBP) will doubtless yield a great deal of knowledge about the productivity of ecosystems. For the present we are mostly confined to more general accounts.

Apart from completely unused land, areas used for *outdoor recreation and nature conservation* represent the condition of least alteration. Where there is a single-use management aim for these, the object is generally to disturb the *status quo* as little as possible, and to maintain the ecosystems as they are at the time of designation or even to restore a former condition. This concern may even lead to the confusion of trying to stop natural processes such as fire or succession in order to preserve particular biota or landscapes even though under natural conditions they would be transient. Limiting factors in this system usually relate either to the numbers of a particularly favoured organism or to the populations of the observers, which if large enough diminish the quality of the crop. In this case it is mainly aesthetic satisfaction: the difficulties over the management of the National Parks of the USA illustrate this point. Most manipulation in these systems involves the control of animal populations which exceed the carrying capacity of the Reserve or Park because its legal limits are unrelated to the true boundaries of the ecosystem of which they are a component.

Requiring little more manipulation is *water catchment*, and indeed in many wildlife areas it is successfully combined with the preceding land use. Apart from the major landscape changes induced by dams and the subsequent replacement of terrestrial by aquatic systems with possible consequent modifications in local climate, the watershed area is often little altered, especially since there is not complete agreement about whether trees are beneficial to water yield (in terms of steady release) or harmful (by transpiring a goodly proportion of the system's water back into the atmosphere). Once caught, the water may be managed to effect far-reaching alterations such as irrigation or industrial growth, but the areally larger watersheds are not often subject to large-scale manipulations.

The *grazing* system represents the large-scale pastoralism of a selected domesticate. All other herbivores, together with the carnivorous predators of the chosen animal, are regarded as pests. Characteristically there is no return of minerals to the soil other than as the excretory products of the animals. (Intensive grazing with highly controlled conditions of herbage yield and fertilizer input is regarded as part of a sedentary agricultural system.) If it is not to degrade the plant cover, pastoralism must be wide-ranging and long recovery times are necessary, especially in arid and semi-arid environments. If flocks are too large and come back too soon to a patch of forage, then trampling may result in puddling of soils and thence their erosion; and selective grazing will certainly eradicate the palatable species in favour of tougher grasses or xerophytic plants such as thorny scrubs or succulents. Manipulation of apparently natural pasture lands has been proceeding for several millennia, in consort with the evolution of domestic herbivores and the use of fire as a management device. Recent research, especially in East Africa, has suggested that a higher amount of living tissue per unit area (biomass) is found under 'natural' conditions, and that as far as animal protein yield is concerned it is better to harvest the native fauna; also they do not degrade the habitat as do domestic beasts. This is one way of altering the whole dimension of a critical limit; more conventionally used are fertilizer input (e.g., by aerial dusting) and vegetation control using various methods of encouraging palatable and nutritious species which help to raise the carrying capacity for stock.

The longstanding but gradual system modifications represented by a pastoral economy are paralleled by one type of *forestry* which 'grazes' through virgin forest, allowing natural regeneration in its wake. On the other hand, modern forest plantation in Europe for instance is more like contemporary farming, exhibiting controlled inputs of nutrients, careful thinning out, lavish use of pesticides and orderly harvesting. So forestry is difficult to place on a gradient of manipulated systems since it can occupy most places from the barely altered to the totally artificial. A reasonable position seems to be to regard it as more manipulative than grazing and less so than agriculture. In biological terms forestry represents the removal of nutrients from the local ecosystem and the disappearance of the dominant of the community. Even if only temporary, the effects are therefore strong: careless forestry can lead to drastic soil erosion and consequent river silting, to quote two well-attested examples. As far as plant nutrients are concerned, the practice of removing and often burning leaf-bearing branches *in situ* means that many of the nutrients essential for tree growth find their way back into the local ecosystem and only the lignified wood is borne away, with its smaller complement of elements likely to be in short supply in the system, whereas soil erosion inevitably carries away mineral nutrients.

Towards the highly manipulated end of the scale must be placed *shifting agriculture*. Although after the plot has been abandoned the system may revert to its original condition, there are suggestions that this is never totally achieved and that small differences in the secondary system always exist. As Geertz (1963) points out, the most interesting feature of shifting agriculture in tropical forests is that the crops planted in the clearing imitated the former community. The miniature forest of crops gives complete cover of the site, so that it is not exposed to the leaching effects of the heavy rainfall. The rapidly fluxing mineral cycling of the forest is not initiated, since the plot is cultivated until the nutrients are more or less exhausted and it is then abandoned to regain higher levels under the secondary forest. In the normal working of the system the critical points are probably the initial nutrient supply which, in tropical forests especially, is mostly in the vegetation and not in the soil (hence the practice of slash-and-burn) and the maintenance of soil structure. Under present conditions very little is usually done about either of these. The overall critical point comes when population levels make it necessary to re-utilize a plot before its nutrient levels and soil structure have been built up again, and diminishing yields coupled with soil erosion are the frequent consequence.

The most highly manipulated of all the non-urban systems is *sedentary agriculture*. Here, the food chains are subordinated to the monocultural production of a crop which either comes to man as a herbivore or is fed to herbivores for subsequent animal protein yield. Thus all competitors are removed and this necessitates either high inputs of energy, as in weeding and bird-scaring, or of matter, as in the form of chemical pesticides. The monocultures are usually prone to epidemics, so that the high yields of the intensive agriculture areas of the sub-tropics (where usually water is a limiting factor and irrigation is the means of lifting its threshold) and temperate zones are achieved only at the price of high inputs by man. This is especially true of mineral nutrients, for the use of the crop may be thousands of miles from the area in which it is grown, and few of the metabolic products find their way back to the fields: most are dumped in the sea. Although much of the energy gained in this system can be cropped by man, there is nevertheless a great reduction of fixed energy compared with the system which preceded it: compare for example the amount of photosynthetic tissue per unit area of a forest with that of a typical row crop, growing for perhaps five to six months of the year.

In the process of manipulating ecosystems for his own ends and in recovering and processing his resources, man may well affect the systems by the material which he returns to them. Very often these are unwanted and even toxic products and they are generally referred to as pollution. This topic along with other negative features of resource use will also be dealt with in Part II.

Further reading*

BOUGHEY, A. S. 1968: *Ecology of populations.*
BOULDING, K. E. 1966: Ecology and economics.
CROCKER, T. D. and ROGERS, A. J. 1971: *Environmental economics.*
FIREY, W. J. 1960: *Man, mind and land.*
GLACKEN, C. J. 1967: *Traces on the Rhodian Shore.*
GREENWOOD, N. and EDWARDS, J. M. B. 1973: *Human environments and natural systems.*
ODUM, E. P. 1971: *Fundamentals of ecology.*
ODUM, H. T. 1971: *Environment, power and society.*
WATT, K. E. F. 1968: *Ecology and resource management.*
— 1973: *Principles of environmental science.*
WATTS, D. 1971: *Principles of biogeography.*

* Full publication details are given in the Bibliography.

Part II
Resource processes

2

Unused lands of the world

In this section we are concerned with those parts of the world where the terrestrial eco-systems appear to be virtually unaltered by man, either because he is present but does not exert any manipulative effect on the ecology, or because he is, in increasingly fewer places, absent. Men may be settled at a particular point and rely on outside sources for nearly all their materials and hence by their self-sufficiency not exert any resource-using pressures on the environment, as in the case of service camps like the US base at the South Pole which is supplied by air. In another category are the settlements which produce within their own area most of their needed resources and obtain the rest by trade along routes where self-sufficient transport is used. Desert oases with their accompanying trade (traditionally carried by the frugal camel) are examples of this category. At the point of settlement there is admittedly a more or less complete obliteration of the original ecology, but it is limited in area, and there is no tentacular reach into the environment for resources.

Man is also said to function only at an animal level in some ecosystems where he is subject to the same competitive and predatory pressures as other mammals. Only hunting, fishing and gathering cultures can be regarded as belonging to this group, and we shall look at examples of such people to try to assess the validity of the supposition that they do not in fact manipulate the ecosystems to which they belong. A schematic layout of these categories is given in Fig. 2.1.

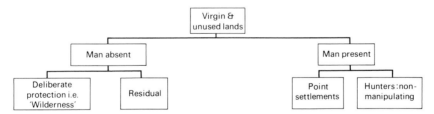

Fig. 2.1 A scheme of the various types of unused land and wilderness referred to in this chapter.

Hunting, gathering and fishing

Hunting and gathering was once the dominant mode of existence of our species, but by AD 1500 only 15 per cent of the world's land surface was inhabited by such peoples, at a time when the ecumene was more or less fully occupied. Today only a few pockets of hunters and gatherers survive, and their culture has almost always been altered by Western contact. Some Indian and Eskimo groups in North America exist largely on hunted products, although contacts with whites are at a high level; less influenced perhaps are people such as the 5,000 Bushmen of southern and south-west Africa who pursue a very largely aboriginal form of life. In such a category also may be placed some of the non-agricultural groups of the 170,000 Pygmies of central Africa such as the Aka, Efe and Mbuti, the Aborigines of Australia, and some Indians of the interior of Brazil and Venezuela. Together with a few other groups, they form possibly about 0·001 per cent of the present population of the world (Murdock 1968).

Such a sample is not therefore the best material for estimating whether or not they exert long-term effects on their ecosystems. To add to the difficulty, most of the studies done on them have been on their cropping as it relates to features of their culture rather than long-term investigations of subsistence patterns and the ways these might have been affected by the hunting and gathering patterns of the people themselves. Most of what follows is therefore inferred from anthropological studies designed for another purpose.

At a very simple level of subsistence are the !Kung Bushmen described by Lee (1968) who live in the Dobe area of Botswana. Here, 466 of them lived in 14 independent camps, each associated with a water-hole. Around this focus, a 9·6 km hinterland (i.e. within convenient walking distance of the water hole) was exploited for subsistence materials. The !Kung practise very little food storage, for rarely more than 2–3 days' supply is kept at hand, and the main foods are vegetable in origin, comprising 60–80 per cent by weight of the diet. The main item is the Mongongo nut, the product of a drought-resistant tree, which contributes about 50 per cent of the vegetable intake and which yields 600 kcal per 100 g edible material and 27 g protein per 100 g. Although many kilograms of these nuts are eaten, many more are left to rot on the ground, so apparently the resource is not fully used up. Of the other sources of vegetable foods, 84 species of edible plants are recognized (including 29 species of fruits, berries and melons, and 30 species of roots and bulbs), but of these 75 per cent provide only 10 per cent of the food value and thus the use of them must be light. There is a parallel situation with regard to meat-eating. The Bushmen name 223 species of which 43 are classed as edible, but only 17 are hunted regularly. It is not said whether this has always been the case or whether such a selectivity represents the end point of a long period of shifting numbers of animal populations. The adjustment of these Bushmen to the resources of their semi-desert environment is successful, for even though 40 per cent of the people do not contribute to the food supply, signs of malnutrition are absent and Lee (1969) estimates that they receive about 2,140 kcal and 93 g of protein per capita per day when an adequate diet would consist of 1,975 kcal and 60 g of protein. No starvation, even of the unproductive people, is necessary because of the basic dependence on reliable vegetable foods adapted to the local ecological conditions. It would seem therefore that no manipulation of the environment is necessary (nor indeed may it be possible) provided the population does not over-use the vegetable resources, and this appears not to happen, though Lee does not comment on any conscious attempts at population control.

In some ways the situation of the Bushmen is paralleled by a community like the Hadza of Tanzania (Woodburn 1968). They also subsist largely on vegetable matter, but meat and honey make up about 20 per cent of their diet. Even in times of drought, the 10 species of plants which contribute the main part of their nutrition do not fail and so there is never any general shortage of food. As with the Bushmen, the predominant activity of the men is hunting but although this brings in a prized food supply, it is scarcely an essential one. No attention is paid to harvesting either plants or game with sustained yield in mind: gathering and killing are indiscriminate. Even so, the ecosystem apparently goes on giving the Hadza adequate nutrition (in a survey of 62 children no evidence of kwashiorkor, marasmus, rickets, infantile scurvy or Vitamin B deficiency was seen), without undue effort on their part: an estimated average of 1–2 hours per day is spent in getting food. Extermination of game is to some extent presumably alleviated by the fact that only a small minority of the adult men do the hunting, and there is no pressure by men upon men to do it or be skilful at it, although keeping a wife may be difficult for an unsuccessful hunter. Further, gambling with metal-headed arrows is a favourite way of passing the time during the dry season and this probably relieves the hunting pressure on the animals.

Some contrast is offered by the subsistence patterns of the native inhabitants of the arctic regions of North America, of which the Netsilik Eskimos who inhabit the tundra regions north and west of Hudson Bay are a sample (Balikci 1968). Their base is essentially a marine-winter (seal) and inland-summer (caribou, salmon trout) movement with elements of substitution should one resource fail. For example, caribou would be hunted across the open tundra with bow and arrow should the normal method of killing them from kayaks at a river crossing fail. The critical period is the long winter, and caches of food for such a period are necessary. Population seems to have been severely limited to those who could be supported readily during the lean times. Thus female infanticide, senilicide and invalidicide were all practised when necessary, especially when travelling was essential. So over very large areas, the population density was quite low: in 1923, the Netsilik numbered about 260, in a region 480 × 160 km in size. In such a context, the harshness of the environment must have meant that the gaining of subsistence in the short term was a considerable struggle and the conscious manipulation of the ecosystem for the long term was scarcely likely. The advent of Western culture has altered the living conditions of most Eskimo, for they can now rely upon imported food from both trade and welfare programmes, and also have access to fossil fuel sources. In a group studied on Baffin Island, Kemp (1970) calculated that in one year the people gained 12,790,435 kcal of consumable food from wild sources. This was backed up by the outside world in the form of 7,549,216 kcal of store food, the equivalent of 8,261,600 kcal in ammunition, and 885 gal (2,815 litres) of gasoline for snowmobiles and outboard motors. In this area hunger is now virtually unknown, although it was in any case rarer than in the harsher terrain of the Netsilik.

In general, hunting and gathering seems to provide a very adequate way of life which can persist for centuries without radical alteration. This suggests that manipulation of ecosystems on a conscious level is rare; unconscious manipulation disturbs the system so little that fluctuations in yield or sudden adaptations to different food sources caused by catastrophes are virtually unknown. Thus obvious, and perhaps even borderline, malnutrition is rare. Even the minimal dietary requirements provided by hunting and gathering often allow such people to fare better than neighbouring groups who subsist on primitive agriculture or who are urbanized. Thus starvation is commonplace only in extremely rigorous climates where wild animals form practically the entire diet. Elsewhere, if there are any selective effects of shortages, they lie in the differential mortality of the old and infirm in the face of the water shortages which are more likely and more frequent than lack of food. Mortality from other causes is not particularly high among hunter-gatherers. Chronic diseases, traumatic deaths, accidents and predation vary in their incidence but are generally low (Dunn 1968). But in most such societies, social mortality has been part of the population–resources equation, with infanticide the most widespread practice. If, therefore, we have a tendency to regard hunter-gatherers as the members of the original affluent societies then it is because they did not attempt to populate their territories up to the limits of the carrying capacities of the lands (Deevey 1968). Either populations were kept down by systematic infanticide or else groups moved elsewhere (Birdsell 1968). Under such conditions, manipulation of environments, though not by any means impossible, becomes much less likely.

The evidence from modern hunters is so scanty and of such an indifferent kind for our purposes that it is scarcely possible to come to a firm conclusion about whether lands occupied by them are virgin lands, i.e. have unmanipulated ecosystems. In practical terms, since they are such small groups, it does not perhaps matter. Theoretically, however, there ought to be a point where the shift is made from man as an animal component of an ecosystem to man the changer of the ecosystem. The factors involved are very diverse, but two have major significance: the population numbers and the fragility of the ecosystem. The importance of the first of these is seen in the population control mechanisms exerted by many groups. Quite possibly experience at a past time had shown them that to grow too large in numbers was to exert an influence on the local ecology which was inimical to future food supply. The fragility of the ecosystem is another variable: semi-arid and arctic areas are particularly vulnerable, whereas temperate zones tend to have greater powers of recuperation after man-wrought alteration. The overall picture presented is of a mosaic in which the presence solely of hunters cannot automatically be taken to imply unaltered ecosystems; but most of the evidence which would enable more precise investigations to be made has now been overlain or wiped out by later changes.

Unused lands today

The 'unused' or 'virgin' lands of the world at present can only be found where human settlement is sparse. Not only is absence of man, or his presence at a very low density, necessary but also his use of either a simple level of technology or a 'point' settlement which is self-contained or relies on outside sources for its materials.

Let us differentiate between two types of 'virgin' lands: those which remain wild because they are residual lands of no value to contemporary resource processes, and those where there is a deliberate preservation of the wild for its own sake or for some other non-exploitative purpose. This second category is often described as wilderness: a term which although equally apt for the first set of lands is perhaps more useful where a particular concept of the role of wild terrain in relation to human purposes is envisaged. We shall deal with these two sets of virgin terrestrial ecosystems separately; the most pristine set of ecosystems of all, the sea, is treated individually later in the book.

Sparsely settled biomes

The largest more or less continuous single area of 'unused' land not deliberately preserved belongs to the arctic and subarctic zones of Eurasia and North America. These lands are mostly in the possession of the USSR, Canada and the USA (Alaska), with contributions from Finland, Sweden and Norway. The region has only relatively recently emerged from glaciation and is often characterized by immature soils and poor drainage. The characteristic vegetation type is the tundra, although many wetland and mountain communities also exist. Southwards, a belt of hardy deciduous forest like the birch scrub of Lapland may intervene between the tundra and the coniferous woodlands of the boreal forest biome. The animals are all adapted to survival over a long and very cold winter.

Like the high arctic and polar lands of perpetual snow and ice beyond them, these northern territories are sparsely settled. Modern incomers mostly live at 'point settlements' supplied by air or sea; the native peoples have always been few in number, although more wide-ranging at ground level both inland and across the ice-covered seas than immigrant whites. Both groups have had some effect on the ecology of the northern wilderness, though of different types. The native populations were largely dependent upon animals such as reindeer, caribou and seals for their subsistence. The number of people was small and the herds of animals immense so that probably no permanent change was effected in the natural ecosystems unless the biota were at a low level: the decline of the musk-ox in the Canadian tundra may have been due to native overhunting, although protection has now allowed it to regain higher population levels.

The advent of industrial man to the north has meant both direct and indirect change. Direct alteration of areas comes from mining, trapping and logging, although the last two need not wreak permanent change on ecosystems if carried out with due regard for sustained yield; inevitably such policies have often been neglected. Indirect changes come from incidental operations: fires from logging which run up onto lichen-clad slopes and destroy the winter feed of caribou, for example. The explosions from seismic testing for petroleum scare away the arctic fox, according to many Eskimo, and there is now the possibility of large-scale oil contamination from the finds on the arctic slope of Alaska and Canada's North-West Territories. In such a cold climate, the longevity of spilled oil is not known and might persist for decades. The same development is producing plans for pipelines across the tundra carrying heated oil, and the effect this will have on the permafrost is not properly known. At point settlements such as drilling rigs, considerable erosion of the tundra can be caused by vehicles and temporary dwellings if the permafrost is not protected by a thick pad of insulating material such as gravel. The wastes from such places are also apt to attract scavenging animals such as polar bears which then tend to end up as rugs. The northern lands, therefore, are still vast wildernesses of mostly natural systems, but exploitation is eroding these wild areas, and agricultural expansion in their climatically more favourable parts is still an aim of some governments. The ecosystems are generally so simple and specialized that it takes very little to cause their breakdown: this can be seen to a minor extent in Iceland, where there has been no impact of heavy industry on the land to disturb the sparsely vegetated surface, but where sheep grazing has nevertheless caused shifts in vegetation towards more open communities and hence an increase in the surfaces susceptible to sub-aerial erosion processes. We must conclude that the fragility of these northern areas needs careful consideration in any proposals to develop them, whether it be for minerals, biotic resources or tourism.

Similar in many ways are the high mountain areas of the world, such as the Rockies, Andes and Himalayas. In general the human impact has been very much less than in arctic and subarctic regions because high relief is added to harsh climate, but apparently unsettled lands may have undergone grazing by domesticated animals. This may produce the symptoms of overgrazing because the ecosystems are fragile and easily changed: so in the nineteenth century John Muir was moved to write of sheep in the Sierra Nevada mountains of California as 'hooved locusts' and to point out the soil erosion that followed in their trail. Today, recreationists may outnumber sheep, but their effect can also be strong. Numerous boot-clad feet can wear away mountain vegetation and allow erosion, and pack animals can do the same damage as other domesticated livestock. In winter, animals may be frightened away from their feeding grounds by motorized incursions on vehicles such as the snowmobile, which may also be used for hunting; by extending the range of hunters in winter it may help reduce the populations of some animals since they are likely to be in poor condition, although if predators like the wolf are killed then species like deer may expand beyond the carrying capacity of their habitat. In northern Ontario, some isolated lakes have been virtually fished out because of improved access during the winter by tracked vehicles.

Some forested areas of the world are also lacking in any density of settlement. The largest of such areas are the boreal forest zones of Canada and the USSR. This zone comprises several different vegetation types, ranging from an admixture of moss-floored forest and bog to an open forest with a dry lichen-heath ground layer. The short summer inhibits the activity of the soil fauna and flora and so a considerable depth of humus is characteristic of many parts of this formation. Along with fallen branches and trees, this layer is potential fuel for wild fires, and when set by humans or lightning these can destroy large areas of forest. They tend to be even more damaging when a management policy of instant fire suppression has been carried out for some years, since this allows the forest floor material to build up. Some populations of animals, such as moose, may build up to extremely high levels when a man-induced predator control programme is effective, as has been that of the wolf in Canada. The herbivores may then seriously affect forest regeneration and growth because of the intensity with which they browse. Even minimal human occupance can therefore lead to quite far-reaching ecological change.

In the remaining stretches of tropical forest considered 'natural', such as those of Amazonia and the highlands of New Guinea, the most disturbing influence has been shifting cultivation (see pp. 196–7). After abandonment, the plots recolonize with secondary forest and if not eventually re-used for agriculture then they become climax-type forest again. It is not certain whether the secondary forest ever regains the exact composition of its virgin state, but if not then reserves may eventually contain the only truly natural tropical forest and all the rest reflect the influence of an unconscious management system, as do most temperate forests even if they are apparently 'natural'.

Possibly the most 'unused' land of all is in the desert areas of the world. Their biological productivity is low, and apart from some hunting and pastoralism human use tends to be confined to mineral exploitation and especially in North America, recreation. Extraction of minerals such as petroleum is a 'point' activity and pipelines do not alter the desert very much, although the arid climate means that any hardware left lying around will persist for a long time, witness the tank hulks in North Africa and the beer cans in Arizona. Recreational use of deserts in the USA, especially in California and Arizona, centres around activities involving four-wheel drive vehicles and, in sandy terrain, 'dune buggies'. The former do not change the ecology very much themselves but import people into another type of fragile ecosystem where, for example, the trampling of succulents or the gathering of dried cactus 'skeletons' for firewood disturb large numbers of niches for a very long time, since plant growth rates are so low. Dune buggies may easily change unfixed dune systems quite radically, but the wind soon rectifies the situation; on the other hand, partially vegetated dunes are soon converted into 'blow-outs' after a few vehicles have torn up the root systems of the grasses binding them.

Islands, particularly those isolated in large oceans, might be thought to be likely candidates for pristine status, but this is rarely so. As Elton (1958) pointed out, such islands generally have a depauperate biota, with the result that unstable ecosystems change very rapidly as a result of direct human activity or the man-induced introduction of alien plants and animals. The coming of the pig and goat to many tropical islands resulted in a revolutionary destruction of vegetation; likewise the rat caused a large faunal shift in small coral-based islands. The innate instability of the latter is underlined by the anxiety which resulted from the population explosion of the large Crown-of-Thorns starfish. Such islands as remain in an unaltered state are highly prized for scientific purposes: Aldabra in the Indian Ocean is one example, containing rare fauna as well as an absence of anthropogenic effects (Stoddart and Wright 1967). The plan to build an airstrip there caused a considerable outcry from the international scientific community; it was, however, financial rather than ecological instability which defeated it in the end (Stoddart 1968).

There remain for discussion a few special cases of ecological systems which can be regarded as natural because they undergo constant renewal. Unfixed sand dunes, in an early stage of succession, are one example. Coastal systems such as the Sands of Forvie (Aberdeenshire, Scotland) are examples of such a condition; inland, the White Sands of New Mexico (part of which are under protection as a National Monument) provide another. Any activity of man generally proves very ephemeral in shifting dunes, but once they become fixed by vegetation then they are much more vulnerable to human activity, especially the specialized form of recreation which causes blow-outs. Tidal salt marshes which receive periodic inundation, and hence an input of silt and salt, might also be considered natural, although many of them are subject to grazing by domesticates; in the tropics the mangrove swamps occupy a similar niche, although without the sheep. Large paludal areas are often close to their virgin condition but are increasingly becoming altered by outside influences such as the influx of pesticides or eutrophication agents from their highly manipulated watershed areas.

Wilderness

In this section, some examples of the conscious and deliberate protection of large wilderness areas are discussed. It is difficult to distinguish these from the national parks and nature reserves described in the next chapter, but the main criteria are the large area (whereas parks and reserves can be of any size), the absence of deliberate management wherever possible, and the feeling of wholeness. The set of systems is preserved particularly because of its unity and not for any particular biota, landscape or recreational activity, as is so often the case with wildlife protection and landscape preservation areas (Plate 3).

Motivations

Ideally, wilderness areas should never have been subject to human activity which has resulted in manipulation, either deliberate or unconscious, of the ecology of the areas being considered. But in many cases our knowledge of land-use history is so fragmentary that we cannot honestly say other than 'it looks natural'. Research into Quaternary ecology and land-use history produces more and more evidence of the antiquity of man's imprint, and it becomes increasingly likely that some areas preserved for their 'natural wilderness' quality have in fact been altered by man at a pre-industrial or even pre-agricultural stage in the past.

The reasons given for the setting aside of wilderness areas vary from place to place and from culture to culture, but running through most of the legislation and regulations are a shared set of themes. There is often a declamation of the rightfulness of the independent existence of such areas: not all nature is to be perceived as a profitable or potentially useful resource and it should be allowed to persist on its own terms without any interference from man. In the last phrase is implicit the absence of any deliberate management of the areas designated and, like so many such hopes, this is often more pious than practical. This ethical strand of thought frequently stems from or is accompanied by religious motivation.

The most persuasive non-scientific argument in Western countries has been the advocacy of the spiritual aura of such lands. It is evident that their nature is changed by the incursion of large numbers of people, so their virtues reside either in their being experienced by small numbers of people as a special form of recreation which is basically spiritual refreshment, or in being symbolic. Then they do not need to be visited, they are just there as 'the wilderness beyond'. At one extreme, wilderness advocates may insist that experience of great natural areas is a spiritual essential for every person. This is unlikely and, nowadays, impractical. A more balanced point of view regards wilderness as being just as much a state of mind as a condition of nature; the beholder's response becomes paramount and hence the type of person determines the necessity or otherwise of wilderness experience. Although a pristine condition is a requirement of consciously preserved wilderness areas, the desire of people to visit them soon leads to ecological changes, and this possibility brings about conflict with another major set of reasons for wilderness protection, which are scientific in origin. There are three main strands to these propositions. There is firstly the need to keep a gene pool of wild organisms, both plant and animal, to ensure present and future genetic variety. Circumstances under which new strains may be needed cannot be foreseen and by

Plate 3 A wild area under protective management: Mount Hood, Oregon, USA. Habitats such as this mountain meadow may experience recreational pressure severe enough to impoverish the biota and spoil the aesthetics; thus restriction of access becomes essential to prevent certain types of change. *(Grant Heilman, Lititz, Pa)*

reducing diversity the possibilities for future choice are much restricted. Large wild areas ensure that a reservoir of potentially useful sources of breeding material for human use is preserved. Secondly, there is an emphasis upon the maintenance of animal communities in their natural surroundings in order to facilitate research upon their behaviour. In changed habitats the animals act differently and the chance to study specialized patterns as the product of a particular ecological niche is lost. This argument is similar to that advanced for many national parks and nature reserves, but here the emphasis is on the large area of the wildernesses and the increased chance that the whole life-span and seasonal cycles of the animal are completed in undisturbed conditions. Thirdly, sharing the last set of motivations and constraints, is the absolute necessity of protecting undisturbed ecosystems of all kinds for research in ecology. Many of man's activities consist of tinkering with his environment, and the prime requirement of successful tinkering is keeping all the parts. Much useful research is done in smaller areas, but large wildernesses are essential not only for pure research but also for applied work. Efforts to increase the productivity of crops, for example, may gain much from an understanding of the functioning of natural ecosystems.

As some of the examples will show, different reasons have been responsible for the legal designation of wildernesses in different places. In some, such as Antarctica, scientific reasons have been dominant. In the case of the National Wilderness Preservation System of the USA, the recreational-aesthetic reasons won the day. Also, some wildernesses may be called by names such as National Parks; in differentiating them from the areas to be reviewed in Chapter 3, we shall try to follow the criteria of size, lack of settlement, and absence of management policies and practices.

The USA and other nations

'The Wilderness' has always played an important part in the symbolic life of North Americans (R. Nash 1967); the rapidity with which the continent was settled and exploited meant the disappearance of most virgin land except in marginal environments. Even here, in remote forests, unyielding deserts and high mountains, the determination to log, mine or graze was often successful even if only temporarily so. The erosion of the wild led to a rising groundswell of public opinion which resulted in the passage through Congress of the Wilderness Act of 1964 (Simmons 1966). This immediately established a National Wilderness Preservation System and placed in it 54 wildernesses, wild and canoe areas, totalling about nine million acres (36,450 km²). All additions to the System have to be approved individually by Congress: by 1970 the System totalled about ten million acres (40,500 km²). The areas thus set aside are to have no economic uses, except where mining has been previously allowed, in which case it has to be removed by 1983; the President may allow other economic uses but only in times of considerable emergency. The criteria for establishment include a normal minimal size of 80 mi² (207 km²) and the Act's formal definition of ecological condition requires

> . . . an area where the earth and its community are untrammelled by man, where man himself is a visitor who does not remain . . . [and] without permanent improvements. . . .

The wilderness areas are to contain no roads, nor use of motor vehicles and aircraft except in an emergency; wilderness users were divided in one survey about the desirability of telephones for emergency use, and none have yet been installed. The terrains designated are mostly in the west of the USA. This is where the wild country is, and where the Federal Government, especially the Forest Service of the Department of Agriculture, has its largest holdings. The wildernesses are mostly forested at their lower elevations but with an alpine terrain of high peaks, cirques and snowfields at the upper levels. An exception is the Boundary Waters Canoe Area in the Quetico-Superior area of Minnesota-Ontario. Here a maze of natural waterways intersects coniferous forest, and canoe travel is the only method of transport permitted.

The Act makes it quite clear that the wilderness areas are recreative in purpose as well as scientific, for it speaks of 'outstanding opportunities for solitude or a primitive and un-confined type of recreation' as well as 'features of scientific, educational, scenic or historical value'. Thus, although wilderness and ecological purity are equated, there is a considerable amount of human incursion either on foot or with pack or riding animals. The convention of wilderness recreation seems to be that the area is crowded if you see people other than those of your own party, and so the constraints on carrying capacity are narrow. Even with such small numbers of users, management of the wildernesses may present problems. For example, natural lightning fires are probably a regular feature of the ecology of western coniferous forests, but these can of course engulf people. Should such forest fires (as distinct from man-set ones, if the distinction can easily be made by a dragged-out-of-bed Ranger who has to decide whether to call in the fire-fighting services) be suppressed or let alone even if there is risk to human life? These and other difficulties, such as refuse and sewage disposal, and the overgrazing of fragile mountain meadows by pack stock, pose formidable problems for those whose task it is to keep the wildernesses wild, for even low levels of use is scientific in purpose, and for example the helicopter used to ferry people, together such as the suppression of fire or the construction of primitive camp sites. Only where the use is scientific in purpose, and for example the helicopter used to ferry people together with their gear and food, can the USA wildernesses be likely in the long run to remain truly inviolate in an ecological sense. Rationing of recreational visits to wilderness areas is now being practised in some of the most popular areas of the Western Cordillera.

Some other examples of the conflict between designated wilderness areas and the need to manage visitors are provided by some of the mountain National Parks of Sweden and Czechoslovakia. In Sweden, the northern wild Parks, administered by the Forest Service, are probably not totally natural since their lower areas are Lapp territory. Nevertheless an information brochure states,

> they must not be visited in such a way that . . . the land loses its unique character, and that any of what we can perhaps best express by the word 'mood' is lost.

Inaccessibility is a feature of Parks such as Sarek (470,490 ac/1905 km²) where provisions for a week have to be carried, while access is forbidden to parts of the forest land and mire complex of Muddus National Park (121,577 ac/492 km²), especially to protect bird life. In the Tatra National Park, jointly managed by Poland and Czechoslovakia, the high inner-most zone can only be entered on certain paths and these must be kept to. Again, such areas were set aside with proper wilderness intentions, but their very designation has probably attracted some of the people whose numbers make management necessary.

Antarctica

The world's southern extremity is perhaps the best example of a deliberately protected wilderness (Plate 4). For many years following the early explorations it was an unconsciously preserved wilderness owing to its hostile nature, although the establishment of an increasing number of scientific bases by many nations meant that some destruction of biota ensued. The great impetus given to international scientific co-operation by the International Geophysical Year (1957–8), when research and observations in Antarctica played an important part, led the nations with territorial interests in Antarctica to conclude the Antarctic Treaty in 1959 (Heatherton 1965, Roberts 1965, Holdgate 1970). Even before the treaty the basic conditions for wilderness were in fact met: all settlement is 'point' settlement, supplied from

Plate 4 Antarctica: the last great wilderness. Even this remote region is not immune from residual pesticides and its research-orientated function is being complicated by the advent of tourism. (*Aerofilms Ltd, London*)

outside, and much transport is by air; none of the local resources is used for food or building purposes except in an emergency. None the less, even this remote polar ice-mass is not totally exempt from man's less disinterested activities. Tourist visits to Antarctica are becoming common, and the body tissues of the penguins contain DDT which has presumably come via oceanic food chains. In addition the major commercial resource of Antarctica, the pelagic whales of its waters, are exempt from the Antarctic Treaty.

The Treaty itself affirms the principle of international co-operation in occupance of the continent for scientific purposes. There is to be no military use or training, although military equipment may be used to aid research; no nuclear explosions or dumping of nuclear waste are to take place. No specific provision, however, is made for any terrestrial commercial resources should they be found: coal is the most likely, although this is highly baked and of a marginal quality. The protection of the ecosystems comes in the Agreed Measures which are annexed to the Treaty and which aim at minimizing any disturbance to the plants, mammals and birds of the Treaty Area. No mammal or bird may be killed, wounded or maimed without a permit, for example; dogs must be inoculated against, *inter alia*, rabies and leptospirosis, and are not allowed to run free. Helicopters are not to approach large concentrations of animals, and all the signatories agree to try to alleviate pollution near the coasts and ice-shelves which are the sites of most of the bases. Particularly noteworthy is the prohibition of the importation of non-indigenous species, except for laboratory use. There are also Specially Protected Areas where no vehicles are allowed and where even plants may not be collected 'except for some compelling scientific purpose', and Specially Protected Species, such as fur seals and the Ross seal, which are thought to be especially deserving of preservation. Overall, therefore, the Measures aim at the perpetuation of the variety of species and the maintenance of the balance of the natural ecological systems. The extent of their success is difficult to estimate but is probably high, since no large-scale ecological changes in the Antarctic appear to have taken place.

A wider context

It is unequivocally clear that the amount of 'unused' land in a 'natural' state is declining, and the rate of its disappearance is quite fast although precise data are lacking. The preservation of virgin land must therefore be a deliberate act, thus bringing it into the cultural-perceptual phase of resource allocation. The 'wilderness' idea is obviously culturally relative: many cultures see no virtue in the preservation of a large area of wild terrain just for its own sake. In many cases it is clearly a 'fringe benefit' for richer countries which poorer ones cannot afford if there are any resources at all in the wild areas. Are there, then, any strong reasons for the protection of wilderness areas other than those which are extensions of the arguments put forward for the designation of land as parks and nature reserves? Apart from the genetic pool idea, a suggestion which seems to have a world-wide validity is the role of wild areas, especially those with a high biological productivity, as 'protective' ecosystems which counterbalance the less stable 'productive' systems, a classification suggested by E. P. Odum (1969) and further discussed near the end of the book (pp. 367–9). A similar role has been postulated for the oceans. The exact role of these biomes is not known, but if there is any possibility that these wild ecosystems might be crucial then no deleterious action should be taken until more knowledge is available. The firm pressures of the numbers of people and their demands for materials militate against such action, for few nations or indeed individuals subscribe to Henry David Thoreau's motto for the preservers of wilderness, that,

> . . . a man is rich in proportion to the number of things he can afford to let alone.

Further reading

BRYAN, R. 1973: *Much is taken, much remains.*

ELTON, C. S. 1958: *The ecology of invasions by animals and plants.*

LEE, R. B. and DE VORE, I. (eds.) 1968: *Man the hunter.*

NASH, R. 1967: *Wilderness and the American mind.*

ODUM, E. P. 1969: The strategy of ecosystem development.

PARKER, B. C. (ed.) 1972: *Conservation problems in Antarctica.*

ROHMER, R. 1973: *The arctic imperative.*

SATER, J. E., RONHOVDE, A. G. and VAN ALLEN, L. C. 1972: *Arctic environments and resources.*

3

Protected ecosystems and landscapes

In the previous section we considered that change was an accidental, if widespread, feature of wilderness areas and unused land. Since management was reduced to a minimum the ecosystems were insulated from anthropogenic changes. We now discuss certain classes of ecosystems where change is acceptable and management a necessary feature but where there is protection from certain kinds of alteration. Such action generally results from a desire to keep an ecosystem or set of systems in a valued state, and so is very much dependent upon cultural factors. The aim may be to preserve a species, assemblage or habitat which is rare, or typical, or symbolic, or perhaps to keep unchanged a traditional landscape because it occupies a high place in the values of those who see it or are responsible for it. Such ecosystems are usually wild rather than obviously man-made. Plants, animals, water and soil are, or are thought to be, relatively undisturbed and the terms frequently used of such areas are 'natural' and 'semi-natural'. In fact, a significant number of protected landscapes are cultural landscapes which exhibit distinctly the work of man, but this need not prevent them from being valued highly.

The desire to protect wild species and favoured landscapes usually resolves itself into two practical elements. The first group is nature protection (for which wildlife protection/preservation/conservation, nature conservation/preservation are synonyms) in which it is desired to perpetuate either a taxon or a group of taxa, or a particular habit. Species protection has a tendency to concentrate on the rare and unusual and habitat conservation upon the typical, but many exceptions can be found. The desire for protection is especially strong if the species is endangered (IUCN 1970, Fisher *et al.* 1969). The second element may be termed landscape protection where a particular view or piece of country is protected from undesired despoliation or simply where change of any sort is restrained. These areas are sometimes used also for outdoor recreation, but that set of activities often requires much more manipulation and is considered separately in Chapter 4. As with wilderness, scientific and educational reasons are often advanced for the protection of biota and landscapes, partly for their study value as relatively undisturbed systems from which we may learn the better to manage intensively used systems, and partly for their role in maintaining the stability of the biosphere. Spiritual and aesthetic, even ethical, considerations also lie behind many protectionist movements: there is no denying the pleasure which many people gain from seeing wild rural landscapes, from Kinder Scout through Yosemite Valley to Fujiyama, and the popularity of bird-watching is such that in some crowded parts of Europe the great migration stopovers sometimes attract as many people as birds. Neither can economics be omitted: the public will line up to see rare fauna, as demonstrated by the nest of the Loch Garten ospreys in Scotland (free, in fact, but donations welcome), and in scenically beautiful areas they spread a lot of cash around the periphery in payment for souvenirs, film, food, lodging and public toilets. In a few instances, such as the CSSR, the right of the people to enjoy unspoiled nature and to see beautiful scenery is enshrined in the constitution of the Republic. In the capitalist world the statement of national purpose is rarely as explicit, but is implied in many legislative acts to create nature reserves and protected landscape areas.

Nature protection

Nature protection stems from a desire to perpetuate certain biota indefinitely (Dorst 1970, IUCN 1971). The object of concern may range from a single species living in a very restricted area to a set of complex ecosystems covering a large tract like a mountain range. Such a continuum can only be divided arbitrarily, but for this discussion a differentiation will be made between species protection, where the resource manager aims to keep a viable population of a particular taxon, and habitat protection, where the whole is more important and fluctuations in the populations of component species or in features of the inanimate environment are not considered detrimental. A capricious feature of wildlife conservation is nomenclature: nature reserves, game reserves, national parks, nature parks and several other terms are used by the private and governmental organizations which manage land and water resources with the purpose of perpetuating wild nature. For example the term National Park covers systems managed for many diverse purposes, all the way from wilderness to intensive outdoor recreation. In this account the purpose of management will be stressed rather than the details of designation.

Species preservation

Nature reserves are usually designated in order to give protection to a species of plant or animal which is rare (on a variety of scales from the regional to the global) and which it is thought can be preserved in this way. Animals, especially birds and large mammals, are most often thought of in this connection, but plants may qualify for the same treatment, especially in densely settled lands where many of the wild mammals have disappeared. Typical early instances of such reserves are the nesting sites of rare birds, although general legislation preventing the killing of particular species is commonly passed before the setting up of reserves. In Britain, for example, a law protecting seabirds was passed by Parliament in 1869 and wild birds generally in 1880, but there were no National Nature Reserves until after the founding of an appropriate government agency, the Nature Conservancy Council, in 1949. Privately owned preserves such as those of the Royal Society for the Protection of Birds were earlier in the field (Fitter 1963). Single-species conservation in Britain is dominated by plants and there are reserves owned or leased by the Nature Conservancy or bodies such as the County Naturalists Trusts or the National Trust which are dedicated to protecting, for example, a good fritillary meadow or particularly rare buttercup (Stamp 1969). In the field of animals, the Farne Islands off the coast of Northumberland are a sanctuary for the grey seal: these islands have a long history of management for the benefit of wild creatures, starting with St Cuthbert in the seventh century AD.

Elsewhere in the world, animals tend to dominate single-species preservation mainly because they dominate worldwide concern, largely of a sentimental nature. In northern Alberta and the North-West Territories of Canada, for example, the Wood Buffalo National Park preserves in a wild and almost roadless terrain one of the few remaining herds of North American bison. The herd is culled regularly in order to keep it within the carrying capacity of the National Park area and also to try and keep down the diseases to which the herd is subject. Elsewhere, many other sanctuaries exist and it is often the first step in protection measures taken by undeveloped countries: two small islands in Sabah, Malaysia, protect frigate birds, for example; in north-east India the Kaziranga Sanctuary preserves the Great Indian rhinoceros; and the last 25–40 Javan rhinos are in a reserve at Udjung Kulon-Panailan in western Java, established in 1921 (Talbot and Talbot 1968).

Management of such reserves is usually limited. Where possible a fence is put up, a warden or ranger installed and the area left alone. Where management is practised then it is usual to manipulate either the habitat or the population of the protected species. At Havergate Island in Suffolk, England, the RSPB have created pools in stretches of shingle in order to extend the conditions favourable for the breeding of the avocet, a bird rare in Britain. Further north, the National Trust periodically culls the grey seals of the Farne Islands in order that mortality said to be due to overcrowding should be reduced, and to keep down damage allegedly done to local salmon fisheries. The usefulness of this management policy has been strongly questioned, since others (Coulson 1972) hold the view that natural mechanisms can be relied upon to keep the populations stable.

The protection of assemblages

Rather more common are reserves to protect an assemblage of species. These merge imperceptibly with those in which a whole habitat or set of habitats is preserved, but a distinction can perhaps be made on the arbitrary grounds of size: habitat reserves are large relative to the assemblage ones. The assemblages may have some linking affinity: wildfowl refuges, for example, which cater for the nesting or migration of many species of ducks, geese and waders (Plate 5). High mountain reserves often protect a very diverse suite of alpine plants, sometimes with their attendant fauna. Although wild terrain is often sought for such reserves, the behaviour of wild animals often makes it necessary to set aside man-made habitats and quite frequently suitable places are of commercial value. The case of wetlands which are sought for reclamation as industrial land, airports or garbage dumps can be seen in many parts of the world: the value of the tidal marshes of Essex, England, as a wildfowl habitat rather than as the basis of the third London airport was strongly argued in 1971. Tidal estuaries are also among the most productive ecosystems in the world and clearly deserve special attention on this account.

The USA has a system of National Wildfowl Refuges which are placed on or near the major flyways which run north–south across that continent (Fig. 3.1). They are designated

Plate 5 Wildfowl. Unpriceable but invaluable? *(Grant Heilman, Lititz, Pa)*

in concert with Canada, on whose northern lands (along with those of Alaska) many of the birds nest. Their management is designed to provide maximum cover and food supply for the migrating birds and to provide refuge from hunting so that while sufficient numbers reach the waiting guns to satisfy the hunters (who pay for 'Duck Stamps' and a tax on all equipment in order to finance research and land-acquisition programmes), there are sufficient escapees to return to breed in the following year. Some limited hunting may be allowed on the Refuges along with a restricted variety of other recreational activities. Experience has shown that most populations of ducks and geese can replace hunting losses quite satisfactorily provided the cropping levels are planned in accordance with the breeding success. This necessitates a fairly sophisticated cropper who is able to distinguish between one species and another and between males and females, which surveys by management authorities have shown not to be axiomatic. Plant assemblages are often protected in reserves, especially where some of them are rare on a regional or national scale. In the

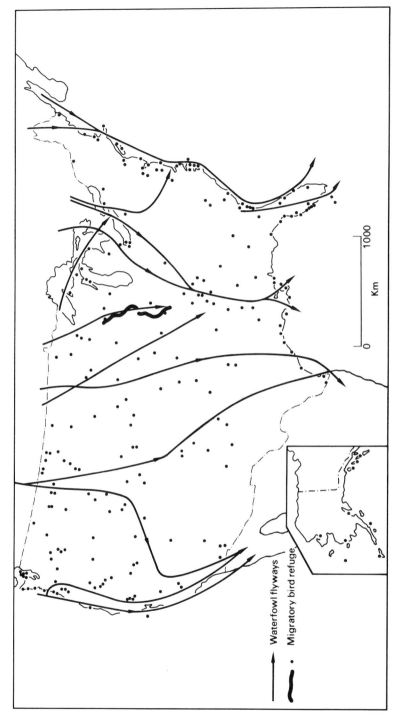

Fig. 3.1 Wildfowl refuges in the USA and the main 'flyways'—the annual migration routes of these birds. The refuges are principally aimed at perpetuation of a particular assemblage of avian species.
Source: Dasmann 1972

Upper Teesdale area of northern Britain, an assemblage of arctic-alpine plants, most of which are found relatively frequently in the Scottish Highlands and commonly in the Alps and Scandinavia, but not elsewhere in England (Piggot 1956), was designated first an SSSI (Site of Special Scientific Interest) under the authority of the National Parks and Access to the Countryside Act of 1949, and then a National Nature Reserve. Because of other interests in the land (especially grouse shooting), management will consist mostly of the traditional practices which include regular firing of heather (*Calluna vulgaris*) which is the food of the grouse. Experimental enclosures which relieve grazing pressure by sheep and rabbits first give a tremendous surge of the rare flora, but this then tends to be suppressed by the vigorous growth of the accompanying plants, often very common grasses. Land-use practices may therefore have been strongly influential in the continued existence of some elements of this flora, and complete protection by withdrawal of other land uses would be likely to entail the loss of some plants by competition. A piece of woodland thought to be typical of a region is also a candidate for preservation, especially if it is thought to be substantially unmanipulated. This is particularly so in Europe, where most woodlands have been either removed to make way for agriculture or intensively managed for centuries. In southern Bohemia, for example, the ČSSR has designated as a reserve the last fragment of beech-spruce *urwald* at Boubinsky Prales. A fence has been erected to keep out deer; the result has been rapid regeneration of the beech but not the spruce, and so other management devices are clearly necessary. The difficulties of ensuring regeneration in small woodland fragments are also illustrated by some of the relict pinewoods of Scotland in the care of the Nature Conservancy. Regeneration of the dominant *Pinus sylvestris* is confined to woods on bouldery slopes; elsewhere the raw acid humus appears to inhibit the seedlings. Here again is a case of *laissez-faire* being unsuccessful in perpetuating a particular plant.

Habitat preservation

Reserves which are large and diverse enough to protect whole sets of ecosystems which are either rare on a national or world basis, or thought to be especially typical of the country where they occur, are often designated as National Parks, although nature protection is often not the sole purpose of such places.

Few reserves in Britain are able to qualify for this category. The possible exceptions are some National Nature Reserves in Scotland such as the Cairngorms, Beinn Eighe and the Isle of Rhum. The first two are mainly mountainous terrain, with grasslands, mountain heath, and relict pinewood on the lower slopes. The red deer is the largest mammal and is in general too high in numbers for the amount of winter feed. But the Nature Conservancy is unable to carry out effective management policies since its leases do not confer complete control over animal management and because animals transgress the boundaries of the Reserves. This is not true of the Isle of Rhum, where it controls the grazing: the sheep which were overgrazing the open moorlands have been removed, and planned management of a herd of red deer substituted. One result has been an increase in the yield of animal protein per unit area together with a recovery of the pastures (Eggeling 1964). Some of the National Parks of the USA are devoted mainly to conserving a series of wildlife habitats. This is particularly true of the Everglades National Park in Florida, which comprises a complex of wetland areas such as coastal mangroves, tropical saw-grass marshes and 'hammock' forests on the slightly drier areas a few centimetres above flood level. The 4,856 km² (1,200,000 ac) park supports a wide variety of animals also, such as the rare Everglades kite, the roseate spoonbill, alligators, manatees and the many fish that are the basis of a sizeable industry. Until recently management was confined to the channelling of the ever-increasing numbers of visitors, and to measures like the protecting of alligators from would-be makers of handbags. But the large size of the Everglades and its proximity to the popular holiday area of Florida mean that pressures to alter the ecology are intense. Apart from proposals (which were allowed to lapse after a considerable controversy but which in 1973 showed signs of reviving) to build an airport on one fringe, the main threat has been the loss of its freshwater input and thus the possibility of the wetlands drying out. The main water source is Lake Okeechobee and the water in this lake has been cut off from the Park in the name of flood control further north; surplus water was released into the ocean instead of into the Everglades. Pressure from concerned people has allowed the tapping of an aquifer and the restoration of some of the lake water, but the future of the Everglades as a set of natural ecosystems remains in doubt (Dasmann 1968, Harte and Socolow 1971).

On a still larger scale are some of the National Parks and Game Reserves of eastern, central and southern Africa, in such countries as the Republic of South Africa, Tanzania, Zambia, Uganda and Kenya (Fig. 3.2). Here the desire to ensure the survival of the fauna, especially the large mammals, is reinforced by two strong economic considerations. Firstly, most of these countries (especially the newly independent republics) make a great deal of foreign currency from tourism; for some it is their largest earner, and the visitors nearly all come to see the animals. Secondly, it has been shown that controlled harvesting of wild animals not only helps to ensure their preservation, since their ranges are being restricted by various forms of development, but also that the wild game can yield more protein per unit area than domesticated animals and with less damage from overgrazing. This is a fairly revolutionary concept and is not widely acceptable at grassroots level. Groups such as the Masai of Kenya, for example, are reluctant to give up their tradition of cattle-herding since the animals are not only meat and milk but also money to them (Pearsall 1957, Huxley 1961). The potential of controlled cropping is discussed in Chapter 5.

Asia too has many parks devoted to protecting mountain and forest areas, along with the associated fauna, in a natural state. Even countries like South Viet-Nam had two National Parks. The large one, of 78,000 ha at Bach-ma Hai-Van, near Hue, was of virgin monsoon forest (Nguyen-van-Hiep 1968). It is presumably necessary to use the past tense when referring to these Parks, and probably those of some other south-east Asian countries also. The course of shifting cultivation and logging have also injured many park areas in Asia where insufficient park personnel and wild terrain mean that control of these inimical land uses is scarcely possible. A further reason for preservation of upland forests is found in their protection of watersheds: if deforested they add to the flood hazard of urban and agricultural lands downstream and increase the silt burden as well. They also form reserves for research into management of Asian wild lands, and although they are not yet tourist attractions on the scale of the African parks, there can be little doubt that their turn will come in the course of the upsurge of world tourism (Talbot and Talbot 1968).

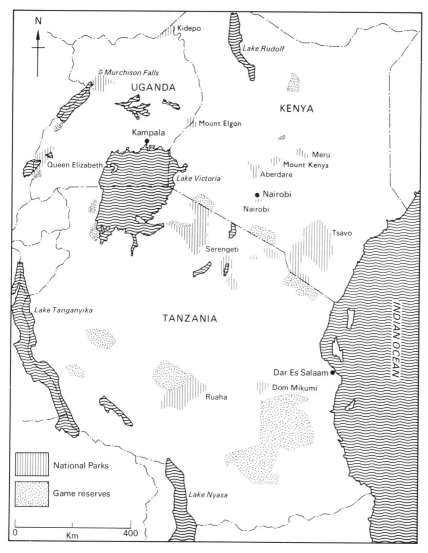

Fig. 3.2 The major National Parks and Game Reserves of Kenya, Uganda and Tanzania in 1970. The large areas which they occupy are symbolic of their role in the economy of the nations concerned as well as environmental considerations.
Source: Morgan 1972

The preservation of habitats is also the main function of the natural areas of the USSR which are withdrawn from economic utilization for scientific research and for cultural-education purposes. In 1966 there were 68 of these *zapovedniki*, totalling 4,300,000 ha, and the predominance of scientific research as their main purpose was well established, in such fields as the breeding and propagation of animals that are rare or threatened with extinction, the study of both unusual and typical vegetation types, the investigation of the total ecology of particular regions, and the preservation of unique geological or archaeological features. Certain 'open' *zapovedniki* accommodate tourism, but they are limited in number and recreation appears to be a secondary consideration. A long-range plan for new reserves was presented in 1957, but so far few of its recommendations have been implemented (Pryde 1972).

Difficulties

The preceding paragraphs have given particular instances of difficulties associated with the management of ecosystems for nature protection, and some of these have a more general applicability. As with wilderness areas, deliberate designation is necessary but mere legislative enactment is insufficient. Apart from the obvious protective measures such as the prevention of poaching or picking, there are more subtle ecological interactions. For example, the removal of a particular type of pressure from a desired species may cause it to 'bloom' in an explosive fashion and crash thereafter. The mule deer of the Kaibab Plateau of Arizona are one much-chronicled example (Fig. 3.3). In an effort to increase their numbers, predator control was introduced and numbers of wolves were exterminated. The deer herd rapidly grew in size and outstripped its food supply, with a subsequent population 'crash' down to very low numbers (Dasmann 1964b). Similar difficulties have been

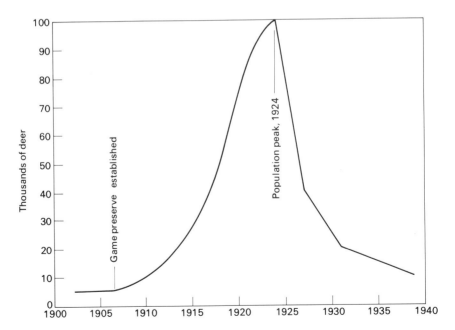

Fig. 3.3 The population expansion and 'crash' of the deer of the Kaibab plateau of Arizona, following the application of predator control.
Source: Dasmann 1964b

experienced when the enclosure of rare plants has been followed by the discovery that they have survived because grazing pressure has kept down competing species. An example of this is given by some species of orchids in the chalk grassland of southern England. In the absence of sheep this plant association soon becomes long grassland and then scrub, so that the orchids characteristic of the short-grass stage disappear very quickly once succession starts to take place. In this case, management measures for the preservation of orchids consist either of re-introducing sheep or of mowing the nature reserve. A classic instance of the imperfections of designated reserves occurs when an animal spends part of its yearly cycle outside the reserve. A large mammal may spend its winters in a reserve where predators are protected but the rest of the year on a range outside the reserve which it shares with domestic livestock and where predator control, as of the wolf or the coyote, is maintained. The populations of the mammal are thus liable to build up to levels which cannot be supported by the winter feed, and the predators are incapable of trimming the population sufficiently. In such cases, management must be undertaken, either by culling a number of beasts or by feeding them artificially. The elk of Yellowstone National Park in the USA have had to be treated in this way: in this instance culling by the Park staff is undertaken, much to the chagrin of local hunters.

Such problems basically arise from the fact that legislative boundaries rarely coincide with the natural spatial limits of the ecosystems which it is desired to protect; this may also be manifested in the operation of watershed influences which originate beyond the limits of the reserve but which penetrate into it. An obvious case would be the spraying with a persistent insecticide of agricultural land upstream from a protected lake. Similarly, the addition of large quantities of chemical fertilizer would probably result in the eutrophication of the lake. If the protected system is a forest, then commercial logging up to the boundaries of the reserve may possibly mean that the remnant area is too small to function as a natural unit—e.g. there may be insufficient territories for a viable population of a particular species. As a further example, in connection with the establishment of a Redwoods National Park in northern California in 1968, the Secretary of the Interior is authorized to enter into agreements and easements with the owners of the watersheds whose ecology affects that of the Park, in order to protect certain features of the Park itself (Simmons 1971). Apparently destructive influences such as fire and flood, whose origin is frequently outside the reserve area, often pose problems for the managers of protected ecosystems. Fire may in some places be a part of the natural ecology, especially in coniferous forests where it seems to have an important role in mineralizing organic matter piled up on the forest floor, and in aiding tree regeneration. (Several species of conifers have cones that only open and release their seed after subjection to very high temperatures.) The giant redwood (*Sequoia gigantea*) of the western slopes of the Sierra Nevada in California is a case in point. Nearly all the remaining specimens of this tree are in State or National Parks, but regeneration has been sparse since the seedlings of the tree were shaded out by faster-growing competitors. Following the realization that lightning-set fires had been a normal component of the local ecosystem, managers began programmes of controlled burning. Along with some restrictions on access to prevent trampling, these appear to have encouraged some regeneration of this rare and exceptionally impressive tree.

Although the presence of wild nature is becoming more and more valued, it does not yet take precedence over more directly economic uses of land and water resources, and so conflicts over the conversion of use arise. The most common of these is the encroachment of industry on formerly wild lands which may have been under protection. Examples of this are particularly common on tidal lands and freshwater wetlands, both of which are commercially cheap and easily 'reclaimable'. Wetlands are especially vulnerable when surrounded by agricultural land, owing not only to substances dissolved in the drainage water, but also to the need to drain the agricultural land. If a 'perched' water-table is to be achieved in isolation from the surrounding drier lands, then considerable engineering works are a necessary prelude to management. This has been achieved by the Nature Conservancy at Woodwalton Fen in eastern England, where a remnant of original fen vegetation is maintained as an island in a sea of intensively farmed agricultural land (Duffey and Watt 1971).

Purposes

The aim of much nature protection is the avoidance of species extinction at one or more scales, and we may legitimately ask whether the disappearance of a species represents an inevitability or merely a failure on man's part to be sufficiently sensitive to the web of living organisms of which he is a part. Scientific reasons for the perpetuation of such organisms exist in terms of interest and possibly of short- or medium-term 'usefulness': it may be very helpful in terms of agricultural development to know how a rare species has adapted itself to a very hostile environment such as a saline desert. On the other hand its very scarcity means that the disappearance of a rare component is unlikely to cause instability in the ecosystems of which it was a component unless it is a key species of the type described by Paine (1969). However, Western culture recognizes that the quality of our lives is enhanced by having around us a rich diversity of organic life, including rare, strange and beautiful forms. Another 'useful' purpose perhaps needs to be stressed most. In Westhoff's (1970) words:

> nature conservation itself has one main end: preserving the stability of the ecosystem where such is required and thus maintaining the diversity of biotic communities, which is necessary for preserving all organisms living on Earth.

To this end, the designation of nature reserves is an initial step.

The protection of landscapes

The placing of whole landscapes under some form of legislative or regulatory protection comes from the desire to maintain or enhance a scene which is of great value, often for various types of recreation or for aesthetic purposes, and so emotive and symbolic values are of considerable importance. Highly valued landscapes do not have to be 'natural'. Some of them are mostly virgin terrain, for example the National Parks in the western cordillera of North America like the Yellowstone and Rocky Mountain Parks in the USA and the Banff-Jasper Parks in Canada. Others are landscapes which are thought to be natural but which closer investigation reveals to be man-made, even if they are extremely wild, like the moorlands of England and Wales. Lastly there is the frank preference for the man-made landscape which exhibits aesthetic qualities that makes it worthy of special attention. The combination lake, wood, field and village in parts of Denmark, the small-scale neatness of rural England, the patterned richness of Lancaster County, Pennsylvania, the staircase of rice paddies flanked by cherry trees in rural Kyushu, all exemplify this type. The perception of the landscape, and the value then attributed to it, are obviously all very important in the decision to protect it. Management may (or may not) thereafter be carried out on scientific principles, but the initial motivation is inspired by a particular set of cultural values.

National Parks

One expression of the desire for protection is the designation of entire landscapes as 'scenic areas', 'areas of natural beauty' or 'national (state, regional county, country) parks' in such a way that the dominant purpose of management becomes the preservation of the qualities of the scenery. This 'total protection' is most often done with natural landscapes, since the lack of other uses produces fewer conflicts than in areas with more directly economic utilization. The legislation is therefore necessarily strong, since it must confer upon the manager the power to exclude all manipulations and changes which are deemed to be inimical to the perpetuation of the values of the landscape. In practice this usually means government ownership of the land and its recources, and the outstanding example of this category is the National Parks system of the USA (Fig. 3.4). Not only does it exemplify the way in which protection has taken place, but it also illustrates some of the conflicts which may arise within the framework of protection, even after the decision to remove the park resources from the ambit of commerce has been taken.

The first of the National Parks, Yellowstone, was designated in 1872. Others followed and the system grew to the point where an Act of the Federal Government was necessary to establish a National Parks Service to administer the system. The wording of the organic Act of 1916 enshrines the purpose of the Parks as being to:

Conserve the scenery and the natural and historical objects and the wildlife therein and to provide for the enjoyment of the same in such manner and by such means as will leave them unimpaired for the enjoyment of future generations.

The system has grown to include not only the National Parks which are the chief concern of this section, but National Monuments, National Recreation Areas, Seashores and many other features. National Parks are, however, still being added (e.g. Utah Canyonlands in 1964, Redwoods and North Cascades in 1968), although it was intended to complete the system by 1972. In 1970 there were 35 National Parks, with a total area of 59,086 km² (14·6 million ac), of which the Federal Government owned over 90 per cent, the difference being accounted for by privately held inholdings within the park boundaries. The types of terrain enclosed in the system are those generally acknowledged to be outstanding examples of the American scene: Yellowstone, Glacier, and Rocky Mountain National Parks in the Rockies, for example; Shenandoah and the Great Smoky Mountains in Appalachia; Grand Canyon, Bryce Canyon, Zion, and Canyonlands in the arid south-west; Yosemite, Kings Canyon-Sequoia, Lassen, Crater Lake and Mount Rainier in the far western ranges of the cordillera; and many more, including the Florida Everglades discussed earlier in this

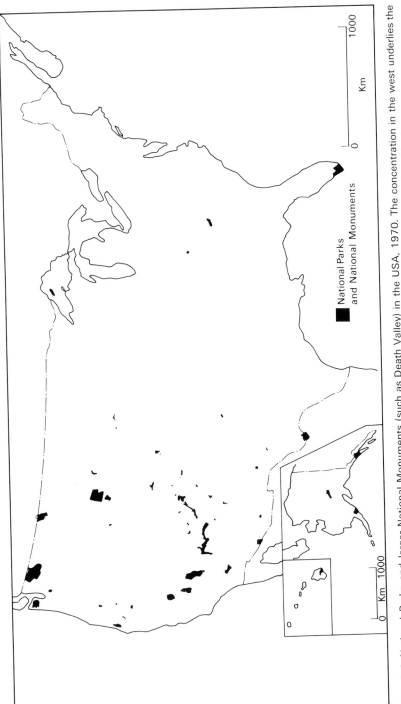

Fig. 3.4 National Parks and larger National Monuments (such as Death Valley) in the USA, 1970. The concentration in the west underlies the class of resource under this type of management, but the very small proportion of the nation so protected is evident. Source: US National Parks Service 1970: *Areas administered by the National Park Service and related properties as 1 January 1970.* Washington, DC.

National Parks and National Monuments

section. Hunting is not allowed, but the Parks are popular for many other recreational activities, of which the main one is the viewing of the scenery and its component natural elements which are the *raison d'être* of these Parks. Their popularity is such that visitor numbers have been rising by about 10 per cent each year, i.e. doubling every seven years.

In spite of these pressures, active manipulation of the Parks has been limited to relatively small areas. Forests and water-courses are little altered and there is neither grazing nor mining. In surroundings with such little change, wildlife is comparatively abundant, although sometimes the protection leads either to an overall superabundance, as with the Yellowstone elk, or to undesirable concentrations, as where a species turns to scavenging upon the leavings of the visitors and occasionally predating upon the visitors themselves, as has happened with grizzly bears (*Ursus horribilis*). Because most of the visitors stay close to the roads, campgrounds and other 'developed' parts of the Parks, wilderness can also be a feature, and most of the Parks have large back-country areas which are only infrequently visited since they have to be traversed on foot or horseback. Inevitably, the more accessible areas are the most popular and here the demands of visitors have in large measure been met: there are car parks, campgrounds, stores, hot showers, cabins, nature trails and other interpretive facilities. Fishing is so popular that all the streams have had to be kept stocked. The story is told of the angler in a National Park who had fished for five days and caught nothing. In a similar situation was another angler. When the first expressed disgust at his lack of fortune and said he was leaving the area, the second is reputed to have said, 'Well, I'm stayin'. Tomorrow's the day they put the fish in.' The catering to visitors extends in many parks to a hotel or park lodge and in some to a luxury version, like the Ahwahnee hotel in Yosemite National Park. To go with such developments there may be a golf course and for many long years summer nights in Yosemite were momentarily enlivened by the famous firefall, when glowing ashes from a large wood fire were pushed in an incandescent stream over the edge of a highly U-shaped valley. It was an unusual, if over-rated, form of scenic *divertissement*. With so many functions to perform it was inevitable that conflicts between them arose, especially under the relentless escalation of visitor numbers. Under the politically useful if ecologically contradictory slogan 'parks are for people', many developments were made which threatened wilderness values, such as roads into remote parts. More campgrounds intruded into wildlife foraging areas, sometimes those of easily angered animals such as bears, and the problems of sewage and garbage disposal from the campers and day-visitors in a few places resembled those of a small town (Bourne 1970). Such conflicts were the subject of a special advisory committee to the Secretary of the Interior (A. S. Leopold 1963). Their special concern was wildlife, but their report had far-reaching effects upon the long-term purposes of the Parks. They concluded that the management goal should be

to preserve or where necessary to re-create, the ecologic scene as viewed by the first European visitors, . . . in order to . . . 'enhance the aesthetic, historical and scientific values of the parks to the American public, vis-à-vis the mass recreational values'.

In line with these aims, a new set of policies appeared, designed to avoid land-use conflicts arising from confusions of purpose (National Park Service 1968). Three major types of area within the National Parks system have been designated (natural, recreational and historic) and the administrative guidelines for the 'natural areas' emphasize the protection of the ecological systems, in such terms as,

(1) Safeguarding forests, wildlife and natural features against impairment or destruction.

(2) The application of ecological management techniques to neutralize the unnatural influences of man, thus permitting the natural environment to be maintained essentially by nature.

(3) Master planning for the appropriate allocation of lands to various purposes in a park and location of use areas as needed for development.

Some of the measures taken to achieve these ends included the formulation of control programmes for ungulate populations, the use of prescribed burning to pre-empt dangerous wildfire, and the gradual removal of service facilities outside the park boundaries. In due course the motor car is to be restricted: in the summer of 1970 an area of Yosemite Valley was sealed off and a minibus service substituted and further plans envisage a 'de-development' at popular areas such as the Old Faithful geyser at Yellowstone National Park. It remains to be seen whether the public image of the National Parks as all-purpose scenic-recreation-resort areas is maintained or whether their avowed role as the jewels in the crown of protected lands with a special, even élitist, role can be substituted. Their remarkable nature and distinctive purpose (it must be remembered that the USA gave the world the National Park idea) requires a farseeing intellectual effort on the part of managers and an understanding attitude from the visiting public. As Darling and Eichorn (1967) conclude,

> certain forms of decorous behaviour should be accepted and not questioned. . . . The national parks . . . represent the glorious creations of nature and no expediency or misconception of their beauty must endanger the world heritage of which they are so shining a part.

Protected landscape areas

The amount of land that can be placed under restrictions of the kind reviewed in the previous section is, by present cultural criteria, limited. Elsewhere, economic considerations may apparently dictate land and water use. Some of the landscapes created by economic usage are nevertheless highly valued, and the desire arises to prevent changes which threaten the areas which have evoked such reactions, for some landscapes exhibit in their aesthetic dimensions a quality which adds to their conventionally utilitarian worth. The type of protective measure which seeks to protect such landscape values while not interfering with the farming or forestry or other commercial use could perhaps be described as 'cosmetic', since it deals with the treatment of details of the surface, rather than with the underlying structure. A more conventional term is 'development control'. Development control seeks to minimize conflicts between the normal processes of economic use and the principally aesthetic appeal which the landscapes hold. Thus control conferred by legislation or by agreement seeks to preserve the familiar and well-beloved by preventing change which is deemed to be ugly, and by clearing up unwanted relics of the past. As examples, we may quote the banning of advertising billboards along roads in Denmark, the control exercised over certain types of agricultural buildings in parts of England and Wales, and the grants available in many countries for the camouflaging of auto junkyards in rural areas and on urban fringes. There are basically two ways in which such controls can be applied: by wholesale prohibitions and regulation over the whole of an administrative area; or by designating certain regions with a distinctive character and concentrating on the protection of that particular place. In the case of the latter, some distinguishing title, such as Protected Landscape Area, Area of Outstanding Natural Beauty, or even National Park, is given.

The control of outdoor advertising is one of the fields in which cosmetic control is exercised. Although the USA is frequently excoriated for this contribution to the scenery, it is worth noting that by 1968 some 31 states had enacted legislation controlling billboards, neon signs and similar paraphernalia outside the commercial zones of towns and cities. Vermont and Hawaii have banned all off-premise outdoor advertising signs, and the city of Aspen, Colorado, has installed a successful sign wall to replace billboards along a State Highway. The constitutionality of restricting outdoor advertising has been affirmed by courts in the states of Washington and Hawaii, and the pursuit of high aesthetic standards as a community goal has thus been endorsed (US President's Council on Recreation and Natural Beauty 1968).

In the case of areas of a particular character which it is desired to protect *in toto* from certain landscape changes, the two main aids are development controls and the provision of governmental aid to clear up detrimental features (Plate 6). Thus one of the major aims of the National Parks and Access to the Countryside Act 1949 of England and Wales was to secure control over most types of development such as non-agricultural buildings, advertising, and caravan sites, in the areas which were to be designated (Fig. 3.5) as National Parks (Darby 1963). Money for clearing up eyesores, mainly wartime remnants, was also available to planning authorities. Regions of slightly lower value, Areas of Outstanding Natural Beauty, have also been designated. As it has turned out, the major landscape changes in the National Parks to which many people have taken objection are exempt from the provisions of the Act. These were large-scale afforestation with coniferous trees, reclamation of open moorland for agriculture and the erection of large-scale farm buildings to take advantage of new developments in intensive farming. Because of the importance of retaining the economic life of the National Parks, even the Countryside Act of 1968 did not provide for control of these changes.

In Denmark, the protected landscape may, if small, be part of the system of nature reserves. Larger units are called 'Naturparker', and the aim is to preserve a total environment or milieu with both cultural and natural features in which the Dane will feel at home. As Bjerke (1967) puts it:

> The individual forms his own impression of the Danish landscape, and this impression is influenced by impressions from the landscape of his childhood and later connections. ... The impression of landscape formed by an individual rests upon past experience, and often also upon knowledge of the dynamic composition in what was experienced. Expectations are thus generally limited to existing landscape forms and often restricted, when compared to the expectations an individual may have towards landscapes in other countries.

Plate 6 Derwentwater in the English Lake District. Apart from the lake this is largely a cultural landscape, but one so valued that it enjoys protection from certain kinds of change by virtue of its designation as a National Park. As can be seen from some of the mountains, afforestation is not subject to control. *(Aerofilms Ltd, London)*

The formation of a 'Naturpark' takes place under the 1969 Preservation of Nature Act which makes possible the designation of large areas (10–15,000 ha, for example) in all parts of the country. The chief aim will be the preservation of current characteristics, and to that end farming and forestry will continue, with new buildings and other developments strictly controlled. Management aims will allow the integration of recreation areas where these are compatible with the primary purpose. An early example of a Naturpark is the Tystrup-Bavelse area of Zealand, known as 'Sjaellands grønne hjerte'. It is an area of

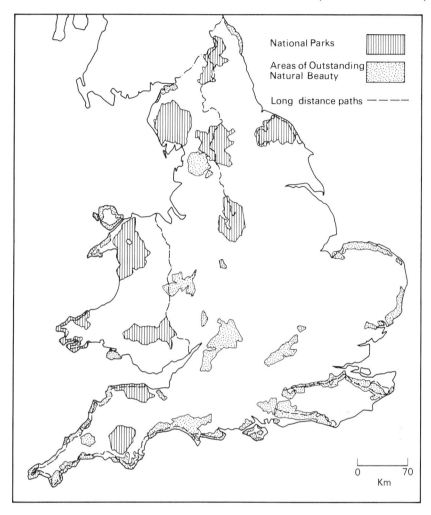

Fig. 3.5 National Parks and Areas of Outstanding Natural Beauty in England and Wales (1972), where strict development control is practised. Although a large proportion of the land surface is protected by these designations, economic activities are supposed to continue unabated.
Source: Countryside Commission of England and Wales 1972: *Annual Report 1971–72*

farmland, woods and villages comprising 12,000 ha around a lake, the Tystrup Sø. Until the 1969 Act it was not possible to pay compensation to landowners materially affected by the emparking, and the character of the area was maintained largely by voluntary agreements, but this legislation has made the position of both government and landowners clear.

Needless to say, there are many problems associated with the preservation of landscape values. Take for example the implication that a landscape should be kept as it is. Unless it is a totally natural landscape, then it has come to its present state in response to operation of past economic processes. If the needs now change, why should not the landscapes alter? What justification can be found for fossilizing a cultural landscape as it is now? The answer that present values demand it raises the question of whether such values are permanent, which they clearly are not. If we agree that uncontrolled alteration of landscapes in response to every economic whim of a *laissez-faire* economy is unacceptable, but that fossilization is also undesirable, then we have to find criteria for distinguishing allowable change from that which must be stopped (Simmons 1967). Although development policies can be defined and adopted democratically (or autocratically), not every demand for change will fall neatly into an allowable or prohibited category, so that many *ad hoc* decisions have to be taken. In the face of pressures for a new industrial development such as a newly discovered mineral deposit, it is almost impossible to uphold a protective set of regulations, witness the controversies over the North York Moors National Park (Statham 1971), and the concern over the copper and gold extraction explorations of RTZ in the Snowdonia National Park in the early 1970s. Sometimes the viewers of the landscapes create the greatest problems, especially if they are present in sufficiently large numbers (Duffey 1967). The unwitting damage which they then do, such as trampling and the scattering of litter, is made worse by the presence of numerous vehicles (Bayfield 1971, Streeter 1971). These not only damage the ecology unless properly managed: in open areas they represent a highly unaesthetic intrusion. But only small numbers of careless or malevolent visitors are needed to create damage of a vandalistic kind. Examples of this are very familiar, and include direct economic loss to farmers as when stock are allowed to stray or are harassed by dogs; or when palatable but lethal rubbish such as some types of plastic are left behind for domestic animals like cattle to eat.

Ideally, the protected landscape is a non-consumptive resource: the crop is of a visual nature, and when this has been taken by the onlookers, the resource remains; the aim of management is to perpetuate this attribute.

Conflicts

The mention of landscape-protection areas which embrace forestry and farming provokes the discussion of the possibilities of multiple-use schemes which embrace a measure of wildlife or scenic preservation. Clearly, given goodwill and the possible loss of income from compromising with that aim, farming and forestry can be carried on along with nature parks, National Parks and the like. Any severe restrictions, such as the control of agricultural buildings or the enforced planting of hardwood screens around conifer plantations, need compensation payments if they are to be reasonably willingly adopted. Recreation and watershed management may also usually be integrated into scenery preservation if firm control can be exercised over the siting of developments. Reservoirs may of course come into the category of unacceptable alterations of the landscape: tastes vary from country to country. Nature protection often fits well, as when small reserves are embedded in a matrix of preserved landscape. Some resource uses are decidedly incompatible with the protection of landscapes: military use almost invariably results in considerable damage, and industrial plants can rarely be given sufficient screening to render them unobtrusive. Large quarries are generally inimical developments, producing dust and noise as well as large holes, and even solution mining of minerals such as potash causes large scars in wild country where the pipelines are buried. Processing plants are likewise highly intrusive and often sources of environmental contamination. So while landscape protection and nature conservation elements can and should be a part of every development scheme, rural or urban (as it is in the Netherlands where the Forest Service has a national responsibility for landscaping), the opposite case, where the valued scene and wildlife are the primary objectives of management, needs careful attention.

The effects of increasing human populations are both direct and indirect. Directly, there are more people, usually with more vehicles either public or private, wanting to visit the protected places, and they are often concentrated at especially popular times like the summer weekends and holidays. This intensifies their impact upon the ecological systems which form the landscape, and in large enough numbers they become a feature, usually undesired, of the landscape itself. Indirectly, more people want more jobs, more housing, more water and the like. Even when regional or national planning is efficient, these pressures cannot be for long diverted from valued landscapes. The patterns of world trade and interdependence exert effects too, so that agricultural development in LDCs* stimulates demand for fertilizer production in DCs, whose industrial anabasis in turn requires more water and hence more reservoir construction in areas of high landscape value which inevitably will sometimes be in areas of considerable scientific interest, with an area of flora and fauna being threatened with damage or extinction (R. Gregory 1971). Despite considerable opportunities for creative planning and public education there remains among resource managers, in the West at least, no doubt that landscapes and nature can in the end be kept untrammelled only by restrictions on the number of people who come into their presence and by the slowing down or cessation of the competing demands for space created by higher populations with rising material expectations.

* Throughout this book the abbreviations LDC (less developed country) and DC (developed country) will be used.

Further reading

BUSH, R. 1973: *The National Parks of England and Wales.*

DASMANN, R. F. 1964: *Wildlife biology.*

DUFFEY, E. and WATT, A. S. (eds.) 1971: *The scientific management of animal and plant communities for conservation.*

FRASER DARLING, F. and EICHORN, N. 1967: *Man and nature in the National Parks: some reflections on policy.*

GREGORY, R. 1971: *The price of amenity.*

IUCN 1970: *United Nations list of National Parks and equivalent reserves.*

JARRETT, H. (ed.) 1961: *Comparisons in resource management.*

KRUTILLA, J. (ed.) 1972: *Natural environments.*

PRYDE, P. R. 1972: *Conservation in the Soviet Union.*

4

Outdoor recreation

The urge to spend leisure time in rural surroundings, thus creating a demand for the use of land and water resources, even if not exclusively for that purpose, has probably existed since the beginning of an urban way of life. In pre-industrial times, even the city dwellers were in relatively close contact with nature, but with the coming of the factory and the urban explosion of the nineteenth century, the working masses became confined to their towns except for holidays, for after the long hours of work there was time only for eating and sleeping. The waggonnette and then the train became cheap means of escape to seaside and countryside, and the working classes began to acquire that taste for fresh air and rural surroundings which hitherto only the rich had been able to enjoy. The developments of the twentieth century have further entrenched the recreational desires of all strata of society in the West (Revelle 1967), to the point where Gabor (1963) listed leisure among the dangers to civilization along with war and overpopulation.

Leisure, affluence and mobility in the twentieth century

At the turn of the century, the 60-hour working week was common in the West. In Holland and Denmark, for example, this was the usual figure, and similar hours were worked in most industrial countries. In the USA, for example, the fall in hours worked, along with increase in average daily leisure time, is given in Table 4.1. The present situation is summed up in Table 4.2, from a Danish source, which gives for slightly different dates (mostly 1964–6) the relevant figures. The daily hours of work, the annual holiday and the occasional free days mean that individuals are now able to plan a very different time-budget from that which was common earlier in the century. In 1900, Clawson (1963) reports, 26·5 per cent of the time of US citizens could be classed as leisure (time after work, sleep, housekeeping and personal care); by 1950 this proportion had risen to 34 per cent and is likely to rise to 38 per cent by the year 2000. In Britain, the 1967 proportion is about 31 per cent (BTA–Keele University 1967). The pattern of leisure that is developing seems to be common to most north Atlantic countries. Daily after-work or after-school leisure is currently least important for outdoor recreation, but its contribution is growing, especially with increase in second-car ownership; weekend and special holiday leisure is extremely important and contributes substantially.

   Forecasts of work and leisure suggest a continuation of present trends. Sweden expects a 40-hour week by the 1970s with at least 4 weeks' vacation; in the USA, projections

TABLE 4.1   Work and leisure in the USA 1920–60

Date	Work hrs/day	Leisure hrs/day (averaged for year, including vacation)
1920	49·7	5·7
1930	45·9	6·4
1940	44·0	6·7
1950	40·0	7·4
1960	37·5	7·8

Source: Scheider 1962

TABLE 4.2   Working hours and holidays

Country	Normal weekly working hours	Yearly number of vacation days	Yearly number of free days (weekdays or holidays)
Denmark	42·5	18	9–10
England	40·0–42·5	12	6
Netherlands	45·0	12	7
USA	40·0	6–24	6–8
Finland	40·0–45·0	18	12
Sweden	43·3	24	11
Norway	42·5	24	10
Belgium	42·0–45·0	18	10
West Germany	40·0–42·0	15–18	10–12
France	40·0	18	5–10
Italy	44·0–45·0	12	16
Luxembourg	42·5–44·0	18	10
Iceland	44·0	18	?
Ireland	48·0	12	6
Spain	44·0	7–12	13
Switzerland	44·0–46·0	12–24	6–8
Australia	40·0	18	10
Israel	47·0	12–18	9–11
Japan	44·0–48·0	6–20	?
USSR	41·0	15–24	?

Source: Arbejdsministeriet Danmarks 1968

suggested by the Outdoor Recreation Resources Review Commission (ORRRC) in 1962 are given in Table 4.3. Other countries will no doubt follow at varying rates; lower-paid workers are usually willing to exchange leisure time for extra income and the proportions of different income groups among a population are therefore likely to influence the rate at which the 'standard' working week decreases in length.

TABLE 4.3   Projected working hours and holidays

Year	Weekly working hours	Weeks' holiday	Individual free days
1976	35·4	2·8	8·5
2000	30·7	3·9	10·1

Source: ORRRC 1962b

The basic richness of some industrialized countries is emphasized in Table 4.4, and together with the other criteria of leisure and mobility it enforces the view that the use of resources for outdoor recreation is primarily a phenomenon of industrial nations; particularly those of the West, along with Japan, some of the highly urbanized Asian states, and the richer nations of the southern hemisphere. For the present purpose the relevant part of the richness is the disposable income, and Table 4.5 shows the increase in disposable personal income in the USA and its forecast level for 1976. Within the disposable category, expenditure on recreation as a whole appears to vary only within the 4–7 per cent bracket and is surprisingly constant for all income levels. Definition makes difficult the separation of outdoor recreation expenditure, but it appears that in the US there is a steeper rise in the proportion spent on outdoor recreation than on recreation in general. Nobody expects that the rate of expenditure on leisure activities will do anything other than rise, war and monetary system collapse permitting. In Britain, for example, real income per head in 1985 is expected to be 175 per cent of the 1960 figure.

TABLE 4.4   Per capita GNP (mostly 1969 data; US dollars)

Western countries		Socialist countries		Non-Western countries	
Canada	2,650	USSR	1,200	Brazil	270
Denmark	2,310	Czechoslovakia	1,370	Nigeria	100
UK	1,890	Hungary	1,100	Indonesia	100
Netherlands	1,760	Poland	940	India	110
USA	4,240	Rumania	860	Japan	1,430

Source: Population Reference Bureau 1972

TABLE 4.5   Disposable personal income, USA (billions (= 000 million) 1959 dollars)

1946	1950	1957	1976
222·48	246·9	316·0	702·5

Source: ORRRC 1962b

As far as outdoor recreation in the West is concerned, possession of a private motor vehicle is a paramount factor in participation (Table 4.6). In eastern Europe and Japan, public transport is still the most important conveyor of recreationists, but in the West the outdoors is visited largely in the company of the internal combustion engine. Even if the gasoline engine becomes a museum-piece within the span of projections now being made, possession of private individual transport seems to be very firmly tied into the patterns of outdoor recreation which have become familiar and desirable to the inhabitants of the West.

TABLE 4.6   Passenger cars in use (thousands)

	1953	1963	1970	Persons per car 1970
Canada	2,513·8	4,788·9	6,602·2	3·03
Denmark	157·5	605·0	1,076·1	4·52
Great Britain	2,797·7	7,482·6	11,666·0	4·62
Netherlands	187·6	865·5	2,500·0	4·58
USA	46,460·1	68,683·0	88,840·5	2·28
Japan	114·7	1,234·0	8,779·0	10·18

Source: United Nations 1972

Activities

Outdoor recreation consists of leisure-time activities undertaken in relatively small groups, in a rural setting. The second two of these conditions are not capable of precise delimitation, for the number–units run from the solitary walker to the members of a sailing club. The major activities are included in Table 4.7.

Although some of these require considerable manipulation of the natural resource or heavy investment in equipment, it can be seen that an important element in every activity is a 'natural' substance, be it fields and forests, water or snow; this is the difference between these forms of activity and the nature-divorced pursuits such as bowls, cricket, and football of all kinds. Hence, extra-urban areas are the locations for the activities, particularly since just being out in rural surroundings doubtless forms a major source of attraction, although not one easily assessed by questionnaire survey.

In Western countries where surveys of participation in these activities have been carried out, we can gain an idea of the number of people who take part in outdoor recreation. Table 4.8 gives such data as are reasonably comparable. From the extensive list of activities and the relatively high proportions of people undertaking them, we can readily visualize that land and water resources are demanded by people for their leisure time. There has always been an element of this kind of 'non-productive' use in most places: in medieval England there were the Royal Forests, strictly preserved for the King, and areas of lower status like Chases and Warrens for the lesser aristocracy. Later, the great landscape gardens of

TABLE 4.7   Major outdoor recreation activities (no ranking is implied by the order)

Driving for pleasure	
Walking for pleasure/Hiking	This is a useful distinction—the latter is the serious version.
Outdoor games	These should be of an informal nature, requiring little or no fixed equipment.
Swimming	Includes sub-aqua activities. It is implied that a 'natural-looking' water body is involved, not a 'pool'.
Bicycling	
Fishing	
Nature study, archaeology	
Nature walks	Includes both guided walks and self-guiding nature trails.
Boating/Sailing	This category means motor-boats on inland waters and sea.
Canoeing	Inland water.
Sea sailing	Sail only.
Sightseeing	Of cultural interests rather than appreciation of views, etc.
Caving	Restricted to limestone pothole country.
Hunting	This is an American term, and is used there mainly for deer-shooting. For use in this book it will be taken to be synonymous with shooting and to exclude fox-hunting.
Horseback riding	Including pony-trekking.
Camping	Including 'day-camping', not easily separable from picnicking; also caravaning: difficult to separate in North America.
Picknicking	
Ice skating	Outdoor only, on naturally frozen water.
Tobogganing	
Snow skiing	
Mountain climbing	Synonymous with rock climbing: fell-walking and scrambling under hiking.
Motor sports	Hill trials, motorcycle scrambles over informal courses.
Water skiing	

Sources: ORRRC 1962a, BTA-Keele University 1967. This latter survey also includes activities such as archery, bowls, golf and athletics which are considered as urban phenomena and are not dealt with here.

the seventeenth and eighteenth centuries became backgrounds for the less lusty pursuits of the contemporary gentry. The ruling classes of most ages have had their resource-using pleasure gardens, whether rural or urban, as with the pleasure-dome of Xanadu, presumably a sort of early Havasupai City. By contrast with the requirements of the numerically insignificant rich, the demand to transfer resources into leisure use now emanates from a large proportion of the population in industrialized countries. Another way in which the dimensions of man–environment relations have altered with regard to leisure is the hardware involved. Once a pair of nailed boots and a woolly sweater (or solar topee in the tropics) sufficed. Now, trailbikes, dune buggies and snowmobiles extend mobility off the roads into most kinds of terrain; aqualungs allow penetration under water (there is a sub-marine National Park in the US Virgin Islands); and the humble tent is being ousted in favour of a caravan or an integral-chassis camper. In North America it is not uncommon to see a large integral camper with a boat on the roof, two trailbikes slung on the front,

Plate 7 Perhaps most people's ideal of outdoor recreation? An isolated lake and a lone fisherman-camper, communing with nature. *(Grant Heilman, Lititz, Pa)*

and a small Japanese motorcar being towed behind. The impact of all this technology upon some of the recreation resources can easily be imagined.

The types of ecosystems which people like to be in for their outdoor recreation are very varied, according to both taste and availability, but certain preferences emerge. Overriding them all is the attraction of water (Plate 7). The pull of the seashore or the sandy edge of large lakes needs no stressing, but the presence of a small inland lake or river adds immeasurably to the value of a recreation area inland. There is, too, a preference for wild or seemingly wild vegetation such as woods, dunes and heaths, providing that the woods have ample openings or 'edge'. In climates with inhospitable tendencies some sort of shelter is demanded, so that the picnic tables at White Sands in New Mexico have reflective shades over them; in part of the Netherlands a very popular region is that where forest is found in the lee of sand-dunes so that people can move inland if the weather turns chill. It is not of course the actual nature of the ecosystem which attracts people so much as their perception of it, and varying degrees of alteration and change are acceptable for different recreation activities. While it is usually only possible to describe outdoor recreation use of resources in objective terms, therefore, it must not be forgotten that just as important are people's ideas about the sort of surroundings they choose, or would choose if alternatives were available. For example, Lucas (1964) showed that the two major groups of users (those

TABLE 4.8   Comparisons of participation

Activity	USA 1960	1965	Netherlands 1966	Sweden 1963	Canada 1966–7	GB 1960–4
			Selected activities per cent of population			
Walking for pleasure	33	48	25	73		
Swimming	45	48	29	65	34	10[1]
Camping	8	10	11[2]	19	13	6
Sightseeing	42	49			29	
Driving	52	55	50	73	47	56[3]
Fishing	29	30	14	37	26	6
Hiking	7	9			11	5
Sailing[4]	2	3		24	7	6
Skiing	2	4		41	6	1[5]

[1] Will include some use of urban facilities.
[2] Includes use of country cottage.
[3] An estimate for Whitsun 1963.
[4] Not motorized (Sweden, motorists included); includes rowing where this is separated.
[5] All winter sports.
This table is compiled from a variety of sources.

with and those without motors on their craft) of a wilderness canoe area in Minnesota–Ontario have different perceptions of the amount of human interference with the forest and of the effect such alterations have upon their enjoyment.

Classification of outdoor recreation areas and users

One classification of outdoor recreation resources is in terms of their actual or potential use; this method was adopted by the ORRRC (1962a) of the USA and distinguished six types of area:

Class 1: High Density Recreation Areas: areas intensively developed and managed for mass use

Class 2: General Outdoor Recreation Areas: areas subject to substantial development for a wide variety of specific recreation uses

Class 3: Natural Environment Areas: various types of areas that are suitable recreation in a natural environment and usually in combination with other uses

Class 4: Unique Natural Areas: areas of outstanding scenic splendour, natural wonder or scientific importance

Class 5: Primitive Areas: undisturbed roadless areas, characterized by natural wild conditions, including 'wilderness areas'

Class 6: Historic and Cultural Sites: sites of major historic or cultural significance, either local, regional, or national

Another method takes account of social factors such as accessibility from the users, and the classification to be used here has been developed by Knetsch and Clawson (1967). It is basically a *user-resource* method in which the two major elements are the characteristics of the users in terms of the time when they use the resource—whether it be afternoon, day or weekend use, or in their longer vacations—and the physical and ecological characteristics of the resource, especially its degree of wildness and of manipulation away from the natural state. The classification has three categories: user-orientated, dealing with the shorter periods of use; resource-based, treating the longer holiday periods; and intermediate, not unnaturally discussing the class in between—mainly the weekend and short vacation periods.

User-orientated recreation resources

The recreation areas deemed to be user-orientated are characterized by being as close to the homes of users as possible, and thus make use of whatever resources are available. The activities become the most important feature and a great deal of alteration is acceptable, and often necessary to protect the area against the damaging effects of heavy use. Activities such as golf, tennis, swimming and picnics, walking and horse riding, small zoos and model farms or railways and general informal play are the most usually found. The intensive use of what are often quite small areas, at most a few hundred hectares, with many smaller units, comes after school or after work and at weekends. Such areas are commonly owned by city or county governments or their various equivalents. The city park forms the innermost element of the structure. Its nature is very variable and the present tendency is away from the starched formality of traditional city parks. The value of such areas of open space as Boston Common, Central Park in New York and the Royal Parks of London is probably best judged from the fact that they are still not yet built upon.

Examples of recreation areas near cities

Parks and recreation areas on city fringes are difficult to acquire because of the high cost of land which is also valuable for housing or perhaps industrial use; but some cities have happily acquired, been given or converted from dereliction suitable tracts of land and water. The Amsterdam Forest ('Het Amsterdamse Bos') on the south-east side of that city is a large (900 ha), totally artificial recreation area, converted from polderland. Since 1934 (Fig. 4.1) the major pattern is of woods with informal footpaths and cycleways interspersed with grass fields and water-bodies, some irregular and informal, others regular as in the case of a rowing course. The developed facilities include a sports stadium, riding school and open-air theatre. There are roads and car parks, but access by public transport forms the commonest pattern of use. In the same country, the theme of conversion is echoed by a water area just outside Utrecht, called Maarseveense Plassen. Under the auspices of the national authority carrying out land-consolidation plans, a former wetland area of peat cuttings and intervening baulks has been dredged out to form a swimming and boating lake. The margins are landscaped, either with woodland containing cycleways and footpaths or with lawns

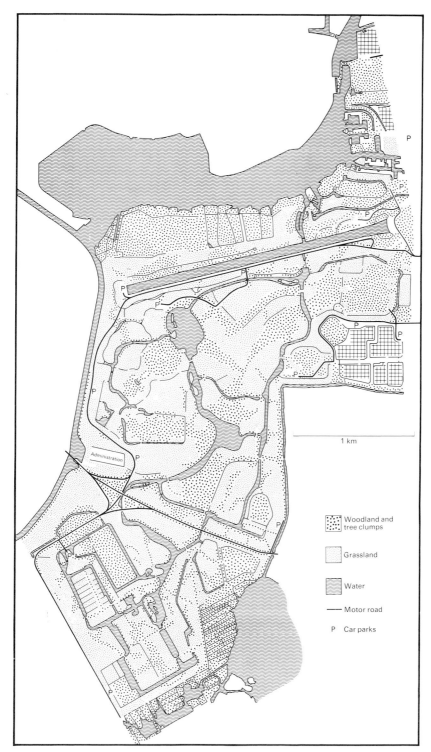

Fig. 4.1 The Amsterdam Forest: a completely man-made recreational facility which by use of trees and water creates a rural atmosphere in some parts. More urbanized and formal areas for games and a rowing course are also part of the area.

Source: Dienst der Publike Werken Amsterdam 1960: *Het Amsterdamse Bos*

leading from the facilities (toilets, changing rooms and café) down to the diving boards and shallow-water zone. Use is heavy, averaging some 30,000 people per annum in the first years of its use during the 1960s.

The valley of the River Lee slices through the eastern suburbs of London and here a scheme to develop a rather ill-assorted agglomeration of reservoirs, a canal, gravel pits, football pitches, refuse dumps and small industries like scrap-metal reclamation into a Lee Valley Regional Park has been initiated (Civic Trust 1964). The Park will have some nature reserves but will in general be highly developed, with playing fields, indoor sports halls, water-sport pools, restaurants, and possibly animal collections of special interest to urban children, like cows and horses (Fig. 4.2).

These are more or less spatially isolated instances, and actual park systems on the edges of urbanized areas are rarer. One example is the East Bay Regional Park District on the east side of San Francisco Bay in California. The hills behind cities such as Oakland, Berkeley and Albany are naturally grass- and chaparral-covered, with some redwoods, but since the nineteenth century eucalyptuses have become naturalized. In this setting, a series of parks has become established catering mainly for user-orientated recreation but admittedly overlapping into the intermediate zone. The most user-orientated parks in the system are Tilden Park and Redwood Park. In the valleys nearest to the cities, development of features such as a swimming lake, steam-powered railways, golf course, a carousel, a miniature farm, and riding stables has taken place. Further in is a less developed zone with picnic sites, group camp sites and a botanic garden of a relatively informal kind. Beyond these the park is largely wild in appearance, with a few trails striking off into the chaparral and wooded areas. Here, deer herds exist probably along with their natural predator, the bobcat or mountain lion. The development of Tilden Park, for example, shows a distinct series of development zones aligned parallel to both the topography and the adjacent cities (Fig. 4.3). Another unit in the system consists almost entirely of a swimming pool and adjacent facilities, open-air but formal in character, near to the edge of the Bay Area conurbation.

Possibly the largest class of user-orientated recreation areas are beaches at the seaward fringes of seaside cities. These are very cheap resources since there is generally perpetual renewal of the essential elements by the sea. Where this action breaks down then sand has to be brought in and an artificial beach maintained, which is costly but usually essential for the viability of the resort. In Japan, for example, a first priority in open-space acquisition for public use is the provision of beaches which will be easily accessible to the people of the great conurbations.

Changes wrought by recreational use

The designation of a unit of land or water as a recreation area within this present category usually means that changes will occur in the local ecosystems. At a deliberate level, most changes have to be made in order that the area can withstand the intensive use which it receives. Thus circulation routes are inevitably hard-surfaced, and it may be necessary to plant trees and shrubs which can withstand compaction of the earth over their roots and the loss of a branch or two by vandalism. Picnic tables if installed have to be specially strong, and concrete frames, if not tops, are common. Biota rarely receive management in

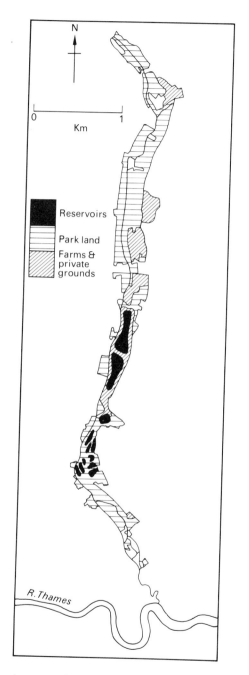

Fig. 4.2 The proposed redevelopment of the Lee Valley in east London: a mosaic of reservoirs, private lands and parklands for intensive use by the population of the urban areas which surround the valley. Source: Civic Trust 1964

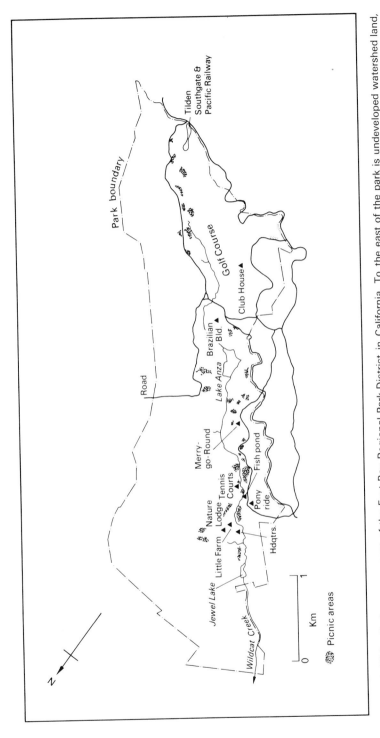

Fig. 4.3 Tilden Park, a component of the East Bay Regional Park District in California. To the east of the park is undeveloped watershed land, to the west the urbanized areas of the East Bay (e.g. Berkeley, Albany, Oakland). The concentration of developed facilities along the western edge is evident.

Source: East Bay Regional Parks District n.d.: *Charles Lee Tilden Park* (pamphlet)

such places, although a pair of nesting swans can be inimical to other uses of water-bodies in spring, and in many countries the numbers of pigeons and starlings attracted to such areas may be undesirable. Beaches may of course suffer from polluted water, and enlightened municipalities endeavour to remove the source of pollution, which may be not only unaesthetic but a positive danger to health.

Intermediate-type recreation resources

The zone of recreation resources available to the city-dweller for use on day outings and weekends is called by Knetsch and Clawson (1967) the Intermediate zone. The actual distance travelled by users will vary according to the road system, since transport by private auto is all-important for this type of use. Within the time–distance limitation, preference is shown for the best resources that are available, in terms for instance of scenery, water and forests. These are generally larger in size than the user-orientated areas, running from a few hundred to several thousand hectares. Emphasis is put on activities such as camping, picnicking, hiking, swimming, hunting and fishing, and there is also the pleasure of driving to get to the chosen location. Although public resources managed by governmental agencies are perhaps the most common feature of this category, the private sector is often involved. The degree of manipulation away from the natural state tends to be less than in user-orientated areas, and acceptance of quasi-urban features is lower. Insistance on a natural environment is of course impossible in continents like Europe and here high value is placed on areas which are obviously wild even if not natural, or on areas like heaths and moors which are popularly thought to be natural even though they are anthropogenic in origin. The pressures resulting from recreation may still be intense over a small area of the resource, but there is more often a large area of back country into which the less gregarious can escape.

National Parks in England and Wales

Although dealt with once under the heading of protected landscape, the National Parks of England and Wales come under this heading too (Darby 1963). People come to them not only to view the scenery, but for many active recreations as well. Driving for pleasure, walking and hiking, climbing, potholing, boating, natural history pursuits and many other activities are carried out in these 11 designated areas. Most of them are within the day-use zone of a major conurbation, yet several receive some usage of a resource-based category. Most of the valley land within the Parks is private and obviously so, which means that use is only by direct permission of the owner unless walking along a public right of way is contemplated. Even the owner may be under restrictions since, for example, the placing of caravans requires planning permission. The majority of farmers in the Parks do not welcome recreationists, however, because of the trouble caused by their ignorance of the working nature of rural areas. It is not surprising therefore that much recreation tends to be concentrated in the unenclosed zones which are altitudinally above the farmed lands. Such lands are often common land to which there is a *de facto* but not *de jure* right of public access (Fig. 4.4). It is here that most people like to set off on walks, to picnic or simply to sit in their cars. Since until the late 1960s there were few places where cars could pull off the usually narrow roads, such spots as there were frequently received very heavy pressure. The installation of car parks and toilets in many of the attractive villages that are found in the lower areas of the Parks has meant an alleviation of the congestion of narrow and picturesque streets by fleets of visitors' cars. In some of the Parks, the planning authorities have taken the lead in such actions as providing official but limited camp and caravan sites in order to prevent a rash over all the countryside. Experiments are being undertaken to control car access to some of the most popular but narrow roads in the interests of general public amenity: the Goyt Valley in the Peak District National Park is an example (Countryside Commission 1970).

Even with such measures, it is difficult to avoid the conclusion that at peak times some of the National Parks (the Lake District and Peak District especially) are reaching their carrying capacity for outdoor recreation. This is especially so for people with cars, but queues to climb particular crags and to descend certain potholes suggest that the pinch is also being felt in other activities. Under the aegis of the Countryside Act of 1968, county councils are empowered to designate another kind of Intermediate-class recreation area, the Country Parks. The degree of development of these facilities can be varied according to the circumstances, and it is hoped that the National Parks will be relieved of some of their recreational pressures and be visited more for their unique attractions rather than for activities which can be pursued equally well in other areas. The Country Parks will amplify a role already played in some parts of the country by the plantations of the Forestry Commission. During the last few years there has been a revolution in the policy of this body regarding recreation, so that picnic sites, camping sites, trails and visitor centres are now often found, as at Grizedale in the Lake District, Allerston Forest in North Yorkshire, and many other places. As these areas have distinct boundaries, it is often possible to make a charge for facilities and this is usually done. In this context, recreation presents fewer problems as an element of multiple use than with farming: young forests are very susceptible to damage but are not very attractive for recreation, and wildlife is not particularly abundant in monocultural coniferous forests.

The Dutch experience

The role of recreation in re-afforested parts of Europe is carried to a considerable length in the Netherlands, where 25 per cent of the area managed by the State Forest Service (Staatsbosbeheer, SBB) is managed primarily for timber production, and the remainder mostly for recreation and nature conservation, especially the former (SBB 1966). Apart from the customary facilities, the SBB has created large informal swimming holes out of sandy lands, an example is to be found at Nunspeet. In at least one case the hole represents the further use of a borrow-pit resulting from motorway construction. Most of the State Forests of the Netherlands come into the Intermediate category although some are near enough to towns to be thought of as user-orientated and development is correspondingly intensive. In both situations, however, the Dutch love of food is exemplified in the

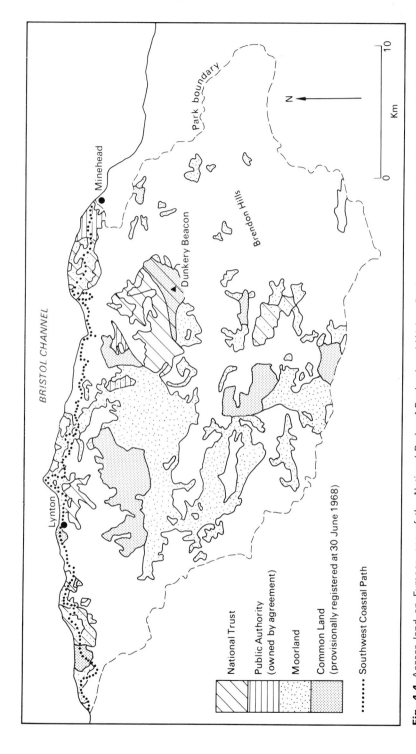

Fig. 4.4 Access land on Exmoor, one of the National Parks of England and Wales. *De jure* access is to National Trust and Public Authority land; *de facto* access exists to moorland and commonland but, strictly speaking, such access could be withdrawn. The Coastal Path is a public right of way for those on foot.
Source: Patmore 1971.

Legend:

- National Trust
- Public Authority (owned by agreement)
- Moorland
- Common Land (provisionally registered at 30 June 1968)
- ••••••• Southwest Coastal Path

BRISTOL CHANNEL

Lynton

Minehead

Dunkery Beacon

Brendon Hills

Park boundary

N

Km

0   10

provision of refreshment kiosks and restaurants in places where British and American experience and preference would find them a little intrusive.

State Parks in the USA

Most states have such a system of State Parks, but their effectiveness and range of utilized resources vary greatly. In general, the richer the state, the more complex the State Parks system will be: the states of New York, Michigan, Minnesota, Oregon and California are generally recognized to be the leaders. In all such systems these are areas of primarily historical or cultural interest (such as some of the Franciscan Missions in California), and in some the system embraces nature protection as well. For recreation, State Park systems usually enclose the best scenic and recreational resources which are not already within the Federal system and develop them to cope with heavy pressures, especially at summer week-ends; winter sports may also be catered for at selected locations. Nearly all outdoor recreations are carried on in these Parks, with some emphasis on camping, fishing and hiking. Hunting is rarely permitted in them. In states like California, with a high diversity of eco-systems, generalizations about the pattern of resource use are difficult to make. Forests have a clear attraction especially for summer shade, and in this connexion the northern coast redwood parks are popular as cool places quite apart from the magnificence of *Sequoia sempervirens*. Water is another attraction, whether on the few public beaches (those of southern California are very crowded in summer) or inland at reservoirs or natural lakes such as Clear Lake and Lake Tahoe, both of which have State Parks along part of their otherwise privately owned shores. The desert Parks are naturally popular in winter, as are skiing, tobogganing and other snow-based sports.

The second home

The possession of second homes in rural areas is a rapidly growing phenomenon in the West. In Europe it reaches the apogee of its development in Scandinavia, but it is burgeon-ing everywhere (Fig. 4.5). Weekend cottages, beach-houses, cabins, caravans and their kin are almost by definition part of the Intermediate zone; and because their owners wish to be in rural surroundings but also to have most home comforts such as electricity and mains drainage (or at least a cesspool or septic tank), they pose resource management problems. The aesthetic one of screening to avoid the appearance of a rather tatty suburb is one difficulty, and where zoning laws do not exist it is often impossible to prevent a variegated scatter of bungaloid growth in favoured spots. Economically they pose problems in terms of the services which their owners demand, while often paying relatively low local taxes. The communities in which they exist are therefore likely to have to subsidize them.

Ecologically their effects are most profound when a new area is opened up for cabins around a desirable place such as a lake. It is unlikely that regulations about waste disposal are in effect and so raw sewage will be discharged into the lake with consequent eutrophica-tion and aesthetic damage. The actual placing of the cottages may have less effect since there is a desire to preserve trees and other biota.

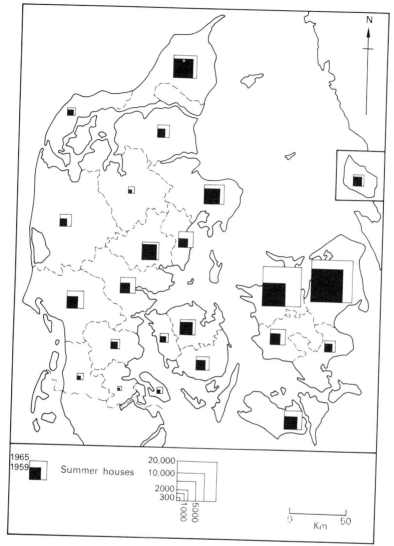

Fig. 4.5 Summerhouses in Denmark, by counties, 1959 and 1965. The concentration in Sjaelland (especially near Copenhagen) and in east Jylland is noticeable. Most of these summerhouse areas were not subject to planning control.
Source: Landsplanudvalgets Sekretariat 1965: *Strandkvalitet og Fritidsbebyggelse*

Resource-based recreation

In contrast to the previous two categories, resource-based recreation takes place where the outstanding resources are to be found, independently of the distribution of population. This may well be some distance from the majority of users, although some people may live in the backyard of an outstanding resource which others travel thousands of miles to visit. It follows that the longer vacation periods are the commonest use periods and that activities are consequent upon the resource offered: major sightseeing is perhaps paramount, along with scientific and historic interest, even if these latter two are very inchoately realized. Hiking and climbing, fishing and hunting may also be pursued because of the superlative qualities of the particular place; camping may be an end in itself or a cheap way to visit the resource area. The qualities of the attractive area are generally extensive: typically a resource-based recreation area may range from many thousands of hectares in size to ten times that magnitude. It is not surprising therefore that the resource is usually publicly owned and that the agencies of the national government are usually the managers. Exceptions to this are sometimes found in water frontages along large lakes and the sea.

As the environment is all-important, it should be a feature of the designated areas that human impacts resulting in alterations to the ecology should be minimized. This is generally so, except where visitor numbers are very high and require particular management responses. But highly developed zones are usually small in relation to the proportion of wild back-country.

National Parks in North America

The world's most famous examples of the designation of resource-based recreation areas are the National Parks of the USA and Canada, especially those of the western cordillera. The range of terrains is immense, but all the Parks share the property of being very wild and in most places natural or at any rate affected only by aboriginal economics in the form of hunting and burning. Economic activities on a large scale have never been permitted, although some early grazing may have left erosive scars, and there are numerous private inholdings which complicate management.

The major problems of the National Parks come from the great mass of visitors. In 1910, about 0·2 million people visited a US National Park system of about 9,308 km² (2·3 million ac), in the 1960s about 95 million a year went to a system that was still below 80,940 km² (20 million ac) in size. Such numbers initiate immense demands for roads (since most use private cars), for accommodation, food, gasoline, water and other services (Plate 8); in turn they produce sewage, garbage, litter, car exhausts and traffic jams (Cahn 1968). These effects, together with the presence in some National Parks of luxury hotels and golf courses, eventually led to the reappraisal of National Park policy in the USA described in Chapter 3, which has resulted in the designation of recreation areas within a park system whose function is primarily protective. Thus recreation is being de-emphasized, and eventually perhaps most developed facilities will be withdrawn beyond the park boundaries. Under the impetus of public opinion, the master plans for the National Parks of Canada include large wild areas and developed areas are being kept to a minimum (Fig. 4.6).

Even before such changes in policy, these National Parks were unequal to the recreation pressure they were being expected to carry. One result, analogous in function to the Country Parks in Britain, has been the development within the USA Federal system of National Recreation Areas. In 1971, there were 17 units comprising 14,164 km² (3·5 million ac), representing outstanding opportunities for resource-based recreation within the Federal

Plate 8 Perhaps most people's reality of outdoor recreation? The area near Old Faithful geyser in Yellowstone National Park. The Park Service now aims to 'de-develop' this part of the Park. *(Grant Heilman, Lititz, Pa)*

system at areas not suitable for designation as National Parks. The selection criteria involve consideration of the size of an area, its ability to provide a high carrying capacity for recreation, and a location usually not more than 400 km from large urban centres. A natural environment is not required and many of the areas are primarily for water-based recreation along artificial impoundments such as Lake Mead, Lake Powell, and the Shasta Dam and Lake in California.

Multiple use with recreation as a primary purpose of management is represented in the USA Federal system by the National Forests. Most of their 752,742 km² (183 million ac) are in the west and they often form the matrix within which the National Parks and National Recreation Areas are set. Since recreation is only one of the purposes of management (the others are wildlife, grazing, water and timber production), the multiple use tends to be a mosaic pattern, with developed recreational facilities and roads within a much larger area of undeveloped country. Even where campsites and picnic grounds are developed, they tend to be more simple than in National Parks and National Recreation Areas. Hot

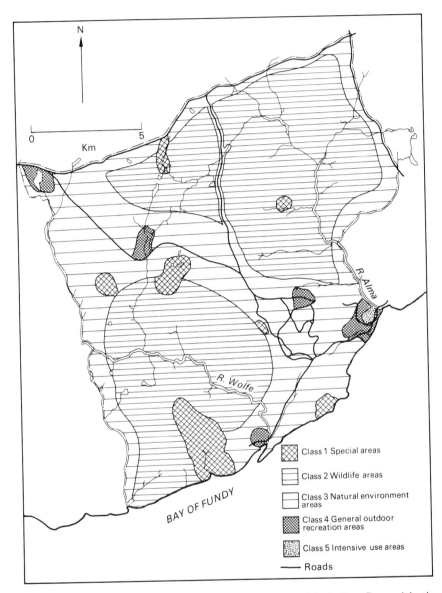

Fig. 4.6 The proposed master plan for the Bay of Fundy National Park, New Brunswick, showing the division of the park into zones. Developed areas are kept to a minimum consistent with the use of the park for recreation. Such a plan is a public document and the subject of public hearings.
Source: National and Historic Parks branch kit for hearings on Bay of Fundy National Park Master Plan, Ottawa, 1968

showers and launderettes are not found in National Forest campgrounds, and the deep-pit toilet replaces the flush type. Thus the local ecology is usually less modified than in the Parks and Recreation Areas, a feature which commends the National Forests to the more hardy campers. The National Forests in fact extend well beyond the forested zone in mountainous terrain and so enclose the alpine meadows and slopes and the high alpine country itself. Recreation activities are hence very varied in kind and range from the highly popular to the more eclectic such as river-rafting and wilderness back-packing.

Europe

In more densely settled parts of the world like Europe, resource-based recreation areas are harder to find and are mostly confined to high mountain areas such as the Alps, Pyrenees, Carpathians and the Norwegian *fjells*. Each of these regions attracts many people both winter and summer for recreation. Management varies, but in general there are a few areas within each region which are particularly designated for the protection of wildlife (e.g. the Tatra National Park in ČSSR–Poland, and the Swiss National Park) and then development of recreation in the rest is subject to the ordinary planning laws of the country.

Within Europe, one area with potential for resource-based recreation is Lapland. At present relatively few people visit it except for such specialized activities as bird-watching and tourism based on the few roads. The same can be said of Iceland. Both these places have very fragile ecosystems with short growing seasons, and any development must recognize this if irresponsible damage is not to be done. On a European scale it would probably be best to make most of both areas into formally protected wildernesses.

A small yet densely populated region like the British Isles fares badly for resource-based recreation, but fortunately the unequal distribution of population confers a sense of remoteness upon places like the Western Highlands and Hebrides of Scotland. The roadless nature and low population density confirms the 'otherness' of these areas and the result is their function as a resource-based recreation region. This has been emphasized by the development of the Cairngorms as Britain's leading winter sport area. Some of the Scottish National Forest Parks attract a nationwide clientele, and a study of the National Forest Park at Beddgelert in North Wales (Sinden and Sinden 1964) showed that many campers were taking their annual holiday, a pointer to one of the functions of the mountains of North Wales generally, although they are probably most heavily used as Intermediate areas by the population of Lancashire and the industrial Midlands.

An immense country like the USSR has enormous recreation resources; yet protected areas for recreation which have nationwide importance have been slow in coming. Pryde (1972) discusses the planned creation of two National Parks ('Russian Forest' south of Moscow, and Lake Baykal in eastern Siberia) which would be devoted primarily to vacation use by the Soviet people. Another 13 sites have been put forward as suitable areas, which would be at least 10,000 ha in size and would be divided into developed and undeveloped sections, with a central semi-wilderness having only trails and designated camping sites. The 'Russian Forest' Park, about 100 km from Moscow, will cater for more intensive use which will be combined with educative functions such as a demonstration forest.

Japan

In all essentials, Japan shares the West's tastes in outdoor recreation. Given a small country with a high density of population, particularly in the Tokyo-Osaka axis, there are large numbers of outdoor recreationists, whose quantity is increasing steadily with the advent of more leisure time and income. The only areas of the country which were specifically designated in 1972 as being available for outdoor recreation are the 26 National Parks and 46 Quasi-National Parks (QNPs), together with 286 prefectural parks; about 13 per cent of the surface of Japan is thus designated. The Parks function through all three user-resource recreation zones, but some especially are of the resource-based character. In these, the cultural attractions are generally less than in the intermediate zone, assuming not unreasonably that Fujiyama has a significance far beyond that of being a mountain. The resource-based National Parks are all distant from the major population axis of Japan; thus the Aso National Park and Unzen-Amakusa National Park in Kyushu, the Towada-Hachimantai National Park in northern Honshu, and the Daisetsuzan and Akan National Parks in Hokkaido are all composed largely of the natural environment of mountain, forest and lake. Nevertheless all the National Parks and Quasi-National Parks are probably accessible for weekend use if overnight trains or planes are used, and all are penetrated by public transport often to an intensity not now common in the West. In the case of Japan, the dilemma of development or preservation centres around two factors: the ownership of the land, and the application of zoning (Senge 1969). Where the land is in national ownership then it is frequently under the control of the Forest Agency, which places a high priority on economic timber production and tends to use clear felling as a method of harvesting; this conflicts at least temporarily with recreational activities as well as spoiling some of the visual attractions of the landscape. Thus the National Parks Agency is frequently at loggerheads with the Forest Agency over resource management in the National Parks. Where there are large areas of private land within the National Parks, the Parks Agency has little control over the development of hot springs, hotels and inns, restaurants, cafés and souvenir shops; these tend to be very frequent elements of the landscape at the nodal points of the National Parks, such as around Lake Shikotsu and Mount Showashinzan in the Shikotsu-Toya National Park in Hokkaido. Another example is at the transport-mode interchange station high on the slopes of Mount Aso in Kyushu. Under the impact of the recreation-seeking element of the population of Japan, there seems at present to be an impetus towards development, and the appreciation of the virtues of the natural environment as a milieu for recreation which has characterized recent movements in the West does not yet seem to have penetrated: there is consequently considerable ecological change wrought by developments made in the name of the provision of recreation facilities.

Changes caused by recreation

As with other types of recreation, the activities and development may affect the ecosystems within which the recreationists operate. At a conscious level, developments to cope with large numbers in popular areas are probably the most noticeable. In Yosemite Valley there is a small village catering to visitors; and in the Canadian Rockies earlier policies established two small towns (Jasper and Banff) which are currently suffering expansionist pressures. In such Parks there is then the somewhat incongruous sight of sewage works and solid waste disposal areas. As pressure increases so more management has to be undertaken, necessitating more notices, more hardtop and generally less nature. Another deliberate policy stems from the desire of some managers to make as much country as possible accessible to as many people as practicable. The building of roads is therefore undertaken, with considerable effects on drainage lines, soil stability and many other features. A road through tundra may have unstable banks which are then seeded with a commercial mixture containing exotics and so the potential for very large biotic invasions may be created. Trees may often be felled to give a clearer view; conversely, insecticides may be used to preserve trees which have a special landscape significance or other associations. Hardware such as gondola lifts require the clearing of a swathe of forest beneath them like a fire-break; and fire roads themselves may be cut for the maximum travel efficiency of fire-fighting crews rather than with regard for the ecology.

Unconscious effects are numerous. The effect of human feet is perhaps the most noticeable, especially where plant roots are susceptible to compaction of the upper layers of the soil, as happens with the California coast redwood. In this case, redwood bark chip mulches have to be laid along the major pathways. In many popular resource-based areas, one animal develops the role of scavenger, to become dependent for its food on the leavings of the visitors: yellowhammers at Tarn Hows in the English Lakes, brown bears in western America. Bears can be dangerous, if surprised or with cubs; harmless-looking animals like ground squirrels and chipmunks may have rabies. At the other extreme are creatures which are driven out of their habitats either because of alterations brought about by visitors or simply by the presence of large numbers of our species. Either way, the ecological patterns which are so valued in 'natural' resource-based recreation areas are disrupted. Plants may suffer even more and after a few years' use a forest campground does not regenerate: there are no seedlings and usually the surface is trodden too hard for germination to take place. A period of 'rest' with management techniques such as scarifying the soil and burning off excess litter (of the natural variety) may be necessary.

These few examples, and many more which could be quoted, serve to highlight the basic dilemma of resource-based recreation: that too great a number of people destroy what they come to seek. The resolution of this in the short term lies in better management of the visitors and, where possible, in the transfer of additional resources from other uses.

Outdoor recreation as an element of multiple use

The non-consumptive nature of most outdoor recreation activities means that it is sometimes possible to combine them with other resource uses. Multiple use may be of two types: either the use of one piece of terrain for several purposes, or a densely interwoven mosaic of different uses. Occasionally both can be found. In general, the compatibility of different use varies according to the intensity of the uses, i.e. the degree of ecological manipulation the systems have undergone. Thus generally compatible resource uses include watershed land, provided the recreation does not cause erosion leading to high silt yields. Water stored in reservoirs can also be used for most types of recreation, although swimming may be dis-couraged where the water is for drinking purposes and is near to its delivery point. Simi-larly, the preservation of scenery is usually compatible with recreation, except where exten-sive development of a visitor-orientated kind has to be undertaken. Nature conservation may be compatible with recreation, but there is a good deal of variation; and the fugacity of animals or the resistance to damage of plants and animals under protection differ in the amount of visitor pressure they can withstand without harm. But such compatibilities are not axiomatic, and careful distinction of the management aims of recreation areas from those of nature conservation and landscape protection are necessary: it is folly to lump them together under a single 'conservationist' label. Certain resource uses are clearly highly incompatible with recreation. The protection of delicate or rare species needs often to be accomplished in secrecy, not least to be hidden from keen botanists and birdwatchers. A more commonly irreconcilable land use at present is agriculture. The damage inflicted on farming operations by either malicious or ignorant visitors to rural areas is a constant complaint of farmers in industrial countries and the eradication of their just cause for concern is difficult. Education is one solution, but it is a long-term process; in the mean-time, areas of very high agricultural productivity are probably best kept underdeveloped as far as recreation is concerned. It seems that farmers who suffer loss because of recreation, or who voluntarily manage their farms so as to take account of it, are increasingly likely to be compensated out of public funds, as are woodland owners in the Netherlands who receive freedom from certain estate duties if they maintain footpaths through their property. Obviously mineral extraction is inimical to all forms of recreation, but we may note that after-treatment of abandoned workings may bring them very successfully into resource processes. Landscaped wet gravel pits are very popular for sailing in many places; old quarries and dry pits may house car parks or sheltered picnic sites and day-camps, and with the queues at the bases of popular rock climbs there may be a demand to create new faces by management of suitable quarry walls. Lastly, the military use large areas of land and water which would otherwise be suitable as recreation resources. Heaths in the Netherlands and south-east England, wild terrain in Utah and south-west England, coast-lines in most maritime countries, all form the habitat of *Homo aggressor* rather than *Homo ludens*. Pressures to move them on are occasionally successful and compromises over access can sometimes be reached (Please do not step on unexploded shells), but large areas are still devoted to the training of the military and appear likely to remain so.

Multiple-use schemes containing recreation, if carefully planned and managed by a body representative of all the interests concerned, can be highly successful. In industrialized countries where demand especially for intermediate and user-orientated recreation facilities is increasing so quickly, such schemes may represent, in the short term, the only way of providing anything like an adequate supply of resources and may in turn serve to take some pressure off the resource-based areas whose nature generally makes them very susceptible to damage. In recreation, damage is the only form of consumption, and the continuing pressures of use make reparation by natural processes very difficult.

Effects of increasing populations

Although in the short term more recreation resources can be created by shifts of land and water from other uses, this process cannot be carried on indefinitely. Other more basic demands like housing, industry and agriculture cannot be deprived of their share. Rising populations exert an increasing pressure upon resources because demand for recreation in industrialized countries appears to rise at approximately five times the rate of population growth. In poor countries fewer people participate and so the dimensions of the interaction are much smaller. An increase in the number of people hammering at the park gates is immediately caused to a great extent by increases in leisure, affluence and mobility, and in recreation areas they cause crowding with subsequent loss of satisfaction from the recreation experience; at popular times the peak loading causes tremendous management problems, and the intensity of use may lead to loss of biotic diversity. Environmental contamination may even result, since sewage and refuse disposal systems are unlikely to have been built to deal with such peak loads. People who come to enjoy wild places and rural environments seem inexorably destined to destroy them.

In a more long-term perspective, recreation and the protection of wild ecosystems are essential components of what industrial countries call 'environmental quality'. Inasmuch as the demands for material resources are, per capita, the highest in the world, and that such desires seem to conflict with the maintenance of environmental quality, it is not surprising that population growth has been called the fundamental cause of the overloading of park and recreation systems. It is argued that just as LDCs suffer from certain material or 'quantity' deficits, because of their increases in population size, so even the relatively slow growth of population in the DCs is fundamental to the steady attrition of environmental quality. Such a train of thought is hard to prove quantitatively, since so much can be done to alleviate the problems by allocating more resources and by improved management. But as populations and expectations continue to rise, it appears inevitable that competition for land and water resources, including those at present of value for recreation, will rise. The more basic demands are likely to prove victorious in any such conflict. Similarly, if the quality of recreation declines because of pressure, there are few substitutes that can be brought into this particular resource process. While it is scarcely possible therefore to argue that a cessation of population growth is essential for the persistence of outdoor recreation as a cultural activity, it certainly appears that slower growth with its consequent redistribution of age classes would make available a high quality of outdoor recreation experiences much further into the future than would be possible with a rapidly expanding population.

Further reading

ADAMS, A. B. (ed.) 1964: *First World Conference on National Parks.*
BRACEY, H. C. 1970: *People and the countryside.*
CLAWSON, M. and KNETSCH, J. L. 1966: *Economics of outdoor recreation.*
OUTDOOR RECREATION RESOURCES REVIEW COMMISSION 1962: *Recreation for America.*
PATMORE, J. A. 1970: *Land and leisure in England and Wales.*
REVELLE, R. 1967: Outdoor recreation in a hyper-productive society.
SENGE, T. 1969: The planning of national parks in Japan and other parts of Asia.
YOUNG, G. 1973: *Tourism: blessing or blight?*

5

Grazing

The products of this resource process consist of both edible and potable substances (meat, fat, milk, blood and various other delicacies) together with materials such as hides, wool and other minor non-edible items, and are taken by culling populations of domesticated or semi-domesticated herbivorous mammals. The planned cropping of certain wild mammal populations is also discussed at this point.

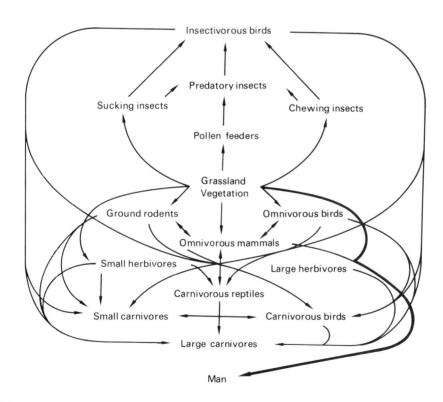

Fig. 5.1 A simplified food chain for a grassland system, with man's cropping pathway added and emphasized. In order to enhance his offtake, man will often eliminate other energy pathways and hence simplify the ecosystem.
Source: Lewis 1969

The grazing systems discussed in this section are divided from the utilization of herbivorous animals in an intensive agricultural context by the absence of deliberate nutrient return to the soils by the resource managers. The animals themselves may contribute to the biogeochemical cycles by way of excreta and the odd carcass, but most of the soil nutrients which reach the body of the selected animal are removed from the site of intake. Even though other manipulations of the local ecosystems may occur (either deliberately as with stock water management, or unconsciously as with gradual shifts in forage composition due to selective grazing by certain species), fertilizer input is unlikely except in the richest countries. This major criterion does not conflict with the definition of the grazing resource formulated by the American Society of Range Management (1964) as 'all land producing native forage for animal consumption and lands that are vegetated naturally or artificially to provide a forage cover that is managed like native vegetation'. Alteration of the ecology of areas utilized by pastoralists has often been slow and unconscious, thus earning its position among the less manipulated of the ecosystems discussed in this book. As Fraser Darling (1956) says, man's ecological dominance of wild lands through the medium of domesticated animals

> takes a long time to develop its expression, and is not always conspicuous in process, so that its influence is often unappraised in both biological and administrative assessments....

The most obvious form of deliberate ecosystem manipulation which takes place is the struggle against competitors for the crop of herbivores, or 'predator control'. This gives us the clue that although the food chain of plants–herbivores–man is very simple, it is in fact part of a more complex web (Fig. 5.1).

Biology of grazing

There is a high variety of biomes in which grazing by domesticated animals is important, although the various types of grassland (Fig. 5.2) form the main source of forage (C. W. E. Moore 1964). Of the total land surface, some 28 per cent is covered by forest which is grazed by wildlife and/or domestic stock for at least part of the year; and 47 per cent is suitable only for grazing by wild beasts or domesticated stock, having no potential for any more intensive use (Lewis 1969). FAO estimates of 'permanent meadows and pasture' give a rough indication of the continental distribution of grasslands (Table 5.1). On a world scale, it has been estimated that domestic stock get 75 per cent of their forage needs from such extensive grazing resources.

The ecology of extensive grasslands is complex. It is dominated by grasses and herbs, sometimes with trees or shrubs, especially at the transitions to forest or desert. The plants form a closely knit cover over the soil, with their roots penetrating to considerable depths. The sod thus formed protects the soil from physical removal although the root system may be inadequate to prevent podzolization in wet and cool climates. On the other hand, where evaporation exceeds precipitation, minerals move up the soil profile: the humus content and the presence of upward-moving calcium carbonate give the chernozem, a most characteristic grassland soil, its particular qualities including a pH in excess of 7·0. As Fig. 5.1 shows,

Fig. 5.2 A world map of grassland types. Some of the 'modified community' grasslands are used intensively (e.g. in Europe) and so fall outside the definition of the grazing system used in this chapter, which thus deals mostly but not exclusively with the 'natural community' grassland.
Source: C. W. E. Moore 1964

Grasses prominent in the natural communities which can be grazed with little or no modification

Grasses not prominent in the natural communities which have been more or less modified to produce grasslands

TABLE 5.1   Geography and biology of grazing

Grasslands by continental distribution (1,000 ha)		
	Land area	'Permanent meadows and pastures'
Europe	493,000	93,000
USSR	2,240,220	374,000
North and Central America	2,241,000	372,000
South America	1,784,000	413,000
Asia	1,797,000	322,000
China	956,100	177,000
Africa	3,030,000	844,000
Oceania	851,000	464,000
World	13,392,000	3,059,000

Source: FAO *Production Yearbook No. 25* (1971), Table 1

this vegetation is the starting point of a complicated ecosystem of which the grazing sub-system is the part in which man is primarily interested, to the point of trying to eliminate wild mammals which are also grazers and which he perceives as competition for the forage. The primary productivity of the grasslands is of course the key feature of the system whether it is being valued for its natural or man-managed features, and it is highly variable,

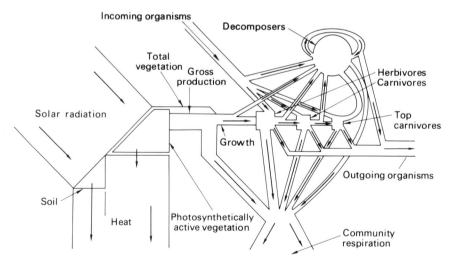

Fig. 5.3 A diagram of a Lindemann model representation of a natural grassland ecosystem. The usual features of such models are present, including the considerable losses (as heat) at the primary producer stage and the overall conversion of concentrated energy to the dispersed form of heat. A special grass-land feature is the importance of the decomposers, and boundary difficulties are acknowledged by the presence of flows from incoming and outgoing organisms.
Source: Lewis 1969

being dependent upon minerals, water, climate and other factors. Much of it goes into subterranean parts which are not available to most grazing animals: in *Andropogon* prairie in Missouri, USA, the energy production for the above-ground parts of the grassland was 1.962×10^6 cals of biomass/yr, whereas the below-ground portions yielded 2.389×10^6 cals biomass/yr (Kucera *et al.* 1967). On a world scale grasslands do not come very high in biome productivity ranking (see p. 19) and a single instance illustrates this (Table 5.2). The low production of the grassland compared with the other forms, all within the same environment, is emphasized by Ovington *et al.* (1963) when they point out that the greatest mass of potential food for grazing, and hence the highest rate of secondary production, is in the savanna because the shelter of the scattered trees resulted in a very high primary productivity at ground level. Here can be seen a fundamental reason for the high densities of wild animals in African savannas, particularly when specialist grazers of swamps and tree tops are added to the ground-level suite. Because they are adapted to use a greater proportion of the forage than domestic livestock, the biomass of wild herbivores on extensive grazings is nearly always greater than domestic stock, a fact which will be referred to again later in this section (Plate 9).

TABLE 5.2   Comparative production of some North American ecosystems

Cedar Creek, Minnesota, primary productivity $(kg/ha^2/yr)$		
	Max.	Min.
Prairie grasslands	9,700	6,100
Savanna	63,200	54,400
Oak forest	257,100	224,200

Source: Ovington *et al.* 1963

In a grassland, as in other ecosystems, the cycles of water, carbon, oxygen, nitrogen and other kinds of matter are very complex but stable. Energy flows through the system at a rapid rate and through many strands of the web, yet all the energy is dissipated in the life processes of the living components of the ecosystem (Fig. 5.3). The way in which the energy flows of a grassland are tapped by domesticated beasts is little quantified. One of the best studies for our purpose is that of Macfadyen (1964), who attempted to quantify the energy exploitation of a reasonably fertile grass field under British conditions. It thus belongs rather more to an intensive agricultural system than to real pastoralism, but it will serve as a guide which will point to features of grazing systems, and Fig. 5.4 shows his results, using the Lindemann structural model of ecosystems, and Standard Nutrition Units as measures. Some of the main features of the diagram will be expected from the discussion of ecosystems on pages 6–12: the fact that, out of 2,500 SNU/ha/yr of incident radiant energy, only 40 SNU/ha/yr appears as grass will not be surprising. The very low proportion (0.2 SNU/ha/yr) appearing as beef stock is worthy of more comment. Bullocks select only about

Plate 9 A natural grassland in South Dakota, grazed by the aboriginal large mammal herbivore, the bison. Most major grasslands had a similar mammal or marsupial in such a niche. Compare the condition of the sward with Plate 10. *(Grant Heilman, Lititz, Pa.)*

one-seventh of the available herbage, reject about two-thirds of the ingested food as faeces and respire 90 per cent of what they assimilate. If the stock becomes unhealthy all the desired crop may go to the decomposers. So if the initial grass production is of the order of 5,000 cal/m²/yr, then a successful resource manager is going to harvest only 30 cal/m²/yr. In a commercial (as distinct from subsistence) system much of that will be unusable products such as hoof and bone. An annual-type California range studied by W. A. Williams (1966) exhibited an energy flow of the same order, where over a 3-year period the efficiency of conversion of solar energy in the vegetation was 0·09 per cent and in animal stock 0·004 per cent (Table 5.3). Another outstanding feature of Macfadyen's diagram is the accumulation of organic matter in the soil, mostly at its surface. This is mainly humus from the grasses, but animal excreta are an important component too. This large amount emphasizes the importance of soil flora and fauna, especially micro-organisms, in mineralizing this matter and making it available again for uptake by the grasses. Macfadyen (1964) says that it is the activity of the decomposers which limits the productivity of the whole system and so clearly this 'hidden' factor must be taken into account when assessing rangeland or diagnosing its ills. Quantitative budgets of nutrients in contrasted grazing systems are also difficult to find. One example is the work of D. T. Crisp (1963) in a Pennine moorland catchment. Here the input and output of key nutrients into a peat-covered watershed of 83 ha at about 600 m ASL with a rainfall of 2,130 mm/yr was studied. Especially noteworthy was the immediate loss of most of the nutrients in runoff, but by contrast the proportion of the nutrients which was removed in the form of the sheep, which were the

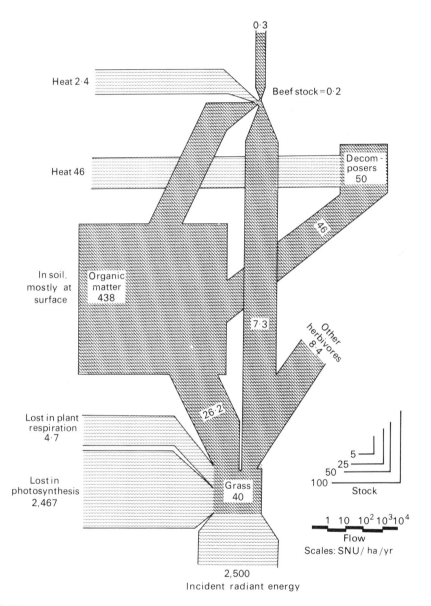

Fig. 5.4 Schematic diagram of energy flow in an intensively managed grassland-cattle ecosystem, expressed in SNU/ha/yr, where 1 SNU represents adequate caloric nutrition of 1 person at a rate of 2,460 kcal/day (900,000 kcal/yr). The darker shading represents flows and storages of organic matter, the lighter shading being flows of radiant energy or heat. The low quantity of incident radiation which becomes beef stock is apparent, as is the importance of the decomposer level at the soil surface, as suggested in Fig. 5.3.

Source: Macfadyen 1964

principal grazing animals of the watershed, was very small, about 1/200 of the incoming phosphorus, for example, being taken off in this manner. Pastoralism here is obviously an insignificant part of the ecosystem in terms of nutrient loss, although the sheep may alter the system in other ways, as by altering the species composition of the vegetation. In eco-systems with lower inputs of nutrients from precipitation, the removal of animals may constitute a higher proportion of the budget of essential elements.

TABLE 5.3   Energy flow and conversion in a California range

	kcal/m²/yr	%
Total incoming solar radiation	1,600,000	100
Available solar radiation of suitable wavelength	700,000	44
Net primary production[1]	1,410	0·09
Net secondary production	69	0·004

[1] Before the introductions of legumes and fertilization with sulphur, net primary production was 0·04 per cent.
Source: W. A. Williams 1966

These studies, doubtless to be amplified by results from International Biological Pro-gramme (IBP) research, point to certain generalities about pastoral grazing systems. Most striking is the generally low efficiency of the process. The large domestic herbivore appears to be an inefficient converter of greenstuff to animal protein: it is too selective in its intake of forage, it passes out too much of it as faeces and dissipates too much of the assimilated energy by running about. On the other hand the tissue produced is high in animal protein, the insufficiency of which is often the cause of malnutrition in humans. With such con-straints it is not surprising that commercially produced protein is expensive, and so other sources must be found for those malnourished because of its lack. Animals which are omnivorous scavengers or detritus feeders (such as pigs and molluscs) become ecologically if not culturally more attractive propositions for development.

The crop of domesticated animals

The ubiquity and absolute numbers of domesticated animals, including the grazers, are such that accurate statistics are not to be expected. The FAO figures given in Table 5.4 allow some estimate of the overall totals for different beasts, but they include animals from intensive agriculture systems and of course represent numbers of animals and not numbers killed for produce. They do total the number of beasts which are utilizing the grazing resources of the continents, and include a large number of work animals used in agriculture which may consume extensive grassland resources close to the land upon which they work.

The major extensive grazing animals are distributed largely in accordance with the

TABLE 5.4   Major livestock numbers 1970–71 (millions)

	Horses	Mules	Asses	Cattle	Pigs	Sheep	Goats	Buffaloes	Camels
Europe	7·7	1·1	1·7	122·6	139·4	127·5	12·6	0·3	—
USSR	12·8	—	0·6	99·1	67·4	137·9	5·4	0·5	0·2
North and Central America	14·2	3·1	3·6	172·0	95·2	26·8	13·6	—	—
South America	18·0	6·0	5·4	203·3	83·3	123·5	28·0	0·1	—
Asia	8·4	0·7	8·1	288·9	49·1	210·4	146·5	92·9	4·1
Africa	3·2	2·2	10·8	158·4	6·9	140·4	119·4	2·1	10·0
China (mainland)	5·3	1·6	11·7	63·2	223·0	71·0	57·5	29·4	—
Oceania[1]	1·3	—	—	33·7	3·5	237·2	0·2	—	—
World	66·3	14·7	41·9	1,141·2	667·7	1,074·7	383·0	125·3	14·6

Source: *FAO Production Yearbook No. 25* (1971), Table 104A

[1] Australia, New Zealand and the islands of the Pacific

availability of pasture, competition from other land uses and cultural preferences. As stated before, many of the Asian cattle do not enter resource processes except as symbols, but such animals are not users of extensive grassland areas.

The general inadequacy of animal protein supplies in the LDCs and the high cultural demand for meat in DCs has led to an ambitious programme for livestock being incorporated in the Provisional Indicative World Plan (IWP) of the FAO (FAO 1970). The basis of their proposals is the calculation that although by 1975 90 per cent of the projected demand for animal protein will be met, by 1985 (the last year of the IWP period), only 77 per cent can be catered for. The shortfall is caused partly by factors such as the poor suitability of forage and the bad management of herds: on the savanna of Guyana the cattle : land ratio is 1 animal : 17 ha; and on African savannas as a whole it is c. 1 : 8–10. In Tanzania, for example, only about half the cows calve annually, and about 50 per cent of the calves die shortly after birth. Malnutrition of the animals themselves, disease and bad herding practices are all important. External economic factors also loom large in this system. Demand is high and rising as overall prosperity in DCs increases, but the grazing system has been unattractive to investors in LDCs because of the low turnover and return on capital. Rates of increase would therefore have probably been very low, even supposing environmental limitations were exerting no constraints.

In determining the IWP objectives, religious customs were stressed as far as culturally inedible animals like cattle in India and pigs in Islamic countries are concerned. These factors, together with the low efficiency of the ruminants, have meant that a great increase in production of poultry is suggested (Table 5.5), since it is a very efficient converter of a great many types of foodstuff, and the same can be said of pigs for the non-Muslim areas. Thus intensive production of animal protein by moving from an emphasis on the grazing system to the agricultural—or even industrial as is happening in DCs at present—is proposed. Nevertheless, protein deficiencies in LDCs by 1985 are still likely, and the

TABLE 5.5   Proposed growth rates in output of livestock products[1] 1962–85 (per cent p.a.)

Region	Ruminant meat	Pork	Poultry meat	Total meat without offals	Milk	Eggs
Africa, south of Sahara	3·1	4·1	6·3	3·4	2·4	4·9
Asia and Far East	2·2	4·4	5·6	3·5	2·8	5·9
Latin America	2·9[2]	3·5	4·7	3·1	3·1	4·1
Near East and north-west Africa	2·9	−1·8[3]	7·0	3·2	2·6	4·4

[1] These growth rates exclude retention of stock to build up inventories.
[2] This figure rises to 3·2 per cent if Argentina is excluded from the analysis.
[3] This decline is attributable to the fact that pork is only eaten in non-Moslem communities and in some of the countries (particularly in north Africa) such communities are expected to decline in numbers during the lifetime of the Plan
Source: FAO 1970.

DCs are probably going to be short of beef and veal, so that the relatively unconventional methods of protein production and the harvest of the seas are clearly going to suffer no diminution in importance.

Ecological shifts caused by grazing

In the absence of deliberate management of pastures, changes in vegetation and subsequently in other ecosystem components are likely. The plants which prove most palatable to the stock are grazed frequently, and those weakened by cropping are replaced by species which are able to withstand such attention. These are taxa capable of rapid immigration into areas of lessened competition and which escape being eaten because of features such as low stature, a short season of growth, low palatability, poisonous properties, or spines (Klapp 1964, Moore and Biddiscombe 1964). Concomitant changes involve the reduction of the mulch cover of the soil. The microclimate then becomes drier and more severe, and so many invaders are plants of xeric habit: in semi-arid areas they are frequently plants of the desert biome such as succulents and thorny shrubs. The absence of humus cover may mean that the mineral soil surface is heavily trampled when wet, producing puddling of the surface layers, which in turn reduces the infiltration of water into the soil and accelerates its runoff, producing drought. These changes all contribute to the reduction of the rate of energy flow, and the disruption of the stratification and periodicity of the primary producers results in a breakdown of the biogeochemical cycles, especially those involving water, carbon and nitrogen. A final stage of total system breakdown may occur where a very dry microclimate is accompanied by extensive water and wind erosion.

The advent of domestic flocks onto extensive pastures formerly grazed only by wild animals may alter the vegetation completely. In New Zealand, for example, the aboriginal vegetation of the plains of South Island was tussock grassland dominated by species of *Poa* and *Festuca*. The introduction by Europeans of grazing animals such as sheep, rabbits, red deer and goats, and the use of fire as a management technique, has resulted in a more or less complete replacement of the native flora. The chief forage is now introduced grasses such as *Anthoxanthum odoratum*, *Festuca rubra* and *Holcus lanatus*, and on the whole this type of vegetation cover is now less complete than formerly. Introduced wild animals have also destroyed the natural stability of their new habitats, especially forests and alpine grasslands, rendering these lands unsuitable for the grazing of domesticates and accelerating erosion. Table 5.6 gives some information on the species ranked as 'problem animals' (Howard 1964). As another instance we may quote the deforestation of Iceland in the course of sheep grazing, which has meant the denudation of 30–40 per cent of the soils; the annual loss of soil and vegetation cover is still greater than that regained through plant recolonization and management efforts (Thorsteinsson *et al.* 1971).

Shifts within a native flora are also common. The deforestation of the Scottish Highlands produced a moorland vegetation of hedges, grasses and heather. The selective grazing of sheep leaves ungrazed material which has to be burnt off, and together with the differential effects of the foraging habits of the animals this produces a change from the mixed vegetation to one in which *Nardus stricta* and *Molinia caerulea* are dominant. The first is unpalatable and the second deciduous. The xerophytic *Erica tetralix* then becomes important and finally the useless *Scirpus caespitosa* dominates the vegetation. Thus the calcicoles have disappeared, the herbage is deficient in minerals and protein, yet the attempt continues to extract protein directly as meat and wool (Fraser Darling 1963, McVean and Lockie 1969).

Intensive grazing which results in increased areas of bare soil creates a new habitat in which burrowing animals may flourish. In North America, mice, jackrabbits, gophers and prairie dogs all probably benefit from overgrazing; predator control applied to wolves or coyotes may also have released their numbers and so the levels of these rodents reach almost epidemic proportions. In their increased burrowing they render sterile thousands of hectares of forage land, and control measures aimed only at their direct extermination are clearly ecologically unsound. Although there is no direct evidence, we may also speculate about the connection between intensive grazing in semi-arid areas and locust plagues. The presence of loose sandy soil is necessary for oviposition in locusts and heavy grazing produces such conditions. Thus the pastoralists of antiquity may have been creating some of their own plagues rather than having Jehovah do it for them.

TABLE 5.6   Browsing mammals established as 'problems' in New Zealand

Species	Origin	Date introduced	Abundance	Degree of damage
Brush-tail oppossum (*Trichosurus vulpecula*)	Australia	1858	Abundant	Acute
European hare (*Lepus europaeus*)	Europe	1867	Abundant	Acute
Goat (*Capra hircus*)	Europe	18th century	Common	Acute
Thar (*Hemitragus jemlahicus*)	Asia	1904	Common	Moderate
Chamois (*Rupicapra rupicapra*)	Europe	1967	Common	Acute
Red deer (*Cervus elephas*)	Europe	1851	Abundant	Acute
Pig (*Sus scrofa*)	Europe	18th century	Common	Acute

Source: Howard 1964

We can see that the potential of pastoralism for vegetation change of a deleterious character is great (Plate 10). Beyond a certain intensity, the pressure of grazing animals produces effects which are labelled 'overgrazing'. These changes are very varied in nature, and this term may apply to the forage resource or to some symptoms exhibited by the stock itself. As far as the grassland is concerned, 'overgrazing' consists of an intensification of the trends already noted. The incidence of such overgrazing may not be uniform in a given area: within a mosaic a particular species may be grazed out; equally a seasonal overgrazing may occur as when the first flush of spring grass or post-rains grass is immediately

Plate 10 Cattle on an overgrazed range. Virtually all the available forage has been grazed or browsed out and patches of bare soil can be seen. Invasion by xerophytes and soil erosion are both likely in such circumstances. *(Grant Heilman, Lititz, Pa)*

totally consumed. In such conditions, there are likely to be stock 'crashes', when catastrophic declines in the animal population may be observed: these may be absolute in terms of numbers no longer pasturable, or actually dying, or relative in terms of low gain or malnutritive disease. Beyond this stage, an environmental 'crash', in the form of accelerated soil erosion, is the most probable eventuality. Wind erosion produces scoured areas where the bedrock or its upper weathered layers form the ground surface, and the transported material accumulates elsewhere as drifts or even dunes of sandy material. Water erosion produces sheet-wash areas as well as the familiar gullies. In high-latitude and high-altitude areas, overgrazing may remove insulating vegetation cover to the point where freeze–thaw processes are accelerated and heaving then becomes more widespread, increasing the coverage of bare ground at the expense of plant material. Some of these phenomena may of course be produced at the analogous point in agricultural ecosystems by the process of overcropping. The problems associated with severely eroded land do not stop with its abandonment. Siltation of water courses ensues, as in the case of the Mangla Reservoir in

Pakistan, whose planned life of 100 years as an irrigation reservoir has been cut by half due to silt input from the watershed (Brown and Finsterbusch 1971).

Recovery from man-accelerated erosion requires either a long 'fallow' period in which the cause of the erosion is removed and natural processes allowed to heal the scars, or a considerable input of matter and energy by man: the fundamental cause of the erosion must be eliminated as well (L. N. Costin 1970). Natural healing is invariably lengthy since succession has to start from the bare ground stage and a gully system may have acquired an erosive momentum which, following the laws of the development of drainage systems, is unlikely to stop short of its energetic equilibrium point. In the case of Mr Zabriskie's Point, for example, this is well after the forage resource has disappeared. Man-directed schemes of erosion control for grazing lands share some characteristics of those for agricultural systems, but engineering works are less usual owing to the lower return on investment from grazing systems. Wind-eroded areas, however, can usually only be re-seeded if the hard surface ('scalded' is a term sometimes used) is subjected first to a mechanical treatment such as ripping or ploughing. The stabilization of mobile material is akin to the management of coastal sand-dunes and requires a pioneer species which can withstand alternating burial and exposure. If grasses can be successfully planted then the material can be stabilized, and even if good forage does not develop for some time, loose material is at least prevented from burying useful areas elsewhere. In water-eroded areas, the aim of a managed grass cover is to minimize surface runoff and soil loss. To this end grasses with a dense, compact growth habit are most desirable, and their establishment may be aided with cheap mechanical devices such as straw mulches, wire netting and bitumen. The cost of such processes and the technical expertise required ensure that their application is limited relative to the extent of the initial erosion.

Range improvement

The degradation of pastures is a regression to an early phase of succession. The opposite is a progression to a condition of higher secondary production and, on a sustained yield basis, can be induced by manipulation of various components of the grazing ecosystem. Such treatment may be applied either to a more or less virgin system in the hope of increasing the potential crop, or to a degraded area by way of rehabilitation. Geology and landforms may be taken as immutable factors, but climate at the local scale can sometimes be altered by cloud seeding; the certainty of success is not high and there may be difficult legal problems, but experiments at three rangeland sites in Kansas which cost $0.10/ac ($0.25/ha) to produce 0·5-in (12·7 mm) increase in precipitation showed benefit/cost ratios of 22 : 1, 6 : 1 and 25 : 1 respectively (Hausle 1972).

The alteration of components such as the plants, soils and consumer organisms offers most hope for the resource manager wishing to increase his output and at the same time consider the long-term biological productivity of his range, and the management of the crop herbivores themselves is an obvious first stage. The actual species used can be selected if alien species can be brought in: most of the domestic herbivores have been introduced to parts of the world in which their ancestors were not native. Beyond this elementary

TABLE 5.7   Some manipulations of range ecosystems for increased efficiency of energy utilization

Factors	Manipulation
Controlling factors	
Climate	Weather modification, burning
Geological materials	Water spreading, land levelling, terracing, fertilization, ground-water recharge, drainage
Available organisms	Species elimination, introduction and improvement
Dependent factors	
Consumers	
Native biota	Grazing management, wildlife management, insect and rodent control
Livestock	Grazing management, livestock management
Vegetation	Plant control, hay management, plant disease control, revegetation
Soil	Mechanical treatments, nitrogen fertilization
Decomposers and transformers	Antibiotics, growth stimulators (?)
Microclimate	Shades, shelters, mulch manipulation
Human factors	Objectives, management, use of goods and services, economics

Source: Lewis 1969

consideration lies the grazing management techniques applied to the selected animal; these are the heart of successful range management. Thus the numbers of animals, their species and strain, their proportions if pastured in mixed herds, and their distribution in space and time, control the species of plants which are grazed, the time in their life cycle at which they are cropped, and the frequency with which they are eaten. The manager selects his species in the light of the available forage, the preferences of the animal and the prevailing economic factors. He may control their grazing distribution by providing water points, salt licks or specially fertilized patches of grassland. Above all, he may be able to fence or herd animals. All such measures are designed to spread the animals to the optimum density for utilizing the forage. In Australia, one study found that the net primary productivity was greatest at a stocking density of Merino sheep at 20 sheep/ha and least at 10 sheep/ha; at 30 sheep/ha, productivity was slightly higher than the rate for 10 sheep/ha (Fig. 5.5), but seasonal fluctuations were greatest at the highest stocking rate. This suggests there are optimum stocking densities for maximum net primary productivity of grazed grasslands in temperate zones, but that they vary according to the time of year (Vickery 1972). Many plants are easily damaged by being grazed too soon after they have started their growth, yet it is during periods of fastest growth that they are most nutritious. Thus grazing systems (Table 5.8) must be elaborated, either by folk knowledge as in relatively simple societies or by complex socio-legal arrangements as in the Grazing Districts of the United States of America. If a system other than continuous grazing is employed, then additional water developments are usually necessary, as is the fencing of the range into units with

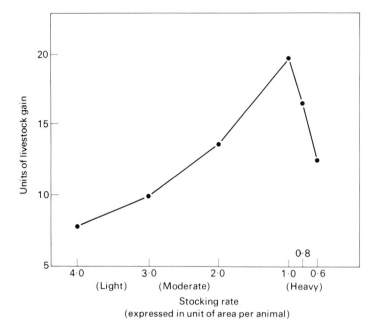

Fig. 5.5 Livestock gains for different stocking rates in the south-west USA. Gains are higher at increasingly heavy grazing densities until a critical value is reached, beyond which there is a 'crash' in production. These results suggest the ease with which the grassland ecosystem can be over-exploited by managers of domesticated animals.
Source: A. B. Costin 1964

more or less equal stocking potential. Scientific range management becomes a very intricate matter in which the cowboy's hip is more likely to be decorated with a sampling quadrat than a Colt ·45.

TABLE 5.8   Classification of grazing systems

I. All sub-units grazed one or not more than two periods per year	
A. Continuous occupation by grazing animals during the same grazing season each year	Continuous grazing
B. Grazing deferred on one or more sub-units	
1. Deferment not rotated	Deferred grazing
2. Deferment rotated	
a. Grazed sub-units continuously occupied	Rotational deferment
b. Grazing rotated in sub-units	Deferred rotation
II. One or more sub-units rested	
A. Rest not rotated	Rest
B. Rest rotated	Rest rotation
III. All sub-units grazed more than two periods per year	Rotational grazing

Source: Lewis 1969

The bringing about of changes in vegetation is another method of manipulating grazing systems, but one which involves longer time-spans than the attraction of stocking rates. The aims are to produce a high proportion of palatable plants, preferably with a spread of maximum growth periods so as to provide a long grazing season, and to reduce the proportions of open ground, unpalatable shrubs or scrub and poisonous or injurious plants. Mechanical control by chaining and cabling may reduce the proportion of juniper and mesquite in places like Arizona, USA; fire may be employed with some success, for mesquite and cactus kills of 50 per cent have been reported; and chemical treatment is increasingly favoured, especially with hormonal herbicides such as 2,4-D and 2,4,5-T. These latter are not without dangerous side-effects, however and the use of 2,4,5-T has now become very restricted in developed countries. Range seeding may seem an attractive proposition where aids such as light aircraft are available, but success appears very variable. A sequence of burning, then seeding coincident with the high rainfall season, and thereafter applying chemical weed control has been followed with some advantage in California and Israel. Similarly, parasite and disease control of range plants may be possible in rich countries with a highly developed infrastructure capable of delivering the correct dosage of a specific pesticide more or less to the correct place.

The soil itself is more difficult to alter than animals or plants but is not beyond treatment. Mechanical treatment such as discing, subsoiling and contour furrowing may help to improve runoff characteristics or provide a niche for more desirable forage species, but improvement of the nitrogen status of the soil is one of the most usual desirabilities. Crops and tame pastures of the world contain about 200 leguminous species, whereas wild range and forest ecosystems have c. 12,000, of which 90 per cent have nodule-bearing roots; thus the encouragement of leguminous species helps to counteract the loss of soil nitrogen. Furthermore, some soils appear to be deficient in mineral elements such as copper, cobalt and molybdenum, which are essential for the nutrition of animals, so that fertilization of intensively used grasslands generally has taken place since the nineteenth century (Barnard and Frankel 1964) and the light aeroplane has extended the practice to extensive forage resources. One edaphic element which cannot easily be directly manipulated is the soil flora and fauna. The importance of these biota was stressed earlier (pp. 13–15), especially in the detritus food chain which is critical to nutrient circulation. Most other management techniques will affect these biota, some adversely.

Many of the management arrangements described above are clearly applicable to both simple societies and more complex, industrially based ones. But many of the most effective are available only to high-energy and high-material-input societies. This limitation needs keeping in mind when improvements to the grazing system are considered, for many of the world's forage resources are outside that particular ambit.

The cropping of wild animals for food

Most domestic animals are very selective in their use of forage; by contrast, many wild animals of potential use for food, particularly ungulates, are much more thorough in their use of the available herbage; even if one species is very selective, it is likely to exist as part of a suite of animals whose combined cropping effectively utilizes the range. The faunas of the savanna and grassland biomes of east and central Africa are the outstanding example of this characteristic, and a considerable amount of research has been done on their ecology (Fraser Darling 1960, Dasmann 1964a, Talbot 1966), although Parker and Graham (1971) point out that such cropping is more talked about than done, and suggest that the case for utilizing wild animals is not so strong as that for improving domesticates.

Africa

A high biomass of wild animals is partly a consequence of the variety of habitats within the biome: although large areas of uniform landscape such as *Acacia* savanna exist, they are broken by swampy zones, by dense bush and other terrain types (Fig. 5.6). Within these units, certain animals are specialized, whereas others move throughout a number of them in a purposeful seasonal or diurnal sequence. The sitatunga, for example, is confined to perpetually inundated swamps, whereas the lechwe ranges from the edge of that habitat through to the outer margins of seasonally flooded riverine plains. Likewise, the klipspringer scarcely ventures forth from rocky hills, whereas zebra will forage in most types of grassland, bush and wooded savanna, though venturing rarely into dense bush. The gross anatomy of species helps to spread their foraging habits: the giraffe is the obvious example, enabled by its long neck to browse off the canopies of trees otherwise inaccessible unless pulled down. At a less obvious level, browsers such as the black rhino stay in bush and wooded areas, thus avoiding competition with the grazers of the open grassland such as the white rhino. Even where the same grass species is a preferred element of several animals' diet, grazing is staggered to avoid competition. The red oats grass (*Themeda triandra*) is a very important part of the intake of wildebeests, topis and zebras. The wildebeests eat the fresh leaves of the grass only, until they are about 4 inches long, avoiding stalks and seed heads. Zebras prefer more mature forage, eating longer leaves together with stalks and heads; however, they avoided the grass when it was dry. The topis exhibit a distinct preference for dry red oats grass, usually at a mature stage and with a large proportion of stalks and heads.

The result of the interaction of a variety of habitats, species and habits is a high herbivore biomass (Fig. 5.7), in which very large numbers are found of some species (hartebeest, wildebeest, zebra) and in which some species (hippopotamus, elephant, rhinoceros) are very large. As expected, predator numbers and biomass are much lower but nevertheless add up to a relatively high density of such creatures: a particularly important feature when the tourist-trade value of the game areas is considered. Table 5.9 considers some data for year-long biomass of the wild faunas of grasslands and savannas and compares it with some figures for domestic stock in similar environments. The poor animals, from badly managed tribal grazing systems, reach at best one-fifth of the biomass of the wild population, and even European management can scarcely bring the proportion to one-half. The discrepancy between wild and domestic beasts in Africa can be further seen from figures for liveweight gain. Species such as eland (0·33 kg/day), wildebeest (0·185–0·28) and topi (0·15–0·19) contrast with domestic sheep (0·05) and cattle (0·13). Cattle reach marketable size in 5–7 years, whereas the flesh of Grant's gazelles and impalas could be marketed in 18 months,

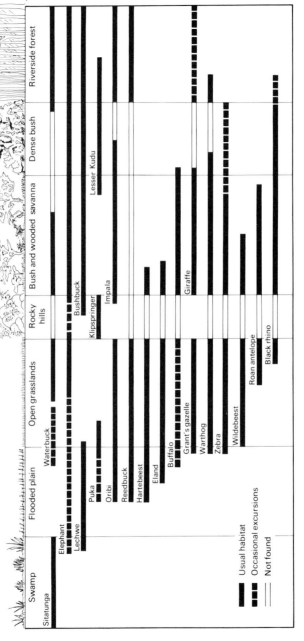

Fig. 5.6 The savanna provides a variety of habitats, some of which are the only forage areas of a particular herbivore, whereas others are utilized by a wide variety of the fauna, which sometimes crop different levels of the vegetation, e.g. the giraffe and black rhino do not compete for forage in bush and wooded savanna.

Source: Reader's Digest Publications 1970

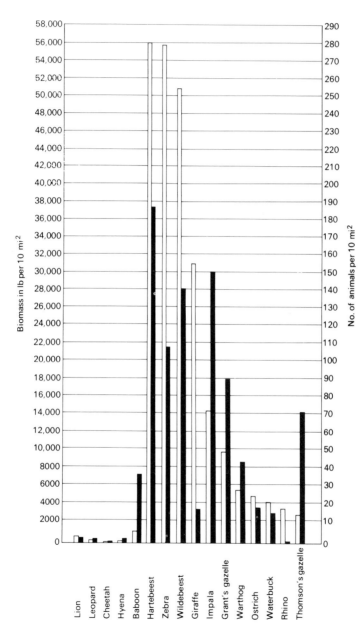

Fig. 5.7 The biomass of animals in Nairobi National Park. The open column represents the weight per unit area and the black column the number of individual animals per unit area. The relatively large herbivore population needed to support a few predators is clearly shown, as is the very high biomass of certain ungulates which might be cropped for food (lb/10 mi² equals approximately kg per 5,000 ha; 10 mi² = 2,590 ha).
Source: Reader's Digest Publications 1970

and wildebeests in 2·5–3 years. Furthermore, the marketable proportion of the carcass is higher for wild animals, they contain more meat and less fat, and the proportion of valuable hind-quarter is also higher than that of cattle raised on the same lands. Transport and marketing generally present the most difficult problems (Talbot and Talbot 1963). The meat of all species of wild ungulates is eaten by Africans and Europeans, although there are some local taboos. Dried meat (biltong) is also a useful product, and experiments with canning hippo have been tried. By-products can also be valuable if properly handled: zebra skins and elephant tusks are but the most obvious examples.

TABLE 5.9   Comparison of biomass of wild and domesticated animals

		Year-long biomass	
Animals	Range type and location	lb/mi²	kg/ha × 10⁵
Wild ungulates	Savanna, east Africa	70,000–100,000	82·2–117·5
Domestic livestock	Tribal savanna, east Africa	11,200–16,000	13·2–18·8
Cattle	European-managed savanna, Africa	21,000–32,000	24·7–37·6
Domestic livestock	Virgin grassland, western USA	26,700	31·3
Bison and ungulates	Prairie, USA	14,000–20,000	16·4–23·5
Red deer	Deer forest, Scotland	4,373	0·14

Source: Talbot and Talbot 1963

Cropping programmes require sophisticated knowledge of the ecology of the animals involved and especially their social structure, so that discriminating culling can be practised: it is a different matter shooting young males of a pair-bonded species, for example, from culling spare males from territorially based harem groups kept together by one male. The role of hunter and predator has to be carefully evaluated, as has the contribution of species such as the elephant which, by virtue of its size and habits, strongly affects the development of habitats. On the one hand, they make forage from high trees available to other species by pulling them down, and they also dig water-holes: on the negative side, they will damage large areas of otherwise edible bush by trampling, will pull up trees which are the habitats of birds, for example, and at high densities wreak a general damage to the environment. Culling of elephants has often been a first step in good game management.

As well as the gains so far mentioned there is the income from tourism, which is the major source of foreign exchange for many east and central African countries. Here is a growing industry, and shooting animals with cameras does not conflict with the use of the game populations for meat. In Kenya, for example, tourism netted $52·5 million in 1971 and is predicted to yield $105 million/yr by the end of 1974; in 1966–7 the rate of return on government assets was a very high 20–30 per cent, and the employment of 20,000 people in 1971 is expected to double by 1975 (Swank 1972). In spite of this, huge game-extermination programmes have been carried out in Africa in the probably forlorn hope of exterminating tsetse fly. Cattle are often then brought in and if managed inefficiently contribute to ecological degradation. Their concentration around water sources means puddling of soils, especially in the wet season, with subsequent soil erosion. This is exacerbated by the use of fire to encourage early growth at the start of wet seasons (Talbot 1972, West 1972). By contrast, native ungulates only degrade environments if their densities are too high, as has happened with hippo and elephants that have moved out of 'reclaimed' areas.

Grazing as an element of multiple use

Although livestock production is the major aim of most range managers, from Arabia to Alberta, other goods and services are also potential crops. Forest lands, for example, often support grazing animals. Advantages which may accrue to the forest manager are the reduction of inflammable undergrowth or the checking of some species competitive with his desired species such as leafy shrubs in a softwood forest, and sometimes the animals are beneficial in scarifying and manuring a clear-felled area before it is re-seeded. Yet there are numerous disadvantages to this form of multiple use (FAO 1953), since damage to the forest stands may take place because of the elimination of seedlings or their deformation, and mature trees may be injured by being debarked. Goats especially can reduce woodland to scrub or completely open land, and sheep are only a little slower. Cattle are much less dangerous and it is said that pigs bury acorns as well as eat them. Grazing in forest lands must be controlled with some care, lest overstocking eventually produces watershed deterioration and soil erosion.

As has been seen from the African examples, wildlife and domesticated animals may be highly incompatible, but under some conditions, sophisticated management may realize that very little competition for grazing resources may occur between, for example, sheep and deer since there is 'forage separation'. In such instances income from game and associated recreation facilities has, in rich countries like the USA, exceeded that from the grazing livestock. The winter or other off-season is generally the critical time when competition for forage may occur and the manager who would have both sheep and deer must face the fact that sometimes the deer's predators will like a change of menu.

Hunting of wildlife is a form of recreation towards which the grazing manager is likely to feel ambivalent. He can raise money from it; but on the other hand hunters are not always careful in their treatment of his fences and water-holes, nor, in the last analysis, of their targets. Tom Lehrer's bag of 'two game wardens and a pure-bred Guernsey cow' is probably not too great an exaggeration. Other forms of outdoor recreation tend to conflict with range management: the hill lands of Great Britain exemplify the problems. Fires, destruction of fences, leaving gates open, worrying by dogs, fouling of water and edible but lethal litter are everyday complaints by farmers. Carried out with due care for the countryside, many outdoor activities do not, however, conflict with grazing. In semi-arid areas with low stocking rates, recreation may well be a compatible use, and carries considerable potential for expansion, as in Australia, where the traditional beach recreation is becoming overcrowded: in 1967 there were 40,000 tourists to the Northern Territory (Box and Perry 1971).

Many grazing lands are also used as watershed lands, and overgrazing reduces their use for this purpose just as it will for further grazing. In particular, high silt yields fill up reservoirs, while poorly vegetated areas produce flash floods and then dry up quickly instead of yielding a steady flow of water. Remedial measures, as with other overgrazed areas, are often expensive and long-term.

Potentials and possibilities

The overriding aim of rational management of the grazing resource is simple: the maintenance of a permanent productive capacity at a level which not only precludes the possibility of decline but also contains the seeds of further improvement. Secondary purposes include the use of forage areas so as not to exclude other uses such as water catchment for which fewer alternative areas are available, or perhaps nature conservation. No changes should be irreversible.

To this end, various measures have been suggested. The detailed range improvements discussed above are very important, for in a world context it seems more profitable to improve existing grasslands than to try to find new ones: indeed the Indicative World Plan for Agriculture (IWP) of the FAO suggests a decline by 2 per cent (25 million ha) in the total grazing resource land during the 1972–85 period. Besides their major features, there are many other components, of the grazing ecosystem, both social and biological, that can be changed. The control of the currently rife overgrazing is a clear priority. The replacement of some phases of the wild grassland grazing with feed-lot ingestion of fodder crops might help with this problem, but prejudice against cereals as fodder crops is strong in many places, and it is scarcely to be expected that such people would take easily to the use of concentrated feeds, even if they could afford them. Similarly, problems of land ownership and tenure may be critical. The minimum economic size of enterprises (in the British uplands no less than in the arid lands of Africa) needs careful consideration. In many places the forage resource is a commons, with all that implies by way of potential for misuse by individuals. Apparently rational developments may in reality be inimical to each other: the encouragement of nomadism and transhumance to avoid overgrazing (Fraser Darling and Farvar 1972, Heady 1972), for instance, is scarcely compatible with the development of an infrastructure that will allow such people to market perishable products like milk and meat. Yet again, diseases act as a drag on animal productivity and we must consider the economic and ecological implications of tsetse which reinforce the idea that wildlife grazing is the proper use of such lands (Lambrecht 1972), and features like the need to eradicate foot-and-mouth disease in the flesh-producing countries of Latin America.

Not so far discussed are the possibilities of domesticating new animals. The present meat-producing domesticates are all members of the order Artiodactyla, and that same order has perhaps the greatest potential for new domestications (Jewell 1969). There are 192 species in the order, of which 92 are African, but even outside Africa there is considerable potential. The various deer are the obvious candidates since they can crop the shrubs, lichens and mosses of the tundra, taiga and boreal forest which are otherwise inedible by man. Of the African species, the most notable example of an attempt at domestication has been the eland, both in South Africa and in the Ukraine. The eland

(*Taurotragus orys*) can thrive in a domesticated state when food, water and tsetse fly make cattle a very poor prospect. Jewell calls the domestication of the African buffalo (*Synoceros caffer*) 'long overdue', and even the warthog has its potential since it is unaffected by the African swine fever which may make pig farming difficult.

We should note in passing that domestication of such wild species will very likely bring about physical and behavioural changes in the animals, so that it cannot be considered a way of protecting wild species which are otherwise threatened with extinction.

The effects of increasing human populations

As far as subsistence graziers are concerned, the effects of an increasing number of mouths to feed is relatively simple: more beasts are depastured (especially on forage resources held in common), there is a lower-quality animal product, and all the effects of overgrazing described above become manifest (L. H. Brown 1971). Basically, the increased number of people help to contravene the rules of successful pastoralism which revolve around the maxim 'once over, lightly' (Fraser Darling 1955). Structural alterations in the system, such as the importation of animal foodstuffs, may alleviate some difficulties, but the important cultural shift is to an acceptance of the possession of fewer animals. Since in many pastoralist societies the beasts possess a value far beyond that of their products, this has proved almost uniformly impossible: death control applied to men and animals in societies based on grazing systems has not been accompanied by the cultural changes which would have prevented widespread ecological degradation.

Commercial extensive pastoralism is less likely to fall into the overgrazing–poor beast syndrome, for its existence depends upon a high-quality product. Higher demand for animal protein caused by both increased populations and raised levels of living will in general mean higher prices, so that greater profits and investment will lead to more efficient production within the ecological limits of the system. Eventually the high prices commanded by animal products may cause subsistence pastoralists to re-evaluate their position and move into a form of commercial pastoralism. Their cultural conservatism can sometimes be changed if the new systems are presented so that they become desirable, and increased nationalism has also been cited as an aid to changing traditional resource processes (L. N. Costin 1970, Semple 1971).

One of the arguments in favour of the grazing ecosystem is that it brings into resource processes all sorts of primary productivity, from lichens to desert halophytes, which would otherwise be uncropped by man. But as experiments with leaf materials (p. 215) have shown, this may not always be so, and in time the direct extraction of useful foodstuffs from present forage resources without the interposition of the animal may be commonplace.

Further reading

BARNARD, C. (ed.) 1964: *Grasses and grasslands.*

DASMANN, R. F. 1964: *African game ranching.*

FAO 1970: *Indicative World Plan for Agriculture.*

FRASER DARLING, F. 1956: Man's ecological dominance through domesticated animals on wild lands.

LEWIS, G. M. 1969: Range management viewed in the ecosystem framework.

MACFADYEN, A. 1964: Energy flow in ecosystems and its exploitation by grazing.

MCVEAN, D. N. and LOCKIE, J. D. 1969: *Ecology and land use in upland Scotland.*

SWANK, W. G. 1972: Wildlife management in Masailand, east Africa.

TALBOT, L. M. 1972: Ecological consequences of rangeland development in Masailand, east Africa.

6

Water

Water occurs naturally in gaseous, solid and liquid phases; man's use of it is nearly all concerned with the last state and is also dominated by his demand for water relatively low in dissolved salts, i.e. fresh water. Of the various conditions in which free water exists, salt water in the oceans claims 97 per cent, in absolute terms 1.31×10^{24} cm^3. The remaining 3 per cent is fresh water, but three-quarters of this is virtually immobilized as glaciers and ice-caps. Of the last quarter, most is ground water, so that at any instant in time surface fresh water (lakes and rivers) accounts for only 0.33 per cent of all fresh water, and the atmosphere 0.035 per cent (Barry 1969; Fig. 6.1). Since our demands, like those of nearly all terrestrial living things, are for fresh water rather than salt, we deal with only a tiny fraction of the total water volume of the planet; yet the absolute amounts are large, and the energy relations of the various phases are such that human intervention is often no easy matter and water management can be very expensive.

The water that is not locked up as permanent ice is continually moving through various pathways in the atmosphere, biosphere and lithosphere, and this set of natural flows is called the hydrological cycle. A pictorial representation of its qualitative aspects is shown as Fig. 6.1. From the point of view of water resources, the quantity of water in each major unit of the cycle and the rapidity of flux between each becomes the important consideration. The cycle can therefore be regarded as a series of storage tanks, interconnected by the transfer processes of evaporation, moisture transport, condensation, precipitation and runoff. Fig. 6.2 presents a simple model of the quantitative flows within the cycle (Barry 1969). It takes as its starting point the mean annual global precipitation of 85.7 cm (33.8 in) and calls this 100 units. Evaporation and transpiration then provide the sources of input into the atmospheric part of the cycle: 84 per cent comes from the oceans and 16 per cent from the continents. The average water content of the atmosphere if rained out all at once would provide a global fall of 2.5 cm (1 in) and *de facto* constitutes about 10 days' supply of rainfall (Barry 1969). Ten days is also the average residence time of a water molecule in the atmosphere. This points at once to a rapidly fluxing cycle of evaporation, runoff and precipitation: the annual precipitation over land surfaces alone is about 30 times the moisture content of the air over the land at any one time.

As far as most water resources are concerned, precipitation onto land surfaces is a critical component of the system since much fresh water falls onto the oceans where there is no possibility of garnering it. Over land the distribution of the various forms of precipitation is uneven and on a world scale, but four outstanding features of the pattern may be noted: firstly, the equatorial maximum, which is deflected into the northern hemisphere;

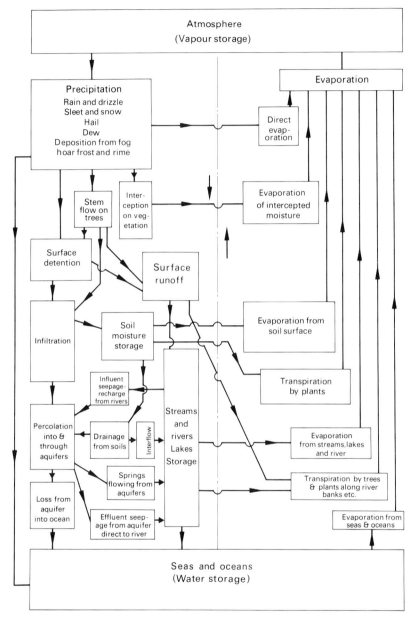

Fig. 6.1 A schematic diagram of the hydrological cycle. The boxes represent both the major storage zones and the transfers between the storages.
Source: Barry 1969

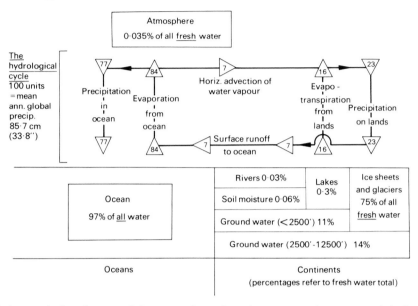

Fig. 6.2 A quantitative diagram of the proportions of total water at various stages of the hydrological cycle. In the top part of the diagram 100 units represent the mean annual global precipitation; the lower part shows how the planet's water is divided up: the fresh water (right-hand boxes) is only 3 per cent of the total water, and 75 per cent of it is locked up as ice sheets and glaciers.
Source: Barry 1969

secondly, the very reliable falls upon the west coasts of continents in the middle latitudes: thirdly, the arid areas of subtropical cells of high pressure where rainfall is not only sparse but sporadic from year to year; lastly, high latitudes become 'arctic deserts' because of the low precipitation from the cold dry air of these regions. The natural flow of water once it has reached the ground is of importance from the resources point of view. Some is re-evaporated, some runs off by way of rivers to the oceans, and a third component enters the ground-water system. If the precipitation falls as snow, then until melting occurs there is a lag between precipitative input and its re-distribution. Globally, water retention on the land surfaces is highest in March–April when there is extensive snow cover and freezing of lakes and rivers in the northern hemisphere. In October there is a rise in sea level of 1–2 cm, when an estimated extra 7.5×10^{18} cm^3 of water are present in the oceans. Water normally spends between 10–100 days on land, unless it enters ground-water circulation, in which case it stays much longer. In the great Artesian basin of Australia, some water in the aquifers has apparently been there for 20,000 years, but both younger and older sources have been found (Barry 1969).

Human use of water

There are two types of 'use' of water. In the first, water is used as a carrying medium in which materials or objects are carried either suspended in the water, or in solution, or by flotation. The last of these, theoretically, leaves the water in an unchanged condition, and from the former the water can be reclaimed by treatment. On the other hand, the use of water may result in its evaporating into the atmosphere and so passing at least temporarily out of a resource process, or being incorporated with some other material to make a new product. Then the use can be said to be consumptive, since the water is effectively removed from the resource process, even if not permanently. Uses of both types are multifarious, since water is one of the most versatile as well as necessary of man's materials. The most basic need is our own metabolic requirement: men die of thirst long before they succumb to hunger. Since our bodies are 60 per cent water, those of politicians and professors included, a daily intake of about 2·25 litres is needed. To this must be added the residential demands of our species. In the LDCs this may not be very great (90 litres/day for the inhabitants of Karachi), but in industrialized countries the amount is much higher: figures of 160 litres/day in the UK and 635 litres/day in the USA are commonly quoted. Activities thus covered include washing, the preparation and cooking of food, and the disposal of household wastes and sewage. Such patterns comprise both consumptive and non-consumptive uses, with some emphasis on the latter. Industrial use of water reaches immense proportions in the DCs. A typical factory will probably use 45–70 litres/day for each of its employees, apart from its needs for industrial processes which include the use of water for energy conversion as in boilers (including those of ships) and especially in the generation of electricity from fossil and nuclear fuels. High pressures ($> 1,000$ lb/in^2; 70 kg/cm^2) call for water of a very high quality free from dissolved solids and silica, and high capital costs demand minimum stoppages for cleaning and descaling. In an industrial country such as the UK, demands on quantity (about 2,300 mgd (million gal per day)/10.4 × 10^6 kilolitres in 1968) and quality are therefore very high (Institution of Civil Engineers 1963, Water Resources Board 1969). Water is also much in demand for cooling, since it is the cheapest available substance for the transfer of heat. Even though recirculation is widely practised, the Central Electricity Generating Board of the UK loses an average of 40 mgd (0·18 × 10^6 kilolitres) to the atmosphere (Water Resources Board 1969). Quality here is not quite so critical as in boiler use, but scaling and corrosion are inevitable consequences of water that is less than pure. Hot water returned to a river alters the ecology for some distance downstream; this is called calefaction or thermal pollution. Industrial processing often requires high-quality water, but the nature of each individual product is critical. Washing of materials and equipment, conveyance of solids, dilution, and the scrubbing of gases to remove unwanted elements are all important here. Water which is incorporated in a product usually needs to be very pure, especially in food, drink and pharmaceutical industries. Some contaminations are, however, permitted in special products as in the case of peat in whisky manufacture and the special qualities of the River Liffey in the case of Guinness. Most modern techniques require a very high water input per unit of product output: for example, 1 ton (1,016 kg) of cement requires 800 gal (36 kilolitres) of water; 1 ton of steel, 25,000 gal (113 kilolitres); and 1 ton of paper, 60,000 gal (272·5 kilolitres). Even a gallon (4·5 litres) of beer uses 350 gal (1,590 litres) of water, much of which appears to remain in the product.

The flotational use of fresh water is largest in timber-producing countries and in industrial waterways. Hence the rivers of Finland form 400,000 km of floatway for logs, conveying 3 million m³ of timber annually; the St Lawrence Seaway is a major traffic artery in North America and in 1966 was used by 60·7 million mt of cargo, while the Rhine is another outstanding industrial waterway, conveying 230·6 million mt in 1965. Such a use is theoretically non-consumptive, but the general contamination caused by shipping (sewage, oil, solid waste and garbage) generally renders the water unusable for other purposes without treatment (Beckinsale 1969a).

A genuinely non-consumptive use of water is the generation of hydro-electric power. This method of electricity generation is extensively used in some LDCs as well as in the West and the socialist countries (Beckinsale 1969b). In Peru, for example, 68 per cent of all electricity comes from this source, and in Colombia 63 per cent. Canada is very dependent with 81 per cent, but Norway heads the list at 99·8 per cent. Although the use is non-consumptive, considerable man-directed intervention in the hydrological cycle at river-basin scale is required (p. 156).

Plants are dependent upon water for their metabolism, and those in the direct service of man as in crops and managed forests no less so. The transpiration from several 'tame' plant communities appears to be of a similar order: 470 mm/yr from short grass, 580 mm/yr from a tall crop and 480 mm/yr from a pine plantation have all been reported from the UK. The absolute amounts depend principally upon climate, and here the supply of water for irrigation may become important. In California, irrigation use may rise to 500–635 mm/yr, and even in Great Britain it has been estimated that 600,000 ha would benefit from supplemental irrigation (Prickett 1963). At the equivalent of 2·54 mm, this would require a water supply of $1·3 \times 10^6$ kilolitres (3,000 mgd) which is similar to the demands of an equivalent area of a densely built-up city. Non-irrigated agricultural use of water is also very high: one pound (0·45 kg) of dry wheat needs 60 US gal (227 litres) for its production; 1 lb rice between 200–250 gal (757–946 litres), and 1 quart (0·9 litres) of milk 1,000 gal (3,785 litres) of water. Neither can the water consumption of animals be dismissed as negligible. A pig of body weight 75–125 lb (34–57 kg) needs 16 lb (7–25 kg) of water per day; a pregnant sow 30–38 lb (14–17 kg) and a lactating sow 40–50 lb (18–23 kg). A lactating Jersey cow requires 60–102 lb (27–46 kg) per day in order to produce 5–30 lb (2·25–14 kg) of milk. By contrast sheep are very abstemious, for on a good pasture they need little if any free water, and on dry range only 5–13 lb (2·25–6 kg) of water per day; on salty range they can be kept happy with a daily input of 17 lb (8 kg) (US Department of Agriculture 1955).

The recreational use of water is analogous to flotation in the sense that it is not consumptive at all except where pollutive contamination occurs. Again, many recreational activities involve floating (more or less) of people or boats. Only sport fishing involves a consumptive crop and even that is sometimes returned to the water. The use of water as a wildlife habitat is non-consumptive too when the wildlife is for scientific purposes or for observational recreation. Fish and fowl for consumption are important as well: fresh-water fish formed 14 per cent of the world's fish catch in 1966 (Beckinsale 1969a).

One theme runs through all these uses: the greater amount demanded in the DCs. It is in these areas that we expect to find the greatest manipulations of the hydrological cycle at whatever scales are manageable with the available technology. In the LDCs the demands are also high in particular sectors, but the development to match these requirements with the supply is often lacking so that large rapidly growing cities especially may suffer inadequacies of both quantity and quality.

Ecosystem modification for water control

In order to divert water from the natural hydrological cycle to his own purposes, man must intervene at those places where technology makes it feasible and where the ratio of benefits to costs is deemed to be favourable. Most phases of the cycle are prone to intervention but naturally the runoff and storage phases of fresh water are the most usual. Others, however, need consideration.

Weather modification

The difficulties of manipulating the atmospheric phase of water are such that, compared with attempts to regulate water flow in other parts of the cycle, its practice is both very recent and small in scale. The methods employed have been dominated by cloud seeding. The statistical significance of results is hard to assess, but one example from Australia shows a benefit of $A2 million to wheat growers who produced an extra 1·8 million bushels ($63\cdot4 \times 10^6$ kilolitres) after a 6-month seeding programme had increased precipitation by 13–25 mm (A. B. Costin 1971). None of the studies mention the fate of the silver iodide used to provide condensation nuclei, but the most immediate difficulties are legal rather than ecological. If precipitation is induced at area A, then area B downwind is unlikely to receive the precipitation it might otherwise have had. At intranational levels this is a fruitful source of profit for lawyers (Maryland has made weather modification a crime, and Pennsylvania gives counties the option of making it so), but internationally it is conceivable that it could be used as a long-term weapon to subdue an enemy by desiccation (MacDonald 1968, Sargent 1969). Ecologically, the effects of one-shot 'weather modification' are unlikely to be serious, but persistent interventions come more into the category of 'climatic modification' and hence shifts in species are likely. Gross vegetation shifts are of course possible, but even more rapid would be those of rapidly disseminating species such as fungi and insects, some of which are bound to be 'pests'. So even meso-scale changes which are artificially induced are likely to produce serious and unpredictable biological consequences; should the technology for larger-scale changes become available, then the prospect is full of hazard.

Watershed management

Once precipitated, water in its liquid form is much more amenable to management. The portion not immediately re-evaporated goes largely through the pathways of the vegetation (transpiration), into water courses (runoff) and into ground-water storage at various levels (Fig. 6.3). In the first two categories, the most usual manipulations involve firstly the alteration of the vegetation of a catchment area or watershed, in order to produce more runoff, and secondly the increasing of the storage capacity in the runoff phase so that water may be held for use in dry seasons or to prevent floods.

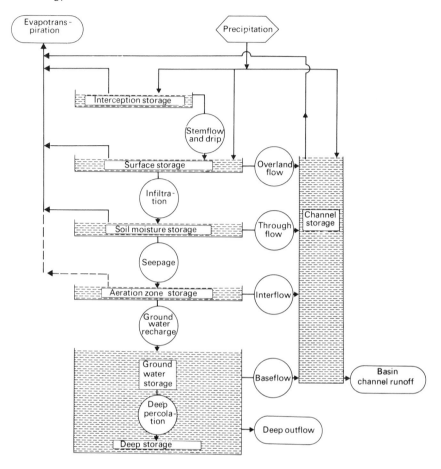

Fig. 6.3 Schematic relationships of the components of the hydrological cycle at the scale of a single basin. Interception storage refers principally to vegetation above the ground but might presumably also comprise buildings in an urban context.
Source: More 1969

The runoff characteristics of catchments are affected by many variables such as slope, soil type and depth, and vegetation cover, of which the last is the easiest to alter. In general, the higher the vegetative biomass the higher the transpiration and hence the greater the water 'loss'. Other factors such as the aerodynamic roughness of the vegetation may be important, but a forest normally transpires much more water than a grassland. On the other hand, a deforested watershed or a grassy catchment may yield greater quantities of unwanted silt than the forested zone, so that the optimal balance point between high water yield and high water quality must always be sought. Flood peaks are usually higher in unforested catchments unless the soil is unusually deep or unusually retentive as with blanket peat on British uplands. Forested mountains are often critical watershed areas because they may accumulate snow during the winter, the melt from which forms a major source of water for lowland areas. Management aims at increasing the depth of snowpack but delaying the melt so as to produce a steady and prolonged yield. It has been found in the western USA that snowpack depth is lowest in the centre of dense coniferous forests and highest (by increases of 15–30 per cent) in openings and lightly wooded areas such as aspen stands. Management techniques used include logging narrow strips on an east-west axis across the watersheds, which may produce 25 per cent more snow (30·5 cm water), and shading the trees over the narrow strips to delay melting; fencing on open watersheds may also increase the depth of snow. A major economic difficulty is that the benefits of such management may not accrue to the landowner but to the down-stream user and so adequate costing is rather difficult; this makes the technique especially suitable for high terrain in public ownership (Martinelli 1964). In brushlands and other semi-arid vegetation, the removal of scrub may increase water flow but the quantity of silt may increase dramatically, and wind erosion may also result unless seeding to grass is successfully employed. The removal of riparian vegetation can be a useful ploy which increases channel flow but affects silt yield very little. In the San Dimas experimental watersheds of southern California, for example, a flow of $86·3 \times 10^3$ m³/day was produced during a wet season instead of $49·3 \times 10^3$ m³/day before the removal of riparian vegeta-tion. The stream flow also continued all year round instead of drying up for the summer months. Such treatment is most effective in semi-arid and arid areas where phreatophytic vegetation (with species such as tamarisk) transpires large quantities of water (Hopkins and Sinclair 1960). Watershed management by vegetation control is not yet an exact science, but computer modelling and simulation are rapidly bringing about a situation where the optimum cover for a given mix of resource uses can be predicted and the major obstacles to successful implementation may then be institutional and social constraints.

Intervention in surface and immediate sub-surface flow

A primary aim of managing water flow over land surfaces is to get rid of any excess. Drainage is therefore important in questions of water supply, although it is not usually done with the object of providing a higher downstream flow. Nevertheless, different methods of drainage will affect many aspects of river regimes, as well as contributing to the quality of the water. Loss through evaporation must have been reduced by the advent of under-draining of fields, and large-scale drainage of wetlands such as the Fens of eastern England must have altered the regime of the rivers of the region. Urbanization has also produced its complex of effects, including the rapid runoff from impervious substances which is partly balanced by high potential evaporation from these surfaces.

Once the runoff from both rural and urban areas becomes committed to a flow channel or a lake, management and offtake become feasible. In effect, streams and lakes are moving storage cells of water, especially since many lakes are temporary widenings of rivers. On a world scale the amount of fresh water stored in lakes and rivers is dominated by the lakes of Africa, which amount to 30 per cent of the world's liquid fresh water at the surface; they are followed by the lakes of North America with 25 per cent, and Lake Baykal (USSR) with 18 per cent. Smaller lakes and the world's rivers comprise the remaining 27 per cent. River channels themselves are distinguished by a relatively rapid flow of water, but as storage cells they are held to be insignificant on a world scale. A world isochronal volume of water in river channels was estimated to be 1,200 km³, compared with 125,000 km³ of fresh water in the world's lakes and 124,000,000 km³ on the world's land areas as a whole, a total which includes some saline water in inland seas. This emphasizes the minute proportion of the planet's water with which man is concerned when he manipulates the river systems, although at regional and local scales the absolute amounts may be very important indeed. The storage capacity of rivers can be marginally enlarged by engineering works such as the deepening of channels and the regulation of flow: these are generally carried out as part of flood-control schemes but may have a secondary effect. Rivers are often the immediate source of water for the world's irrigated areas, which comprise about 202,500 km², although pumped ground water is a significant component as well. Manipulation for irrigation is dominated by mainland China, followed by the USA and USSR, and indeed some 80 per cent of all irrigated lands are in Asia (excluding the USSR). Thus few irrigated lands, actual or potential, occur in very arid regions. Here, and to a lesser extent elsewhere, evaporation losses from the open channels used in most irrigation schemes can assume very high proportions (Beckinsale 1969b).

The technology involved in manipulation for irrigation is very variable, depending upon the access to energy resources of the society involved. At one level are the man-powered devices for lifting water into irrigation channels (e.g. the shadoof), and the small earthen dams or minor streams which merely divert the flow into irrigated areas such as rice paddies; at the other extreme are the giant multi-purpose dams of the world.

Water storage

There can be no doubt that the dam is the most popular of all devices for controlling water supplies on a large scale. The effect is to create a lake whose discharge can be controlled according to the demands placed upon the resource manager (Plate 11). The lake itself may create secondary benefits in the form of fisheries or recreation space to offset the value of the land which is drowned in its creation. The earliest dams, such as the tanks of ancient India and Ceylon, were built solely for water storage, so that water collected during a rainy season could be stored and used during dry periods for irrigation or human consumption. Such a function remains one of the primary purposes of the large-scale control schemes much in evidence today. Even in relatively wet climates, there are advantages in smoothing out river regimes, for example so as to avoid a summer low-flow period when the river may be unable to carry its downstream effluent loads without serious disturbance of its biological communities, and when its dissolved oxygen levels may also be very low. Where a river forms the major source for an industry then it is vital that a year-round supply is ensured so that the processes are not interrupted; the same applies to domestic supplies. The evening-out of the flow may also contribute to the solution of flood-control problems. Particularly in areas with rapid runoff, flash flooding causes serious damage and loss of life, but a dam may retain such waters and thus obviate their damaging effect. Sometimes the efficacy of dams in this respect obscures the need for more rational management of the catchment areas that are contributing the rapid runoff. A steady release of water for irrigation is one of the greatest benefits conferred by storage. In seasonally dry climates it

Plate 11 The traditional way of garnering water for industrial and urban purposes. In this Welsh example, the effect of the reservoir in drowning the sheltered valley lands of the farms can be seen, as can the apparent lack of recreational facilities which might have been a minor consolation. *(Aerofilms Ltd, London)*

may be possible to utilize year-long sunshine for multiple cropping on land formerly rendered agriculturally unusable by aridity. The control of the Sacramento River in the Central Valley of California by the Shasta Dam and associated works of the Central Valley Project has facilitated treble and even quadruple cropping of some fruits and vegetables in the southern half of the Valley. Storage requirements per unit area of land increase in regions of climatic variability, so that per acre of irrigated land Australia stores 6·9 acft (1 acft = 1,233·5 m³), the USA 31 acft, and India only 1·7 acft (A. B. Costin 1971). The generation of electrical power from falling water is much enhanced by the construction of large dams. In industrialized countries there is the frequent advantage that the power can be sold to industry in order to pay for the cost of construction and hence agriculture is made more efficient by its linkage with industry. It is one of the less happy features of some major dam projects in LDCs that no market exists for the power that could be generated.

The numerous purposes to which a large dam can be put, together with its visible presence as a symbol of modernity and apparent mastery over nature, has meant the construction of some very large edifices, together with huge impoundments. Of the 20 largest dams in the world, only one pre-dates 1950, and the Hoover Dam's (1930s) 221 m is dwarfed by several at 300 m. Kariba is the largest impoundment (130 million acft/159·9 × 10⁹ m³), followed by High Aswan (127·3 million acft/156·6 × 10⁹ m³) and Akosombo, Ghana (120 million acft/147·6 × 10⁹ m³), and 13 others above 20 million acft (25 × 10⁹ m³). Areally, the USA now have a greater surface of man-made than natural lakes, if Alaska and the Great Lakes are excluded.

The benefits to be gained from manipulation of the river flow usually overwhelm any suggestion that significant secondary costs might be incurred; indeed much water power is very cheap because the social and ecological costs are rarely reckoned up in the accounting of projects. The effects of large impoundments are wide-reaching and affect the hydrology, the terrestrial system and the aquatic systems of the basin in ways which have not always been beneficial (Lagler 1971). The hydrology of the basin is most altered downstream from a dam, especially if the dam is completely closed during the filling period. Thereafter, the volume of discharge and the current velocity downstream are most obviously altered, with a concomitant reduction in river turbidity. Basin evaporation rates rise, especially in arid and semi-arid countries, leading to the trial of surface films which will transmit oxygen and carbon dioxide, resist wind, be self-restoring after disturbance and be non-toxic. The alcohols octodecanol and hexadecanol from monomolecular films and on small stock dams in Australia have reduced evaporation by 15–70 per cent, decreasing to 15–20 per cent as the impoundment area increases (A. B. Costin 1971). Downstream from a dam, the water temperature may be affected severely if water is drawn off below a thermocline, and the quality of the water will also be changed if the impoundment is chemostratified and draw-off comes from only one depth in the lake. There is also the possibility that large dams may trigger seismic movements, especially in highly faulted regions (Rothe 1968). Silting reduces the life-span of a large impoundment and where possible a silt trap is built into the design; if the sediment piles against the dam, it may be periodically flushed out, with disastrous effects on the ecology of the river downstream. Silt removed by an impoundment may represent a loss of nutrient input to lands lower down and have to be replaced by chemical fertilizer; projected dams on the rivers of northern California would deprive some of the coast redwoods (*Sequoia sempervirens*) of their periodic injection of nutrients and probably prevent them reaching their enormous height (up to 112 m) which is their major aesthetic and commercial attraction. Control of river regimes may also lead to a net loss of soil moisture downstream, although it is sometimes predicted that lateral percolation from the impoundment may increase the groundwater supply to quite distant points.

When the initial flooding takes place there is a biogeochemical enrichment of the water, usually resulting in an explosive growth of phytoplankton and other producer organisms. Some of these are floating water plants such as water hyacinth (*Eichhornia crassipes*), salvinia (*Salvinia auriculata*) and water lettuce (*Pistia stratiotes*). These weeds transpire water which would otherwise remain in the catchment: they and ditchbank plants together transpire $2 \cdot 3 \times 10^9$ m^3/yr, worth about \$40 million, in the 17 western states of the USA. The cost of clearing them is likewise high: only the expenditure of \$1·5 million/yr on herbicides has enabled the Sudanese to prevent the spread of water hyacinth from the White to the Blue Nile. In this region, the loss of water from *Eichhornia*-covered lakes is 3·2–3·7 times that from a free surface. The weeds also prevent algal photosynthesis and hence lead to serious depletion of fisheries. On Lake Volta, water lettuce serves as a habitat for the larvae of several mosquitoes, including the vectors of encephalomyelitis and filariasis (Holm *et al.* 1969). Submerged weeds may create difficulties, especially in irrigation systems, as with the introduction of *Myriophyllum spicatum* into North America from Europe. With other similar plants it causes losses in fishing, hinders navigation, interferes with recreation use, clogs water intake points, smothers shellfish beds and provides habitats for mosquito larvae. Control by herbicides is often used, but it is very expensive and a constant vigilance is necessary: the cessation of spraying of the Congo after the post-independence wars allowed water hyacinth to clog it again very quickly, and some herbicides are also toxic to fish. Mechanical removal is slow and costs 10 times as much as herbicides. Biological control depends upon finding an animal with a voracious appetite for a particular plant: some snails are the subject of experiment, and the sea-cow or manatee is a possibility if enough of them can be found, since conversion into pelts is currently a profitable exercise. The white amuo fish and a wingless aquatic grasshopper (*Paulinia acriminate*) are also specialized feeders, the latter eating only *Salvinia*.

Downstream, the stabilized stream flow favours the survival of sedentary and rooted organisms but disrupts species of fish which spawn in flood water or whose eggs or fry depend upon the occurrence of a nutrient-enriched zone of inundation. Adult fish may be catered for by fish passes round dams, but these have not been universally successful, and young fish going downstream sometimes find them difficult to traverse.

A concatenation of the unforeseen effects of river impoundment have all been observed on the Nile as a consequence of the construction of the Aswan High Dam. The removal of silt has taken away a natural source of nutrients which must be replaced by buying chemical fertilizers, and off the delta, the stoppage of nutrient input into the Mediterranean has caused a decline in fishery yield to Egypt since the sardines have disappeared. In 1962 the Egyptian fish catch was 30,600 mt, but this was reduced by 18,000 mt by 1965. The fishery of Lake Nasser is expected to reach 10,000 mt by the mid-1970s, but this figure probably represents an initial 'bloom' and will stabilize well below that figure. The productivity of the delta lakes has fallen owing to fish kills caused by biocide runoff, and by accelerated eutrophication (George 1972). The Nile delta itself is now in retreat due to lack of building material. The extension of perennial irrigation is instrumental in extending the range of blood-fluke diseases such as bilharziasis which now infects 100 per cent of the population of some areas; it is virtually impossible to cure, and control measures such as improving sanitary conditions, drug therapy or snail control have all been ineffective because of their expense or their incompatibility with cultural patterns (Schalie 1972).

This example could be buttressed with many others where unforeseen effects of impoundments have been detrimental. The W. A. C. Bennett Dam in British Columbia removed the spring flooding of the Peace–Athabasca delta, and thus the muskrat resources upon which the native population depended; a similar project to raise the level of South Indian Lake and drown some Indian settlements became an election issue in Manitoba; the Quebec government's James Bay project (the largest hydro-electric power project in the world) will drown one year's production of timber from the province and many Indian and Eskimo resource areas, but the political symbolism of the project and the chance of selling the electricity to the USA are primary considerations. The examples show that the damming of rivers may have many beneficial results, but that the consequences of the alteration of the many ecosystems to which the river acts as a common thread have rarely been explored and scarcely ever incorporated into the reckoning of costs and benefits.

Floods

One normal condition of the hydrological cycle has been perceived as abnormal by man and labelled as floods. Poor watershed practices have often exacerbated and in some places have been the cause of floods, but it remains true that most rivers have floodplains which get inundated from time to time with varying depths of water and at low levels of predictability. For human purposes, as in Eliot's impression of the Mississippi, quantity is high and quality is low:

> ... implacable
> Keeping his seasons and rages, destroyer, reminder
> of what men choose to forget. ...
> Like the river with its cargo of dead negroes, cows
> and chicken coops.

Human adjustment to flood hazard (White 1964) may take the non-ecological form of moving smartly away, lock, stock and barrel, or *inter alia* of pressuring the appropriate governmental agency to remove the threat by environmental intervention. Flood-control dams are one remedy as are channel widening, channel straightening and deepening, and the construction of by-pass channels. Apart from the three-dimensional aspect, the problem is rather like traffic engineering, but new freeways only create more traffic and concrete riprap does not reforest an urbanized watershed. In sum, flood-control measures rarely control beyond certain well-defined limits at certain places and do not look at the cause of the flood or the real reasons (usually to be found in ecologically unsuitable land-use patterns) why they cause damage and loss of life.

For all-round ease, manipulation at this surface-water phase of the hydrological cycle ranks first. But the essentially limited amount of water at this stage, together with the fact that most of it is not of the desired quality unless treated, means that nations with access to advanced technology are assessing their deep underground aquifers more keenly.

Intervention at the ground-water phase

Relative to other sources of fresh water, ground water is an important phase of the hydrological cycle. One estimate suggests that about 7×10^6 km^3 of such water is recoverable (about half the total thus stored) and indeed ground water comprises about 0·5 per cent of total planetary water, compared with 1·9 per cent (26×10^6 km^3) as ice and 0·0001 per cent in rivers (Nace 1969). Though ground water is essentially a storage phase, it appears to have two components: cyclic ground water, which passes in and out naturally within the space of a year, and inherited ground water, which appears to have a much longer storage period.

One of the most important roles of ground water so far as man is concerned is its role as the major contributor to the base flow of rivers. Without this regular input, the reliability of rivers as resources would be much diminished. Of greater importance regionally is the pumping out of water for all purposes and this is done on many scales: dense networks of pumped wells serve towns and industrial areas in many parts of the world, as they do some major irrigated areas where river storage is not feasible. On the other hand, a single wind-driven pump watering a livestock trough or an isolated farm is a common enough sight in semi-arid parts of the world. Pumped wells have their disadvantages because it is often difficult to estimate the quality and quantity of water available, and, like oil, recovery may be uneven. Near the coast, overpumping beyond a certain level may allow the influx of saline water into the aquifers, rendering them useless for a sustained yield of water. Artificial recharge is one response: water is spread into the aquifer by forcing it down through pumps, but achieving a reasonably even spread of the water through the rock can present problems. Nearer the ground surface, the Dutch, for instance, spread polluted waters from the Rhine system over the coastal sand-dunes, which act as a filter, and the water collected beneath is to some degree purified. Deeper recharge schemes often have the aim of allowing the period of percolation through rock to remove contaminants. Purification depends largely upon porosity, and if a high rate of flow is desired then a high-porosity rock needs to be chosen, which will mean a low efficiency of purification. The inverse relation between flow and purification appears to hold for most types of rock, so that ground-water recharge is not always a great success. Nevertheless, many overpumped aquifers such as the Chalk under London are now subject to recharge schemes.

Intervention at the saline phase

The limitation upon the human use of 98 per cent of the world's water is its content of mineral salts. Comprising all except 1 per cent of that proportion, sea water commonly has

Plate 12 A small desalinating plant in the Channel Isles, UK. Such plants are very useful on small islands low in ground-water resources, especially where there is a peaking of demand caused by a seasonal influx of tourists. *(Senett and Spears Ltd, Jersey)*

35 g/litre of salts, and there are many brackish waters inland with contents above about 2 g/litre which make them useless for most purposes except flotation. In view of the increasing demands for water which is low in mineral salts as well as free from particulate matter, harmful organisms and toxic substances, it is not surprising that attention should have been turned to methods of demineralizing salt and brackish waters (Plate 12).

About 50 plants are currently in use in the world, of which the largest are in places such as Aruba, Curacao and Kuwait. These use multiple distillation of sea water as their extractive technique: one plant in Kuwait produces 6 million gal/day at $US1.76/1,000 gal (4,542 litres) and costs may in similar plants fall to $US1.40/1,000 gal with this method. Multiple-stage flash distillation appears to be cheaper, and a plant in Guernsey, Channel Islands, which is used for 'topping up' during the holiday season produces at 45c/1,000 gal (Pugh 1963); there is a similar plant at Oxnard in California. Another promising method is electrodialysis, in which a series of membranes allows migration of the water but not the dissolved salts. A good yield can be obtained but the price is high: a plant using brackish ground water at Coalinga, California, has a production cost of $7/1,000 gal. The prices quoted are all high compared with the current costs of supply from ground and surface resources: a comparable figure would be 20c/1,000 gal from traditional supplies.

Other methods tried include freezing, using butane as a liquid refrigerant; exchange resins, which will work only up to a salt content of 5 g/litre; and solar distillation, the drawback of which is the large area needed to collect the sun's energy; and plants using natural freezing have been designed in the USSR (Pryde 1972).

Apart from the heavy cost of plant involved, the cost of energy for separating salts from the water is critical, and so nuclear energy is often thought of as a principal source of power for demineralizing water in the near future. One idea is the 'nuplex': this envisages the development of an arid region based upon a 3,000 MWe nuclear reactor to which is coupled a desalination unit, a fertilizer plant producing nitrogen and phosphorus fertilizers for local use and export, electrochemical and electrometallurgical industries, and fisheries, in all supporting a population of 250,000–400,000 (Meier 1969). Such a plant would take about 8 years before it came into full operation and it would be 20 years before any profit was realized. Locations such as Sinai and the Gulf of Kutch have been suggested, and there are problems of the social impact of such a development, particularly since its protagonists consider its main virtue to be a freedom from the institutional and social constraints the region might otherwise possess. The output from distilled sources might not be required immediately it is produced, but in order to be economic a distillation unit would have to be constantly on stream. Thus there would be considerable water losses during periods of storage and stages of transport. Since the water may well be expensive to begin with (one proposal envisages a cost of 28·6c/1,000 gal, another 17c/1,000 gal, but a higher interest rate would force these up to 67c and 32c respectively), then its loss during phases of storage and transport, together with extra energy costs of lifting the water away from the shore-lines where it would be produced, might well make the economics of the whole project unviable; for example, to lift water 500 ft (152·4 m) would cost $3.50/acft for energy and $3/acft for construction. Water which cost, for instance, 60c/1,000 gal at the plant would in reality cost 90c/1,000 gal delivered to the field (Clawson *et al.* 1969). If water were to be lifted for urban and industrial use, one estimate suggests that a payment of 1c/100 m of lift/1,000 litres of water would be necessary, so that Lubbock, Texas (population 150,000, elevation 1,000 m), would have to pay $5 million/yr for lifting, plus $5 million for the horizontal delivery costs (van Hylckama 1971). The type of areas which would both benefit and be able to afford desalination are therefore restricted in number. Urban and industrial areas in high-technology countries may be one of these, but it may be noted that a plant in southern California to be built under a low interest rate (3·5 per cent) and a guaranteed market for 90 per cent of its water and power (150 mgd/0·681 × 10⁶ kilolitres/day and 1·8 million KWe) was deemed uneconomic. If nuclear plants are not viable in such places, where might they be so? The use of desalted water as a catalyst for agricultural and in-dustrial development in poor and arid areas is an exciting prospect, but as the cost of demineralized water is at least one whole order of magnitude higher than present supplies, it seems unlikely to be a cornucopia at any rate until virtually unlimited supplies of extremely cheap energy are available; even such a project would have to reckon with the ecological costs of the return to the sea of immense quantities of hot concentrated brine.

In from the cold?

Van Hylckama (1971) suggests that since icebergs contain so much fresh water they should be considered as resources. The average Greenland iceberg has an initial volume of 15×10^6 m³ or enough to supply a city of 60,000 people for one year. Their shape would make them difficult to tow, but the flat-topped antarctic bergs might be easier: an iceberg of dimensions $3,000 \times 3,000 \times 250$ m might be towed to Australia in 1 month for a cost of \$US1·5 million. Even if half of it melted there would still be 1×10^9 m³ of water or enough to supply 4 million people for one year at an average cost of \$1.50 per annum. Even better figures might be obtained for the dry west coast of South America, where ocean currents might be used to aid transport. Early in 1973 the USA Government was reported to be setting up a feasibility study of towing icebergs from Antarctica to the west coast; it was criticized on the grounds that lines of weakness in the bergs would cause them to crumble long before they reached their proposed destination.

Scales of manipulation

The simplest and earliest forms of intervention in the hydrological cycle were at a series of single points. Wells, shadoofs, Archimedean screws and similar devices tapped the water at one place and it was then borne to the site of use by pipe, container or channel. It is a measure of their effectiveness and of the recency of much water-control technology that they are still found around the world, though often with a motor attached to reduce the labour. At a high intensity, such as closely spaced pumped wells, the effect on the water storage can be very great; point manipulation in rivers affects flow rather less.

Another scale of manipulation involves much more intervention, but the control is confined to one basin. Dams for irrigation, flood control and the various other purposes discussed above, irrigation schemes fed from wells or impoundments, and underground transfer lines such as the *qanats* of the Middle East (especially Iran) are examples of this scale of diversion (Beaumont 1968). As the effectiveness of technology increases and planning sophistication soars, so the proportion of water under control in the basin becomes greater so that multiple-use schemes for whole basins of varying sizes become feasible. The Tennessee Valley Authority scheme (quoted still so often as if it were the only example of a multi-purpose basin development) is one example, and those prepared for the Jordan basin and the lower Mekong others; the last two are problematical because of the political boundaries which transgress the natural water-control unit. The creation of large fresh-water lakes behind barrages at coastal estuaries is another major intervention that is especially popular in low-lying countries without steep-sided inland valleys to flood. The IJsselmeer and Delta schemes of the Netherlands and the studies for Morecambe Bay, the Wash and the Solway Firth in Britain are contemporary examples.

A still larger scale is the transfer of water between river basins, sometimes involving an ascent stage which necessitates pumping. The earliest examples of such interbasin transfers were usually to ensure a good head of water behind a particular dam which was being used for power production or irrigation, or both. The Conon Valley scheme in Scotland (Fig. 6.4) is a scheme designed to develop power from the flow of tributaries in the same basin

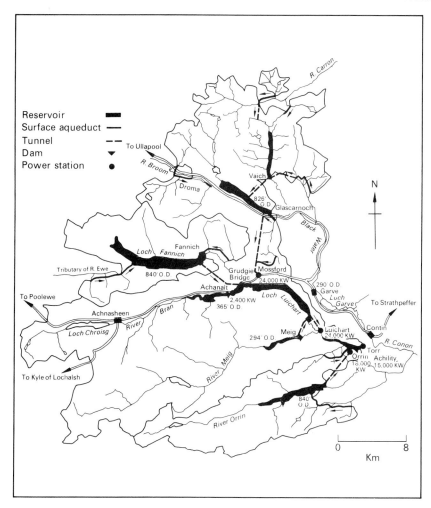

Fig. 6.4 The Conon Valley scheme in Scotland. Transfers within the basin (e.g. from Glascarnoch to Mossford) as well as from outside it (e.g. from tributaries of the River Ewe into Loch Fannich and from the headwaters of the River Carron to those of the Black Water) are used to provide the maximum head of water for hydropower generation.
Source: Aitken 1963

by tunnelling water across watersheds, and also bringing it by tunnel and surface aqueduct from other basins: water from the Ewe (which drains to the west coast) is tapped for Loch Fannich which drains to the Moray Firth. Glascanoch water is piped into Loch Luichart, its parallel eastward-flowing system. Of the scheme's total catchment area of 119,140 ha, 5,957 ha belong entirely to other basins (Aitken 1963). The road to the isles nowadays is accompanied by the skirl of a different sort of pipe.

A larger-scale set of diversions can be seen in schemes planned for Alberta and north-east England. In both there is relatively ample water in the north and a thirsty south, with

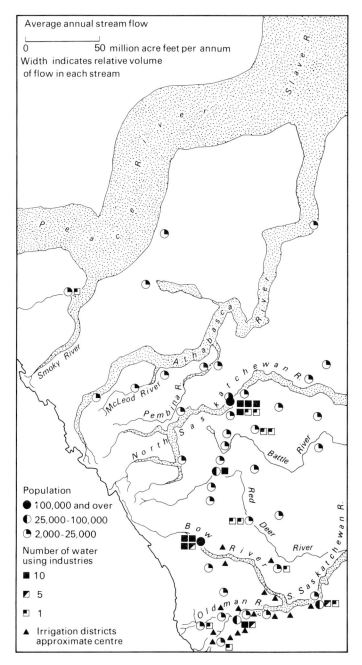

Fig. 6.5 The volume of prairie rivers in relation to user groups. The spatial discrepancies provided the impetus for a scheme of interbasin transfer, progressively transferring water southwards. This scheme (PRIME) has now been incorporated into a larger project.
Source: Province of Alberta 1969

parallel west–east rivers. Plans exist therefore to transfer water from the northernmost stream via intermediate rivers to the middle reaches of the southernmost artery. In the case of north-east England the transfer is from the north Tyne via the Wear to the Tees (Water Resources Board 1970). Alberta was the centrepiece of PRIME (Prairie Rivers Improvement Management and Evaluation), in which the great untapped flow of the Peace River (Fig. 6.5) was to be the northernmost source of a set of interbasin transfers. Water from the Peace was to be fed via Lesser Slave Lake to the Athabasca and thence to the north Saskatchewan; there was also a transfer planned further west between the Athabasca and the north Saskatchewan, and water was to be fed from the north Saskatchewan to the Red Deer River as well. In the south of the province many tributary streams of the south Saskatchewan will have dams in order to supply irrigation districts (Province of Alberta 1969). This scheme has been subsumed into a much larger project for the whole of the Saskatchewan-Nelson basin which is the fourth largest basin in Canada (Saskatchewan-Nelson Basin Board 1972).

Such schemes are puny compared with some of the ideas put forward for large continents, particularly where a small number of political units is present. The USSR is an obvious

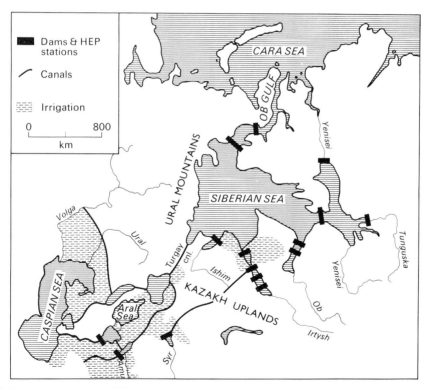

Fig. 6.6 A plan for the use of Siberian rivers to irrigate large areas of central Asia and also to generate hydropower. Considerable controversy has arisen over such massive schemes because of the quantity of land drowned and because of possible changes in climate.
Source: Simons 1969

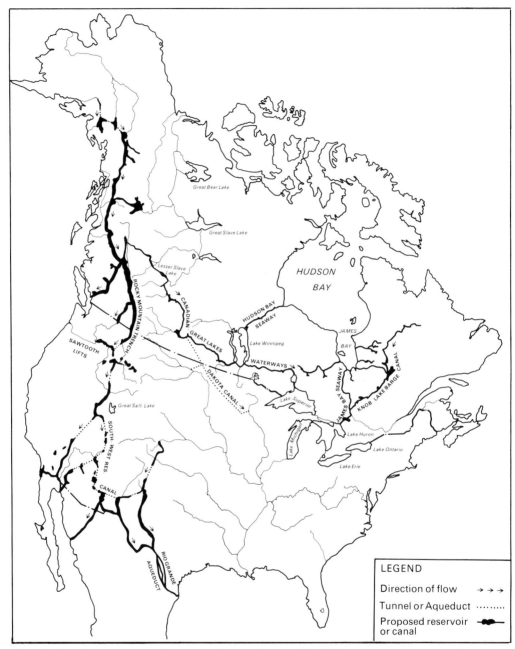

Fig. 6.7 The North American Water and Power Alliance (NAWAPA) scheme which would divert water from northern Canada and Alaska and use it to supply southern California, northern Mexico and the upper Great Lakes region. Navigation projects are also proposed. The effects of drowning the Rocky Mountain Trench upon wildlife, recreation, forestry, communications and earthquake frequency are hard to predict. Source: Province of Alberta 1968

instance, and here engineers have suggested diverting the northward flowing Ob, Yenesei and Irtysh rivers to the south in order to irrigate large areas around the Caspian and Aral Seas (Fig. 6.6). A major problem would be the repercussions upon the climate of 60,000 km² south of the Steppes, where there would be a net loss of heat to plants and where the continentality of the climate would be reduced, and the west Siberian water-table would doubtless rise to the point where large areas would become swamplands (Micklin 1969). However, the discovery of oil and gas in areas which would have been flooded has caused the apparent dropping of the scheme. Another example of continental plumbing is the Parson's Company plan for taking 'unused' water from the northern rivers of Canada and feeding it as far as the Great Lakes, New York, Los Angeles (inevitably) and Chihuahua in Mexico (Fig. 6.7). Virtually all the western rivers of North America would be reservoirs or strictly controlled, and the centrepiece would be a flooded Rocky Mountain Trench in Montana and British Columbia, 914 m ASL (Province of Alberta 1968). The objections range from the geological doubts about the ability of the Trench to withstand such a weight of water to the complaints on aesthetic grounds that the great playground of North America would not have a wild river left and that much wildlife habitat would be destroyed. Figs. 6.8 and 6.9 also show some 'geographical engineering' projects for North America. At 1966 prices, the NAWAPA (North American Water and Power Alliance) scheme was estimated to cost $800 million; an even more potent objection, however, is the rising Canadian nationalism, which seeks to free Canada from economic dominance by the USA. Like many such schemes it presupposes that urban/industrial growth is an ever-expanding consumer which must be supplied, and that it is more necessary to take the water to the sites of use than *vice versa*. Apart from its engineering *folies de grandeur*, NAWAPA appears to be devoid of useful thought about water resources.

Economic and social constraints

More than most resource ecosystems, the water crop is subject to difficulty by virtue of economic pressures. These often derive from the status of water as a free good in economic terms. It costs nothing itself, but manipulating it and treating it may be very expensive: a typical municipal scheme may incur costs of land acquisition and compensation at the site of a headwater reservoir, dam construction and maintenance, pipelines to the city, treatment plants, storage space near the city and distribution costs within the city itself. Inevitably, the greater the distance from source to user the greater the costs; not only is the initial supply system expensive, but its maintenance is likely to absorb large quantities of money. In the south-west of the USA water costs 5–15c per 1,000 gal (4,542 litres) per 100 miles (160 km) to transport, thus making some 'project water' sell at $1 per 1,000 gal, compared with the usual price of 50–70c for industrial water and 5–10c for agricultural supplies. Small wonder that many authorities try to generate power at their dams in order to sell the electricity to pay for the costs of the water-supply system. In the face of supply shortages and rising costs, the search for effective methods of cleaning effluents from water so that it may be re-used downstream is an important development, as is the technology for recycling water used at one site, for example as a cooling agent in an industrial

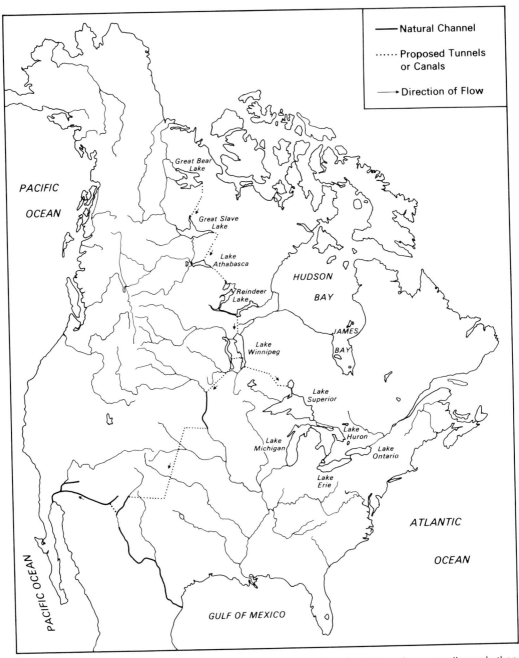

Fig. 6.8 Another large-scale water diversion scheme for North America. Although on a smaller scale than NAWAPA (Fig. 6.7), its magnitude is nevertheless impressive in conception.
Source: Province of Alberta 1968

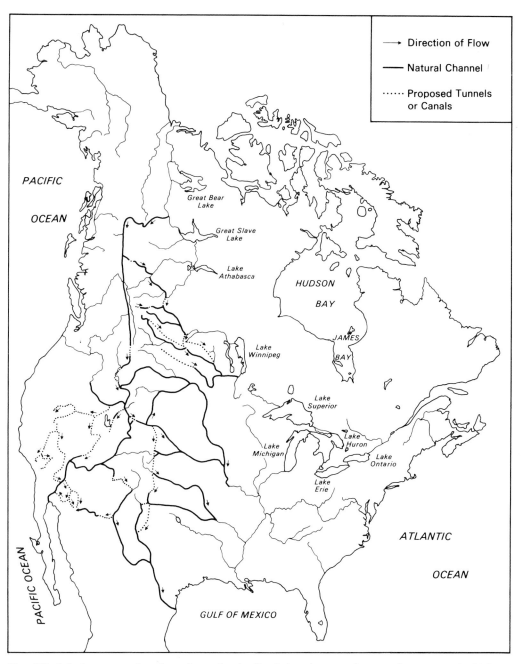

Fig. 6.9 A further water diversion scheme for the North American continent, to be compared with Figs. 6.7 and 6.8. None of these three schemes has as yet proceeded towards any form of implementation. Source: Province of Alberta 1968

plant or thermal power station. On the River Trent in England, water containing sewage effluent can be used by power stations for cooling, and it is successively re-used by power stations downstream at intervals of 16–32 km. The operations have to be regulated so that the river temperature does not exceed a prescribed limit of 30°C. Cooling towers themselves achieve re-use within a power station: the water is cooled partly by evaporation, which means a loss of just over 1 per cent of the amount of water being circulated through the tower. This amounts to 14 mgd (0.066×10^6 kilolitres/day) for a 200 MW power station and is usually made up from a riverine source. The large bulk of water required for nuclear power stations has meant that coastal sites have been favoured, bringing them into conflict with recreational and wildlife resource uses.

Treatment of waste waters is more fully dealt with in the section on water pollution (pp. 295–7), but the economic constraints appear in the costs of the full treatment needed to return water from, say, domestic sewage to a high degree of purity. The necessity for the introduction of full treatment can be deduced from the fact that such processing is usually five times as cheap as the supply of new water. Here therefore is a major source of supply of potentially high-quality water: theoretically a town could recycle its own fluids on a closed-system basis. This argument can probably be applied to many polluted waters, particularly if the authorities responsible for sewage charge the true costs of treating industrial effluents.

The different values put on different uses of water or catchment areas often exert a social constraint on water manipulation. The most frequent instance of this is a controversy over the loss of land under a reservoir impoundment. Settlements may be lost, as in the Tsimlyansk reservoir in the USSR which necessitated the relocation of 159 towns, villages and hamlets (Pryde 1972); or the loss may be cultural as with the Abu Simbel temples which would have drowned beneath Lake Nasser in Egypt, but were saved by international action; it may be more narrowly economic as with the disruption of farm units when bottom land is drowned in upland Britain; it may be scientific as with the Cow Green reservoir in Upper Teesdale (northern England) where part of an assemblage of arctic-alpine relict plants was destroyed; or it may be scenic as with the drowning of Glen Canyon in Arizona, and the proposals to put dams in Bridge Canyon and Marble Canyon near the Grand Canyon of the Colorado River. In all these cases, and many others, there has been fierce opposition to the proposed water-management scheme, and the opposition to the building of dams especially has become vocal and well informed. In industrial countries, therefore, we are likely to see social pressures influencing large manipulation schemes to a greater extent than hitherto and hence accelerating the move towards closed-cycle re-use. If the benefits of wild country and natural ecosystems are considered at their true value, then the case against some impoundments may be stronger.

The effect of increasing human populations

The very vastness of the quantity of water on the planet gives it an aura of an illimitable resource. Regionally this is clearly not so, but is not the total amount so great that improved distribution would bring about plentiful supplies for every purpose? But only 3 per cent of this great amount of liquid is fresh water, and obstacles exist to the use of the salted variety. In the industrialized nations particularly, vast quantities are needed to sustain the urban-industrial life-cycle. In the USA, for example, Wollman (1960) estimates that 15,000 gal/day/person ($68·1 \times 10^3$ litres/day/cap) are used, out of a total resource of 28,000 gal/day/person (127×10^3 litres/day/cap). Projections of demand for the near future reveal vast increases in the quantities of water required, much of it of high quality (Table 6.1). At the current rate of use in the USA, even if all the nation's water resources were utilized, a population above 230 million (1970 level: 210 million) would begin to notice losses in water quality. Regional shortages are already apparent and are the moving force behind some of the continental plumbing schemes like NAWAPA.

TABLE 6.1   Estimated water withdrawn and water consumed, USA 1980 and 2000 (mgd—1 million gal = 4,542 kilolitres)

Use	Withdrawn		Consumed	
	1980	2000	1980	2000
Municipal (public supplies)	29,000	42,000	3,500	5,500
Industrial	363,000	662,000	11,000	24,000
Agricultural	167,000	184,000	104,000	126,000
Local uses, e.g. hatcheries, wetlands	—	—	71,000	97,000
Totals	559,000	880,000	190,000	253,000

Source: Wollman 1960

On a world scale all known sources of fresh water have been estimated to total $4·5 \times 10^{13}$ imperial gal or 20,000 km³. At a present per capita use this could support a world population of 20,000 million, a number arriving in about AD 2040 from a growth rate of 2 per cent p.a. (Simons 1969). The slightly larger estimate for the earth's annually renewable waters of 37,000 km³ (Kalinin and Bykov 1969) only alters the prospect slightly. They suggest that, by the year 2000, half of the above total will be in use by men (Table 6.2).

Within the envelope of these global limits much can be done to procure essential water supplies. New technology will probably reduce demand in some industrial processes, as in the halving of water used per KWH generated in England between 1900 and 1965. Much pure water is now used for purposes which do not require such pristine conditions, as in carrying industrial effluents and domestic sewage for example; and the provision of separate supply channels for pure and not-so-pure water, as already happens for effluent in the Ruhr area of West Germany where one river is maintained clean as a recreational stream and urban supplier while a parallel water-course acts as the regional cloaca (Fair 1961), is a development which may have wider application. The purification of contaminated water would provide a major source of supply possibly equal to half that needed by industrial nations.

TABLE 6.2   Annual world water requirements by 2000 A.D. (km³)

Usage	Total	Lost by evaporation
Irrigation	7,000	4,800
Domestic	600	100
Industrial	1,700	170
Dilution of effluents and wastes	9,000	—
Other	400	4,000
Total	18,700	5,470

Source: Kalinin and Bykov 1969

We must not lose sight of the possibility that water supply could be a limiting factor on population levels, especially at a regional scale. Even given unlimited re-use the time taken to recycle would be critical, and use of all known sources for economic purposes (including, as Borgstrom (1965) suggests, the large quantities needed for producing food) would cut across the rising expectations of those who demand water for recreation and wildlife, or for its scenic value, particularly where it is untouched by man. If shortfalls begin to occur, whether of quality or quantity, we must remember that technological substitutes for water are not very likely and it does not appear to exist in recoverable quantities on other planets even if the cost of space water-carts could be borne. We must at the very least disprove the validity as far as water is concerned of the Chinese proverb:

> Water and words . . .
> Easy to pour
> Impossible to recover.

Further reading

CHORLEY, R. J. (ed.) 1969: *Water, earth and man.*

CLAWSON, M., LANDSBERG, H. H. and ALEXANDER, M. T. 1969: Desalted water for agriculture: is it economic?

HOLM, L. G., WELDON, L. W. and BLACKBURN, R. D. 1969: Aquatic weeds.

VAN HYLCKAMA, T. E. A. 1971: Water resources.

LAGLER, K. F. 1971: Ecological effects of hydroelectric dams.

SMITH, K. 1972: *Water in Britain.*

US DEPT OF AGRICULTURE 1955: *Water.*

7

Forestry

About one-third of the world's land surface (4,028 million ha) is covered with forests (whose continental distribution is outlined in Table 7.1), which we may intuitively define as ecosystems dominated by trees, reflecting the status of some of those organisms as being among the biggest living things in the world: both species of redwood are examples, and the bristlecone pines of California are certainly the oldest living organisms in the world at about 4,600 years. The size of trees subjects all the other elements of the forest system to a hegemony which is reflected in the organization of the layering of the forest plants: the canopy of the dominant trees may be penetrated by only a limited amount of light to be absorbed by shrubs; patches of light on the forest floor allow the growth of shade-intolerant elements of the ground flora. In deciduous forests a temporal element may be noticed in the herbs that flower, shed seed, and die down before the trees come into leaf.

TABLE 7.1   Forest lands (000 ha)

Europe	140,000
USSR	910,009
North and Central America	815,000
South America	908,000
Asia	458,000
China	76,600
Africa	639,000
Oceania	81,000
World	4,028,000

Source: FAO *Production Yearbook 25*, 1971. See also Fig. 7.1.

The leaves of the trees themselves are the fundamental element in the system since they are the site of photosynthesis. Growing in Switzerland, spruce trees (*Picea abies*) need 2,300 kg (fresh weight) of leaves to produce 1 m^3 of freshwood, and the average dry weight of leaves in measured forests is 7,000 kg/ha (3 tons/ac) (Ovington 1962). These organs are also important in the food webs of woodlands, since the stem of the tree contains few nutrients and is physically intractable to many animals as food. The nutrient-rich leaves and twigs hence form the first level of most of the food chains of the forest, both predatory and saprophytic: defoliating insects thus have an important role to play in natural forests.

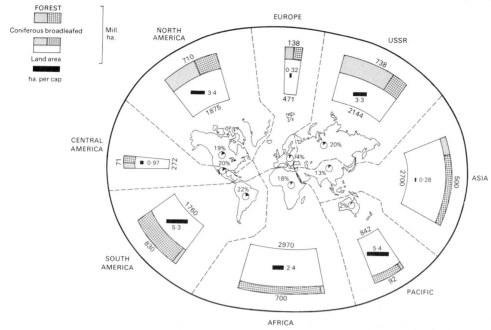

Fig. 7.1 A diagram of forest area and distribution in the world. The divided circle located in each major region indicates the proportion of the land area devoted to forest. The outer segments show (reading outwards) the total land area (million ha), the number of hectares of forest per person, the division of forest between conifers and broadleaved types, and the total forest area. The area of the segment itself is proportional to total land area, subdivided into forest and non-forest sectors. The predominance of the USSR and North America in terms of the coniferous trees so much in demand for paper and paper products will be noted. The dependence of Europe on outside resources in this field (as in so many others) can easily be inferred.
Source: FAO 1963

It follows that the biota of the forest floor are very important factors in the dynamics of forests, for they exist mainly among the leaf and twig litter and are responsible for its mineralization and re-use by the tree and for providing some of the energy pathways through the ecosystem. In temperate woodlands, for example, they decompose 3,000–4,000 kg/ha of autumnal leaf fall by the next spring (Ovington 1965), and in evergreen tropical forests their activity keeps the ground surface virtually free of dead organic matter. Larger animals, too, may have vital roles in the ecology of the forest: the populations of small mammals, which feed on for example acorns and beech mast, will affect recruitment to the next cohort of young trees and so the populations of the predators of these animals such as owls can also be critical. An overpopulation of deer can damage and disfigure a whole generation of young trees by browsing off the leading shoots, while a population explosion of insects can strip a forest of its leaves and alter the ecology of a woodland for many years.

A forest is one of the most complex of natural ecosystems, and in man's use of natural forests and his attempts to imitate or improve on them these intricacies must be borne in mind, since manipulation of the ecosystem for resource purposes can easily bring about deleterious effects which were not foreseen.

Energy flow and nutrient circulation in forests

Because forests are so interesting and because the accumulation of organic matter in the tree stems forms the most important forest resource, more studies on woodland energetics have been done than on many other ecosystems. Forests are reputed to be very efficient users of incident solar energy because of the stratification of photosynthetic surfaces and the high density of chlorophyll-containing tissue. The maximum thermal efficiency of photosynthesis here, as elsewhere, is about 14 per cent, however, and of the net radiation received, a tree expends 60 per cent in transpiration, and the actual processes of photo-synthesis account for only 1·5 per cent (Ovington 1962). The balance between photosynthesis and respiration determines the accretion of organic material in the tree, and this depends not only on the season but on the age of the tree. The rate of accumulation of organic matter is greatest at the dense pole stage of young forest, becoming slower in mature woodlands. A climax forest may attain 400,000 kg/ha of dry matter; in energy terms, forest plantations have been found to contain $22-156 \times 10^{10}$ cals/ha. Animal biomass is much lower and probably does not exceed 1,000 kg/ha in the temperate zones of the world (Ovington 1962). Table 7.2 shows the annual energy budget for a plantation of Scots pine.

TABLE 7.2   Annual energy budget for Scots pine (*Pinus sylvestris*) plantation 26 years old

	1×10^8 calories per hectare
Income of short-wave radiation	76,700
Net long-wave radiation loss	32,000
Net radiation assuming a reflection coefficient of 0·25	25,500
Energy flow through organic matter	
Captured during photosynthesis of trees and under-storey plants	1,890
Released by respiration of trees and under-storey plants	890
Contained in organic matter produced by trees and under-storey plants	1,000
Accumulated in tree stock	339
Accumulated in under-storey plants	6
Accumulated in A_0 horizon	32
Removed in trunks of harvested trees	172
In roots of harvested trees	72
Released by litter decomposition	378

Source: Ovington 1965

   The processes of the biota cannot be considered separately from those of the soil, since there is a reciprocal relationship. The importance of soil organisms is corroborated by the fact that the overwhelming energy use in the soil is in the breakdown of organic matter.

Nevertheless, the soil humus is an important store of energy: in Devon, England, the annual leaf fall was calculated at 4,000 kg/ha (Ovington 1962), and in very wet climates the depth of organic matter in needleleaf forests (such as those of the west coast of North America) may be so great as to form a peat. Weathering processes in soil rank second in their consumption of energy, followed by the hydrothermic cycle and the transport of substances in the soil profile.

In summary, most of the incident radiant energy is used in the metabolism of the tree. A small proportion (1–3 per cent according to Ovington (1962)) is used for the critical phase of accumulating the organic matter which is the basis of both the forest resource and the forest food web. The subsequent pathways are dominated by the stem and by forest humus, which both accumulate energy over long time-spans, and by the leaves, which have a shorter turnover period and a lower energy content. Some actual figures which demonstrate this are shown in Table 7.3.

As with energy studies, quantitative investigations of the circulation paths of essential elements, such as calcium, potassium and nitrogen, have been undertaken in many different types of forest. The basic flow consists of inputs from rain and subsoil weathering, circulation within the forest–soil–animals system, losses by way of crops of plants or animals, and runoff in both dissolved and particulate forms. The exact quantities in each pathway vary greatly according to the species involved and environmental factors like precipitation. In wet climates, for example, there is often a high input of certain cations from rainfall, but rapid runoff removes much of this quite quickly. Fig. 7.2 shows some pathways of potassium in two different kinds of British woodland. Different rates of processing mean that essential elements need not be distributed evenly in both parts of the forest–soil system. In tropical forests, for example, the amount of calcium in plant shoots is 20 times greater than in the roots, and phosphorus 10 times greater. In temperate forests the order of difference is usually 2–3 times, and in a strand of Corsican pine in Scotland the nitrogen content of the trees was estimated to be only 0·4 per cent of the total nitrogen content of the ecosystem (Ford 1971). So the tropical forest is regarded as having evolved a circulation system which reduces nutrient loss from leaching and runoff by keeping most of the minerals locked up in the vegetation. The total nutrient budget is high in such places: tropical forests have been estimated to accumulate 2,000–53,000 kg/ha of minerals, whereas dry savannas reach only 1,000 kg/ha (Bakuzis 1969). The long-term stability of the forest ecosystem depends upon a successful balance between output and input of nutrients. If there are high losses these need to be replaced, but it is more common to find that they are small in undisturbed forest. A small area of New Hampshire with an average slope of 26 per cent, which included some slopes of 70 per cent, lost on average only 14 mt/km²/yr of nutrients. Clear felling accelerated the nutrient drain by factors of ×3 to ×20 for various cations, and in the first year after felling an amount equivalent to a whole year's turnover of nitrogen was lost (Bormann et al. 1968). Within the forest itself the cycling of nutrients involves uptake by the plants, storage within the organisms, and return to the soil via dead organic matter. The quantities of nutrients at various stages are important in resource processes because they determine the quantities of minerals removed if the tree is harvested and taken elsewhere. Table 7.4 shows some comparative data for different European species, from which it can be seen that storage is the smallest of these stages and

TABLE 7.3   Plant biomass of woodlands

Trees	Pinus nigra	Pinus sylvestris	Betula verrucosa	Quercus borealis	Picea abies	Nothofagus truncata	Pseudotsuga taxifolia	Evergreen gallery forest
Location	North-east Scotland	Eastern England	Moscow, USSR	Minnesota, USA	Sweden	New Zealand	Washington State, USA	Thailand
Status	Plantation	Plantation	Natural	Natural	Natural	Natural	Natural	Natural
Age of trees (years)	48	55	67	57	58	110	52	n.a.
Tree height (m)	14	16	26	17	17	21	17	29
Number of trees/ha	1,112	760	n.a.	800	924	490	1,157	16,200
Oven-dry weight (000 kg/ha)								
Tree leaves	5.6	7.2	2.8	3.5	9.1	2.7	12.0	19.0
Tree branches	11.2	12.3	11.3	49.5	14.3	42.0	17.9	50.0
Tree trunks	95.1	96.7	156.7	111.9	85.2	224.8	174.8	225.2
Shrubs and herbs	7.0	2.6	2.0*	0.6	1.0*	0*	0.1	0.2
Roots	34.0	34.1	43.1	15.0	60.0*	39.2	12.3	88.5
Dead branches on trees	10.0	10.0	2.0*	21.9	2.6	1.1	11.2	n.a.
Organic matter on ground	22.0	45.0	3.0	36.7	78.0	16.7	117.3	3.0
Total	184.9	207.9	220.9	239.1	250.2	326.5	345.6	385.9

* Estimated from other woodlands
Source: Ovington 1965

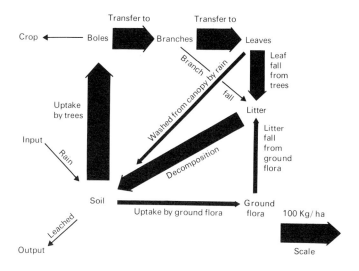

Quercus robur aged 47 years

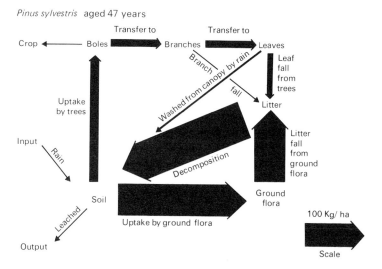

Pinus sylvestris aged 47 years

Fig. 7.2 The circulation of potassium in adjacent woodlands under similar conditions, showing the dominance exercised by the trees over the movement of essential elements. The oak trees, for example, take up much more potassium than the pines, where the ground flora (in this case, of bracken fern) is considerably more important in its flow.
Source: Ovington 1965

TABLE 7.4   Annual cycling of nutrients in forest stands (kg/ha)

Process	Species	Nitrogen	Phosphorus	Potassium	Calcium
Uptake	Pine	45	5	7	29
	Beech	50	13	15	96
	Oak	87	6·5	79	95·1
Return	Pine	35	4	5	19
	Beech	40	10	10	82
	Oak	55·6	3·1	58·6	82·8
Storage	Pine	10	1	2	10
	Beech	10	3	5	14
	Oak	27	3	13·9	0·8
Removed by thinning	Oak	5·1	0·4	6·5	10·5

Source: Bakuzis 1969

hence cropping of the stem, which in turn has the lowest proportion of nutrients, involves the least of these elements. See also Fig. 7.3.

The nutrient flow of the forest may be summarized by emphasizing that under natural conditions it is cyclic and loss is nearly always in balance with gain. If forests are to be used as crops, then an ecologically sound resource process must ensure that this cycle is perpetuated; artificial forests must either establish their own cycles or be aided to do so by forest management. In all cases, the soil fauna and flora are a little-noticed but vital part of the mechanism of nutrient flow in the ecosystem: this is exemplified by the findings of Stark (1972) on the role of soil fungi as nutrient sinks for different kinds of forest (see p. 13).

In spite of the effects of man, enough forest remains to give us a clear idea of the nature and functioning of the natural forest. Some details of the diverse forest types of the world therefore form a necessary background to an understanding of their potential as a source both past and present. This information is summarized in Table 7.5. The nature of the forests is perhaps epitomized in the values for diversity and biomass, which decline poleward as climatic conditions become less favourable for tree growth. The tropical forests have easily the highest production of organic matter, but the forests of the subtropics and temperate zones do not greatly lag behind; the boreal conifer forest has a lower productivity, but even so it is higher than non-forest vegetation types such as savannas (66,000 kg/ha), tundra (5,000 kg/ha) or shrub desert (4,300 kg/ha) (Rodin and Bazilevic 1966).

Man's demand upon the forests can be divided into two categories, of which the first comprises the direct uses of the wood itself, gathered almost entirely from the stems of the trees. The second category consists of indirect uses such as water yield and animal products which have come from the forested area and in whose ecosystems the trees have played an important part. The cropped forests of the world have an annual growth potential of 4,500 million mt, of which 1,626 million mt are estimated to be harvested (Weck and Wiebecke 1961). In Europe the deciduous trees appear to have the most efficient foliage,

TABLE 7.5   Some characteristics of the world's main forest types

Forest type	Regime	Structure[1]	Typical dominants	Spp/ ha	Tree biomass[2] (kg/ha)	Typical fauna	Soil type	Uses
Moist tropical forest (e.g. Congo; Amazon basins)	Evergreen broad-leaved	3TL OSL OGL climbers, epiphytes	Mahogany Ironwood *Morea*	200	500,000	Stratified: Canopy: flying squirrels, monkeys Trunk: martens, baboon Ground: tapir, anteater, deer	Variable. Nutrient-poor	Selected hardwoods, e.g. mahogany; shifting cultivation; clearance for agriculture; simplification, e.g. rubber
Subtropical broad-leaved forests	Deciduous broad-leaved	2TL 1SL 1GL	Teak Pyinkado	n.a.	410,000	Canopy: monkeys, civets Ground: tiger, elephant	Variable. Nutrient-poor	Dominants, e.g. teak, have commercial value; shifting cultivation; clearance for agriculture; watershed protection
Temperate zone coniferous forests	Coniferous needle-leaved	1TL 1SL 1GL	Douglas fir Redwood	1–5		Black bear	Leached brown-earth	Dominants have commercial value; clearance for agriculture; watershed protection; recreation; grazing
Temperate zone deciduous forests	Deciduous broad-leaved	1TL 1SL 1GL	Oak Beech Lime Chestnut	20–40	370,000– 400,000	Deer; small rodents; owls; insect-eating birds	Brown-earth; leached brown-earth	Dominants have commercial value; clearance for agriculture; watershed protection; recreation; simplification for plantation, e.g. oak, beech; grazing of cattle, pigs
Boreal forest	Coniferous needle-leaved	1TL 1GL	Spruce Firs Pines	1–5	200,000	Moose; wolf; woodland caribou; reindeer	Podzol	Dominants have commercial value; recreation

[1] TL = tree layer; SL = shrub layer; GL = ground layer.
[2] Source: Rodin and Bazilevic 1966

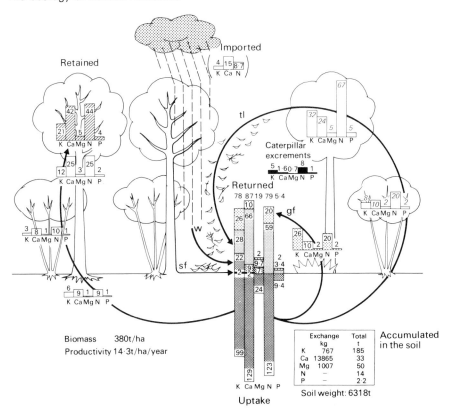

Fig. 7.3 The annual cycling of selected minerals (in kg/ha) in a Belgian forest of oak and ash with an understorey of hazel and hornbeam. The retention of the elements is in the annual wood and bark increment of both roots and above-ground portions of the trees and the 1-year-old twigs. The pathways of return are tree litter (tl on the diagram), ground flora (gf), washing and leaching of canopy (w) and stem flow (sf). Imported flow is from rainfall. The italic figures on the right of the diagram are for crown leaves at full growth in July, at which time defoliating caterpillars are an important part of the return flow. Uptake is equal to the sum of the retained and returned portions of the circulation. (The tons (t) are metric tons.) At harvest, it is largely the stem component of the larger trees which is removed.
Source: Duvignéaud and Denaeyer-De Smet 1970

for 880 kg of fresh foliage will produce 1 m³ of solid merchantable wood; even-aged spruce stands require 3,000 kg for the same production and Scots pine 1,200 kg (Bakuzis 1969). Table 7.6 shows the area and growth potential for the various forest types of the world. The dominance of the lowland equatorial forests is apparent, as is the subordinate status of the rest: possible exceptions are the summergreen (i.e. temperate deciduous) forests and mountain conifers, but an order of × 2 separates them from the tropical rain forests. This growth potential is not equivalent to harvesting potential since species diversity and accessibility are very important too. The latter is self-explanatory; with regard to the former it must be remembered that the number of species per unit area in tropical forests is so much higher than in the boreal conifer forests that harvesting is costly. By contrast, the immense stands of one or two species of pine and spruce in subarctic Canada provide a uniform product much more evenly distributed.

TABLE 7.6   Estimated forest area and estimated growth potential[1] for different formation classes of the forests of the world

| Formation class | Estimated area | | Estimated growth | | |
	Million ha	%	mt/ha yr	Total million mt/yr	%
Equatorial rain forest, lower range	440	18	3·5	1,540	35
Equatorial rain forest, mountain range	48	2	3·0	144	3
Monsoon forests and humid savanna	263	11	1·8	474	11
Dry savanna and dry mountain forests in tropics	530	21	1·0	530	12
Temperate rain forests and laurel; precipitation below 1,000 mm	20	1	7·2	143	3
Sclerophyllous forests	177·5	7	1·0	178	4
Summergreen forests and mountain conifers	393	16	2·2	865	19·5
Boreal conifers	605·5	24	0·9	556	12·5
Total	2,477			4,430	100

[1] In tons of dry matter production per hectare and per year.
Source: Bakuzis 1969

Wood

Fig. 7.4 sets out the main uses of forests. Among the high number of direct uses, the use of wood for fuel has probably been the most significant until relatively recently. The average figures for the 1960s show that industrial wood (i.e. all uses except fuel and products such as cork and waxes) accounted for 54 per cent of the world's crop, so that fuel is slightly overshadowed (FAO 1969). Nevertheless it remains an enormous consumer of forest and one in which there is little selectivity, for almost the whole tree can be used. It can be removed from its growth site, so any return of mineral nutrients to the soil is precluded, and although some trees are better fuel wood than others, in places of scarcity any tree or bush will be utilized (Openshaw 1974). In many countries the wood is converted to charcoal before being sold: India and Japan are instances, and in rural Japan a large proportion of domestic heating still comes from the charcoal-burning *hibachi*. Table 7.7 states baldly the magnitude of recent increase and the proportion of industrial wood, and Table 7.8 the regional components of the total production. Of the uses of industrial wood, lumber is the

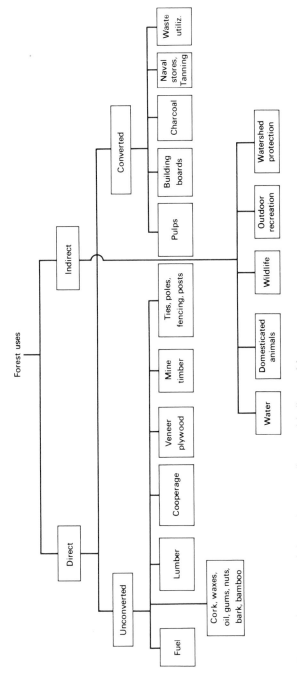

Fig. 7.4 A diagram of the major uses, direct and indirect, of forests

TABLE 7.7   Removals of wood 1959 and
1969 (000 m³)

Year	Total wood	Industrial wood
1959	1900·1	1009·0
1969	2184·7	1219·4

Source: FAO *Yearbook of Forest Products 1969–1970*

TABLE 7.8   Total wood production 1969 (000 m³)

Area	Quantity
North America	448,030
Western Europe	243,511
Developed Oceania	20,510
Other developed areas	60,541
Central America	41,285
South America	233,025
Africa	237,231
African Near East	21,560
Asian Near East	30,892
Far East	213,244
Developing Oceania	4,713
Eastern Europe	628,624
USSR (1968)	380,400
Other centrally planned economies	175,675
World	2,184,739

Source: FAO *Yearbook of Forest Products 1969–1970*

most important, especially in the construction of housing, and the furniture industry is also a major market for both soft and hard woods. Other industrial uses include cooperage (a declining use due in part to the regrettable rise of beer sold in glass or metal kegs), veneer and plywood which consume about 10 times less wood than lumber but are a very large industry on a world scale, mine timber, railway sleepers or ties, posts, poles, fencing and various minor products such as cork, waxes, nuts, resins and bark. The uses of converted wood are dominated by the practice of converting wood to pulp in order to make paper. In 1968 a total of 90,409,000 mt dry weight of pulp was produced. By far the largest proportion (80,034,000 mt) came from the market economies of the West and Japan, with the centrally planned economies following at 8,576,000 mt, and the developing countries producing relatively little at 1,799,000 mt (FAO 1969). The rank order of the major producers of pulp in 1968 was USA, Canada, Sweden, Japan, Finland, USSR. The consumption of paper and paperboard products in the Western-type economies is enormous (Table 7.9), and increased 50 per cent during 1955–67. Most of it is converted eventually to ash and CO_2 and recycling has been little practised outside a few environment-conscious cities in Europe and North America. The profligacy of use is illustrated by the story of the

TABLE 7.9   Per capita consumption of paper and pulpboard products

	1967: mt/1,000 cap		
USA	226·3	Denmark	115·4
Sweden	168·9	UK	115·2
Switzerland	126·8	Norway	110·0

Source: FAO *Yearbook of Forest Products 1969–1970*

little old lady in Idaho who came across a recently logged forest. As she walked among the debris of the former woodland, seeing the great stumps of decapitated trees, she wept. She cried so hard that she used up a whole box of Kleenex tissues. Among the other uses of converted wood, the various kinds of particle board and building board have a very high growth rate. Not only is waste from lumber used up in this way but trees which have a relatively low market value as lumber can be used too, providing industry for places that might otherwise be economically remote. The whole question of waste utilization is important: sawing lumber produces large quantities of sawdust, and up to 35 per cent of total harvested timber may in fact be waste which at present is often used as a fuel at sawmills but which may be converted into a saleable product in future. The leaves of the trees are traditionally not used. They contain much protein, however, and experiments have been conducted into the feasibility of harvesting them for food, discussed in Chapter 8. The roots are never used and may either be left *in situ* or gathered up. The trunk of the tree is thus the source of nearly all the forest products which are harvested directly.

As the major consumer of wood, the West's tastes and technologies obviously affect the ecology of the forests which they use. Some changes in demand may eventually be reflected in the types of forest which resource managers try to produce. Modern housing, especially apartments, uses less sawn lumber than individual houses, so that the trend of the 1960s, when half the new housing in Europe (except the UK) was apartments, is towards a lower demand for sawn wood. Similarly, particle boards are absorbing much of the market for sawn wood in the housing and furniture fields. Mining timber output is falling, but the same kinds of wood are being absorbed into the enormous increase in pulp production. In Europe during the period 1950–75 the proportion of logs used for pulping will rise from 18 to 44 per cent, and as high as 50 per cent for smaller logs. These trends have their repercussions in the move to the planting or manipulation of forests to bring about pure even-aged stands of fast-growing trees such as poplars, certain conifers, teak and eucalypts. Such forests are of course monocultures and, while possessing the economic cheapness associated with uniformity, are also subject to the ecological instabilities and aesthetic inacceptabilities which accompany a lack of diversity.

Crop ecology

The use of the forest for wood inevitably removes energy-rich material from the site on which it has grown. However, this loss to the local ecosystem is probably not of great consequence provided regeneration eventually takes place. In nature the removed tree trunks would eventually provide energy for decomposer organisms whose populations are probably linked to the available organic detritus and so fluctuate within wide limits. Thus the food webs based on the flora and fauna of the litter horizons must be deprived of energy by the practice of forestry. It has already been noted that forest trees utilize only 1–3 per cent of total incident energy for the production of matter; at harvesting a lot of this is left on site as litter, seeds and roots. The proportion of incident energy which is cropped is thus very small, and so forests are certainly not efficient ways of gathering winter fuel. Industrial users of wood are not of course interested in its energy content; but of the total assimilated matter of the forest, only about 32 per cent appears as usable wood even under very good conditions, since respiration accounts for 45 per cent, litter 16 per cent, roots 3 per cent, seeds 1 per cent, and 3 per cent is lost in logging and transport (Polster

Plate 13 Modern forestry has strong ties to industrial energy sources as seen in the heavy equipment portrayed in this photograph from the USA. Although most of the nutrient-rich parts of the tree are being left on site, the bark is being removed. The traditional suitability of winter for forest operations is confirmed here, as is the commercial suitability of relatively uniform stands of coniferous trees. *(Grant Heilman, Lititz, Pa)*

1961). This last figure is much higher in places with a tradition of inexpert logging and in the Soviet Union has been placed at 33 per cent, including 50 million m³/yr wasted at the cutting areas (Pryde 1972). So the final crop of wood from a mature forest (a fast-growing one is accumulating energy as organic matter more rapidly) is of the order of 0·1 per cent of the incident solar radiation (Plate 13). Mineral nutrients in the natural forest are cycled, so cropping in this case may remove elements in short supply from the plant–soil system. Losses through harvest are highly variable, according to Duvignéaud and Denaeyer-De Smet (1970), and vary with the type of tree: 100-year-old stands of some European species had different amounts of certain nutrients in their trunks (Table 7.10). These data show broadly that a good proportion of the nutrients in the forest are removed by stem harvest but equally that the leaving on-site of much of the crown provides a source of organic matter to be recycled. What is not shown by figures is whether any particularly scarce element in the ecosystem is removed which cannot quickly be replaced by subsoil weathering or precipitative input. There is at present no evidence to suggest that this is so, but the base status

TABLE 7.10   Nutrients in 100-year-old forest stands

	Kg/ha in trunks and roots, and total for stand					
	Calcium		Potassium		Phosphorus	
Deciduous hardwoods	257	1,283	121	320	20	70
Conifers other than pines	129	676	102	375	10	70
Pines	84	283	45	138	8	30

Source: Rennie 1955

of the local rainfall and soils must inevitably be critical. Forestry operations may involve the elimination of designated trees (selective logging) or the removal of whole stands (clear-cutting), although the so-called Montana definition of the former is, 'You select a forest and then you log it.' Clear-felling has been unequivocally shown to accelerate silt and nutrient loss into the streams of the forest. In a New Hampshire deciduous forest nutrient loss was accelerated by several methods (Bormann et al. 1969). Transpiration was reduced so the amount of water passing directly through the ecosystem was increased, root surfaces able to remove nutrients from the leaching waters were reduced, and in some cases more rapid mineralization of added organic matter increased the loss. (Microbiological processes in the soil may also lead to an increase of dissolved nitrate in waters and eventually exceed levels of 10 ppm in the runoff, thus causing algal blooms, i.e. bringing about eutrophication.) In many forests, however, the immediate losses of precipitative input in rainwater and the possibilities of luxury consumption by trees suggest that harvesting may not in the long term be deleterious to the ecosystem providing that the input in precipitation can be intercepted and stored in the soil, and that nutrient-rich but unwanted parts of the tree are left to mineralize on site; Likens and Bormann (1971) show that, for example, 36 per cent of the total calcium in the deciduous forest they investigated is incorporated in the stem bark of the trees. Forest practices which are inimical to such processes need to be eliminated, and in any case monitoring of the nutrient flows of all exploited forest is essential if sustained yield is to be maintained. Existing forests may be very strongly manipulated in order to increase their yield of desired benefits, especially in the case of timber production where man-directed inputs of energy and matter may be of an almost agricultural intensity. Attention to the trees themselves involves 'weeding', i.e. the elimination of species which might compete with the seedlings of desired species; thinning, i.e. the eradication of individuals of the same species; and brashing, i.e. the removal of leafless lower branches especially in conifers. These levels of control are applied only in intensively managed forests, but other influences may affect extensive tracts of more or less natural forest. Chief among these is the application of chemical technology against insect parasites and damaging fungi. Beginning with tar washes and Bordeaux mixture earlier this century, the advent of the aircraft and the organic pesticide has escalated warfare against creatures such as the spruce budworm to a very high degree. Some of the spraying has had untoward side-effects, along with many other uses of persistent pesticides. Fire control has also been ruthlessly practised on all forms of forest despite the fact that in many coniferous forests fires appear to be a normal part of the ecology. The cessation of fire due to a policy of suppression may produce two major effects in fire-adapted ecosystems. The first is to bring about a shift in species composition. This may favour trees less attractive from a commercial point of view, or, to take an example from the field of nature protection, the remaining trees of the fire-tolerant *Sequoia gigantea* more or less ceased to regenerate because their saplings were shaded out by competitors which were not fire-resistant and which would have been destroyed if fires had taken their normal course. A second consequence may be the piling up of humus and litter to great depths on the forest floor. When such a thickness is ignited the temperatures are very high, and 'jumping' to produce a crown fire which is the most destructive form of forest fires is likely. More regular burning of a thin layer of humus and litter does not lead to such damage. One result of these discoveries has been the careful introduction of prescribed burning into some sophisticated forest management schemes. Such a practice may well be much cheaper than fire suppression: the US Federal Government spent $186 million in 1968 on suppression but an average of 1·9 million ha still burn every year, and in 1968, Alaska suffered 1·7 million ha of burnt forest (Oberle 1969). Even spatially minor forest exploitation works may have effects on the forests. Roads for logging are one example: if badly sited they act as channels for water and eventually as initiators of gulley systems in steep terrain. Together with careless logging and fire, enough silt may be shed into streams to render them aesthetically unattractive, kill the fish populations (especially salmonids), and contribute markedly to the silting-up of impoundments.

The net effect of manipulation of natural and semi-natural forests for timber yield is generally to simplify them by reducing undergrowth, eliminating 'weed' species and controlling herbivorous animals who feed directly upon the trees. The ecological analogy of an intensively managed forest is an agricultural crop like grass, and indeed cropping such a forest is very much like grazing with domesticated animals.

On the other hand, the new forests which are the result of the afforestation of previously unforested land are analogous to crop agriculture. The ground is carefully prepared by ploughing and perhaps by applying chemical fertilizer; the trees are planted as seedlings from nurseries, weeded and carefully protected from grazing and browsing animals, sprayed with insecticides and generally pampered. The reasons for establishment of such forests are generally either production of cheap softwood or soil conservation, or both. Countries like Denmark and Britain which down the centuries had become denuded of forests undertook extensive planting of new forests, generally of native or imported (usually North American) conifers. In Britain the intention was principally to build up a strategic reserve of timber after the 1914–18 war, a reason only officially abandoned in 1972. In the south-eastern USA, great areas of pine plantations have stabilized some of the soils most affected by erosion following overcropping for tobacco and cotton, and they form the basis of pulp and furniture industries. In New Zealand about half the indigenous forests of the islands were removed in the century 1850–1950 (12·1 million ha to 5·7 million ha) and the establishment of large forests of exotic species, mainly pines, was undertaken after 1896 with the result that, by 1950, 360,450 ha of exotic forest had been planted, half by the State (New Zealand Forest Service 1970).

New forests are usually highly productive because the species have been chosen for their suitability for the prevailing climate, their ability to grow fast and their conformity to market demands. Some doubts about their long-term efficacy as wood producers still remain. One of these is the worry that the establishment of monocultures (necessary for the reduction of short-term costs) may make the forests prone to particular types of ecological instability. For example, small environmental shifts may allow new pests to spread rapidly and become rife. Their uniformity also means a constant fuel supply for an established fire. In addition, the short cropping cycle of 30–40 years on which forests for pulp production are maintained may take away too many nutrients for production to be sustained, especially in cool temperate latitudes where podzolic soils are part of the coniferous forest ecosystem. In such cases chemical fertilization will become a standard procedure, showing these forests to be indeed a form of intensive agriculture.

Forestry as a land use

The external and reciprocal interconnections of forest land with other land uses are of interest and significance. Its relation to agriculture and pastoralism, for example, is and has long been ambivalent. As Sears (1956) phrases it:

> The forest . . . was prized for the material it yielded and for some of the functions it performed, but it was also regarded as a rival to the space needed for crops and flocks. This two-mindedness about the forest has continued to confuse humanity down to the present day.

On the one hand, therefore, agricultural pressures have meant the clearing of forest, whether it be the great medieval clearances of Europe, the opening up of the interior of eastern North America, or the patchwork of shifting cultivation that covers so many hillsides in Asia and South America. The forest removal may be temporary, as in shifting cultivation on a relatively long rotation period, or permanent as in Europe. The result may be the substitution of a stable ecosystem such as European agriculture, or total ecological collapse through soil erosion. By contrast, forests have taken over from agriculture in some places. The abandonment of fields in Black Death Britain or twentieth-century Sweden allows forests to recolonize, and on a larger scale commercial forestry may become competitive with agriculture on marginal land during a period of agricultural intensification. Thus in upland Britain or on the sandy moraines of Denmark, farms are being replaced by forest.

The key to the interchangeability of forest and farmland may lie partially in the nutrient distribution within the natural system. In temperate latitudes where a good proportion lies in the soil and litter, stable agriculture may often replace forests provided due care is paid to the nutrient and organic matter status of the cropped soils. In the tropics, however, an ecosystem deprived of its forest vegetation loses most of its mineral nutrients and those that are left are rapidly leached away or converted to laterite. Successful 'development' of tropical forests has been largely confined to replacing a type of mixed natural

TABLE 7.11   Amount (kg/ha) of mineral nutrient required to produce 1 ton of forest and agriculture crop

	Nitrogen	Phosphorus	Potassium	Calcium
Forest	4–7	0·3–0·6	1–5	3–9
Field crops	10–17	2–3	8–26	3–8

Source: Bakuzis 1969

forest with a less diverse man-made one: rubber is the obvious example; the maintenance of a simplified forest ecosystem will also allow some cultivation beneath the dominants. Most attempts at agriculture on the European pattern have failed, since without trees the richness of the equatorial lowlands appears to be illusory. Although we cannot do without our crops, we might recall the efficiency of the forest relative to agricultural land as an energy fixer and add to that the information that trees are conservative users of minerals (Table 7.11). In time to come, this thrifty habit may find a new relevance.

The structure of the forest, and the relatively little damage that can be done to it (compared with field crops for example), have encouraged resource managers to think of multiple use as a normal aim of woodland management. Some of the possible combinations are set out in Table 7.12, which also attempts to assess the compatibility of the various components. Water is probably the most important accessory use, since undisturbed forest catchments have low silt and mineral yields and hence give water which requires little treatment. These considerations have to be balanced against the enhanced losses from transpiration, and the balance of benefits and costs probably depends upon the other uses of the forests. Domesticated animals may be grazed in forests provided that the numbers are kept to a level which does not inhibit regeneration and that areas planted with young trees are fenced.

TABLE 7.12　Compatibilities of elements of multiple use in forests

	Grazing	Water	Hunting	Wildlife observation	Recreation
Logging	Not compatible at immediate site	Long-term compatibility OK	Not compatible at site, long term OK	Not compatible	Not compatible
Grazing		OK	Not compatible	Not compatible if predators	Compatible
Water catchment					
Wildlife hunting			OK	OK OK but difficulties	OK Difficulties but separation possible
Recreation					

The use of the forest for recreation is one of the fastest-growing demands made upon the resource. A notable example of this is the Netherlands, where the State Forest Service now manages about 75 per cent of the area of its larger forests primarily for recreation, nature protection and landscape enhancement (Staatsbosbeheer 1966). Small blocks of forest have also been planted in the Netherlands purely for landscape and recreation purposes in such places as the shores of newly embanked land in the Delta project and on the edges of agricultural land in the new polders of IJsselmeer. More commonly recreation is one element of multiple-use schemes. If it is to be compatible with the other functions, it seems essential that mass recreation should be managed as part of a mosaic of different uses of the forest rather than as one of several uses of the same stand of trees. Recreation affects forest ecology in many ways, the most noticeable of which are the increased number of fires and decreased incidence of regeneration. In spite of such difficulties one study indicated that a forest area in California could increase its recreation capacity 10 times and suffer a loss of timber production of only 13 per cent (Amidon and Gould 1962). If such a conclusion were to be true of most forests, the outlook for compatibility of these two resource processes is very good.

Established forests act as a reservoir of wildlife, both plant and animal. Although the animal biomass is not very high in relation to that of the plants, some of it is very visible in the shape of birds and of mammals such as deer. Natural and semi-natural forests with plenty of glades and 'edge' habitats are particularly valuable from this point of view. Forestry operations are rarely deleterious in the long term to such animal populations, unless very large areas are clear-felled. The exceptions are the rare cases where an animal cannot tolerate humans anywhere in its vicinity: the California condor now confined to the Los Padres National Forest in California is an instance, and special status has been given to the forest land around its remaining eyries. Reciprocally, wildlife populations such as deer must usually be managed if they are not to endanger tree growth. Browse-lines are a common sight in forests where there is perhaps insufficient predation, and in such cases controlled culling is essential.

Forest policies

The importance of forests and their products is such that many countries have adopted national forest policies, and even in the LDCs one of the better legacies of the colonialist era has often been a technically competent forest service. However, it is the DCs which have on the whole evolved the more detailed national schemes.

In the USA, for example, the Forest Service of the Department of Agriculture operates principally under the Multiple Use–Sustained Yield Act of 1960. A mosaic of uses is maintained, with accessibility by motor car the determinant of facility development. The Forest Service operates only on land belonging to the Federal Government: 75·7 million ha, out of a total of 186·3 million ha, is commercial forest area. The national resource process is thus dominated by private landowners, whether in the shape of giant timber corporations or woodlots attached to farms. Both state and Federal governments influence private owners however, through taxation structures and forest practice legislation. In such a large country, with complex patterns of ownership and fragmented levels of legislation, an overall picture is impossible except to say that in general the large forest landowners are very conscious of the importance of their management programmes, and that in this they are influenced by an articulate and concerned public which expects the Forest Service to set the standards for the nation (Frome 1962).

In New Zealand, the national forest policy concentrates on the long-term management of both indigenous and exotic forests for timber production, recreation and water yield (New Zealand Forest Service 1970). In addition, however, the Forest Service is responsible for control programmes exercised on 'noxious animals'. The principal offenders are deer, whose large populations eradicate mountain vegetation and induce serious soil erosion (see p. 126). The Forest Service is also concerned with the reclamation of sandy areas, and co-operates with the National Parks Authority to preserve examples of natural forest eco-systems and scenic reserves. One sanctuary of 5,112·5 ha contains the rare kauri, and kiwi and blue-wattled crows are similarly protected by the Service. Countries with low population densities and large areas of forest need devote little attention to development for recreation. An example is Finland, where policy is to develop timber production and at present allow the recreation to look after itself. In the subarctic part of Finland, for example, there are 55 million m³ of timber with an annual growth of 870,000 m³. This growth is quite slow and regeneration uncertain in the northern part of Finland, so that investigations of climatic fluctuations, the encouragement of regeneration and the selection of suitable strains all become critical, especially as timber is the major export of the nation. Seeding using selected strains may become important even in wild terrain like Lapland (Mikola 1970). Another aim of the national policy for the northern forests is the maintenance of reindeer grazing, which plays an important role in the northern economy. A different example is the Sudan where, apart from in the south, forests do not grow easily, where the overwhelming demand upon trees is for fuel, and where government policies must be directed at securing an orderly flow of trees for this use at a reasonable price. In the 1960s a typical annual consumption of firewood and charcoal was 42 million m³, contrasting with a sawn timber production of 153,000 m³. Continued pressure on the woodlands and savannas of the Sudan is causing soil and wind erosion, sandstorms and the encroachment of the desert (Faris 1966). A major product is gum arabic, of which the Sudan is an important exporter (production in 1968 was 58,000 mt, of which 50,736 mt, value $22 million, was exported). Fortunately, gum trees (*Acacia senegal*) are regarded as 'garden' trees and are mostly grown in rotation with crops, so they share the protection afforded to agricultural crops.

As a last example we may discuss the USSR, an industrial nation with strong centralized control of resource processes. The forest lands belong collectively to a State Forest Reserve of 1,238 million ha, of which 738·2 million ha are actually tree-clad and 171·8 million ha are burned and unreforested logged areas. There are three categories of forest: group I (5·6 per cent of the total) which enjoys maximum protection and preservation and is often largely for amenity and shelter purposes; group II (7 per cent) which consists of forests covering important watersheds and woodlands in lightly forested areas of European Russia; group III (87·4 per cent) are the main productive forests subject to intensive timber harvest, and are mostly in northern European Russia, the Urals, Siberia and the Far East.

The forests are controlled by the State Forestry Committee, and out of a resource of 76×10^9 m³ an annual cut of $350–400 \times 10^6$ m³ is taken. According to Pryde (1972) there is a lack of effective sustained-yield harvesting practices, and overcutting is noticeable: a cut of 150–200 per cent of the annual growth is not uncommon in group III forests. In 1960 it was said that 10 million ha which had been cut in the previous decade had no regrowth. Forest land is also lost to fire (1 million ha/yr), insects, and reservoirs (a total of 18 million ha), as in many other countries. In spite of a centralized bureaucracy, the control exerted upon the field managers appears to be insufficient to inculcate modern forest management methods, especially in the face of what locally must be perceived to be an inexhaustible resource.

Effects of increasing human populations

Population pressure upon the world's forests is inextricably linked to scale, and three areas of concern at different scales will be examined. The first of these is the local scale in LDCs, where the pressure of population growth results in extensive deforestation. Woods are cut for fuel and building material, cleared for agriculture and subject to attrition from grazing by domestic animals. Forest policies at any scale are often absent and if they exist are unenforced. The relationships of the DCs to their forests at the national scale are rather different. Fuel needs are at present catered for mostly by fossil hydrocarbon and hydro-electric power, so that the forest becomes a supplier of timber, pulp and a desirable environment. In many places secondary forest becomes a desirable habitat for suburban houses: New England is a prime case. Virgin forest is even more desirable for second houses in the mountains or by lakes. Thus not only the trees but the whole forest ecosystem enters the economic-social-political realm and conflicts over priorities of use and manipulation assume large dimensions, especially since publicly owned forest lands become subject to pressures from all the citizens who consider they have a right to say how they should be used. Approximately 70 per cent of the world's forests are currently in public ownership (FAO 1963), although the extraction of their resources may frequently be in the hands, legal or otherwise, of individuals and companies.

If substitutes for timber are likely, but for paper less so and forest recreation not at all, then the pressures on the forests of DCs will come mainly from the conflicts between recreational use of forests and the short-cycle uniform softwoods needed for pulping. If spatial zoning can be achieved, so much the better; but the size of management units is crucial, particularly where some of the nations of Europe are concerned.

On a global scale, forests are responsible for about half the photosynthesis of the world, which means a much higher proportion of the terrestrial photosynthesis. If, as seems very likely, the balance of gases in the atmosphere is a biological artefact then the role of the forests in absorbing CO_2 and producing O_2 is very important. Just how the increase of CO_2 in the atmosphere (see pp. 283–4) and the decrease of forest area affect this balance is not known, but it seems likely that forests have an important place in the carbon and oxygen cycle of the planet. No suggestion is made here that a breakdown is imminent, but careful research into the global importance of forests is an obvious necessity. There seems to be no shortage of practical reasons for at least maintaining or at best enhancing the forest area of the planet even without acknowledging intangible values such as those exemplified by Charles Darwin in his *Journal During the Voyage of HMS Beagle*:

Among the scenes which are deeply impressed on my mind, none exceed in sublimity the primeval forests undefaced by the hand of man. No man can stand in these solitudes un-moved and not feel that there is more in man than the mere breath of his body.

Further reading

BAKUZIS, E. G. 1969: Forestry viewed in an ecosystem concept.

DUVIGNÉAUD, P. (ed.) 1971: *Productivity of forest ecosystems.*

HOLDRIDGE, L. R. 1959: Ecological indications of the need for a new approach to tropical land use.

FROME, M. 1962: *Whose woods these are.*

MEGGERS, B. J. *et al.* (eds.) 1973: *Tropical forest ecosystems in Africa and South America: a comparative review.*

NEW ZEALAND FOREST SERVICE 1970: *Conservation policy and practice.*

OVINGTON, J. D. 1965: *Woodlands.*

PRYDE, P. R. 1972: *Conservation in the Soviet Union.*

REICHLE, D. (ed.) 1970: *Analysis of temperate forest ecosystems.*

RICHARDS, P. 1952: *The tropical rain forest.*

RICHARDSON, S. D. 1970: The end of forestry in Great Britain.

WESTOBY, J. C. 1963: The role of forest industries in the attack on economic underdevelopment.

8

Food and agriculture

Humans need food as a source of energy and for tissue replacement, like any other animal. Unlike them, our intake can be divided into metabolic food, necessary for the maintenance of the organism, and cultural food where preferences, taboos and excesses are manifested. The nutritional requirements of *Homo sapiens* vary according to size, age, and the kinds of activities which each individual undertakes: Table 8.1 shows the range of energy requirements for various tasks in an industrial society, and Table 8.2 the areal energy expenditures of some subsistence agriculturalists. If the individual is to function successfully an adequate energy intake must be complemented with sufficient protein to ensure the continuous replacement of tissues and, at certain times, to enable growth to take place. Some vitamins and mineral salts also appear to be essential, and water too is an indispensable part of the human diet. Table 8.3 sets out some recommended daily allowances for various ages and conditions. Such figures must be treated with caution, since it appears that some people are quite healthy even when receiving much lower amounts, especially of energy-yielding foods: nevertheless the figures are indicative of the level of intake considered necessary by Western nutritionists.

Cultural food is the translation of our metabolic requirements into such foods as are available and, for areas where food is plentiful, into choice between different kinds of food even to the point of the onset of diseases of obesity rather than dietary deficiency. On the other hand, people receiving barely adequate nutrition will avoid certain potential foods (Kerala exports millions of protein-laden frogs' legs every year) and prehistoric hunting societies may have limited their populations to the number that could be supported by the preferred food supply rather than by the total available nourishment (see Chapter 3). Our species also ingests various organic substances derived from natural or man-made ecosystems but which are not strictly food, such as medicinal and social drugs.

TABLE 8.1   Energy requirements (kcal/hr)

Writing	20	Cycling	180–600
Dressing	33	Coal mining	320
Ironing	60	Sawing wood	420
Walking	130–240	Walking upstairs	1,000
Polishing	175	Running quickly	1,240

Source: Pyke 1970a

TABLE 8.2   Energy required for agricultural tasks (kcal/ac)

The Tsembega of New Guinea, 1962–3	
Clearing underbrush	56,628
Clearing trees	22,650
Fencing garden	34,164
Weeding and burning	18,968
Placing soil retainers	14,476
Planting and weeding until end of harvest	180,336
Other maintenance	46,000
Sweet-potato harvest	44,835
Taro harvest	5,608
Cassava harvest	2,184
Yam harvest	15,700
Cartage	119,764

Source: Rappaport 1971

TABLE 8.3   Daily dietary allowances

	Energy-yielding foods (kcal)	Protein (g)	Others
Man, 25 yrs	2,900	65	
Woman, 25 yrs	2,300	55	Calcium, iron
Woman, pregnant	2,700	80	Vitamins A and D, Thiamine, ribo-flavin, niacin, ascorbic acid
Children, 4–9	kg × 110	kg × 3·5	
Boy, 16–20	3,800	100	
Girl, 16–20	2,400	75	

Source: Pyke 1970a

Sources of food

The source of much of the food consumed by man is terrestrial agriculture. This represents the most manipulated of all the non-urban ecosystems, in which the energy and matter pathways are directed almost entirely to man and where he maintains a high level of input of matter and energy to keep the system stable in order to yield his preferred crop. Fig. 8.1 shows a schematic representation of the energy pathways in an agricultural society. Not only is the ecosystem man-made, but the plant and animal components of it have usually been genetically altered by man in the course of their domestication. There are two main types of agriculture: crop agriculture, in which the plant production is harvested for use by man either directly or after processing; and animal agriculture, where a crop from a

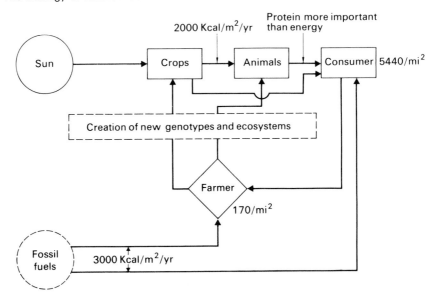

Fig. 8.1 The major flows of energy in modern agriculture. The flow of fossil power is not only applied directly by the farmer; it also fuels other activities of the consumers which result in feedbacks such as fertilizers, pesticides and improved varieties. With the aid of the fossil fuel subsidy, this agriculture can support a population density 32 times that of the farming people (1 mi² = 2·59 km²). Simplified from H. T. Odum 1971

highly manipulated ecosystem is fed to domesticated animals. (Herein lies the difference from grazing systems, where the forage is more or less wild vegetation.) Ecologically, terrestrial agriculture presents man either as a herbivore or as a third trophic level carnivore, and Fig. 8.2 shows the energy harvest from different ecosystem levels.

Considering the importance of agriculture, it appears surprising at first sight how little of the surface of the continents is cultivated (Table 8.4). Closer inspection reveals the relatively small areas of land which can be subject to the manipulation required by agriculture and still remain as stable systems; furthermore the tolerances of domesticates are inevitably rather narrow, although increasingly accurate breeding methods may aim at widening them. The proportion of land under cultivation, which includes rotation grassland and fallow, is not an infallible guide to the production of agricultural crops since multiple cropping may be possible in tropical and subtropical latitudes.

Terrestrial agriculture is not our only source of food: grazing (Chapter 5), the oceans (Chapter 9) and the so-called 'unconventional' foods (pp. 214–18) are all important, but the relative proportions vary enormously with locality. Together with terrestrial agriculture these sources also supply 'industrial crops', consisting of non-food materials such as pyrethrum, sisal, ornamental flowers and pearls. This section is concerned entirely with food, and will concentrate largely upon terrestrial agriculture and 'unconventional foods'. In passing, we should note the sometimes important but usually unquantified contribution of 'wild' foods in some societies, usually rural, although the blackberrying and bilberrying of urban Europeans forms a traditional exception.

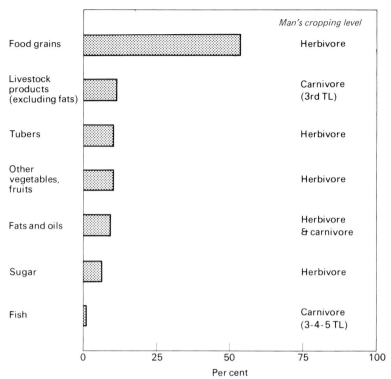

Fig. 8.2 Man's cropping level for food: his harvest is dominated by grains since wheat and rice each supply a fifth of his food energy, but offtake from other trophic levels is also common, including very high carnivore levels in the case of some fish. Yields are low compared with crops at the herbivore level. (TL = trophic level)
Source: L. R. Brown 1970

TABLE 8.4   Agricultural land (000 ha)

	Continental area, incl. inland water	Arable land, incl. fallow, non-permanent grassland, shifting agric.	% arable
Europe	493,000	14,500	29·4
North and Central America	2,242,000	27,100	12·0
South America	1,783,000	8,400	4·7
Asia	2,753,000	463,000	16·8
USSR	2,240,000	227,600	10·1
Africa	3,031,000	214,000	7·0
Oceania	851,000	47,000	5·5
World	13,393,000	1,457,000	10·8

Source: FAO *Production Yearbook 26*, 1972

The ecology of contemporary agriculture

Basic types

Agricultural systems today exhibit a major division into shifting and sedentary types. In the former, total manipulation of the natural system is practised over a limited area but for only a short (1–5 years) period of time. Thus the agricultural path is spatially and temporally enclosed by wild vegetation. Sedentary agriculture, on the other hand, aims at a permanent replacement of the natural systems by the man-made ones. Partial reversions may occur in the shape of fallow periods, but a pioneer stage of recolonization is usually all that is achieved especially if domesticated beasts are allowed to use the fallow land for grazing.

Shifting cultivation

Shifting agriculture today is largely confined to tropical forests, savannas and grasslands, although its demise in temperate zones is not particularly ancient. Its ecology has been conceptualized by Geertz (1963), who visualizes it as a miniature imitation of the closed plant community which it temporarily replaces, and this is especially so of the forest clearings. The crops are planted in a mosaic of different heights and times of fruition so that the plant cover of the soil remains as complete as possible throughout the year in order to reduce the leaching effect of heavy rainfall. The importance of mineral nutrients is emphasized by the burning which follows the clearing of the natural vegetation, for this mineralizes organic matter and allows its uptake by the crops. In virgin tropical forests most of the mineral nutrients at any one time are in the vegetation, and so 'slash and burn' provides a method of translocating some of these elements to the soil. The drain of nutrients by leaching and crop removal is traditionally the reason for the abandonment of the plots, although competition from weeds may be a more immediate factor (Cassidy and Pahalad 1953, Watters 1960). The natural diversity of the forests is imitated by the variety of crops which are grown by some shifting cultivators. Conklin (1954) describes the Hanunoo of the Philippines as recognizing 430 cultivates, of which 150 specific crop types were found in the first year of a slash-and-burn plot. Tropical crops favoured include rice, beans, root crops, shrub legumes, tree crops, yam, taro, sweet potato, vines, bananas and sugarcane, together with European-contact crops such as maize, groundnuts, tomatoes, melons and pumpkins. This cornucopian productivity is not maintained everywhere that shifting cultivation is practised: in the highlands of New Guinea, for example, there is a considerable dependence upon the sweet potato (*Ipomea batatas*), to the point where it usually provides 77 per cent of the calorie intake and 41 per cent of the total protein. Where a mixture of crops is grown then the food supply is abundant and varied, as Conklin (1957) says,

> over the first two years, a new swidden produces a steady stream of harvestable food . . . from a meter below to two meters above the ground level. And many other vegetable, spice and non-food crops are grown simultaneously.

The major disadvantage of such a system seems to be the inability to store surpluses, even when partly processed to paste and flour form. The grains are more stable but highly vulnerable to insects, bacteria and scavenging rodents. Buffering against a poor season is made very difficult by the lack of technology and even worse for groups who have come to depend largely upon one crop. In normal years, calorie intake is sufficient but there may be protein deficiency, especially in newly weaned children (2–3 years) and in adolescents: the groundnut was introduced in order to help combat this problem, especially since animal protein (pig) usually forms only 3 per cent of their protein ingestion (Conklin 1957). Breakdown of this agricultural system appears to occur when plots are re-cultivated too soon or when the system is extended into less humid areas where trees cannot re-establish themselves and a grassland establishes itself as the fallow vegetation. In both cases the mineral nutrient cycles never build up to their former levels and fertility is lower when the plot is cultivated again. The breakdown manifests itself in either or all of three ways: in malnutrition of the people, in emigration from the district, and in ecosystem disintegration particularly in the form of soil erosion. The population levels at which such a breakdown occurs are of considerable interest, but few generalizations can be made. In the forest area of Ghana, Hunter (1966) has estimated that emigration occurs when densities exceed 363–88/km², but 259–518/km² and even 777/km² appear to be carried in the New Guinea study areas. In Java, 20–50/km² has been quoted. Local circumstances vary greatly, but the general conclusion is irresistible: that shifting cultivation is an ecologically well-adapted system in forested lands where the trees regenerate easily when the plots are deserted, and where an equilibrium population has been established. Given a rapidly expanding population, the system cannot cope with the more intensive crop production needed and will either break down ecologically and socially or undergo transformation into a basically sedentary system.

Sedentary cultivation

Sedentary agriculture represents the permanent manipulation of an ecosystem: the natural biota are removed and replaced with domesticated plants and animals (Plate 14). Competition by the remnants of the original biota or by man-introduced organisms may still remain, and considerable effort may be needed to keep these weeds and pests at an acceptable level. In dryland agriculture the soil assumes an importance which it did not have in shifting systems, for it now becomes the long-term reservoir of all nutrients and is constantly depleted as crops are harvested and removed. The nutrients must be replenished either by the addition of organic excreta or chemical fertilizers. The former have the additional advantage that they usually help maintain the crumb structure of the soil as well as adding the elements necessary for plant growth. In contrast there is the important paddy-culture of rice, where the soil is very largely a mechanical rooting medium for the plants and the water supplies the essential mineral nutrients; it often contains blue-green algae which fix nitrogen, for example. Essentially this is an aquarium system with the boundaries made of earth instead of glass; it works particularly well when the catchment areas of the streams which feed the paddies drain from nutrient-rich rocks or soils. Thus paddy rice can be grown on a substratum which is very poor in essential elements and productivity can be maintained for long periods of time, since the cycle of cultivation practices ensures the replenishment of the mineral nutrients (Geertz 1963). The variety of crops grown under the various forms of

TABLE 8.5   A classification of farming systems

	Tree crops		Tillage with or without livestock	
	Temperate	Tropical	Temperate	Tropical
Very extensive Examples	Cork collection from Maquis in southern France **2**	Collection from wild trees, e.g. shea butter **1**	—	—
Extensive Examples	Self-sown or planted blueberries in the north-east USA **2**	Self-sown oil palms in west Africa **2**	Cereal growing in Interior Plains of North America, pampas of South America, in un-irrigated areas, e.g. Syria **4**	Unirrigated cereals in central Suda
Semi-intensive Examples	Cider-apple orchards in UK; some vineyards in France **4**	Cocoa in west Africa; coffee in Brazil **4**	Dry cereal farming in Israel or Texas, USA **4**	Continuous cropping in gested area Africa; rice south-east Asia **4**
Intensive Examples	Citrus in California or Israel **4**	Rubber in south-east Asia; tea in India and Ceylon **4**	Corn belt of USA; continu-ous barley-grow-ing in UK **4**	Rice and ve table-growir in south Ch sugarcane p tations thro out tropics
Typical food chains (see p. 201)	A	A	A, B	A

Ecosystem type: **1** Wild, **2** Semi-natural, **3** Man-directed, temporary, **4** Man-directed, permanent. Based on Duckham and Masefield 1970

sedentary cultivation is very high, and changing patterns of agriculture together with shifting trade flows and altered rates of consumption make a world kaleidoscope of infinite variety (Laut 1968). Table 8.5 reproduces one classification of farming systems, together with the degree of ecosystem manipulation they represent and the economic context (subsistence or commercial) in which they occur. This pattern is dominated by certain elements and Table 8.6 sets out the major crops from each of the main groups of foods and beverages, together with the totals for the group where appropriate.

Alternating tillage with grass, bush or forest		Grassland or grazing of land consistently in 'indigenous' or man-made pasture	
›perate	Tropical	Temperate	Tropical
·ting cultivation ·legev Desert, ·el **3**	Shifting cultivation in Zambia **3**	Reindeer herding in Lapland; nomadic pastoralism in Afghanistan **1**	Camel-herding in Arabia and Somalia **1**
	Shifting cultivation in the more arid parts of Africa **3**	Wool-growing in Australia; hill sheep in UK (sheep in Ireland); cattle ranching in USA **2**	Nomadic cattle-herding in east and west Africa; llamas in South America **1**
·on or tobacco ·livestock in ·south-east ·; wheat with ·and sheep ·ustralia **4**	Shifting cultivation in much of tropical Africa **3**	Upland sheep country in North Island, New Zealand **2**	Cattle and buffaloes in mixed farming in India and Africa **4**
·ated rice and ·s beef farms in ·tralia; much of ·eastern and ·hern UK, the ·herlands, north-·France, Den-·k, southern ·den **4**	Experiment stations and scattered settle-ment schemes **4**	Parts of the Netherlands, New Zealand and England **4**	Dairying in Kenya and Rhodesia highlands **4**
·, C, D	A (C)	C (D)	C

The table confirms what has already been hinted at in the discussion of domestication and what we should expect from the trophic structure of ecological systems. Firstly, in spite of an overall diversity of crops a very few of them dominate the agricultural production: the three major cereals comprise seven-ninths of the world grain crop and the three major oil-seeds likewise provide seven-ninths of the world output of this group. Secondly, meat is a very much scarcer product because it comes mostly from domestic herbivores which are inefficient users of energy, whether cropped from pastoralism or from more intensive

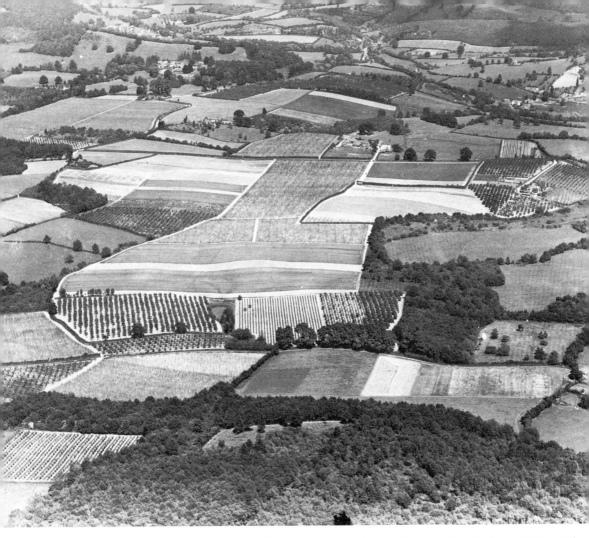

Plate 14 An agricultural landscape of high diversity near Cradley, Herefordshire, England. Fields, woods, orchards and hedgerows provide not only aesthetic pleasure but an ecological buffering system as reservoirs of predators upon the pests of man's crops. *(Aerofilms Ltd, London)*

agricultural systems. The world's dependence upon these few major crops in which there is at present a great deal of variety of plant type and technical practice to suit local circumstances is probably increased by current agricultural trends. Comparison with shifting agriculture of the numbers of people supported by sedentary agriculture is scarcely possible since so much trade is carried on. One of the most intensive of all, wet-rice paddy, appears however to be capable of supporting 2,000 persons/km² under subsistence conditions in favourable areas like Java. Odum and Odum (1972) calculate that the requirements for an American diet need 1·5 ac/cap, which would mean a density of 166/km².

TABLE 8.6   Estimated world production of certain agricultural commodities (million mt)

Average 1961–5[1]; 1972

Wheat	228	*348*	Soya beans	32·5	*53·0*
Rice	242	*295*	Cotton-seed	20·1	*24·1*
Maize	207	*301*	Peanuts	15·9	*16·8*
Total grains	924	*1,275*			
Potatoes	237	*280*	Coffee	4·3	*4·9*
Sugar (cane)	471	*581*	Tea	1·0	*1·3*
Citrus fruits	23	*35*	Cocoa beans	1·2	*1·4*
Milk (cow)	327	*375*			
Meat (beef, mutton, pig)	68	*88*			
Eggs	15	*22*			

[1] Grains for 1961 only
Sources: Duckham and Masefield 1970; FAO *Production Yearbook 26,* 1972

Agriculture as food chains

General

A simple way of viewing agriculture ecologically is to use the model of a food chain with man as the end member (Duckham and Masefield 1970). There are four of these, of which chain C (Fig. 8.3) represents the grazing ecosystem dealt with in Chapter 6. The others are chain A: tillage crops—man; chain B: tillage crops—livestock—man; and chain D: tillage crops and grassland—livestock—man. Fig. 8.3 shows the inputs of energy and matter for each of these chains and the alternative pathways through which the energy-rich organic matter comes as food to man. Examples of chain A are cereals, potatoes and sugarbeet; of chain B, bacon pigs and barley-fed beef; of chain C either a nomadic pastoralist group or an intensive beef herd on carefully managed pasture; and of chain D, a mixed farm with dairying as the main enterprise. The economics and research input of agriculture have made it possible to compare the energetics and output of each of these chains, and some information is shown in Table 8.7. The general notions about trophic structure discussed in Part I are borne out here: man as herbivore in chain A has access to far higher quantities of energy and plant protein than when he acts as a carnivore in the other chains. In these, milk is the most 'efficient' product in terms of both energy and protein, and meat is obviously a great waster of energy and a relatively poor source of gross protein, although the special nutritional qualities of animal protein make it particularly valuable. The table also hints at the basic problem of agriculture, which is that none of these chains is very efficient at energy conversion, and Table 8.8 shows some food outputs as a proportion of energy input from solar radiation; it is evident that even the

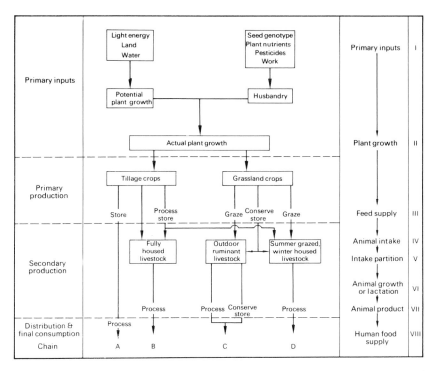

Fig. 8.3 The four food chains which characterize agriculture, with the basic stages set out on the right of the diagram. Where chain C derives its plant growth from grasslands not intensively managed then it falls into the class of the grazing system (Chapter 5). In the case of chain A, the absence of a box at the secondary production stage means that direct cropping by man at the herbivore level is practised. Source: Duckham and Masefield 1970

TABLE 8.7   Relative outputs of food chains in UK

Chain	mcal of food per 100,000 mcal solar radiation	mcal of food per acre (= ×0·405 mcal/ha)	Edible protein lb/acre (= ×0·184 kg/ha)
A (Tillage crop—man)	200–250	4,600–6,500	230
B (Tillage crop— livestock—man)	15–30	440–840	55–80
C (Intensive grassland— livestock—man)			
Meat	5–25	200	20
Milk	50–80	2,250	250
D (Grassland and crops— livestock—man)			
Milk	30–50	800	90

Source: Duckham and Masefield 1970 (1 mcal = 1,000 kcal)

herbivore chain is losing a potential energy yield, as would be expected, by respiration loss and by photosynthesizing for only part of the year. The harvest from indoor livestock and intensive milk production comes from the close attention paid to the feeding of pigs and their penning so as to avoid energy loss by movement, a feature also of intensive cattle-rearing, as is the avoidance of animal crop loss by disease, in which antibiotics play a large part.

TABLE 8.8   Energy production as a percentage of annual solar radiation

Chain	Production	Percentage of solar radiation	
A	Rice: Egypt	0·17	
	Cereals: UK	0·16	
	Potatoes and sugarbeet: UK	0·21	Energy inputs on UK farm:
B	Pig meat	0·03	Manpower: 0·001%
C	Fat lambs	0·01	Power and electricity: 0·017%
	Summer milk on experimental farm	0·08–0·15	
D	Summer and winter milk	0·05	

Source: Duckham and Masefield 1970

Individual chains

Since man is acting as a herbivore, chain A should be the most efficient at producing food. The gross energy disposal of a potato crop in the UK, excluding disease and wastage, is as follows (Duckham and Masefield 1970):

Total organic dry matter formed per acre	24,750 mcal	100%
Respiration loss	9,000 mcal	37%
Unharvested vegetation	3,750 mcal	15%
Post-harvest loss	2,250 mcal	9%
Household waste	2,250 mcal	9%
Net human food (1 mcal = 1,000 kcal)	7,500 mcal	30%

The 30 per cent of the photosynthate which becomes available as human food represents about 0·22 per cent of the total solar energy received. With such losses it is scarcely surprising that agricultural development strategists for areas of nutritional stress concentrate if possible on multiple cropping as the sure way to increase energy uptake. The potato crop referred to above was used in the UK, and therefore a lot of cultural waste occurs which might be obviated in poorer countries: peeling the tubers is quite obviously wasteful, and the above-ground parts are burnt.

Turning to chain C, a much lower efficiency is observed, as would be expected from the trophic structure of ecosystems. This example (Duckham and Masefield 1970) is an intensive grass crop grazed for beef production:

Total organic dry matter formed per acre	28,000 mcal	100%
Respiration loss	9,000 mcal	34%
Unharvested roots and stubble	3,000 mcal	11%
Uneaten grazing	4,000 mcal	14%
Faecal and urine loss	4,000 mcal	14%
Animal metabolism	5,000 mcal	17%
Tissue conversion loss	1,000 mcal	4%
Slaughter and household waste	500 mcal	2%
Net human food (1 mcal = 1,000 kcal)	1,500 mcal	4%

So this chain, cropped at carnivore level, yields 4 per cent of total photosynthate as food, which represents about 0·02 per cent of the solar energy received. Chains B and D show comparable efficiencies: pig meat from chain B may represent about 0·03 per cent of total solar radiation; milk from chain D, 0·05 per cent. All these are considerably more efficient than modified range ecosystems, where yields of 0·004 per cent of solar radiation as cattle have been found by W. A. Williams (1966).

In attempts to increase the yields of food, inputs of energy from human and fossil sources and from abiotic substances such as fertilizers and pesticides are almost universal.

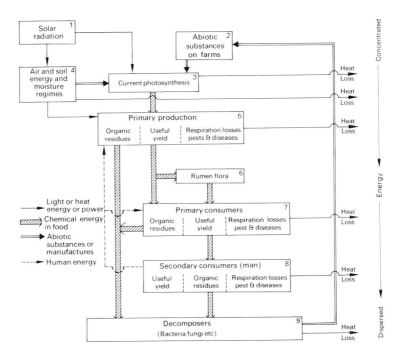

Fig. 8.4 Qualitative flows of energy and matter in a simple farming system in Uganda. In this case the crop is taken at a carnivore level via domesticated animals. Compare with Fig. 8.5, where equivalent boxes have the same numbers in them.
Source: Duckham and Masefield 1970

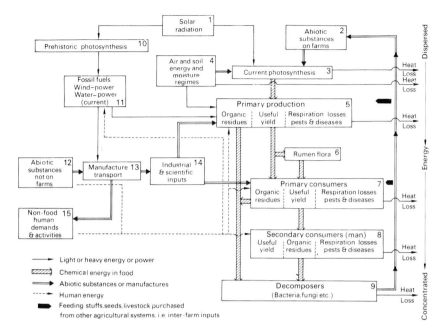

Fig. 8.5 Qualitative flows of energy and matter in a complex farming system in the UK. The greater complexity derives mainly from its linkage with the urban-industrial economy as shown on the left of the diagram. Inputs from other farms are represented by the two broad arrows on the right.
Source: Duckham and Masefield 1970

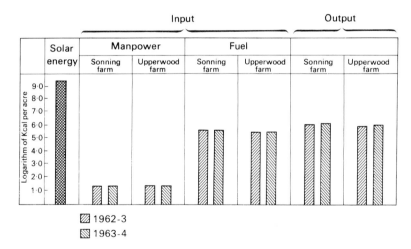

Fig. 8.6 Comparison of energy inputs (from the sun, manpower and fossil fuels) and output from two intensively managed farms in the UK for two successive years. (The vertical scale is logarithmic.) The role of fossil fuels is clear.
Source: Duckham and Masefield 1970

In a simple farming community in Uganda there is little input from outside the system: there are no fossil fuels nor any interfarm transfers of energy-rich substances like animal feeds (Fig. 8.4). In an industrial society, the farm's energy and matter relations are more complex, and the input of fossil fuels, animal feeds, pesticides and fertilizers is of considerable importance (Fig. 8.5). The latter system is much more efficient: whereas one family took 3·2 ha to feed itself in the Ugandan system, 8 workers on 178 ha in the industrialized farm produced enough food, including a high proportion of animal products, to feed 220 families (Duckham and Masefield 1970). The farm's dependence upon fossil-energy supplies for this high yield is very strong, and the relationship of manpower and fuel inputs to food output is shown in Fig. 8.6.

Constraints and buffers

Constraints and buffers operate at all scales, adding further to the diversity of agricultural types in the world. The possible constraints are both natural and man-made and the biggest is probably climate, which forms an overall frame of reference for the tolerances of the plants and animals selected and, in some areas, for the agricultural operatives too. Within the bounds of a climatic type, daily weather is also of importance in determining the crop to be taken from an agricultural system, for a deviation from the expected at a critical time in the life-history of a cultivar may be instrumental in delaying growth or even causing death. The unusual occurrence of a spell of bad weather at the time of parturition in a free-ranging domestic animal is an instance. Except in technologically complex societies the means of forecasting such eventualities are lacking, and even in the industrialized countries some farmers prefer aching toes to inaccurate broadcasts. Diseases and pests are another constraining factor which it may take large amounts of energy and matter to combat. Fossil supplies of the former are increasingly used to apply the latter, as in mechanical spraying, but the traditional energy inputs of a small boy waving his arms, or the contribution of the wind as exemplified in the *haiku* of Hagi-jo,

> His hat blown off . . .
> How pitiless the pelting
> Storm on the scarecrow

are still important in subsistence agriculture. Human constraints are of many types, most more appropriately discussed in economic or culturally oriented work, but infrastructural elements should perhaps be mentioned: if, for example, there are no roads to a farm, it is unlikely to produce cash crops or to make use of an industrial infrastructure which might make fertilizers and pesticides available. Simple economic problems may present themselves, as in the widespread case of the lack of purchasing power of the urban poor in underdeveloped countries. Thus not only do they remain malnourished, they do not stimulate increased production from traditional agricultural systems. Lastly there may be constraints resulting from the lack of knowledge of the farmer, his poor cognition of the limitations (or potentials) of farming in his locality, or simply prejudice against change.

In LDCs, food losses after harvest may significantly reduce the amount available to people. Estimates must of necessity be viewed with caution, but micro-organisms have been held to account for the deterioration of 1 per cent of the world's grain after it has been gathered. Insects are particularly likely to feed upon grains during storage, and in east Africa, corn losses of 9–23 per cent during 6–7 months' storage have been reported, along with 50 per cent losses of sorghum in the Congo during 12 months' storage and 25 per cent of rice in Sierra Leone, also during 12 months. Rodents are voracious feeders upon harvested crops, and it is suggested that 3·55 per cent (33·5 million mt) of the 1961–2 world grain-crop was lost to them; in India a loss of 20–30 per cent of stored grain from the same cause is reported. Mechanical damage is also of significance, as is the activity of mycotoxins such as those which produce aflatoxins in peanuts, possibly as an antidote to the allegedly aphrodisiac qualities of peanut butter which caused some concern in South Africa in 1971. One overall estimate suggests that if only half the post-harvest loss of food grains were prevented, the additional food would be an adequate source of calories for 500 million people in LDCs (US President's Science Advisory Committee 1967a).

To be put against these problem-inducing elements is a whole set of developments which buffer agriculture against such difficulties and stretch its capability. Energy inputs by man were the first of these and remain important, especially in some intensive systems such as paddy rice. Even here, however, the advent of the internal combustion engine has produced considerable change, and some of the crops of the 'Green Revolution' (p. 212) are heavily dependent, as is practically the whole of Western agriculture, upon fossil fuels. Storage is another buffer with an ancient history and one in which the technology is constantly being improved to prevent loss or deterioration of the crop. Not only man's food, but that of animals of lower stages in the food chains, can be stored against a rainy day or a very dry one. Dehydration, heat sterilization, radiation, fermentation, brining, smoking, freezing and chemically controlled ripening all spring to mind in this context. Continuous work on plant and animal breeding constitutes another attempt to improve the 'stretchability' of agriculture. Higher yielding strains, varieties higher in protein content (see Shapley (1973) for developments in sorghum), individuals more resistant to weather or pests, and even intergeneric hybrids like Triticale (wheat × rye), are all part of a post-Neolithic programme given added impetus by the discoveries of genetics. Molecular biology too may yield important advances in such botanical fields as the fusing of desired genetic characteristics (e.g. nitrogen fixation or resistance to a disease) into a receptor plant which then retains these important features. The use of messenger RNA to induce the high peroxidase levels which are associated with disease resistance in plants is an example of the early work (Galston 1971) which may be of considerable future significance, since such 'boosted' plants would be self-sufficient with regard to either fertilizers or pesticides and thus alleviate pollution problems such as eutrophication and the build-up of toxins. Machinery of all kinds has helped to improve agricultural production nearly everywhere, not the least being well-drilling equipment, which has made possible the extension of agriculture at the expense of other ecosystems and a greater intensity of production. Some undesirable results occasionally come to light, as in the breakdown of soil structure in European countries under a regime of continuous cereal cropping with the use of physically heavy machinery. Notwithstanding such objections, present levels of nutrition could not be achieved without the great inputs of fossil energy which is canalized through machines.

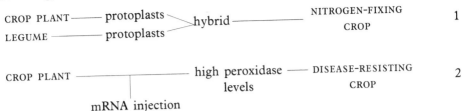

The selection of a stable agricultural system for any one place must, as with all resource processes, satisfy three main conditions. Firstly, it must be ecologically feasible in the long term and must not lead to degradation of the ecosystem by means of such processes as soil erosion or structural breakdown. Secondly, it must be economically gainful to the operator: either he must make money at it, if it is a commercial enterprise, or he and his dependants must not die of starvation if it is a subsistence farm. Lastly, the system must be culturally acceptable both to the operator and to the society in whose context he farms. He may not adopt a new system because he fears the wrath of the gods, or the spirits of his ancestors, or the chilly disapproval of his neighbours. In these days of instant communication, neighbours may extend to non-farming people: witness for example the disapproval of 'factory-farming' systems which has sprung up in some Western countries: this may have persuaded a few farmers not to switch to such enterprises. The sifting produced by each of these variables should in theory produce a stable, economic and culturally accepted agricultural system in each part of the world: perhaps the most remarkable fact is the number of places where it has done so.

Food shortages and agricultural responses

Calorie and protein deficiencies

In the case of an insufficient amount of production from the other parts of the ecosphere discussed in this book, the remedies are fairly simple: give up that particular crop (e.g. cease seeing wildlife), accept a lower-quality product (a more crowded beach) or find a substitute material (silver instead of gold). But with food, the first and last possibilities do not exist since we are dealing with a metabolic resource for which there can be no substitute. Moving to a lower quality of nutrition is a possibility, one forced upon many people with varying frequencies: it usually means a diet which may be adequate in calories but deficient in protein, especially animal protein. Beyond lower-quality food lie severe malnutrition, undernutrition and starvation. The fact that food shortages exist is undisputed, but their extent in terms of population, of temporal duration and of their relation to the needs of the deprived people rather than the possibly artificial norms of Western observers is not so well accepted. Shortages of vitamins and mineral elements such as calcium seem to be due to lack of education rather than any real deficiency in most parts of the world, although the lack of iodine (causing goitre) in some areas could only be cured by importing the element. Deficiencies in calories are difficult to pin down because of the different requirements of different people and a certain (limited) ability to adapt to lower intake levels. FAO have estimated a norm at an average of 1,990 kcal/day for LDCs and 2,520 kcal/day for DCs, but even these have been disputed as too high. The effects of deficiency of calories are sluggishness and probably a reduced resistance to disease, but fertility appears to be unimpaired. In the 1962 base year of the IWP only Japan among the A zone countries was calorie deficient, and this has now doubtless been altered by the new strains of rice. The C zone countries, the LDCs, had an overall deficit of 6 per cent for calories. North Africa had only 88 per cent of its needs, central Africa 91 per cent and east Africa 93 per cent, India was lower at 90 per cent and Pakistan very poorly supplied at 85 per cent. Other areas of the world had only small deficiencies such as west Africa at 97 per cent and Africa south of the Sahara at 95 per cent, or a surplus such as South America at 106 per cent and, highest of all, Oceania at 124 per cent. Probably about 20 per cent of the population of LDCs are undernourished in terms of calorie supply, according to FAO.

More serious shortfalls are in protein supply, the lack of which leads to deficiency diseases of which kwashiorkor is the best known. The average shortage of protein in C zone countries is 7 per cent, in which central Africa features as being able to supply only 68 per cent of its requirements. India and Pakistan are also low, at 86 per cent and 89 per cent respectively; Asia generally has a shortfall of 12 per cent. Oceania again scores highest with 127 per cent. The totality means that one-third to one-half, perhaps even 60 per cent, of the population of the LDCs suffer at some time from protein deficiency. Since proteins are less abundant in foods than starches, oils and fats, and particularly because some amino-acids (notably methionine, threonine and tryptophan) are present in large quantities only in animal proteins, they must be cropped from a higher trophic level. Production of extra protein therefore presents more difficulties than extra carbohydrate.

FAO has estimated that by 1975 the shortfalls in calories and protein for the LDCs (given certain assumptions about population trends and income levels but taking into account improved cereals) will equal 30 kcal and 4 g of animal protein per day. Thus stated the amount sounds small, but the latter estimate is equivalent to 3·6 million mt of animal protein, more than was eaten in 1962 by all the inhabitants of the EEC nations. Rising populations and higher incomes have led FAO to call for an overall increase in food production in the LDCs of 140 per cent by 1985 over 1962: an annual rate of increase of 3·9 per cent. At the end of 1972 a maximum overall rate of 2 per cent had been achieved in the LDCs; per capita production had declined, especially in the Far East.

All the evidence, however, points to malnutrition as a multifactorial problem whose causes have local variations. In some places the diet is well balanced but inadequate in quantity; in others there is a seasonal deficiency of protein; and in any of them endemic disease may prevent absorption of available nutrients. Elsewhere the social structure of a community may direct the available protein away from children and the poorer people. The complexities of malnutrition will be solved only by understanding the social and behavioural environment of the consumers as well as the provision of more calories and protein (Payne and Wheeler 1971).

Extension of agriculture

The extension of the world's agricultural area seems an obvious way to resolve some of the problems. Improved machinery, irrigation, better roads, reclamation from the sea, trans-

TABLE 8.9   Effect of various combinations of factors limiting food production

Individual factors	Land area adapted to food production: 109 ac (1 ac = 0·405 ha)	%
Adequate sunlight	35·7	100
Adequate CO_2	35·7	100
Favourable temperature	29·5	83
Favourable topography	22·7	64
Reliable rainfall	16·6	46
Fertile soil	16·3	46
Adequate rainfall	15·5	43

Combinations of factors		
1. Adequate rainfall + sunlight + CO_2	15·5	43
2. Adequate and reliable rainfall + CO_2 + sunlight	12·2	34
3. Temperature + adequate and reliable rainfall + CO_2 + sunlight	11·4	32
4. Topography + temperature + rainfall + CO_2 + sunlight	7·4	21
5. Fertile soil and all others	2·6	7

Based on data in Pearson and Harper 1945

TABLE 8.10   Selected sub-regional totals for potential arable land

	Arable land 1962 Percentage of potential arable land	Proposed arable land 1985 Percentage of potential arable land	Potential arable land	
			Million	% of total area
Central America	64	76	46	19
South America	19	26	524	30
North-west Africa	100	100	295	6
South Asia (excl. Sri Lanka)	93	96	201	48
South-east Asia (incl. Sri Lanka)	44	57	47	47
Far East	81	97	4	28

Source: FAO *Indicative world plan for agriculture* 1970, **1**

formation of other ecosystems, all ought to provide a greater agricultural area. Inspection of the potential reveals, however, a relatively small area of 'virgin' land suitable for modern agriculture. On a world scale, the ecologically limiting factors are set out in Table 8.9. All the world has adequate sunlight and CO_2 for some form of photosynthesis, but when all other necessities like topography and soil are considered the proportion of the terrestrial surface suited to agriculture falls to 7 per cent. This is probably a pessimistic estimate since *de facto* about 9 per cent appears currently to be thus utilized, but some of it doubtless would be more stable as forest or grassland ecosystems. Regional estimates for the expansion of arable land in the LDCs are given in Table 8.10. The increases are mostly modest but greater than the expectations of the previous table, owing to advances in agricultural technology and resource appraisal. Nevertheless in three regions the 1985 total is at or near to the limit of potential and so further expansion will be nearly impossible. Again, the expansions suggested may need considerable cultural adjustments such as the resettlement of graziers and nomads as well as the relatively easier tasks of drainage or tsetse eradication. Irrigation will of necessity play a large part in agricultural expansion, and if schemes are not to end up choked with salt and silt then considerable technical skill in both planning and day-to-day management is required. Irrigation already accounts for 11 per cent of the world's cultivated land, and two-thirds of the world's population live in the diet-deficient countries which contain 75 per cent of the irrigated land, so that its importance to the malnourished is greater than world statistics imply. IWP envisages a faster growth rate for new irrigation schemes than for non-irrigated harvested lands, together with equally important investments in modernizing existing schemes. All such expansions, in the words of the Indicative World Plan, are unlikely to be 'easy, rapid or cheap'.

Intensification

Most authorities agree that this process holds most promise of improving food yields from existing cultivated lands. It is a complex sequence of events which brings a low-yielding traditional agriculture into connection with the technology and economics of industry. Thus a great deal of capital and management skill are needed for success in applying developments such as irrigation, flood control, drainage, erosion control, mechanization, fertilizer and biocide use and the raising of improved varieties of plant and animal (Plate 15). The keys to intensification are energy availability, both on-site and in the places where tractors, pesticides, pumps and the milk are made; a steady effective demand for the products of the farming system; and good communications between the source of supply of the input, the farm, and the consumers. The doubling of agricultural production in the LDCs in the period 1966–85 will require an increased application of plant nutrients from 6 million mt to 67 million mt, and from 120,000 mt to 700,000 mt of pesticides, representing capital outlays (in 1966 US dollars) of 17×10^9 and 1.87×10^9 respectively (US President's Science Advisory Committee 1967b). This assumes the availability of the appropriate materials: in discussing phosphates Eyre (1971) notes that 80 per cent of the phosphate fertilizer was used in western Europe, North America and the USSR in 1968–9, and that north German agriculture received twice as much as the combined systems of

India, Pakistan and Indonesia. 'One must doubt,' he says, 'the feasibility of so expensive a commodity being made available in vast quantities to poor countries.'

The best-known intensification is the so-called 'Green Revolution', the development of new high-yielding and high-protein crops of basic cereals, especially the wheats bred by the International Corn and Wheat Improvement Center in Mexico and rice strains evolved at the Institute of Rice Research in the Philippines (Harrar and Wortman 1969). Of these the development of IR-8-288-3 ('miracle rice') is the most famous. The highly bred grain matures early after rapid growth and is insensitive to day length so that in the tropics and subtropics two to three crops per year become practicable; resistance to lodging is another important characteristic. IR-8 was developed from a cross between two *Indica* rice strains, and matures in 120–30 days. Its top yield averages 1,067 kg/ha (5,800 lb/ac) compared with the 368–405 kg/ha (2,000–2,200 lb/ac) of its parents and 239–331 kg/ha (1,300–1,800 lb/ac) of most local varieties in the Philippines. IR-5 is also an important new variety

Plate 15 An agricultural landscape of low diversity in the Noord-Ost polder of the IJsselmeer scheme of the Netherlands. This also shows one of the major sources of creation of new land for agriculture—from the sea. *(Aerofilms Ltd, London)*

since it cooks dry and fluffy, whereas IR-8 tends to become soggy as it cools and thus is culturally less acceptable in some places (zu Lowenstein 1969). Such yields can only be obtained with careful cultivation. Fertilizers are the key element: IR-8 needs 13·0–16·5 kg/ha (70–90 lb/ac) of nitrogenous fertilizer applied at particular times, together with a continuous water supply, and the use of biocides; the traditional criteria for harvesting time have also to be abandoned. In spite of these sophisticated requirements the spread of new varieties of cereals has been rapid, as is shown by the estimated figures for Asian acreages planted to all new grain types (Ehrlich and Ehrlich 1972).

1964–5	200 ac	81 ha
1965–6	37,000 ac	14,985 ha
1966–7	4·8 million ac	1·9 million ha
1967–8	20 million ac	8·1 million ha
1968–9	34 million ac	13·7 million ha
1969–70	44 million ac	17·8 million ha

Equally important is realization of higher yields per capita (Table 8.11), although sober reflection reveals the harsh fact that population can expand far more steadily than any agricultural output, which tends to come in surges with development of new technologies.

TABLE 8.11   Impact of production using new seeds

	Annual production of selected cereals using new seeds (lb/person of total population (1 lb = 0·4536 kg))			
	India, wheat	Pakistan, wheat	Sri Lanka, rice	Mexico, all cereals
1960	53	87	201	495
1961	55	83	196	496
1962	59	87	213	525
1963	51	86	218	546
1964	46	83	213	611
1965	56	90	150	639
1966	46	71	188	649
1967	49	80	216	655
1968	76	116	247	680
1969	80	121	n.a.	n.a.

Source: Brown and Finsterbusch 1971

Two biological dangers are inherent in the 'Green Revolution', both of which stem from the lack of genetic diversity in new crops. Hitherto, individual farmers selected their variety according to their own idiosyncrasies and so a mosaic of different strains was produced. With the new types large contiguous areas are planted to one strain and so pathological susceptibility is multiplied. A small change in climate allowing the expansion of the range of an insect or a new strain of rust would cause a major disaster: the new wheats of India, Pakistan, Iran and Turkey might all fail at the same time, although more likely are less extensive failures such as the failure of 10 per cent of the hybrid corn in the Middle West in 1971 because of southern corn leaf blight (Dasmann 1972). Also, the breeding of the new strains means that the genetic diversity present in the old varieties is in danger of being lost, and a programme of cultivation and storage of seeds of all geno-types is absolutely essential (Frankel 1969). If such fears do not materialize then production will be very high indeed, and many modifications to current marketing practices, pricing structures and trade patterns must be made: what, for example, will become of the tradi-tional rice-exporting nations of Asia? On the one hand the potentials unleashed are immense; on the other the price paid for the increased production is an enhanced risk of widespread catastrophe, particularly if the cornucopian aspects are used as an excuse to lessen the emphasis upon population control programmes in cereal-dependent nations (Wharton 1969). Socially, the introduction of the new varieties in a nation like India have swept away a great deal of conservatism on the part of farmers, but the selective impact of the agricultural changes has created unrest on the part of the many who want to be part of the new deal but cannot find the means to get started. Problems of land tenure have also been exacerbated, since rents have often risen as high as 70 per cent of the new crops and some owners would now like to get rid of tenants altogether. The introduction of a technical revolution without understanding of its cultural context is always likely to be fraught with problems (Ladejinsky 1970). There needs to be effective demand from consumers: the penniless cannot buy all the IR-8 in the world. And beyond this there is the concomitant problem of how all the people displaced by even moderately efficient agriculture are to be employed: industrialization to give them all jobs would have to be on a totally unprecedented scale, although the development of a mechanized, industrially based agriculture could come to involve 30 per cent of the working population as it does in the USA (Paddock 1971).

New sources of food

Biological resources

Even if the rapid development of conventional agriculture is sustained, most authorities agree that protein deficiencies will continue to exist. A search for supplementary sources of both plant and animal proteins is therefore in progress, with some emphasis on the latter since their amino-acid make-up is closest to man's requirements. Animal flesh has the further advantage that it is usually the more easily assimilable, since the plant proteins are locked away behind a cell wall of cellulose not easily broken down by the action of the human stomach. Animals have thus been a means of harvesting the plant protein in a digestible form, and so have considerable dietary advantages in spite of the energy losses due to their position in the trophic structure of an ecosystem: looked at economically, the livestock industries of DCs are gigantic welfare societies for domestic animals which return only 10 per cent of the energy invested in them by way of foodstuffs. If animals are to be avoided, a food source which will yield plant protein in a digestible form or from which the majority of cellulose has been removed is clearly attractive. Fungi appear to be easily assimilated and contain a good deal of protein by comparison with some other sources (Table 8.12). Other advantages are that they do not absorb much human or fossil energy in production, can be grown independently of environmental factors in places such as caves and abandoned railway tunnels, can readily be stored in dried form and require little sophisticated knowledge or technology (Pyke 1970b).

TABLE 8.12   Comparative yield potential of mushrooms

	lb/dry protein/ac/yr ($\times 0.184$ kg/ha)
Conventional methods of beef production	70
Fish farming	600
Mushroom growing in UK	60,000–70,000

Source: Pyke 1970b

Requiring rather more technology but readily available are leaves which are not normally cropped or which are fed upon by animals. Within their cells is a considerable harvest of protein if this can be separated from the fibrous material of the leaf and made palatable. Pirie (1969) notes that protein was extracted from leaves as early as 1773, but that the effort devoted to it by modern research is minimal. Leaves which are the by-products of another crop could be used and the fibre returned to the soil as a texture-maintaining essential, or otherwise unused grasses, shrubs or marginal aquatics might be harvested. Thus any leafy plant becomes a potential protein source, providing it is susceptible to propagation and harvesting. The potential of the tropics is especially high and the cropping of leaf protein would make attractive the retention of much of the forest cover, and help to prevent ecological degradation. Apart from harvesting, the major industrial input required is processing the extract to the point where it becomes palatable either by itself or as an additive to other foods. This need not be difficult but inevitably adds both to the cost and to the number of trained technicians who are needed (Pirie 1970). The potential is immense and probably greatly undervalued, since protein yields of 1,200 kg/ha/yr have been obtained with legumes in Britain, and 3,000 kg/ha/yr should be possible in the tropics; these harvests could be raised to 2,000 kg/ha/yr and 5,000 kg/ha/yr respectively if nitrogen fertilizer were added to the appropriate ecosystem (Arkcoll 1971). Algae are groups of plants which have received a good deal of attention as possible sources of food, especially the noncellular varieties which under optimal conditions have exceptionally high rates of primary productivity. 5 m² devoted to algae production could feed one man 10^6 kcal/yr, whereas it would take 1,200 m² of grain and 4,000 m² of pork to reach the same level. Since algae would be cultured in tanks, non-agricultural surfaces such as roof-tops might become food-producing. The potential yields have, however, been stressed at the expense of the drawbacks. Production of algae would be a very technical process, requiring stirring, bubbling of carbon dioxide, sophisticated machinery and skilled man-power (Pirie 1969). All things considered, the net energy input might be higher than the output and only if this were an acceptable price to pay for protein would the process become economically gainful; unquestionably it would depend upon the continued supply of cheap fossil-energy supplies. Algae are demonstrably not the panacea that has been claimed for them, especially in terms of dependence as in Nigel Calder's book, *The environment game* (1967).

Energy-wasters though they are, animals retain many desirable characteristics as cellulose-converters and as saliva-inducers. That so few species have become domesticated is often a source of wonder, and only recently has the potential of many wild animals been realized. If sustained-yield practices are adopted, together with minimal amounts of processing, many wild animals come within the ambit of possibility: most are eaten somewhere. Birds such as young colonial seabirds, reptiles and amphibians are probably under-utilized, and a larger beast like the aquatic manatee which might feed on such nuisances as water hyacinths is also a feasibility. The large South American rodent *Capybara* (about 1·3 m long) which feeds on aquatic weeds is another candidate of Pirie's (1969). New domestications, among which the eland and the African buffalo rank as favourites (Jewell 1969), would be useful too, particularly if they ate plants which currently go unharvested.

Fresh-water and brackish-water fish are other sources capable of development, especially in the tropics (Tables 8.13 and 8.14), where high yields are taken from fertilized ponds (Table 8.14) (milkfish in the Philippines are a good example). Israel and the USSR are also intensive raisers of fresh-water fish, whose protein content is very high (Hickling 1970).

TABLE 8.13   Comparisons of milkfish (*Chanos chanos*) yields (lb/ac (× 0·184 kg/ha))

Country	Milkfish total	Fish total	Total edible protein (dry weight) %	
Java	180	280	15·1	Unfertilized
Taiwan	958	958	51·7	Fertilized
Philippines	300	300	16·2	Unfertilized
Agric. land: swine		450		
cattle		250		

Source: Walford 1958

TABLE 8.14   Yields of milkfishes and various shads (000 mt)

Country	1964	1966
Taiwan	30·7	19·0
India	9·9	8·5
Pakistan	7·1	4·7
South Korea	2·0	6·4
Philippines	62·7	146·0
USSR	324·0	344·6

Source: FAO *Yearbook of Fishery Statistics 28*, 1969

In Asia, yields seem to be declining, possibly as a result of pesticide runoff and of conversion of the ponds to rice-growing; fish were harvested from rice paddies under some traditional systems of agriculture, but multiple cropping has cut into the life cycle of the fish and so this additional protein source is no longer available. In Hong Kong, small ponds have suddenly begun to be very popular with farmers, who also keep ducks which enrich the water and are marketable as well. The remaining aquatic source of food, detritus feeders, is dealt with in the chapter on the sea.

Where industrial technology is available, the choice of organisms for food can be widened, since close control of growth conditions and subsequent processing can be achieved. A first stage in industrialized food is the processing of otherwise unpalatable materials to yield either desirable food or a neutral substance which, if not exactly mouth-watering, is at least not repellent. For example, the soya-bean is high in protein and also highly adaptable, so that its content of plant protein can be disguised as (*inter alia*) turkey or pork sausages via flavouring, colouring and texturizing. It is also cheaper than another alternative, Fish Protein Concentrate. Many unmarketable fish can be defatted, deboned and dehydrated to a white tasteless powder that can be further processed or sprinkled on food as a powder additive. Its disadvantages include a complex and expensive processing procedure, but even so the marketed product is cheap if it can be got to places where it is needed without increasing its cost unduly.

Industrial food

Production of food by industrial processes which altogether sidestep contemporary photo-synthesis offers new possibilities. Bacteria and fungi form the basis of the technique, with yeasts as the group upon which most work has been done. The substrates upon which yeasts can be induced to grow under industrial conditions include waste whey, some sugar waste, sulphite liquor and sewage. The cellulose in paper and sulphite liquor could be used to grow yeasts: one-third of the paper waste of the USA could supply one-third of its calories, but protein yields are less satisfactory (Mateles and Tannenbaum 1968). The most satisfactory substrates so far tested on an industrial scale have been the hydrocarbon by-products of petroleum. These are available in large quantities and not being agricultural products are relatively constant in supply and price. Yeasts grown upon them can be processed to a powder of dead cells containing 35–75 per cent of crude protein. Lysine content is adequate or even high, although methionine and tryptophan are relatively low: rumen bacteria offer future possibilities here because of their high content of these amino-acids. The two hydrocarbons which have been selected for yeast production are gas oil and n-paraffins. Gas-oil-grown yeasts give a product which is 70·5 per cent dry weight of crude protein and also contains 2,550 kcal/kg; n-paraffins yield 65 per cent dry weight of protein and 2,550 kcal/kg. (The FAO standard for a 25-year-old 65-kg male is 3,200 kcal/day, so the product is clearly not likely to be a major energy source.) The basic requirements for the process are pure water as suspension medium, the hydrocarbon substrate, access to balanced concentrations of mineral ions and certain trace ions, continuous supply of oxygen and eliminations of excess carbon dioxide, a pH in the range 3·5–6·5 and a controlled temperature of $30° \pm 2°C$. Constant stirring is necessary to mix the hydrocarbons, the water and the oxygen, so that this has to be supplied; however, the consumption of the substrate is correspondingly reduced: 1 kg of sugar will produce 0·5 kg of yeast, whereas 1 kg of hydrocarbon will yield 1 kg of yeast. The gas-oil variant of this process must be associated with an oil refinery, but the n-paraffin substrate can be used wherever the raw materials are available so it would be theoretically possible to site it near a market. A refinery-based plant in France is producing 16,000 mt/yr of feed-grade protein (Champagnat 1965; Mateles, Baruah and Tannenbaum 1967; Shacklady 1969). Useful as this process is, it is tied to industrial technology and skill together with fossil-energy inputs, and so the problems of providing cheap protein for those most needing it are very considerable and will not be quickly overcome. Nevertheless cheap sources such as these yeast flours, currently being produced largely as animal foodstuffs for non-ruminants like pigs and chickens, offer large-scale possibilities for food fortification programmes. Together with other concentrated sources of food they can be added to traditional diets which are low in protein or added to 'luxury' items such as carbonated soft drinks which are sought by even the poorest people. In such supplementation and fortification schemes, amino-acids produced purely by industrial synthesis are also important, especially lysine; most bread in Indian cities has such an additive, as does 30 per cent of the bread used in Japanese school-lunch programmes. The cheapness of industrially synthesized amino-acids means that they can be fed to poultry and non-ruminant animals instead of conventional animal foodstuffs, soya-bean or FPC products (Pyke 1971). Industrially processed high protein foods may be used: Incaparina has been successfully sold as an infant and child food in Latin America. It consists of cotton seed and maize flour plus vitamins and minerals, and has 28 per cent high-quality protein enriched with lysine. Another product for infants is Duryea, a blend of degermed high-lysine maize flour, soya flour and non-fat dry milk; this costs only half as much as milk protein. The US Government distributes overseas CSM and WSB, which are foods on a corn or wheat basis plus added vitamins, minerals and protein, usually of the order of 20 per cent. Most of these foods and additives have been developed in the West; few LDCs have their own plants for such products (Altschul and Rosenfeld 1970).

The effect of increasing human populations

Population growth is more often considered in terms of the future availability of adequate nutrition than any other factor. The result is a complete lack of unanimity in forecasts, from famine in 1975 to enough and to spare. The effects of the Green Revolution and of industrial sources of food production cannot yet be assessed with any long-term meaning, and as C. Clarke (1967) demonstrates, if nutrition patterns are reduced from the US level to the Japanese standard then it ought to be possible to feed a lot more people. The surpluses of Europe and North America might by 1980 amount to 10 per cent of world food production and be used to make good some of the deficiencies in Asia, provided it was politically acceptable. Such a contribution, either as aid or trade, could only make an impact for a

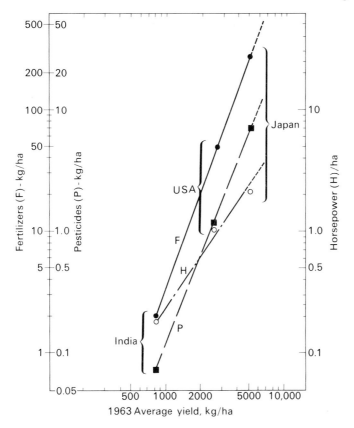

Fig. 8.7 Relationships between yield of food crops and requirements for fertilizer (F), pesticides (P) and horsepower (H) used in cultivation and harvest of crops. Doubling the yield of food requires a 10-fold increase in the use of fertilizers, pesticides and animal or machine power.
Source: E. P. Odum 1971

limited period given a rise in Asian populations of 2 per cent a year: as soon as 1980, four-fifths of the increase in world population will be in LDCs where the food situation is already bad. To these additional people must be added an escalation of demand from developing societies whose better standard of living generates higher expectations, and of those whose aspirations are fuelled by worldwide electronic communications and better levels of literacy; Brown (1971) suggests these may be more potent than population growth. In the face of rapidly expanding food requirements, agriculture must be the main source of food in the foreseeable future, despite contributions from industrial and marine sources; but expansion of production is beset with difficulties both ecological and cultural (Farmer 1969, Hendricks 1969). Extension of the cultivated area is constrained largely by problems of stability of the new systems, where soil breakdown and erosion are common. The greatest reserves of potential agricultural land are in sub-Saharan Africa and the Amazon basin, if the successful management of tropical soils can be achieved and if these lands are not more valuable on a world basis as protective ecosystems; but even in technologically advanced countries like the USA and USSR soil erosion is a problem. In the latter, 30–35 million ha of arable land are affected by water erosion, and 20–25 million ha of cropland are subject to wind erosion; 1·8 per cent of all arable land is classified as 'very heavily eroded' (Pryde 1972). With intensification, the main process is the linkage of agriculture to the industrial world, and some results can be seen in Table 8.15. This comparison is to some extent invalidated by the more recent advent of the new varieties of cereals, but it stands as an example of the differences between an advanced agriculture and a simpler system; in more general terms, the statistics of Table 8.16 show that the production of a fossil-fuel-subsidized agriculture is able to support a much greater number of people than

TABLE 8.15   Comparison of agriculture in Japan and India, 1960

	Yield (kcal/cap/day)	Value of agric. output (US $)	Chemical fertilizers used (kg/ha)	% urban pop.	Tractors per 1,000 ha	Biocides applied (mt)
Japan	2,360	961	303·7	18	1·55	150,000
India	2,060	91	2·3	64	0·21	10,000

Source: Dasmann 1972

TABLE 8.16   Outputs of agricultural systems

System	Yield (kcal/m²/yr)	Persons/mi² supported On farm	In cities
Tribal agriculture	20	50	0
Unsubsidized agriculture	245	600	100
Fuel-subsidized agriculture	1,000	150	2,350
		(1 mi² = 2·59 km²)	

Source: E. P. Odum 1971

one in which there are no ties with the world of industry. Such increases in output are not achieved without costs of various kinds; intensification is expensive for, as Fig. 8.7 shows, a doubling of agricultural output per unit area requires a tenfold increase in the inputs of fertilizers and pesticides. Apart from their monetary cost, such heavy use is likely to create dependence upon an advanced country for supplies which may bring political strings with them. Biologically, the new system will be monocultural and hence prone to instability, and the runoff of surplus fertilizer and pesticides (not always used exactly according to the manufacturer's instructions) creates problems of eutrophication and toxification. In some LDCs the latter may reduce protein supplies, as has happened in Asia, where fish yields of 30–145 kg/ha from unfertilized rice paddies have been wiped out or made unpalatable by the use of γ-BHC to control the rice stem borer (Kok 1972).

Intensification also depends upon a series of inputs of the type described by L. H. Brown (1971) as 'non-recurring improvements'. For example, the ability of plants to respond to fertilizer has an upper limit, as does the capacity for faster growth conferred by hybridization; soya-bean cannot be hybridized and shows a limited response to nitrogenous fertilizer. An inevitable result of any intensification programme is, therefore, an S-shaped yield curve, sometimes for economic reasons like the cost of energy or input materials, sometimes the result of technical considerations like the genetics of a particular crop plant. As a context to the whole development, food prices become critical, especially in relation to the costs of energy, fertilizers, water and pesticides. The role of properly trained personnel at all levels is also an important part of intensification and can sometimes be a limiting factor, as can the gap between the promise of a crop in an experimental farm and its performance under the less controlled conditions up-country. In addition, Borgstrom (1965) has pointed

TABLE 8.17   Water requirements in food production: temperate climates (lb H_2O per lb organic matter) (1 lb = 0·4536 kg)

Millet	200–250
Wheat	300–500
Potatoes	600–800
Rice	1,500–2,000
Vegetables	3,000–5,000
Milk	10,000[1]
Meat	20,000–50,000[1]

[1] Includes water needed for production of foodstuffs.
Source: Borgstrom 1965

out the possibility that water may be a limiting factor on agricultural production: it takes 35 US gallons (132·5 litres) to make a slice of bread, and as Table 8.17 shows, other food crops are high water users as well. To these amounts should be added the water needs of industrially based inputs such as fertilizers where 1 ton (1,016 kg) requires 150,000 US gallons (56·8 × 10⁴ litres) of water in its production, and food processing where 1 ton of edible oil requires 35 tons (35·5 mt) of water (Paddock 1971).

While photosynthesis is the dominant process in supplying our food, there must be an overall limit to the number of people that can be fed: there is considerable scope for trying to improve both the efficiency of photosynthesis and the proportion of it which we garner, but an overall limit must be present. Feeding even larger numbers of people approaching both the present and potential limits, without a considerable safety margin, would seem unwise. The perspective of ecology upon food production thus becomes less 'Can we feed the population we have and are likely to get, given also their rising expectations?' (to which the answer is 'Probably, yes'), but rather 'What are the ecological consequences of doing so?' (H. Brown 1970). Every move towards simplification of ecological systems produces higher chances of wider fluctuations and thus greater risks, many of which inevitably fall upon the LDCs, whose ability to cope with them is less buffered than that of the technologically advanced nations. In the DCs the intensive agriculture which is so successful has suffered from overcropping, and is a source of contaminants via animal waste, fertilizers and pesticide residues. And even assuming success in feeding immensely greater numbers of people (and pessimism is still prevalent (Wade 1973)), there is a fundamental question of purpose: do we want the planet's management to be geared almost entirely to the production of food?

Further reading

BRADY, N. C. (ed.) 1967: *Agriculture and the quality of our environment.*
BROWN, L. R. and FINSTERBUSCH, G. 1972: *Food.*
DASMANN, R. F. *et al.* 1973: *Ecological principles for economic development.*
DE WIT, C. T. 1967: Photosynthesis: its relation to overpopulation.
DUCKHAM, A. N. and MASEFIELD, G. B. 1970: *Farming systems of the world.*
GEERTZ, C. 1963: *Agricultural involution.*
GOUROU, P. 1966: *The tropical world.*
HENDRICKS, S. B. 1969: Food from the land.
LOW, P. F. 1972: Prospects for abundance: the food-supply question.
PIRIE, N. W. 1969: *Food resources: conventional and novel.*

9

The sea

The world's greater water bodies are perhaps less affected by man than any of the terrestrial ecosystems which have been treated so far. Byron could write:

> Roll on, thou deep and dark blue ocean—roll!
> Ten thousand fleets sweep over thee in vain;
> Man marks the earth with ruin—his control
> Stops with the shore.

and we can generally agree, with the proviso that if control stops with the shore, nowadays the ruin certainly does not; but it decreases quite quickly away from it. There are large areas of the oceans unfrequented by man because of their very size: approximately 71 per cent of the globe's surface is composed of the oceans together with the enclosed and fringing seas; volumetrically, this means about $1 \cdot 5 \times 10^{18}$ mt (330 million mi³) of water. The frozen water of the polar ice-caps forms some of the remaining land, although in this case the water is fresh and not salt.

A structurally important feature of the oceans is their depth. Whereas only 2 per cent of the land is over 10,000 ft (3,048 m) above the sea, 77 per cent of the ocean floor is more than that depth below sea level; the great trenches of the Philippines and the Marianas have a depth of 35,000 ft (10,668 m) and hence are deeper than the highest terrestrial mountain. Beyond the coastline there are three main zones: the continental shelves, descending gradually to about 650 ft (198 m) below sea level and the site of most human effects upon marine ecosystems; the continental slope, falling steeply from the edge of the shelf to about 8,000 ft (2,438 m); and beyond that the deep ocean. Being most accessible to the land masses as well as the shallowest part of the ocean, the continental shelf is most often emphasized in studies of marine resources.

The salt nature of the water of the oceans appears to be derived from inwash off the land masses in which soluble minerals and particulate matter contribute to the salinity, which is thought to have been at a virtually stable level during the last 2,000 million years. The organisms of the sea must therefore play an important role in removing minerals from the liquid-soluble phase, otherwise a secular increase in concentration would be expected. The present-day average salinity at $-1,000$ ft (-305 m) is 35 parts per thousand; nearer the surface there are regional effects such as the high evaporation rate and lack of freshwater inflow that produce salinities of 45/1,000 in the Red Sea, or the opposite situation which produces values as low as 10/1,000 in the Baltic. The chemical elements which produce this salinity are endlessly varied, since if an element is present on the land it will sooner or later find its way into the sea. There are, however, enormous differences in concentration, from chlorine as sodium chloride at 166,000 lb/million gallons (19.8×10^3 kg/10^6 litres) down to gold at 0.004 lb/million gallons (0.001 kg/3.7×10^6 litres). The commonest elements are of course the most important, since it is to their presence and concentrations that marine life has had to adapt, and it is they, together with offshore deposits of certain kinds, that constitute the inanimate resources of the oceans. Other resource processes for which the oceans are used include the harvesting of fish, shellfish and other marine life, including water fowl; recreational activities and the provision of aesthetic pleasure; navigation, the dilution and dispersal of wastes, and to a limited but increasing extent the extraction of a domestic and industrial water supply.

Mineral resources

The sea's mineral resources can be divided into three categories: those which are dissolved in the water itself; sediments present on the sea-bed at various depths; and those present at some depth below the sea-floor, beyond the sediments of relatively recent origin.

At present the utility of the dissolved elements is in direct proportion to their abundance and to the relative cost from terrestrial sources. Table 9.1 shows some of the commonest elements present and the 1968 values of the minerals that could be extracted. Common salt immediately springs to mind as one of the resources that has been utilized since prehistoric times for its value in flavouring and meat preservation. At present only salt, magnesium and bromine are being extracted in commercial quantities and the sea does indeed seem to be inexhaustible for these elements: presumably replenishment is taking place at an equal if not higher rate. The first few elements in Table 9.1 offer the highest chances of economically feasible recovery processes, but others lower down, even when they are sought-after metals such as zinc, do not seem a very likely prospect except in the direst of circumstances. For example, 9,000 billion gallons ($34,065 \times 10^9$ litres) of sea water, equal to the combined annual volume of the Hudson and Delaware Rivers, would yield 400 (406.4 mt) tons of zinc. In 1968, 122,400 tons (124,358 mt) of that metal were used in the USA alone (Cloud 1969). It may be possible to lower feasibility thresholds by investigating the capacity of marine organisms to concentrate desired elements (this is done *de facto* for nitrogen used in the form of fish-meal fertilizer and in sea-bird guano), and in the possible exploitation of zones along the sea-bed where fractures allow the escape of unusually high concentrations of mineral ions. As far as minerals are concerned the oceans are more like *consommé* than Scotch broth, and the technology of handling the appropriate volumes of water is poorly developed, but presumably the economic perception of the minerals would be greatly changed by advent of the cheap and ubiquitous power envisaged by Weinberg and Hammond (1971).

Sediments and sedimentary rocks on the continental shelves are sources of certain materials. Placer deposits contain workable quantities of gold, tin and diamonds, and other sediments which may be amenable to exploitation include sand, gravel and shells. The land-use problems created by their extraction from the land would largely be obviated by the use of the sea as a source, provided that the ecosystems of the oceans were not too

TABLE 9.1   Concentration and value of the elements in sea water

Element	Concentration lb/10^6 gal (kg/8·34 × 10^6 litres)	As	Value $/10^6$ gal (10^6 gal = 3·785 × 10^6 litres)
Chlorine	166,000	NaCl	924
Sodium	92,000	Na_2CO_3	378
Magnesium	11,800	Mg	4,130
Sulphur	7,750	S	101
Calcium	3,500	$CaCl_2$	150
Potassium	3,300	K_2O (equiv)	91
Bromine	570	Br_2	190
Carbon	250	Graphite	8 × 10^{-5}
Strontium	70	$SrCO_3$	2
Boron	40	H_3BO_3	3
Silicon	26	—	—
Fluorine	11	CaF_2	0·35
Argon	5	—	—
Nitrogen	4	NH_4NO_3	1
Lithium	1·5	Li_2CO_3	36
Rubidium	1·0	Rb	125
Phosphorus	0·6	$CaHPO_4$	0·08
Iodine	0·5	I_2	1
Barium	0·3	$BaSO_4$	0·01
Indium	0·2	In	4
Zinc	0·09	Zn	0·013
Iron	0·09	Fe_2O_3	0·001
Aluminium	0·09	Al	0·04
Molybdenum	0·09	Mo	0·004
Selenium	0·04	Se	0·2
Tin	0·03	Sn	0·05
Copper	0·03	Cu	0·01
Arsenic	0·03	As_2O_3	0·002
Uranium	0·03	U_3O_8	0·3
Nickel	0·02	Ni	0·02
Vanadium	0·02	V_2O_5	0·04
Manganese	0·02	Mn	0·006

The elements are listed in order of abundance; those in italic type have concentrations valued at $1.00 or more per million gallons of sea water. All others are < 0·02 lb/10^6 gal.
Source: Cloud 1969

greatly damaged by the recovery processes, which create great quantities of silt and also eventuate imbalance in the sedimentary systems of the sea-floor. Phosphates are found as nodules and in crusts where the operation of natural concentration processes brings their recovery closer to economic feasibility. A further resource of the continental shelves is fresh water: large quantities of artesian water may be found in certain aquifers, and although such supplies are currently costly compared with terrestrial sources, a demand may arise for their use in relatively humid lands, just as they are already tapped around some islands and being sought in the Mediterranean. Finally there are petroleum and natural gas, which are already exploited in many offshore waters up to depths of 2–2·5 km, which is the current limit of the techniques used. The minerals of the deep ocean basins are difficult to appraise. The most extensive are the pelagic sediments, which are particles of biological, aeolian or chemical origin that have settled out on the ocean floor. They contain enormous quantities of certain metal elements, but only if they could be easily subjected to enrichment would they enter resource processes under current conditions. The most discussed of them is manganese, which forms in large nodules and crusts in which other metals like nickel, cobalt and copper are incorporated; they occur as a veneer with a mean depth of 4,000–5,000 m, coming up as shallow as 200–1,000 m off North Carolina, but their true extent is unknown, and large-scale methods of extracting the metals from the silica in which they are embodied are as yet undeveloped (Cloud 1969).

In 1964, about 5 per cent of the world's production by value of geological wealth came from the sources discussed above, mostly from oil and gas. That this proportion will increase is not in doubt, but the idea of an unending cornucopia is obviously false. The cheapest source, sea water, contains few elements demanded by modern industry in high concentrations, and access to the other sources is difficult. Any discussion of the extraction of these resources must reckon with the external costs in terms of impact upon the ecology of the seas, for inevitably there would be a risk of destruction of biological resources of considerable value and perhaps greater indispensability.

Biological resources

It is commonplace to see calls for greater use of marine biological resources for food. Yet there are severe limiting factors on biological productivity in the sea. The euphotic zone in which photosynthesis can occur is only about 60 m deep, since from there to 520 m there is only blue light, the other wavelengths having been absorbed. There are very few terrestrial areas where the photosynthesizing zone is 60 m deep, but the primary producers of the sea are scattered very thinly through the water; if they were more concentrated then the euphotic zone would be shallower and so the level is self-limiting. Also limiting is carbon dioxide: as in fresh water, this tends to be scarce and the amount dissolved is dependent upon mixing at the interface between the water and the atmosphere.

In spite of such limitations, the sea supports a great diversity of living forms existing in complex interactive systems; there is in fact no abiotic zone. Figs 9.1 and 9.2 summarize, very generally, some of the main food-chain characteristics in which a number of features stand out: firstly the length of the major predator chain, which has two 'top carnivores', by which stage energy is getting very scarce; secondly, the drifting nature of the first two trophic levels: neither phytoplankton nor zooplankton is able to control its regional movements; and thirdly, the importance of detritus feeding in the continental shelves and in the deep oceans. The primary productivity upon which the life depends is not uniform over the whole ocean area; the open oceans are the least productive and are in fact something of a biological desert, largely because of the small size of the autotrophic zone in relation to the

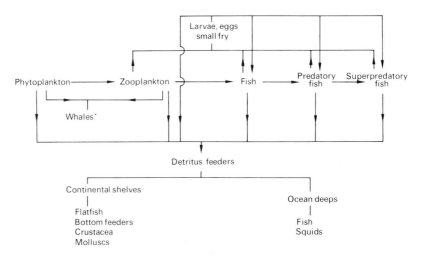

* Some whales are predators upon
  organisms like squids, not
  plankton feeders

Fig. 9.1 Diagrammatic representation of the main food chains of the oceans: the high number of steps in the predator chain is a characteristic feature, as is the importance of the detritus chain on the continental shelves.

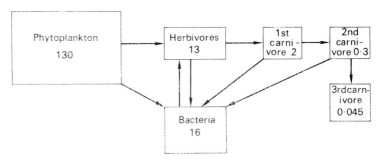

Units are billions of metric tons of organic matter/year

Fig. 9.2 Simple food chain in the oceans showing estimated production (not standing crop) of organic matter/yr at each level (1 billion = 1,000 million).
Source: Ricker 1969

heterotrophic zone in which the cycling of nutrients takes place. The distribution of productivity (Table 9.2) suggests that nutrients may be limiting factors in the ecosystem, which appears to have adapted itself by means of rapid mineral cycling with almost immediate uptake. The most important producer organisms are probably the nanoplankton (2–25 μ in size) which have a short biomass turnover time and rapid nutrient cycling. Corals are also efficient at retaining, for example, phosphorus, presumably because it is recycled between the plant and animal components of the colony. The coastal zone has a higher productivity because of its proximity to the sources of mineral nutrition, and upwelling zones share similar characteristics. Tidal estuaries and mudflats are among the most productive ecosystems in the world. The interpretation of estimates of yearly productivity must take into account the fact that the standing crop is very much lower: in the case of phytoplankton the biomass is probably about 1 per cent of the yearly turnover (Ryther 1969). This contrasts with the terrestrial ecosystems, where biomass of the standing crop may be roughly equal to yearly production as in grasslands and crops, or greater than that measure as with forests

TABLE 9.2   Estimated primary productivity of the oceans

Area	Size (10⁶ km²)	Net primary productivity (gm/m²/yr)	Total for area (10⁹ mt)	Annual energy fixation (10¹⁸ cals)
Reefs and estuaries	2·0	2,000·0	4·0	18·0
Continental shelf	26·0	350·0	9·3	42·6
Open ocean	332·0	125·0	41·5	109·2
Upwelling zones	0·4	500·0	0·2	1·0
Total	361·0	155·0	55·0	160·8

Source: Leith 1972

and desert shrubs. Even if all the phytoplankton were present in the top m of the sea, their average density would be 0·5 gm/m³ of water. Where the actual figure exceeds this greatly, as it does at certain places in particular seasons, direct harvesting by man is technically difficult and hence costs are high. The product is intractable not only on account of cultural factors such as taste and texture, which could be improved by industrial processing, but because of high salt and silica contents. Large-scale direct cropping of phytoplankton does not yet seem to be a very feasible food or fodder source, although use by man at the herbivore level should theoretically give high yields of energy and protein. The removal of organisms would mean taking away nutrients and these would have to be replaced, just as if it were an agricultural system.

As in all ecosystems, productivity falls at higher trophic levels; zooplankton presents similar cropping problems to phytoplankton, and man harvests very little of it. Most of his crop comes at the level of secondary and tertiary consumers, a few species of fish and some molluscs coming from the first trophic level of consumer organisms. The third trophic level yields a great number of the desired species, such as flounders, haddock, small cod, herring, sardines and whalebone whales, while some highly demanded species

Plate 16 Although contemporary fisheries are dominated by the deep-sea fleets with modern equipment, the fish protein supplied to many nations comes from small inshore fishermen operating in a traditional fashion, unlinked to fossil fuel power, as in this part of the New Territories of Hong Kong. *(I. G. Simmons)*

such as halibut, tuna, salmon, large cod, swordfish, seals and sperm whales are yet further along the food chain. At each stage there is competition for the production from taxa which are not important resource species for man: sharks, dogfish and seabirds, for example. A further harvest comes from detritus feeders which scavenge the sea-floor: many flatfish and crustacea belong to this group. World biological production at the levels mostly used by man is estimated variously at about 244–325 million mt fresh weight, mostly of fish. Estimates of the sustained annual yield of the seas vary from 55–2,000 million mt of fish; Ryther (1969) suggests that the length of food chains and the trophic levels at which man crops the oceans will limit the yield to about 100 million mt/yr, an estimate criticized by some authorities (e.g. Alverson *et al.* 1970) as too low. The constraints imposed by economic factors probably mean that the upper range of the various estimates will never be achieved: of the actual capture 80–90 per cent is at depths of less than 200 m and it seems unlikely that commercial trawling could ever extend much beyond 1,000 m. Beyond this level the animals are so scarce in relation to the volume of water that it is probably better to harvest predators which go down to such depths to feed, as do sperm whales on large deep-water squids.

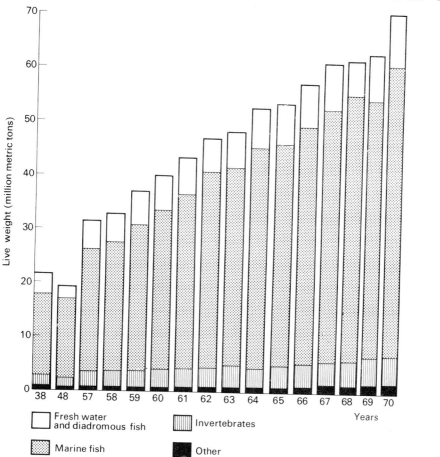

Fig. 9.3 The world fish catch 1938–70. Approximately half the crop is consumed directly by humans, the rest being used as livestock feed (1971 = 69·4 million mt).
Source: Holt 1971, with later additions from FAO data.

In 1971 world fish landings ran at 69·4 million mt (Fig. 9.3), a rate which has risen at about 8 per cent p.a. during the last 25 years, a doubling time of about 9 years. Nationally, Peru and Japan lead, followed by the USSR, China, Norway and the USA; other nations are some way behind. Consumption per person, however, is dominated by Japan, a fact as obvious to the viewer of the wax models outside restaurants in that land as to the avid *sashimi* enthusiast. The averaged figures also conceal the fact that several other Asian nations, such as Burma and Thailand, rely on fish for much of their animal protein (Plate 16). The discrepancy between the landings of Peru and the low overall consumption in Latin America is in part caused by the export of most of the anchovy catch to Europe as animal feed. According to Dasmann (1972) the Peruvian catch could provide a minimal protein intake for 413 million people, although when the Humboldt Current is displaced by the warmer El Nino Current, as happened in for example 1957, 1965 and 1972, the fishery yield is very small and so creates difficulties for Peru, since 40 per cent of her foreign earnings come from fish meal. Domestic consumption has been increasing too, especially since a meat shortage in 1972 necessitated a ban on the sale of beef in the first half of each month. Apart from particular regional and national situations, Tables 9.3

TABLE 9.3   Fishery statistics

1. World catch 1970 (million mt live weight)

Total for world		69·3 (exc. whales)	
For human consumption			42·8
Fresh marketing			19·0
Freezing			9·5
Curing			8·1
Canning			6·2
Other purposes			26·5
Reduction to meal and oil			25·5
Miscellaneous			1·0

2. Catches by nation 1970 (million mt live weight)

Peru	12·6	Spain	1·4
Japan	9·3	Canada	1·3
USSR	7·2	Denmark	1·2
China	5·8 (est. for 1960)	Thailand	1·2
Norway	2·9	Indonesia	1·2
USA	2·7	UK	1·0
South Africa	1·5	Chile	1·1
India	1·7		

3. Catches by fishing area 1970 (thousand mt live weight)

Inland waters	7,620	Indian Ocean	2,780
Atlantic Ocean	23,610	Pacific Ocean	35,330

Source: FAO *Yearbook of Fishery Statistics 1970*

TABLE 9.4   Regional consumption of fish, 1965 (kg/cap)

North America	14·5	USSR	13·1
EEC	12·1	Other central and eastern Europe	6·1
North-west Europe	20·5	China	6·9
Southern Europe	17·2	Latin America	6·0
Japan	53·7	Sub-Saharan Africa	8·2
Oceania	10·7	Near East and north-west Africa	3·2
South Africa	21·3	Asia	7·3
		World average 10·3	

Source: FAO *Indicative world plan for agriculture*, 1970, **1**

and 9.4 show that consumption per head of fish is highest in the developed countries, and since their livestock is also a major user of fishmeal, much of the world's catch is devoted to the industrial nations.

Extension of fisheries

The potential for extending fisheries comes from three sources: the utilization of untapped species, the cropping of hitherto unattractive areas, and the development of more novel methods of culture and harvesting. During recent years a number of new fisheries have started to flourish, such as Peruvian anchoveta, Alaska pollock, Bering Sea flatfishes and herring, and several more. The future for extensions of traditional fishing methods lies, for example, in the cool temperate parts of the southern hemisphere, which only produce about 10 per cent of the world's fish catch (2·7 million mt in 1962 against 25 million mt for the northern cool temperate seas). There are disadvantages, such as the small areas of continental shelf and the lack in some areas of suitable species, but it seems likely that considerable extension of fisheries could be wrought. Even in heavily fished northern areas there are abundant but little-used species: grenadiers in the north-west Atlantic, sandlance, anchovies and sauries in the Pacific, and small sharks like the dogfish in both areas. Even where fish are found that are not very useful for direct human consumption, large-scale catches may mean that they are useful as 'industrial' fish. A protein-rich concentrate can be made that is currently used, for instance, in the broiler-chicken industry. If further processed it can be made palatable and added to protein-deficient diets; at present this could cost less than dried skim milk (Ricker 1969).

Krill

Antarctic whaling has reduced stocks to about one-tenth of their former size and so the presumably uneaten food of the whales is theoretically available to man. Approximately 80 per cent of the prey of blue and fin whales, and even more of humpbacks, is krill, the shrimp *Euphausia superba*, up to 60–70 mm long and 1 g in weight, with a net weight content of 7 per cent fat and 16 per cent protein (Moiseev 1970). Rather rough calculations suggest that between 1964–6, whales ate 148×10^6 mt of krill in antarctic waters, and that the yearly production of nine-tenths of this amount should now be surplus. How much is consumed by other predators is unknown, but no surges in the populations of seals, birds, fish and minke whales have been recorded (Mackintosh 1970); fish and squid may have been the chief benefactors. Since biomass and productivity are not yet known, the sustained yield cannot be calculated, but USSR vessels are already catching and processing krill. Its potential may be very high, even in the same order of magnitude as the Peruvian anchoveta fishery (FAO 1971).

Other less direct ways of increasing the crop of marine resources could be more systematically investigated. When nutrients are limiting, fertilization by the addition of minerals to the sea may bring about higher productivities. Only this type of activity takes fishery management to a state much beyond the largely Mesolithic technology which, give or take a fossil-fuel-powered trawler or two, is still being used.

Aquaculture

The first stage away from a hunting and gathering economy is that of herding, and this is being used in, for example, Hong Kong, the Philippines and Japan. Frameworks are lowered into shallow offshore waters and allowed to colonize with sedentary molluscs like oysters and mussels. With some species, the individuals grow on ropes that hang clear of the bottom so that they are out of the reach of predators such as starfish. Although productive (Table 9.5), such systems are very vulnerable to contamination, and since the organisms filter large quantities of water their ability to concentrate substances toxic either to themselves or to consumers is very high. True aquaculture involves genetic manipulation of the chosen species by keeping them captive throughout their breeding cycle, a difficult though not impossible task. The requirements are unpolluted sea water and a suitable coastal site with adjoining land. Eastern England, for instance, would not suffice because of the degree of exposure, silt levels, low winter temperature and contaminations (C. E. Nash 1970a). The most efficient plant would be large and would require buildings, stores, hatcheries and covered tank complexes on the land, together with enclosed tidal areas and tanks, and ponds or lagoons in deeper water. For preference, use of all the water areas would be possible by housing together algae browsers such as abalone, pelagic herbivores like the grey mullet, and bottom-dwelling carnivores (C. E. Nash 1970b). The possibility of using waste heat to maintain constant water temperatures has been much discussed and tried, and in coastal temperate zones there exists the attractive possibility of raising tropical fish with a high productivity. Even the native species benefit from heated water, as experiments with plaice (*Pleuronectes platessa*) and sole (*Solea solea*) in Scotland have shown: most individuals attained a marketable size in 2 years, which is at least one year before the normal time for wild populations (C. E. Nash 1970b). More complex systems based on other waste products have been envisaged. For example, sewage and other eutrophicatory products might be used as the basis for algal production which forms the

TABLE 9.5   Aquacultural yields (fresh weight, without mollusc shells)

Location	Species	kg/ha/yr	tons/ac/yr
USA	Oysters		
	(national average	9	0·004
	(best yields)	5,000	2·00
France	Flat oyster		
	(national average)	400	0·16
	Portuguese oyster		
	(national average)	935	0·37
Australia	Oysters		
	(national average)	150	0·06
	(best yields)	540	2·20
Malaya	Cockles	12,500	5·00
France	Mussels	2,500	1·00
Singapore	Shrimp	1,250	0·50

Source: MacIntyre and Holmes 1971

food of oysters which then filter the water as well. The oyster droppings are eaten by worms which are the prey of bottom-living fish, whose nitrogenous excretions nourish water weeds which oxygenate the water. In another scheme, carbon dioxide from a power-station chimney is used to enhance production of algae which are fed to clams that then grow rapidly in the heated water which is also the output of the power station. Such designs are all too simple to be true and only limited operational success has so far been achieved.

A general disadvantage of aquaculture seems to be the considerable skill needed for success, and it is therefore yet another competitor in the LDCs for scarce, trained man-power. While we may assent to the principle of the Institute of Ecology's (1972) statement that money would be better invested in aquaculture than larger fishing fleets, the gloomier IWP (1970) statement, that even a five-fold increase in output from aquaculture by 1985 would be only marginal to the world situation (although perhaps being locally significant), seems closer to the reality of the near future.

The IWP on fisheries

The IWP accepts the idea of the oceans as providers of protein, but does not suggest any radical alteration in present trends, as can be seen from Table 9.6. For fish as food, the difference between the production objective and the probable reality in 1985 shows deficits for North America and the EEC countries, presumably as the result of strain upon fisheries of the north Atlantic and north Pacific. Fish for animal feed exhibit even greater deficits, partly for the same reason and partly because of diversion of exports by LDCs to their own use. However, any remaining notions of the seas as repositories of plenitude are dispelled by the generally negative balances for food in the LDCs, especially Asia, where population increase will outstrip virtually any improvements in harvesting. The increases in fodder predicted for Latin America and Africa depend upon the development of demand by indi-genous livestock industries. To achieve the proposed rates of growth, the FAO suggests as main priorities the improvement of vessels, in particular the replacement of traditional craft by powered fleets, together with the development of improved ports and harbours with good storage and freezing facilities. As with agriculture, intensification is to be achieved by the extension of industrial technology, especially in the use of fossil fuels. More rational utilization of fish stocks is a third IWP priority.

In summary, the food resources of the sea can under the most optimal circumstances never be a panacea for all the nutritional problems of the world. Watt (1968) calculates that if we assume 100 g of marine food to contain 100 kcal of energy, and if the crop were to be multiplied 20 times, then about 9×10^8 people could be supported. With a population already at 3.4×10^9 when he wrote, that meant only one-quarter of the present population could be thus fed. In some ways this is a misleading calculation, since the main use of marine food is for protein (9 per cent of the catch weight of fish may be edible protein), and the factor of 20 for future cropping is obviously too high. Estimates of potential yield and role vary but are of the same order, and that of Ricker (1969) seems to reflect a general view. His opinion is that in the next 40 years the 1968 catch can be increased by about 2.5 times, giving an eventual total of 150–160 million mt/yr, contain-ing 20 per cent of usable protein. For a population of the order expected in AD 2000 this could supply about 30 per cent of the world's minimal protein requirements but only 3 per cent of its biological energy demands.

Over-uses of biological resources

The harvesting of marine biological resources is subject to the same constraints as any other wild crop if sustained yield is desired: the population must not be overcropped to the point that its reproduction no longer provides sufficient individuals to constitute a resource (Fig. 9.4). In view of the ecology of fish and sea mammals we might think that over-use

TABLE 9.6   Projected demand and supply of fish and fish products, 1975 and 1985 (million mt)

Region	Projected demand				Demand/ production objective balance	
	1975		1985		1985	
	Food	Feed	Food	Feed	Food	Feed
North America	3·8	4·4	4·6	4·7	− 1·9	− 3·4
EEC	2·7	6·0	3·2	7·5	− 1·3	− 7·4
North-west Europe	2·1	3·5	2·4	3·5	+ 0·5	− 0·5
Southern Europe	2·4	1·4	3·0	2·1	+ 0·2	− 2·0
Japan	6·5	3·0	7·4	3·7	+ 1·8	− 2·9
Oceania	0·2	0·2	0·3	0·2	+ 0·3	− 0·2
USSR	4·3	2·3	5·9	4·5	+ 7·6	− 2·2
China	8·7	—	14·1	—		
Central Europe	0·8	2·3	1·0	3·3	+ 0·7	− 2·9
Latin America	2·0	1·5	3·0	3·5	− 0·2	+ 11·5
Africa south of Sahara	2·6	0·1	4·1	0·6	− 0·7	+ 1·9
North-east, north-west Africa	0·6	0·3	1·0	0·6	− 0·1	− 0·4
Asia	10·3	1·0	18·2	2·8	− 4·2	− 2·6
World	47·6	26·4	69·0	37·5	+ 2·7	− 9·5
(1968 = 64)	74·0		106·5			

Source: FAO *Indicative world plan for agriculture*, 1970, **1**

is not likely, but the gregarious nature of many fish, the large size of whales and seals, and the product desirability of mammals such as sea otters have caused great inroads to be made upon their populations.

Particularly favoured fish species have exhibited considerable declines, as for example the east Asian sardine, Californian sardine, north-west Pacific salmon, Atlanto-Scandian herring, the Barents Sea cod; and a number of others, including the Newfoundland cod, North Sea herring, British Columbia herring and yellowfin tuna, are showing signs of strain (Holt 1971). International regulatory measures are sometimes applied to such species, regulating catch and net size, but these measures are difficult to enforce and once a species has been overfished it may not be possible for it to regain its place in the energy pathways

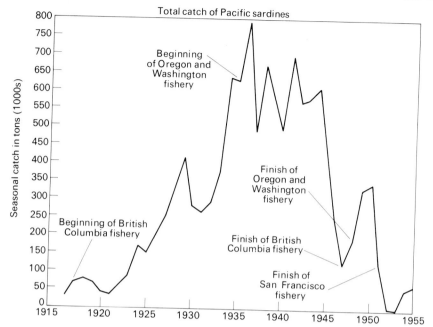

Fig. 9.4 At its height, the Pacific coast sardine fishery was the first-ranking fishery in North America in weight of fish landed, and third-ranking by value after tuna and salmon. The decline is attributed to over-fishing and there has been no recovery in 1955–70. Presumably the niche formerly occupied by the sardine has been taken over by another organism or the breeding stocks are too low to enable the population to gain in size.
Source: Dasmann 1972

of the ecosystem. The Pacific sardine (*Sardinops caerulea*) of the California current system was a major feeder on the zooplankton, and production of the fish aged 2 years and older was estimated at 4×10^6 mt/yr. It was overfished in the 1930s and replaced by a competitor, the anchovy *Engraulis mordox*. At the end of the 1950s the latter's biomass was similar to that of the sardine 30 years before and it has clearly ousted the former species, apparently irreversibly (Ehrlich and Ehrlich 1970).

The increasing number of incidents concerning fishing fleets in territorial waters and the desire of many countries (Peru and Iceland are notable instances) to extend their cropping hegemony to the edge of the continental shelf are obviously indicative of competition for the sea's protein resources. Such an attitude towards the use of the resource may promote ecologically sound harvesting of fish populations if the nation which is enforcing the fishery limit is a good manager, and if the extension of limits keeps out the overfishers, but there is no guarantee of such eventualities.

Sea mammals other than whales have often been the subject of over-exploitative cropping. The porpoise family (Delphinidae) appears to be in no danger, although little is known about its worldwide status: only local populations have been studied. Japan, for example, is taking about 20,000 porpoises per year and the arctic porpoise (white whale or beluga) is extensively used in some northern regions. Fur seals are better documented: the

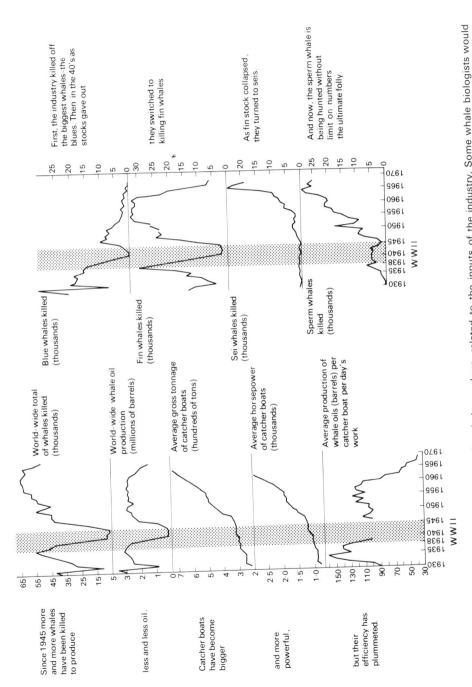

Fig. 9.5 A polemical view of the decline in whale numbers, related to the inputs of the industry. Some whale biologists would claim that the extinction of the blue whale has been averted and that most whales are now being cropped at a sustained-yield level.
Source: Ehrlich and Ehrlich 1970

Guadalupe fur seal was almost exterminated late in the nineteenth century, and the Northern or Pribilof fur seal was reduced from about one million individuals to 17,000 in 1910, since when careful management by the US Government has built the stock up to 1·5 million with a sustained yield of 80,000 animals per year. The true seals are also extensively killed, especially the harp seal of the north Atlantic. Canada, Norway and France share in this resource which, although the subject of controversy, is not in a great decline. The grey seal of the British Isles is also a controversial animal since it eats salmon, and some herds are culled in order to reduce its status as a competitor.

The most outstanding example of the over-use of marine populations is the history of whaling. The products of both baleen (plankton-consuming) and sperm (predatory, mainly on squids) whales have been highly valued in the past: oil, meat, blubber, skin and ambergris have all been used, although effective substitutes could now be found for most of them and whale products were forbidden in the USA in 1970. But a biologically depletive programme of whale cropping, mainly by Japan and the USSR, continues despite falling yields and obviously dwindling stocks. The decline of the whale resource is summarized in Table 9.7 and Fig. 9.5. The International Whaling Commission, which sets catch limits, is fully aware of the depletion of the whale stocks and has set out catch limits and preservation policies such as the complete protection of the Blue Whale (now numbering about 7,000) since 1965. Ehrlich and Ehrlich (1970) argue that exploitation to the point of extinction is occurring, whereas Gambell (1972) suggests that most stocks are stabilized at a sustained-yield level, with the exception of the overcropping of the antarctic and north Pacific fur whales. Such a stabilization is presumably much below the level that could have been achieved if rational management policies had been followed earlier.

TABLE 9.7   Diminution of whale catch

	1933	1966
Catch	28,907	57,891
Barrels of whale oil	2,606,201	1,546,904

Source: Ehrlich and Ehrlich 1972

Effects of contamination

Large as the oceans are, they are not immune from the end-products of man's resource processes. The input of materials into seas is both deliberate and accidental, and only recently has there been much concern about the use of the sea as a garbage can, so that quantitative studies are rare.

The nature and effects of individual contaminants of the biosphere are dealt with in Chapter 11 and here we will mention briefly only those which have been described as creating particular problems in the seas. They are: radio-isotopes, industrial effluents, oil, persistent pesticides, and eutrophication agents such as untreated sewage, fertilizer runoff and detergents. All of them affect coastal waters most markedly, but organochlorine

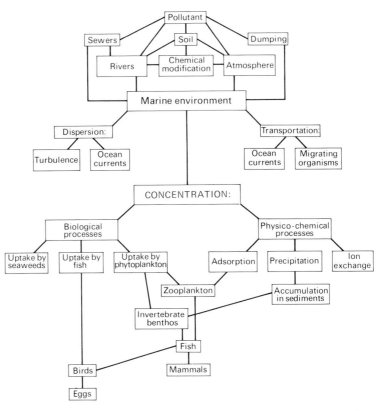

Fig. 9.6 A flow diagram of the pathways by which a contaminant can find its way into the oceans and the ways in which it can be concentrated, with various lethal and sublethal effects.
Source: MacIntyre and Holmes 1971

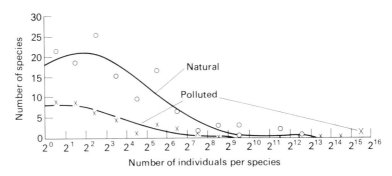

Fig. 9.7 The diversity of diatom communities in natural and polluted waters. While pollution of some kinds such as eutrophication may increase productivity (not shown here), it generally reduces diversity.
Source: MacIntyre and Holmes 1971

pesticides appear to be ubiquitous, having turned up in the fat of antarctic penguins and in the Bermuda petrel, which lands only on its nesting islets and is at the top of a long pelagic food chain. The way in which a marine pollutant is dispersed through the seas is shown in Fig. 9.6.

Pesticides such as DDT have been reported as causing a reduction in the photosynthetic rate of marine algae at very low (10–100 ppb) concentrations (Wurster 1968). Experimental findings such as these are difficult to extend to the oceans themselves, and so this effect of residual organic chemicals is as yet unproven. If reduced photosynthesis or the extermination of certain species were a result of organochlorine residues, then in shallow waters there would probably be floral imbalance and large-scale blooms, exacerbating the effects of eutrophication (Fig. 9.7). Reduced primary productivity must lead inevitably to a lowering of the net biomass of the sea. The effect of substances such as DDT and other marine contaminants is in reality difficult to measure, because the populations of the resident organisms are subject to wide fluctuations under natural conditions (Longhurst et al. 1972). It is thus easy to label a particular substance as a destroyer of sea life, only to be proved wrong and accused of crying wolf. The way is then opened for the complacent to do nothing about trying to discover the objective truth of the effects of contaminants in the oceans.

At a global scale, the effects of reduced rates of photosynthesis in the sea would be very severe, for the role of marine phytoplankton in regulating the CO_2/O_2 balance of the atmosphere appears to be critical. However, the concentrations required to effect any alteration appear to be unlikely to be attained in the open oceans, since the solubility of DDT in water is 1 ppb. If DDT were to be concentrated in a surface oil-film then it might reach levels toxic to plants. The possibilities still exist that DDT may be toxic to phytoplankton species as yet unchecked and that other organochlorines may be more poisonous than DDT and its breakdown products.

Using certain broad-scale assumptions, the 1970 Report of the Study of Critical Environmental Problems (SCEP) calculated that the surface waters of the ocean could accommodate a load of 7.5×10^7 mt of DDT, i.e. about 10 times the total production to date, one-quarter of which is estimated to have entered the oceans. There is every indication that DDT is not uniformly distributed in the surface layers of the sea: it is likely to be concentrated in the surface film, which contains alcohols and fatty acids. From there it may enter the food chains via bacteria and phytoplankton or be absorbed into formerly airborne particles which sink through the water and are ingested by detritus feeders. In the case of the oceans approximately 0·1 per cent of the total output of the chemical has brought about considerable alterations in population structures, particularly of fish-eating birds. Since the rate of decay of the organochlorines in the sea is unknown, a reduction in the amounts reaching the sea would seem to be a wise precaution. Even the SCEP study, not given to alarmism, found that 'our prediction of the hazards may be vastly underestimated'.

A form of eutrophication peculiar to the seas is the dinoflagellate bloom, common under natural conditions where there is an upwelling of nutrient-rich water or disturbance of bottom sediments by tides. The microscopic dinoflagellates may secrete toxins which directly poison the water, may use up all the oxygen in the water if in a relatively confined space, or if filtered through molluscs may build up to high levels. Eating mussels after a 'red tide' allows ingestion of a poison which affects the human central nervous system and to which there is no known antidote. Some recent blooms have appeared in the waters off-shore from known sources of untreated sewage, as off north-east England in 1968 and Nova Scotia–New England in 1972, and although proof is lacking, there is a strong suspicion that human activities can initiate the onset of such phenomena. At any rate red tides put up the price of shrimps by 15 per cent in North America during 1972.

The future value of the oceans

Even under ideal institutional conditions the sea is neither an inexhaustible provider of food and mineral resources nor a bottomless sink for the end-products of resource processes. The ecology of the sea is inimical to the production of large quantities of organic matter per unit volume, as is the volume of water to harvesting of crop, and the sheer immensity of the quantity of water means again that mineral extraction is expensive. If minerals impose any constraints upon the primary productivity of much of the oceans, their removal for industrial purposes could possibly reduce marine harvests, a trend which is likely to be exacerbated by certain forms of pollution of the seas.

Man's 'ecological demand' upon the sea, as upon other biospheric systems, is increasing steadily. Over-use, particularly of fish, seems easy to attain: the adults are overfished and so reproduction is hindered and younger individuals are taken, reducing recruitment to the population. In turn, man's competitors for fish are perceived as pests and if possible their populations are reduced. The eventual effect is likely to be instability in the ocean systems, with large and unexpected outbreaks of 'pest' species and large fluctuations in fishing yields. These symptoms are likely to occur when yields of two to four times the present crop are achieved (Institute of Ecology 1972). Various estimates seem to agree, however, that the maximum world fish catch is 90–100 million mt/yr, out of a biological production of about 240 million mt/year, but do not say whether such a level is a sustainable yield. It is certainly unlikely to be reached if gross contamination of the seas by toxic substances takes place, since the coastal zones are especially vulnerable to pollution and from them come half the fish production and over half the money made on fishing as an occupation. Estuaries are especially fragile ecosystems and are much polluted and reclaimed, but are among the most productive ecosystems on earth, as well as often being important habitats for fish in their early stages of development. These seemingly barren places, haunts principally of wildfowlers and melancholic poets, therefore deserve special protection.

This all supposes rational exploitation of the marine resources, which regrettably does not happen. There are a relatively large number of international agreements about fishing rights and practices (such as the 1958 Geneva Convention on Fishing and Conservation of Living Resources of the High Seas), but loopholes are not difficult to find, and the nature of fisheries has been changing more rapidly than the machinery to deal with them. The International Whaling Convention frequently disregards the advice of its biologists and harvests well above maximum sustained-yield levels; pirate whaling outfits operate without regard to the IWC; Denmark refused to limit her oceanic catch of North Atlantic salmon in spite of the decline in its numbers. Numerous examples, some of them leading to international incidents like the Peruvian seizure of US fishing boats and the British–Icelandic

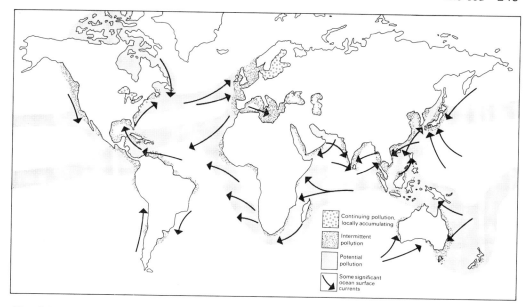

Fig. 9.8 Marine pollution around the world, both actual and potential. The latter refers especially to oil or noxious cargoes along the major shipping lines.
Source: M. Waldichuk and L. Andrèn, reprinted in *Ceres* **3** (3), 1970, 36–7

'cod war' of 1972–3, can be found. At an FAO Conference in 1972, one fish-management scientist was quoted by the press as saying, 'If we wrote a book about our profession, there would be 20 pages of introduction, one page of results and 180 pages of excuses.' The sea, as Garrett Hardin (1968) has pointed out, is a common where every extra exploited unit beyond the ecologically permissible limit is of benefit to the individual cropper but a significant loss to everyone else. New concepts of the 'ownership' of marine resources are probably needed for rational management: the alternatives (Holt 1971) seem to be international ownership or the unprecedented extension of appropriations by nation states. But even given substantial institutional agreement, no improvement in fisheries management is likely for at least 15 years. The first priority, however, is to reduce the already extensive pollution of the oceans (Fig. 9.8), towards which the 1972 agreements on dumping in the oceans was a first step. Thereafter long-term management of the exploitation of fisheries becomes an absolute necessity.

Further reading

CHRISTY, F. T. and SCOTT, A. 1967: *The common wealth in ocean fisheries.*

CLOUD, P. 1969: Mineral resources from the sea.

CRUTCHFIELD, J. A. (ed.) 1965: *The fisheries: problems in resource management.*

HOOD, D. W. (ed.) 1971: *Impingement of man on the oceans.*

INSTITUTE OF ECOLOGY 1972: *Man in his living environment.*

LOFTAS, T. 1972: *The last resource.*

MARX, W. 1967: *The frail ocean.*

RICKER, W. 1969: Food from the sea.

10

Energy and minerals

The energy and minerals dealt with here are from inanimate sources and hence differ in quality from the renewable materials so far discussed. They are often called 'stock' or 'non-renewable' resources, and in the case of minerals this is true to the extent that 'new' materials can only be extracted from the earth's crust once. But even in the transformed states in which they are used, they are not lost to the planet (if we except lunar module junkyards) and so are ideally available for re-use. Energy is somewhat different, since direct solar energy is certainly not cyclically renewable but there is for all practical purposes an unending supply. Stored solar energy as coal, oil and lignite is non-renewable, except on a time-scale of millions of years; in the case of wood the renewability is the same as any other use of a tree or shrub. The raw materials at present used to generate nuclear power are inorganic minerals, and only water power is truly renewable in the manner of an organic resource. Access to energy sources changes the whole of man's relationships to the planet and in particular the use of all kinds of resources, since their extraction, conversion and transport may depend upon the control of large quantities of energy. Access to stored energy sources is the basis of industrialization with all its concomitants in terms of the manipulation of ecosystems by mechanical and chemical means. It also permits penetration to nearly all parts of the planet, making possible such activities as recovering minerals from under the sea-bed or living permanently at the South Pole.

Together, energy and mineral use have also provided the means for man to escape from the surface of the planet and hence the chance to view it from outside, both personally as in the case of astronauts and vicariously as with remote sensing. The effects upon our perception of this planet have yet to be fully appreciated.

Energy

A context

All resource processes can be characterized by quantifying the flows of energy through them, and studies of energetics may be used to link their ecological and economic dimensions (H. T. Odum 1971, Garvey 1972). The increase in organizational complexity of the industrial nations is only made possible by the understanding and application of energy flows, and it is not without significance that the term 'power' is used for energy obtained for urban and industrial purposes. The actual quantities of energy used are measured by the rate of flow of useful energy that can be made to do work; it is a one-way flow and degradation occurs, so that heat sinks are an inevitable consequence. Resource processes should therefore consider the ecology and economics of the whole process, from the 'capturing' of the energy source through to its dispersal into the ecosphere as heat. Table 10.1 shows the increase in energy consumption from the basic metabolism of plants and men to the levels needed to fuel a small car, a symbol of industrialization. The supply of energy to all resource processes which yield a tangible product is so important, and the escalation of use so rapid, that concern is being evinced over the relations between supply and demand both in the near future and in the longer term, even if not in the time-scale of William Blake's dictum that 'energy is eternal delight'. The various sources of power supply must therefore be examined, with the understanding that this, along with mineral science, is one of the areas where the development of technology may change the prognosis most rapidly, albeit on a time-span of decades rather than years. This must be set against a world consumption of energy that is currently doubling approximately every 17 years.

TABLE 10.1   Energy consumption (kcal/day)

Green plant covering 1 m² of ground	4,000
Human consuming food	3,000
Waterfall 10 m high, 10⁵ gal/day	9,100
Small car burning gasoline	900,000

Source: H. T. Odum 1971

Time-use of direct solar energy

The flows of present-day solar energy (Fig. 10.1) are well known from climatic studies. Only 1 per cent or less of the incoming solar radiation is enmeshed in photosynthesis (Woodwell 1970a), and interest has been shown in the direct industrial and domestic use of solar radiation. Its input totals about 100,000 times the world's installed electric power capacity and is virtually constant over long periods, in contrast to the fossil fuels to be treated later. On a small scale, many practical uses can be made of it as in water and house heating, cooking, distillation and photoelectric reactions. The possibility of providing electric power on the same scale as modern generating plants is of a different order. In a solar-electric station the maximum conversion efficiency would be about 10 per cent, so that a plant of 1,000 electrical megawatts capacity would require an input of 10,000 megawatts (MW). If the average solar power at the earth's surface is 500 cal/cm²/day, then the area required to collect 10^{10} watts of solar power would be 42 km², equivalent to a square 6·5 × 6·5 km (Hubbert 1969), and while the whole process is no doubt feasible, its complexity, the cost of the equipment and the effect upon land-use patterns bring into question the practicability of the undertaking. In particular, LDCs short of large-scale energy supplies for industrialization would not be likely to benefit from this source. An improved technique might be to orbit a lightweight panel of solar cells in a 35,880 km (22,300 mi) high orbit, collecting solar radiation 24 hours a day. At a radiant energy collection efficiency of 15–20 per cent, a conversion to microwave energy efficiency of 85 per cent, and a conversion to electricity

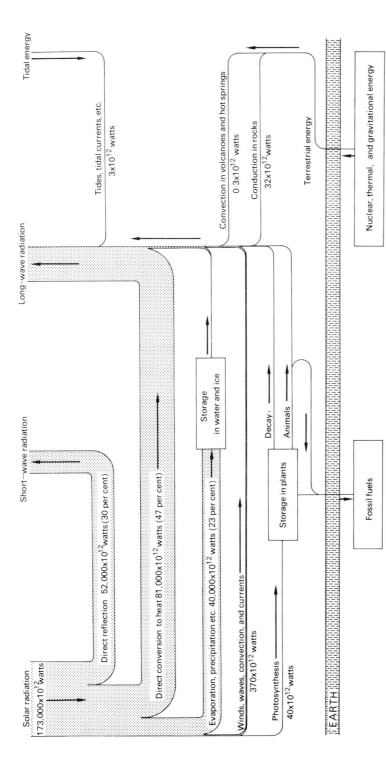

Fig. 10.1 The flow of energy to and from the earth. The overwhelming contribution of solar radiation can easily be seen, as can the small proportion of it which at present enters resource processes, especially via photosynthesis. The thin band leading to fossil fuels reflects their slow rate of accumulation.
Source: Hubbert 1971

efficiency of 70 per cent, then a panel 12·95 km² (5 mi²) with a ground antenna 15·5 km² (6 mi²) could produce the 10,000 MW required for New York City. The projected US demand of 2,500 Gigawatts (GW) for AD 2000 would need 250 such installations and the incremental demand until 2000 could be supplied with 125 of them (Summers 1971). The objections to ordinary solar plant apply to this project too, together with the added difficulties of increasing the density of large orbiting objects. At an early stage of experiment is one device for coupling chlorophyll to a zinc oxide semi-conductor, using the neutron-donating properties of the pigment as in photosynthesis but with an efficiency of 10 per cent. This process is estimated to be 100 times cheaper than orbiting solar cells ('Monitor' 1972). Solar collectors on the earth's surface would not add to the waste heat load; space collection systems would add less than nuclear or fossil sources of energy. Perhaps more feasible is the use of heat absorbed by the seas, to give electric power, fresh water and maricultural products (Othmer and Roels 1973).

Another ubiquitous commodity, though less constant in its presence, is wind, a climatic result of solar input. Again, local use for a specialized purpose is feasible, but production on an industrial scale so puny as to exclude it from serious consideration.

Hydro-electric power

Of the early sources of industrial energy only water remains important in the form of hydro-electric power. Its development since 1900 has been rapid wherever conditions are suitable, and plants of 1,000-MW capacity now exist. Stream-flow determines the upper limit, which for the USA has been estimated at 161,000 MW, installed capacity at present being 45,000 MW. On a world scale, the installed capacity in 1964 was 210,000 MW, about 7·5 per cent of its potential capacity. Table 10.2, for a slightly earlier date, shows the continental distribution of the water-power capacity of the world. A significant feature of these developments is the complementarity they exhibit with coal reserves (p. 253), for Africa and South America both have large HEP potential.

TABLE 10.2   World water-power capacity, early 1960s

Continent	Potential (10³ MW)	% of world total	Development (10³ MW)
North America	313	11	59
South America	577	20	5
Western Europe	158	6	47
Africa	780	27	2
Middle East	21	1	<0·5
South-east Asia	455	16	2
Far East	42	1	19
Australasia	45	2	2
USSR, China and satellites	466	16	16

Source: Hubbert 1962

Hubbert (1969) suggests that in the long term the full development of the world's hydropower potential would produce a quantity equivalent to the present-day total world consumption. If fossil fuels failed overnight, the world could exist at its present industrial level on hydropower, but there would be no scope for growth. Although hydropower is an apparently inexhaustible source of power, climatic shifts could cause regional variations in output and silting is a further detractor from efficiency. In fact, much hydropower potential is a considerable distance from any possible user and the capital required for yet other sites would preclude their development under most conditions.

Tidal and geothermal power

The source of tidal energy is the combined kinetic and potential energy of the sun–moon–earth system, and uses barrages which store up the potential energy of a high tide and then generate electricity upon its release. It shares the relatively benign ecological characteristics of river-generated power, but high tidal amplitudes are not so common that it can be thought of as having other than local future significance. The world potential is about 13,000 MW compared to 2,800,000 MW for conventional HEP—i.e. less than 1 per cent. The first major project is at La Rance in France, which dates from 1966 and has an annual output of 544×10^6 kilowatt hours (KWH) from a tidal range of 8·4 m. The Soviet Union plans to use the 7 m tidal range of Lumborskaya Bay (east of Murmansk) to generate 320,000 KW, while a larger plant on the Mezen Bay of the White Sea will use a 9 m range to produce 1·3 million KW (Pryde 1972). A project has been in the planning stage since the 1930s for Passamaquoddy Bay off the Bay of Fundy with an average tidal range of 5·52 m. An annual output of $1,318 \times 10^6$ KWH has been envisaged (Hubbert 1969).

Large geothermal energy plants have been constructed only in recent decades. Italy leads in this field with an installed capacity in 1970 of 362 MW at Larderel, followed by New Zealand (192 MW at Wairakei), USA (192 KW in northern California), Japan, Mexico and Iceland. The total world capacity was estimated at 752 MW in 1970 (Rex 1971). About 1 per cent of hydrothermal energy, usually in the form of superheated water or steam, can be converted into electricity. Estimates of world potential are difficult to achieve but are of the order of 60 times the present installed capacity. This amounts to about 20 per cent of the present total installed electric power of the USA. As with tidal power, it may be locally significant but can contribute only fractionally to world energy requirements (Cook 1971).

Fossil fuels

Table 10.3 shows that until AD 1800, man's access to energy was mostly limited to recently arrived solar radiation: the metabolism of human or animal food, the burning of wood, animal and vegetable oils, the tapping of moving air or falling water were used, and they possessed the disadvantage that they could not be economically transported nor their energy content transmitted any distance once released. Ecologically the effect of their utilization was usually quite local and small-scale, except where large quantities of wood were used

TABLE 10.3   Energy use during human cultural development (kcal/cap/day)

Emergent man	2,000	Assumes no control over fire
Primitive hunter with fire	4,000	
Primitive agriculturalist	12,000	
Advanced agriculturalist	24,000	Without fossil-fuel input
Industrial man	70,000	For example, 1850–70 period. In industrial regions of Europe and North America only
Technological man	230,000	This is the US figure

Based on Cook 1971

for smelting metals. The ecology of large parts of the Weald of south-east England was changed by iron smelting during medieval times, for example, as were parts of the remaining forests of Scotland in the eighteenth and nineteenth centuries; and nearly half the present wood production of the world is used for fuel, mainly in the LDCs. Use of peat changed vegetation locally, and its continued use for power generation in Ireland (Dwyer 1958) has altered the landscape of large areas, while the transport of 'sea-cole' into the Tudor cities of England foreshadowed later pollution problems. The full realization of the properties of coal led to its use for smelting metals, the development of the steam engine, steam locomotives and ships, and steam-electric power. Only about a century ago the even more malleable fuels, oil and natural gas, were discovered and led to diesel-electric power and the internal combustion engine in all its forms. Once the technology for discovery, recovery and utilization had been produced, use of these major energy sources grew rapidly. Coal was used in negligible amounts early in the nineteenth century, but by 1870 the production rate was 250 million mt/yr; in 1970 it was $2 \cdot 8 \times 10^9$ mt, rising currently at $3 \cdot 6$ per cent p.a. With crude oil, a negligible production in 1890 has risen to a present extraction rate of 12,000 million bbls/yr at a rise of 7 per cent p.a., i.e. doubling every 10 years (Hubbert 1971). Table 10.4 sets out the increases in consumption of the major sources of energy (excluding firewood, wind-power and other miscellaneous sources) during 1925–68. In 1968, the total consumption of 6,306 million mt coal equivalent came $36 \cdot 7$ per cent from solid fuels, $42 \cdot 8$ per cent from liquid fuels, $18 \cdot 3$ per cent from natural gas and $2 \cdot 1$ per cent from hydro-electricity. Nuclear power was less than $0 \cdot 1$ per cent of the total (Darmstadter 1971). Fig. 10.2 shows the absolute amounts of energy and its percentage

TABLE 10.4   World energy consumption in recent decades

	1925	*1938*	*1950*	*1960*	*1968*
Total consumption millions of mt coal equivalent	1,484	1,790	2,610	4,196	6,306
Per capita consumption kg coal equivalent	785	826	1,042	1,403	1,810

Source: Darmstadter 1971

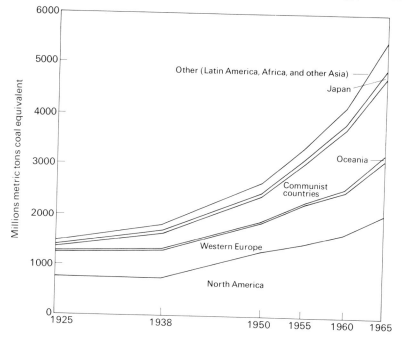

Fig. 10.2 World energy consumption by major regions 1925–65. The dominant position of North America has been maintained for the whole period, although its proportion of the whole has declined slightly. Source: Darmstadter 1971

distribution by regions up to 1968. These figures represent the culmination of annual rates of growth of 2·3 per cent in 1925–50, 5·1 per cent in 1950–65, and 4·8 per cent in 1965–8. The projected rate of growth of consumption 1965–80 for the world is 5·2 per cent p.a., and Table 10.5 shows some regional components of this average, along with the various shares in total consumption for the base and terminal years of the projection.

The consumption of energy is dominated by the USA, which, in any other set of units uses 2·2 million MW/yr out of an estimated total of 6·6 million MW/yr (Table 10.5). This means that much of the rest of the world uses energy barely above the food-intake level (about 100 W/day), compared with the daily per capita use of 10,000 W by each US citizen. If in 50 years' time a world population of 10,000 million were to use energy at contemporary US standards, the energy needed would amount to 110 million MW/yr (Brown *et al.* 1963).

Why worry?

The rates of present and projected consumption of energy sources have led to considerable discussion about the adequacy of coal, oil and natural gas for future industrial and domestic use, and the possibilities of substitution, especially with nuclear fuel. Agreed estimates of reserves are uncommon and most depend upon assumptions about economics, technology

TABLE 10.5   Regional growth rates and shares in total energy consumption 1965–80

Region	% of world total	Annual growth rate 1965–80, %	% of world total, projected, 1980
USA	34·2	3·5	26·8
Canada	2·9	5·5	3·0
Western Europe	20·0	4·0	16·8
Japan	3·3	7·9	4·9
Middle East	0·9	9·4	1·5
Other Asia	2·8	8·2	4·3
Oceania	1·2	4·8	1·1
Latin America	3·5	7·4	4·8
Africa	1·7	6·5	2·0
USSR	15·9	6·5	19·1
Communist eastern Europe	7·1	4·6	6·5
Communist Asia	6·5	7·6	9·1
World	100	4·7	100

Source: Darmstadter 1971

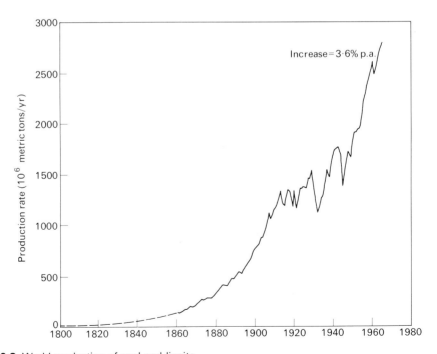

Fig. 10.3 World production of coal and lignite.
Source: Hubbert 1969

and politics that may undergo alteration during the periods about which prognoses are made. The following discussion relies heavily upon the estimations of Hubbert (1969) and Darmstadter (1971).

Coal

The distribution of coal is relatively well known because of the accuracy with which coal deposits can be mapped. The world's resources of minable coal (about 50 per cent of the coal present) are dominated by the USSR (Table 10.6) and the USA. Fig. 10.3 shows the rate of production for the world since AD 1800. Continued growth at 3·6 per cent p.a. is not feasible for much longer, for it would exhaust a minable reserve of 7.6×10^{12} mt in about 30 years. More realistically, Hubbert (1969) calculates that the peak production of coal

TABLE 10.6   Minable coal and lignite (mt $\times$ 10^9)

Region	Estimated resources	Established by mapping
USSR (including European part)	4,310	2,950
USA	1,486	710
Asia outside the USSR	681	225
North America outside the USA	601	70
Europe	377	280
Africa	109	35
Oceania	59	25
South and Central America	14	10
Total	7.6×10^{12}	4.3×10^{12}

Source: Hubbert 1969, Darmstadter 1971

will occur in AD 2220 and that 80 per cent of the reserves will be consumed between AD 2040 and 2380. Such calculations assume no great advances in technology which would make accessible currently unminable deposits, and also assume that no other major energy sources beyond those now known will be discovered. Given these premises, the order of magnitude of time during which coal can be expected to be a major contributor to industrial energy requirements on a world basis can be seen to last about 400 years. This forecast does not preclude the possibility of regional shortages.

The same type of calculation can be carried out for oil and natural gas. Whereas coal is all in the solid phase, this group covers a range from extremely viscous liquids found in tar sands (and the true solid, kerogen, found in oil shales) through the liquid gasolines to gaseous methane. The reserves of these resources are more difficult to calculate than coal because of the erratic manner in which accumulations of oil and gas are found underground. Gas is especially difficult to estimate for anywhere but the USA and calculations have to be based on the assumption that the ratio of natural gas to crude oil is the same as for the USA, and also that these products, often now wasted, will be utilized in future. Table 10.7

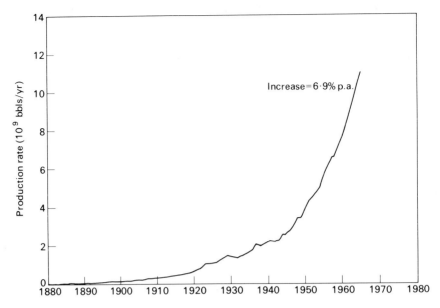

Fig. 10.4 World production of crude oil.
Source: Hubbert 1969

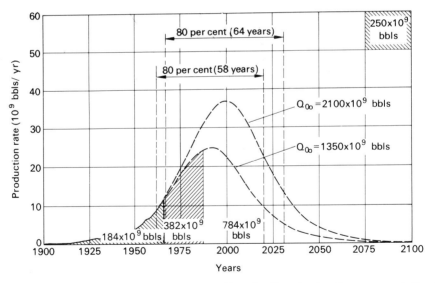

Fig. 10.5 A projection of the complete cycles of world crude oil production. $Q \infty$ represents the ultimate amount of the fuel recovered during the cycle and is given here for different estimates of the $Q \infty$ of crude oil. The difference between them makes little difference to the long-term situation. The quantities enumerated under the curve represent the amounts recovered during various time-segments of the recovery curve.
Source: Hubbert 1969

Plate 17 An oil refinery at Fawley, on Southampton Water in England, with a throughput of 20 million mt/yr. The size of the jetty and the installations underline the importance of fossil fuels to an industrial economy. A few remnants of estuarine marsh (cf. Plate 1) can be seen between the jetty and the plant area. *(Esso Petroleum Company Ltd, London)*

shows some world crude oil estimates which also give an approximate indication of the location of this resource; as Darmstadter (1971) shows, these estimates are conservative, and other calculations increase the ultimate reserve by 3·5 times. Petroleum products may also be extracted from oil shales, bituminous rocks and tar sands, and the world recoverable reserves have been evaluated at 190×10^9 bbls of crude oil, with an estimated ultimate recovery of 15×10^{12} bbls. Oil shales are widespread, especially in North and South America and to a lesser extent in Europe. These present special problems in refining and are not yet an attractive commercial proposition, and so are usually left out of estimates for the oil sector of energy sources. A refining plant exists on the tar sands of the Athabaska River in Alberta, Canada.

The world production of crude oil (Fig. 10.4) is, like that of coal, exponential in nature but has a relatively constant slope of 6·9 per cent p.a. from 1890 to the present, i.e.

doubling every 10 years. Given the accuracy of a projected total recoverable resource of 2,100 × 10⁹ bbls, then the peak production will be reached about AD 2000, with the middle 80 per cent of production being reached between AD 1968–2032 (Fig. 10.5). The estimates are of course subject to many assumptions about technology, but the order of magnitude is thought to be correct. Another set of estimates based on an even lower world resource of 1,350 × 10⁹ bbls puts peak production at 1,990 and the 80 per cent of cumulative production between 1961–2019 (Hubbert 1969). The time-span of the availability of oil and natural gas is thus quite limited, not only as a fuel but for the many other uses derived from its by-products, including pharmaceuticals and the use of hydrocarbons as a substrate for the growing of foods (Plate 17). The diversion of some crude-oil fractions to purposes other than energy generation seems likely some time before eventual exhaustion (Hubbert 1969). The middle 80 per cent of the petroleum family is likely to be gone in about 100

TABLE 10.7   World crude oil

Region	Proved reserves (1967) 10⁹ bbls	Est. ultimate recovery (EUR) 1967 est.[1]
Europe	3·0	20
Africa	31·9	250
Middle East	273·7	600
Far East	15·1	200
Latin America	56·9	225
Canada	10·9	95
United States	113·4	200
USSR and China and satellite states	65·5	500
Total world	571·0	2,090

[1] EUR = produced + proved + probable + future discoveries.
Source: Hubbert 1969

years, but coal will last 300–400 years alongside them (Fig. 10.6), although only 100–200 years if it were to be the main energy source. Thus on a grand time-scale the age of the fossil fuels appears as a transitory phase, even if the most generous estimates of reserves are accepted.

Nuclear energy

Considerable attention has been given to nuclear reactions, since small quantities of raw materials yield very large quantities of energy: 1 g of uranium 235 when fissioned yields 8·19 × 10¹⁰ joules which is equivalent to 2·7 mt of coal or 13·7 bbls of crude oil. An electrical power plant of 1,000 MW capacity would consume U-235 at a rate of only 3 kg/day. Three types of reactor have been built to house the controlled chain reaction in which U-235 is fissioned by the capture of thermal neutrons. These are burner, converter and breeder reactors; the first will use only U-235, which is a relatively rare element, occurring in nature with an abundance of 0·711 per cent of total uranium compared with the

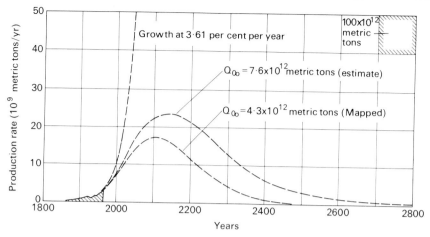

Fig. 10.6 A projection of two complete cycles of coal production for two different values of Q ∞ (see Fig. 10.5 for explanation). The effect upon the reserves of the current growth rate is also plotted. Compared with crude oil, a much longer availability is contemplated.
Source: Hubbert 1969

99·283 per cent of U-238. However, conversion and breeder reactors will use the fissile isotopes U-233, U-235, and plutonium (Pu) 239. U-238 and thorium 232, non-fissile, can be converted into fissile isotopes with an energy yield nearly the same as U-235. Since cheap uranium ores to supply U-235 for burner reactors are at a premium and likely to increase in price to the point of making atomic energy uneconomic in the short term, priority is being given to the development of the fast breeder reactor, or catalytic burner, using U-238 and Pu-239. In addition another breeder reactor using U-233 and thorium 232 is under development. This will allow the use of immense quantities of rock containing low amounts of uranium and thorium: within the USA the energy potentially obtainable from rocks occurring at minable depths containing at least 50 g/mt of combined uranium and thorium is hundreds or thousands of times larger than that of all the fossil fuels combined. One set of granites with a thorium concentration of 30 ppm would provide enough fuel for a world population of 2×10^{10} people using 20 KW/cap/yr for 200 years (Weinberg and Hammond 1971). Transition from burner and converter reactors to breeder types is therefore essential if the energy-producing potentialities are to be realized (Hubbert 1969, Singer 1971).

Atomic fusion may also be a source of energy: the fusion of deuterium and tritium (two isotopes of hydrogen) into helium, with the release of enormous quantities of energy, is called the hydrogen bomb. Regrettably for more peaceful purposes, the reaction cannot at present be controlled. Theoretically, two other reactions should be possible, the deuterium-deuterium fusion and the lithium-deuterium reaction. Using sea water as a source of raw materials in the first reaction, 1 m³ of sea water could yield $8 \cdot 16 \times 10^{12}$ joules, equivalent to 269 mt of coal or 1,360 bbls of crude oil (Table 10.8). 1 km³ of sea water would then equate with $1,360 \times 10^9$ bbls of crude oil, which is the lower of two estimates of world resources of crude oil. The total volume of the oceans would yield energy equivalent to 500,000 times the world's initial supply of fossil fuels. In the second reaction, lithium 6 is in the shortest supply. On a world basis about 2.4×10^{23} joules could be extracted from known lithium 6 deposits, about equal to the world's initial supply of fossil fuels (Hubbert 1971). Given, therefore, the technology to achieve controlled reactions, immense amounts of energy can be forthcoming from nuclear fusion; but the use of energy to perform work is only one part of the resource process. The raw materials have to be garnered and processed, waste matter must be disposed of, and heat is the inevitable by-product. The possible ecological effects of these other sectors of the resource process cannot be overlooked, and their costs should be included in the accounting of the supply industry. Thus estimates like those of Weinberg (1968), that within about 15–20 years there will be inexhaustible and ubiquitous energy at a price something like one-third of the present price of nuclear-generated power, may have to be tempered by the addition of the true costs of the environmental impact of such profusion. Nuclear energy on such a scale also gives rise to numerous fears about the safety of the process, chiefly centred upon the disposal of the radioactive wastes from fission plants (see Chapter 11). Here we will note that proposals

TABLE 10.8   Summary of energy yields from nuclear sources

1. Deuterium-deuterium fusion per atom: yield is 4.96 Mev $= 7.94 \times 10^{-13}$ joules
   or 34.4 g D (1 m³ of sea water) $= 8.16 \times 10^{12}$ joules $= 269$ mt coal $= 1,360$ bbls oil.
2. Lithium 6 per atom: yield is 22.4 Mev $= 3.58 \times 10^{-12}$ joules.
3. Uranium 235 per atom: yield is 200 Mev $= 3.20 \times 10^{-11}$ joules
   or 1 g U-235 $= 8.19 \times 10^{10}$ joules $= 2.7$ mt coal or 13.7 bbls oil.

Source: Hubbert 1969

have been made to site nuclear power stations offshore (Gwynne 1972) and underground (Rogers 1971) for reasons of safety and to avoid some land-use conflicts. Nevertheless, breeder reactors will involve large quantities of plutonium, only a few kilograms of which are necessary to produce an explosive device, and the possibilities of theft, sabotage, wrecking and threat rise with each additional generator; one company was unable to account for 6 per cent of the highly enriched uranium that it was supposed to possess. We might legitimately conclude that much of the enthusiasm about the future of energy supplies based on atomic power are predicated upon rather ideal social conditions. Even Dr Edward Teller, not exactly an opponent of nuclear power, has been quoted as saying in this context that sooner or later a fool will prove greater than the proof, even in a foolproof system.

Ecology of energy use

Any energy source has to be collected, or extracted, processed to a condition suitable for a particular use, transported or transmitted to its site of consumption and made to do work (Fig. 10.7). As a consequence of any of these stages waste products may be formed, and

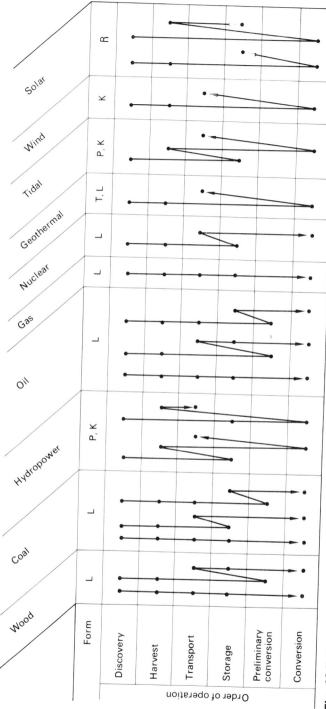

Fig. 10.7 The ecology of energy must also reflect the various stages in its recovery and use. Here the pathways of different energy sources of different forms (L = latent, P = potential, K = kinetic, T = thermal, R = radiant) through the sequence of operations between discovery and use is plotted, showing that alternatives exist for some and that the sequences vary.
Source: Luten 1971

heat is an inevitable result of the transfer of energy from a 'concentrated' to a 'dispersed' condition. Any of these stages may therefore exert their effects on the ecology of the biosphere at various scales. The magnitude of some of these effects is now such that the term 'pollution' is applied, and some will be discussed in greater detail in a later section.

The collection of energy sources is often an agent of ecological change: biota may be altered to capture particularly useful energy-rich organic matter as in agriculture; whole ecosystems may be drowned to provide a constant head of water for hydro-electric power plants. The destruction of large land areas for open-cast or strip-mining of coal and lignite is an analogous procedure. Restoration can take place, as it can for similar types of mineral extraction, but in countries like the USA control is a recent innovation and in Alberta, Canada, no conditions are imposed upon strip coal-mining works in the Rocky Mountain foothills. By contrast the restoration of agricultural land by the National Coal Board in Britain often provides better-drained farmland than previously existed. Although oil and natural gas from underground sources need only a well-head installation such as a derrick, a 'praying mantis' pump, or a simple capping installation, there is inevitably some ecological change in the vicinity of its installation unless, as in Los Angeles, the location is already suburban. In wildlands, however, forest clearance will be undertaken and the installation of the well-head equipment may involve road building and other forms of disturbance from which fragile environments are slow to recover.

Transportation and transmission of oil, natural gas and electricity are commonly by pipeline or overhead transmission lines. Although they can be partially landscaped, the latter share with the oilfield the opprobrium of being aesthetically unattractive, except perhaps to shareholders. Pipelines usually create only temporary disturbance if underground and only a visual intrusion if overground, but in the case of particularly fragile ecosystems certain types of pipeline create considerable problems. The example of the controversial 800-mile, 48-inch diameter (1280 km, 120 cm) pipeline from Prudhoe Bay to Valdez, Alaska, carrying oil across the tundra is possibly the most controversial case (Sage 1970). Oil exploration in the Arctic has shown how easy it is to damage the surface by using heavy equipment, thus compacting the surface layers and allowing increased solar penetration to the permafrost layer, and direct heating might produce similar conditions but more quickly. The Alaskan pipeline will carry 2 million barrels per day, would cross areas of seismic activity, and friction between the oil and the interior of the pipe would generate heat up to 60°C. With 11,000 barrels of oil in each mile (6,831 bbls/km), even perfect locks every 15 miles (24 km) might allow an efflux of 165,000 barrels in the event of a fracture. The construction would destroy arctic flora for 10–20 years even in minimally disturbed areas, use 80 million yd^3 of sand, gravel and crushed rock, and result in a bulk of thawed and muddy earth 6–9 m in diameter. Elsewhere in the USA there were 2,452 accidents in natural gas and liquid throughout pipelines during 1968–70 resulting in 80 deaths, 216 injuries and nearly $10 million of damage (Garvey 1972).

The processing and use of coal, oil, natural gas and nuclear fuels all create by-products of the combustion that is necessary to release their energy. In the case of nuclear energy the waste products are radioactive and require special care. The other energy sources yield mostly waste gases, though with coal there is a great amount of solid matter which is piled into heaps, put back down disused shafts or dumped into the sea. The waste gases are dominated by CO_2, though SO_2 is another common constituent, and the effects of them and other wastes on both local and global scales are discussed in the section on pollution. The greatest waste product of all is heat. This is usually released directly into the atmosphere or into large quantities of water which have been used as a coolant in the industrial process (Singer 1970b). Such calefaction of water changes its ecology drastically but contains the potential for the culture of rapidly growing tropical or subtropical herbivorous fish, provided the water is not so contaminated as to be toxic to the fish or their food (Bienfang 1971).

New techniques may in time revolutionize power production. Electro-gas dynamics, still in the early 1970s at an experimental stage, converts heat energy directly into electricity with high efficiency by sweeping charged particles through an electric field in a stream of gas. The efficiency of EGD generators appears to be independent of size, and the continuous combustion employed would yield 'cleaner' exhaust gases than from internal combustion engines (Musgrove and Wilson 1970). Another useful development might be the direct use of nuclear power to produce hydrogen gas. The basic raw material is water, which is also the chief product of combustion. The hydrogen could be transported by pipeline and stored cryogenically, for both of which the technology is available. Its thermal output is less than that of natural gas, so that one year's supply of natural gas for the USA ($22 \cdot 5 \times 10^{12}$ ft³/$0 \cdot 64 \times 10^{12}$ m³) would have to be replaced by 70×10^{12} ft³ ($1 \cdot 98 \times 10^{12}$ m³) of hydrogen, and four times the electrical generating capacity would be necessary. Hydrogen should also be 70 per cent efficient in fuel cells. Certain flammability problems are associated with its use: for example, certain hydrogen–air mixtures can be ignited by static electricity, but D. P. Gregory (1973) argues that an economy based on hydrogen transmission has distinct advantages for an industrial nation. The process is in some ways analogous to the gasification of coal which produces methane, which may then be transported in gaseous or liquid form.

General remarks on energy

The indispensability of power supplies in the modern world needs little emphasis, for there is no substitute for them, only interchangeability between sources. The suppliers of the resources are therefore in a position to extract a maximum return for their efforts, a fact not overlooked by the governments of oil-producing LDCs. In Britain, the coal miners' strike of January–February 1972 produced such unlooked-for effects as a shortage of eggs, since battery-hen production relies on electric power for lighting and ventilation; a shortage of milk, because of the ubiquity of power milking; difficulties of water supply, due to electrically powered pumps and also pipes burst during surges after cut-offs; and pollution of rivers, because only those sewage works with fermentation plants producing methane had enough power to treat the incoming effluents.

The economic and social factors which surround energy production and use play a large part in determining the cost of energy at a given location and hence the mix of energy sources which is available at a particular time. In the West, for example, the contribution of oil and natural gas has been increasing relative to coal, and in the USA this process has

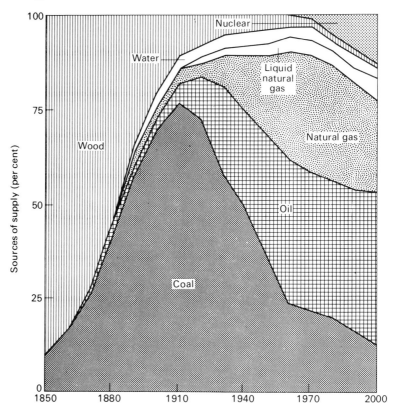

Fig. 10.8 A time sequence of the energy mix (in terms of the relative representation of different source for the USA. The rise and fall of coal is particularly noteworthy, although a renewed interest in it wa evinced during 1972–3. Although nuclear power is much hailed as an important new source, its co tribution to the overall mix is not expected to be particularly high. Resistance by citizen groups to th siting of nuclear power plants is one of the reasons for slow growth of this source.
Source: Singer 1970a

been taken much further (Fig. 10.8). Such shifts invariably cause different ecological effec according to the energy source: a shift to oil, for example, may mean less destructive stri mining of coal but more oil pollution of marine waters. Because of their requirements f water as a coolant, atomic power stations need to be sited on the coast or beside large lake often thus creating conflicts with recreation and amenity values.

Whatever the mix, the trend in energy requirements is inexorably upwards at a wor rate of about 4 per cent p.a. (Fig. 10.9). The main effects of this growth upon the ecosphe are in the substances released into the atmosphere as pollutants, and most important, hea In 1970, the world energy use was $5 \cdot 7 \times 10^{12}$ W, compared with a solar input of $1 \cdot 76 \times 10$ W of which 50 per cent is absorbed at the earth's surface. Man's output of heat was ther fore about one fifteen-thousandth (1/15,000) of the sun's contribution to the heating of th atmosphere (Brubaker 1972). At a rise of 4 per cent p.a. the human-induced proportic would be 1/100 in 130 years, 2 per cent in 148 years and equal to that of the sun in 25

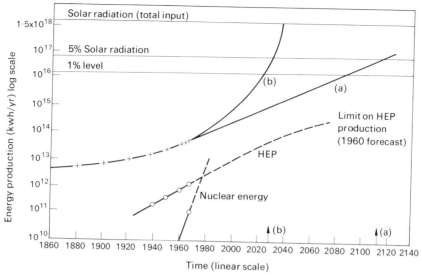

Fig. 10.9 A forecast of the increased heat emissions consequent upon rises in energy consumption. An equilibrium source producing no extra heat burden, such as HEP, is plotted along with a non-equilibrium source such as nuclear power. Curve (a) represents the current doubling time of 14 years; by AD 2028 heat emissions will have reached 1 per cent of the solar flux and by 2120 will be at the 5 per cent level. Curve (b) represents a compound growth law with a steadily decreasing doubling period for the growth rate.
Source: Chapman 1970

years. Pessimistic observers suggest that a 5 per cent level could give a global warming of 10°C which would bring about the melting of the polar ice-caps; Luten (1971) says that the 5 per cent level has indeed been reached over the 1,920 km² of the Los Angeles basin. Holding at or below the 5 per cent level is also suggested by Chapman (1970) since this is the order of temperature change involved in the Pleistocene climatic fluctuation. On the other hand, optimists such as Weinberg and Hammond (1971) calculate that 20×10^9 people consuming 20 KW/cap/yr (which is twice the current US usage) would add only 1/300 of the solar load and raise the global temperature by 0·25°C. The consumption figure may be a little low, since US consumption already appears headed for per capita figures several times the current level. As a perspective upon both points of view, we may note that, as Singer (1970) puts it, 'the atmospheric engine is subtle in its operation and delicate in its adjustments. Extra inputs of energy in particular places can have significant and far-reaching consequences.' Synergistic effects may also intervene; a rising carbon dioxide level (see Chapter 11) will presumably decrease heat loss, since CO_2 has strong absorption bands in the infra-red spectrum of outward-bound heat energy (Ehrlich and Holdren 1969). Shifts from fossil and nuclear sources of energy to 'equilibrium' sources such as solar radiation, tidal and HEP sources might be desirable to reduce risks of atmospheric instability, but their contributions to the totals envisaged by an industrializing world seem to be likely to be small. Acceptance, therefore, of a limit to the use of heat-generating energy requires a radical rethinking of the West's way of life since 1750.

Mineral resources

Stuff for things

The planet is, and has to be, self-sufficient in its sources of materials to make 'things'. Apart from a few kilograms of moon-dust, which has not entered commercial use, all minerals come from the earth's crust, and their transformation also requires a few elements from the atmosphere such as nitrogen, hydrogen and oxygen. The history of mineral use is also the history of man's material culture, dating from the first use of rock tools for killing and dismembering animals, and the origins of present machine-orientated cultures lie in the discovery of how to smelt metal ores. Copper was first, but was replaced eventually by the much harder iron. It was the much later discovery by Abraham Darby of Coalbrook-dale that iron could be smelted using coke as a fuel that set up one of the foundation pillars of the industrial state; today's world can be said with some truth to be built upon a framework of steel.

Wealth from the earth

We demand a great variety of planetary inorganic materials. Chief among these are the ores which are used on a large scale to yield metals like iron, aluminium and copper. To them must be added elements which may not be needed in large quantities but which are indispensable in many modern industrial processes, as for example catalysts and hardeners: vanadium, tungsten and molybdenum are instances of this category. Finally there are non-metallic materials which are vital to industrialized nations such as sand and gravel, cement, fluxes, clay, salt, sulphur, diamonds, and the chemical by-products of petroleum refining.

The distribution of minerals in the earth's crust is characterized by discontinuity. There is, immediately, spatial discontinuity in which deposits rarely coincide with the boundaries of nation states that wish to use them. North America is well supplied with the ore of molybdenum, for example, whereas Asia is not; by way of compensation Asia is rich with tin, tungsten and manganese. Between them, Cuba and New Caledonia have half the world's reserves of nickel, and industrial diamonds are dominated by Zaïre. Such discontinuities are emphasized by temporal patterns of use: the older industrial countries such as the UK are running out of their ore reserves and coming to depend upon imports, and heavy users like the USA face similar problems; in both cases iron ore stands as a good example. The political ramifications are obvious. Another type of discontinuity is exemplified by the richness of an ore. A few metal ores show a more or less continuous grading from the richest ores (which are usually worked first and are cheapest to extract) to the poorest: iron and porphyry copper are examples. On the other hand some ores are either very rich or very poor or both. A simple extension of extraction and refining techniques learned from the rich ores down to the poorest may not thus be possible: a whole new dimension of technology may well be essential (Lovering 1968). In spite of any difficulties of supply and processing, the industrial nations of the world have come to be very large users of minerals of all kinds. Iron and its products are perhaps the most important, and are a good index of industrialization. From 1957 to 1967 the worldwide rate of increase in steel consumption per capita was 44 per cent, from 100kg/cap to 144 kg/cap. Japan, for example, rose by 270 per cent, the USA by 12 per cent (Fig. 10.10). In absolute amounts the USA uses most steel: 634 kg/cap in 1967; this is of course new steel to be added to that already in existence. Analyses of figures of production and of losses suggests that each US citizen is now supported by 9.4 mt of steel, mostly in the form of heavy structure, piling and galvanized sheet metal but about 8 per cent in cars, trucks and buses (H. Brown et al. 1963, L. R. Brown 1970).

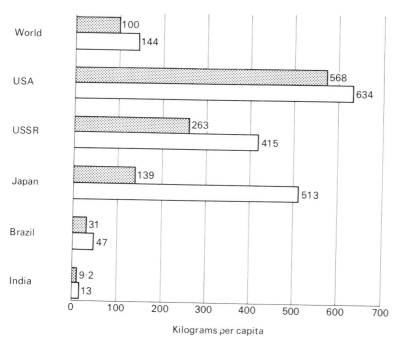

Fig. 10.10 World steel consumption 1957 (stippled) and 1967 (open). The rises were substantial but unevenly distributed, showing the continued dominance of already industrialized nations and the rapid consumption by countries like Japan which was experiencing a phase of fast economic growth. LDCs, by contrast, used little more.
Source: H. Brown 1970

The extension of these levels of use to other parts of the world would place some strain upon resources. To raise the present population of the world to such standards would require an annual increase in extraction of iron by 75 times, 100 times as much copper, 75 times for zinc and 250 times for tin. The iron (18.3×10^9 mt) could theoretically be supplied, although a shortage of molybdenum for the iron–steel conversion process might be limiting; but for the others the quantities involved exceed all known or inferred reserves: 305 million mt of copper, 203 million mt of zinc and 30.5 million mt of tin (H. Brown et al. 1963). Although the LDCs cannot be expected to reach such levels quickly even if they desired, the limiting nature of these statistics in terms of eventual industrialization (some-times proclaimed as a panacea for LDCs) is apparent. Even a level of 1–2 mt of steel per capita represents a formidable programme of capital investment and energy use. And all these calculations assume a static population which seems hardly to be the case. Although figures for the USA are somewhat atypical, they nevertheless represent a level of aspiration in many places. Apart from the steel requirement discussed above, the US citizen is also responsible for the yearly use of 7·25 kg of lead, 3·55 mt of stone, sand and gravel, 227 kg of cement, 91 kg of clay, and 91 kg of salt; in all representing about 20·32 mt of raw material to be extracted from the earth to support each individual (L. R. Brown 1970). Demands upon the planet's resources and space caused by extension of such demands to many nations would be staggering, but under the present system of economics are unlikely to occur.

Future use

Increasing population levels, together with higher per capita use, have led to concern about future supply. Very sober calculations of future reserves of critical materials have been

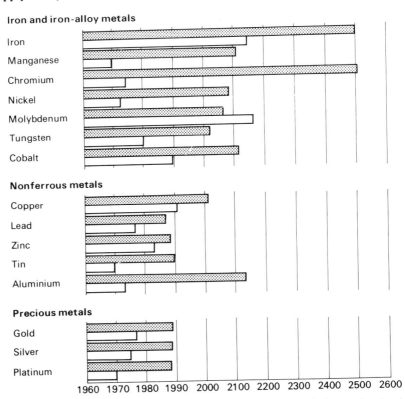

Fig. 10.11 Estimated lifetimes of useful reserves for the world (stippled) and for the USA (open Assumptions include a rising demand created by both population growth and increased per capita use and the discovery of new reserves. US demands are expected to increase four and a half times AD 2000.
Source: H. Brown 1970

made, and the time-span over which such reserves appear to last is shown in Fig. 10.11. The relatively short periods of availability of reserves have thus caused many writers to emphasize the need for conservation of materials, especially metals, which in practice means recycling them after use. New reserves need then only be called upon to replace losses by processes such as friction. (The possible contribution of the seas and oceans is discussed in Chapter 9. Here it need only be repeated that costs will make recovering of all but the commonest minerals virtually prohibitive.) More optimistic views have appeared as well. The work of Lasky upon copper, which stated that as the grade of ore decreases arithmetically, so its abundance will increase geometrically until the average abundance in the earth's crust is reached, led to some euphoria about mineral supply. However, it is only applicable to ores with a continuously decreasing ratio of ore to gangue rock and fails to take into account the cost of energy in extracting the poor ores (Cloud 1968). Similarly, the presence of most mineral elements in common rocks such as granite has led to the suggestion (H. Brown 1954) that specialized deposits can eventually be abandoned and all necessities extracted in multi-metal plants based upon granite. Apart from environmental and storage difficulties (mined rock increases by some 40 per cent in volume), the idea is totally predicated upon unlimited cheap energy, the supply of which is not yet assured. Cloud (1968) sets the costs of high capital investment, power transmission, waste disposal and plant operation against the cheapness of extraction forecast by nuclear-power proponents, and suggests (Fig. 10.12) that increased application of energy does not proportionately increase production of minerals.

In the shorter term, some economists have postulated that since the costs of production of metal ores have been falling, the availability of future supplies cannot be in danger. Furthermore, the promises of technological breakthroughs in techniques of recovery and

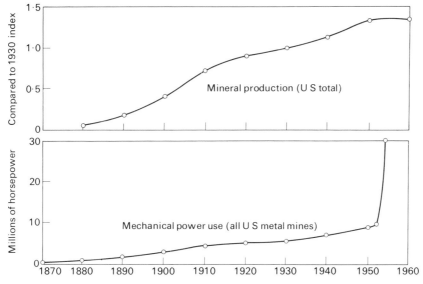

Fig. 10.12 Data produced by Lovering (1969) to suggest that increase in energy input into mining does not increase the output of minerals.

processing, and of substitution if price levels rise too high, are more likely to be kept i this field of endeavour than most; nevertheless Lovering (1968) disputes that unit cos of production of metal ores are declining, and suggests that conclusions such as those Barnett and Morse (1963) that 'the progress of growth generates antidotes to a gener increase in resource scarcity' are not sustainable except where short-term economics ar the only factor in determining the resource processes involved. Granted that materia technology holds a great future, the cornucopian promise (Barnett and Morse 1963) th 'technological progress is automatic and self-reproducing in modern economies' is perhap a little sweeping for most people, and does nothing for the LDCs which are deficient i technology.

A modification of the cornucopian view suggests that supplies will always be availabl though at increasingly higher cost, but that the very fact of their ubiquity will pose seriot threats to apparently inexhaustible resources such as air and water. It is possible therefor to believe in a continuity of mineral supply while advocating the overall strategy propose by the neo-Malthusians.

Ecology of mineral use

As Flawn (1966) puts it,

> Man, like an earthworm, burrows into the earth and turns over its surface; like a bir he brings material from elsewhere to build his nest; and like the pack rat he accumulate quantities of trash.

And most of these activities have side-effects of an ecological nature. Underground minin for example, may include whole new towns among its surface installations: the San Manu coppermine in Arizona necessitated 1,000 dwellings, 19 km of paved streets and thre schools. Timber is cut in forested areas, often leading to soil erosion, and the tailings an mine-waste have to be discarded. Large-size solid wastes can be used as backfill or sold fc aggregates, but tailings usually yield silt particles to wind and water and are often chemicall unstable; the only suitable treatment appears to be to 'fix' them with vegetation. Min waters are often heavily contaminated and have to be treated chemically and physically, c injected into 'safe' rock strata. Either method is expensive and the desire to forgo suc outlays may overcome some mining operators, resulting in ecologically toxic effects. It reported, for example, that the Bougainville mine in the Solomon Islands, extracting 0·4 per cent copper ore, was preceded by the removal of 40 million tons of overburden, inclu ing forest, and two-fifths of all material mined (over 400 million tons) will be dumped i a neighbouring valley. An oval basin 2·1 × 1·5 km will be an end result, as will the chokin of the water courses and silting of the coastline. The lifetime of the project is estimated 25–30 years and the profits to the developer at £20 million/yr (Counter Informatic Services n.d.).

Plate 18 (opposite) The skeleton of the industri world is derived from iron ore. This pit in Minnesot USA, exemplifies the attributes of mineral resourc recovery in holes and heaps, high energy input, and large land area for both the pit and its associate services and housing for workers. *(Grant Heilma Lititz, Pa)*

Considered for the whole world, open-pit mining is more widespread than extraction b
shaft; in the USA, for example, 80 per cent of metallic ores and 95 per cent of non-metalli
minerals and rocks are extracted by this means (Plate 18). The technology has been facil
tated by machines such as dumper trucks with a capacity of 137 mt, coal haulers of 245 m
capacity and draglines with 84 m booms. Thus the biggest operations can extract 101,60
mt (100,000 tons) of ore per day. Waste disposal becomes a major problem to which backfi
is the obvious solution; if the topsoil is saved then restoration to agricultural or recre
tional use is often possible. Where dredging is concerned, disposal of spoil is the mai
difficulty, together with changes in the equilibrium systems of water bodies. The extractio
of sand and gravel from bays has caused the erosion of beaches, and in river beds ha
increased the downstream erosive capacity of the stream. The extra sediment suspensior
created may kill flora and fauna, as with oyster reefs along the Texas coast. The processe
of concentration, beneficiation and refining may all create biological change if variou
products are released into nearby ecosystems. Washing yields sediment and slime-charge
liquid wastes, leaching produces spent acids, flotation is a source of tailings and contam
nated liquids, and smelting gives rise to slags and gases high in elements like sulphur o
even fluorine. Devastated areas like the lower Swansea Valley of south Wales or Copper Hi
in Tennessee are familiar examples. Nearly all these effluents can be treated or put to gainfu
use, usually at some extra cost, but they would be produced in unprecedented quantitie
if 'common rock' such as granite were to be used as a multi-mineral source, for the rati
of waste to usable rock would be 2,000 : 1. If underground leaching were adopted, larg
underground explosions would be needed to shatter the rock, followed by the drilling o
input and recovery wells. Subsequent contamination of ground water with extractiv
chemicals would be difficult to avoid. One further aspect of mineral extraction and proces
ing is the differential invasion of wild ecosystems where competition for other uses ten
to be less and where processing is remote from concentrations of people who might b
harmed. An example is the Canadian shield, a very heavily mineralized region, where th
wild lands are highly valued for their unaltered state. Then controversy ensues, as wit
the constant pressure to open the Wilderness Areas of the USA to mining, or with th
explorations for gold and copper reserves in the Snowdonia National Park in north Wale

Each individual industrial plant, along with the energy use from which it is inseparabl
produces local ecological change by placing a strain on the capacity of the systems of th
biosphere to absorb the concentrations of elements which industrial processes create, an
which economics dictate shall be discarded. Whether there is a worldwide capacity fc
wastes is difficult to assess, but monitoring of potentially toxic elements would seem to b
a minimal step towards trying to avert any breakdown of the biogeochemical cycles of th
planet on anything other than a restricted spatial scale.

Recycling

Increased recovery of mineral elements from scrap and waste is often advocated as a re
ponse to shortages and a way of minimizing the environmental impacts of the extraction o
new materials. Success of the processes depends upon the quantities available in th
recoverable unit (obsolete iron machinery has scrap value but not iron rods embedded i

concrete foundations), and the resistance of the material to chemical and physical break-down. Costs of collection will be high from dispersed sources: thus lead from exhausted vehicle batteries can be reclaimed but not that from lead bullets, except perhaps in Texas.

TABLE 10.9   Scrap metal in the United States

Metal	Approximate annual recovery from scrap[1] (1 ton = 1·016 mt; 1 oz = 28·349 g)	Remarks
Iron	70–85 million tons[2]	In the iron cycle from mine to product to recovery, the loss of iron is 16–36 per cent. About half the feed for steel furnaces is scrap.
Copper	1 million tons	Secondary copper production from old and new scrap ranges from 900,000 to 1,000,000 tons per year, about half of which is old scrap. Old scrap reserve is estimated at 35 million tons in cartridge cases, pipe, wire, auto radiators, bearings, valves, screening, lithographers' plates.
Lead	0·5 million tons	Estimated reserve is 4 million tons of lead in batteries, cable coverings, railway car bearings, pipe, sheet lead, type metal.
Zinc	0·25–0·40 million tons	Zinc recovered from zinc, copper, aluminium, and magnesium-based alloys.
Tin	20,000–25,000 tons	Tin recovered from tin plate and tin-based alloys, 20 per cent; tin recovered from copper and lead-based alloys, 80 per cent.
Aluminium	0·3 million tons	Because aluminium is a comparatively new metal the old scrap pool is small, but it is growing rapidly.
Precious metals	gold = 1 million ounces silver = 30 million ounces	Precious metals including platinum are recovered from jewellery, watch cases, optical frames, photo labs, chemical plants. Because of the high value, recovery is high.
Mercury	10,520 flasks	Recovery is high. Nearly all mercury in mercury cells, boiler instruments and electrical apparatus is recovered when items are scrapped. Other sources are dental amalgams, battery scrap, oxide and acetate sludges.

[1] Includes old and new scrap. New scrap or 'home' scrap is produced in the metallurgical and manu-facturing process; old scrap is 'in use'.
[2] Old and new scrap *consumed* rather than *recovered*.
Source: Flawn 1966

The costs of recycling must be set against those of new materials and at present the latter are generally less. Many of those who hold neo-Malthusian or 'environmentalist' views advocate a minerals tax which would increase the price of new material *vis-à-vis* recycled substances, forcing a shift towards greater employment of secondary sources. Some notion of the sources and quantities of metal recycling in the USA are given in Table 10.9.

Energy and minerals in the face of rising populations

Substances such as metals and concrete are for practical purposes limited in quantity, for only 0·1 per cent of the crust of the earth is accessible by any imaginable means. Clearly, new reserves will be found, new processes for refining lower-grade ores perfected and recyling more pervasively adopted, but such generalities must of necessity be resolved into specifics and the time taken to develop new processes may result in shortages. Again, the demands of an industrializing world may prove very hard to meet and it could be difficult to sustain the situation where nations like the USA with less than 10 per cent of the world's population are using some 30–40 per cent of its material resources.

The past 200 years has seen the development of a fossil-fuel-based foundation to the world economy, and only because of industrial processes can agriculture be intensified: the Green Revolution is essentially an outgrowth of the Industrial Revolution, for it depends upon synthesized fertilizers and pesticides, together with pumped water. The material benefits of energy-intensive industry are so apparent that people in the LDCs, informed by instant electronic communications and every Hollywood film of their desirability, are coming to want them too. Landsberg (1971) argues that energy consumption in the West is related less to population growth than affluence and that a reduction in incomes would be far more effective in slowing demand than zero population growth (ZPG). A Shell Oil Company (1972) report agrees, suggesting that immediate ZPG would reduce demand by only 3 per cent in the USA during 1972–85. Add to this the propensity of the people of the West to be gulled into demanding more than they need, and the basic energy–minerals problem is clear. Two basic attitudes, to be further discussed in Chapter 13, have evolved: a Malthusian attitude which considers that only a stable population practising re-use of all materials, preferably in a frugal way, can provide anything like a satisfactory solution in both material and environmental terms; and a cornucopian view which is predicated upon the discoveries of technology allied to the economics of a society in which expansion of production and consumption is an essential element, although even optimists like Weinberg say that energy abundance must be used to buy time in which to stabilize populations. Whether either of the extremes will turn out to be correct is not yet foreseeable, but we need to remind ourselves of the key role of energy not only in industry but in all resource processes, and the fact that there is no substitute for it, only different ways of harnessing it. It is easier to substitute for materials especially if energy is plentiful, e.g. hydrogen can be used to smelt iron, gasify coal or make a hydrogenated liquid fuel from coal; but the development of new techniques tends to be lengthy, the more so because of the inertia of vested capital in existing processes. Energy is so crucial that its costs (under any economic system) seem likely to be the main element of material costs, whether of mining new metal ore or recycling scrap. Energy availability and price therefore define what is and what is not a resource, and the basic currency of a world in resource stress, whether from shortages of minerals or food or both, is likely to be energy. But its production exists in the real world of a limited biosphere. Its use creates waste products, notably heat, which have to be dispersed, and the capacity of the atmosphere to absorb this without disturbing its balances may be limited. As with agriculture our capacity to increase qualities is, subject to certain overall limits, very great if we will the money and people to work on it, but more than ever the question must also be asked, 'What are the ecological consequences of such expansions of production and use?'

Further reading

BROWN, H. 1954: *The challenge of man's future.*

— 1970: Human materials production as a process in the biosphere.

DARMSTADTER, J. 1971: *Energy and the world economy.*

FLAWN, P. 1966: *Mineral resources.*

GARVEY, G. 1972: *Energy, ecology, economy.*

HAMMOND, A. L. *et al.* 1973: *Energy and the future.*

HUBBERT, M. KING 1969: Energy resources.

LEWIS, R. S. and SPINRAD, B. I. (eds.) 1972: *The energy crisis.*

ODUM, H. T. 1971: *Environment, power and society.*

SCHURR, S. H. (ed.) 1972: *Energy, economic growth and the environment.*

'SCIENTIFIC AMERICAN' 1971: Energy and power issue, **224** (3) (September).

THOMAS, T. M. 1973: World energy sources: survey and review.

11

Wastes and pollution

Everything touched by King Midas turned to gold. By a sort of inversion process, pretty well everything modern men touch, including themselves, turns to a waste product sooner or later. Exceptions are rare, and centre around such things as valued landscape views, and objects of 'high culture' such as Old Masters, priceless buildings and symphonies. Even Michelangelos will crumble some day, presumably, and fed through hi-fi technology Brahms may become noise pollution. In the sphere of material use, the creation of waste products is generally accepted as inevitable: food becomes sewage, automobiles become junked cars, while quarries and mines become derelict land. The ways in which some of the wastes arise in an industrial society are shown in Fig. 11.1.

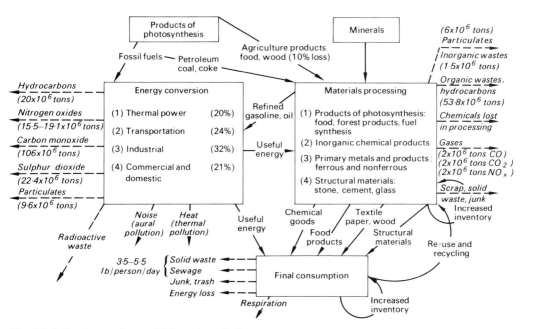

Fig. 11.1 A scheme of material flow through the resource processes of the USA, showing how inputs of energy and materials become converted to various kinds of wastes. Those from energy conversion in particular become contaminants of the atmosphere. Two attitudes to pollution are possible: one seeks to disperse the contaminants over a wide area and hence decrease their effect; the other wishes to increase the magnitude of the 're-use and recycling' loop and possibly erect other loops.
Source: O'Riordan 1971b

Wastes of all kinds may follow one of two paths when they become identified as such. They may be regarded as sources of raw materials (the resource process of re-use or recycling) or ignored as too costly or technically unsuitable to undergo such processing. In the first type of perception, sewage becomes a source of manure, junked cars a veritable treasure-heap of steel, and derelict land an opportunity to create new parkland or housing space. The second perception sees bagged fertilizer as cheaper than dried sludge, new steel as more convenient than reprocessing old cars, and agricultural land as easier to convert to housing than levelled tip heaps; and there is as yet no way of filtering out the organochlorine pesticides from the waters of the oceans. The strategy of re-use is thus heavily dependent upon the relative cost of re-used and new materials and hence of the type of technology used in each process, assuming that supplies *de novo* of the material are still plentiful. Global scarcity would change the relative costs quite strikingly.

Materials and waste heat from energy consumption which currently are not or cannot be re-used are led off into the environment as a means of disposal. Usually the wastes are not put back at the point of first extraction but as close as possible to the processing plant or the sites of use: wastes from coal extraction accumulate at the pit head, garbage in the dustbins of domestic consumers and then at the municipal rubbish dump; heat and gases are dispersed into the atmosphere (Plate 19). Food wastes are usually discarded into water, with or without processing. In fact, the use of flowing water or the ocean margins as sinks for all kinds of agricultural, urban and industrial wastes is the outstanding feature of the world's resource processes: the hydrological cycle ensures the steady movement of all kinds of wastes into the oceans, and the deeps are deliberately used for the dumping of radioactive material and spare barrels of chemical and biological warfare (CBW) agents. Most of the systems of the biosphere have some capacity for absorbing foreign substances, although quantities vary greatly (McGauhey 1968). But each has a threshold beyond which its functioning is altered. Sewage above certain concentrations drastically alters the level of available oxygen in fresh water and thus eliminates certain fauna, for example; likewise toxic fumes poured from an industrial plant may kill vegetation downwind from the point of effluence, and toxins may accumulate with lethal effects in the bodies of animals. When waste substances reach such a concentration that they exert measurable effects upon ecosystems then they are said to be pollutants. The term is also used for waste substances which impinge upon human life, where the threshold is cultural rather than biological. So the presence of high noise-levels near airports, for example, becomes labelled pollution. Similarly, an odour emitted from a pig farm or a chemical factory may be unacceptable, and called pollution, even though it is doing no detectable biological damage to the people. The two kinds of threshold interact. The death of songbirds from pesticide poisoning may not 'matter', since they are not an 'economic' resource and their niche in the ecosystem can be filled by another group, but their loss is culturally unacceptable to many people. There can be no doubt that acceptability of the pollutant by-products of economic activity varies with affluence: it is the already rich nations which are trying to grapple with pollution. Poor countries and the poorer regions of the industrialized nations are prepared to tolerate the effects of pollution if their living standard is raised by the operation of the earlier parts of the resource process: loss of wildlife through use of DDT brings little sorrow to Asians freed from malaria, and the cessation of pollution from pulp-mill waste is

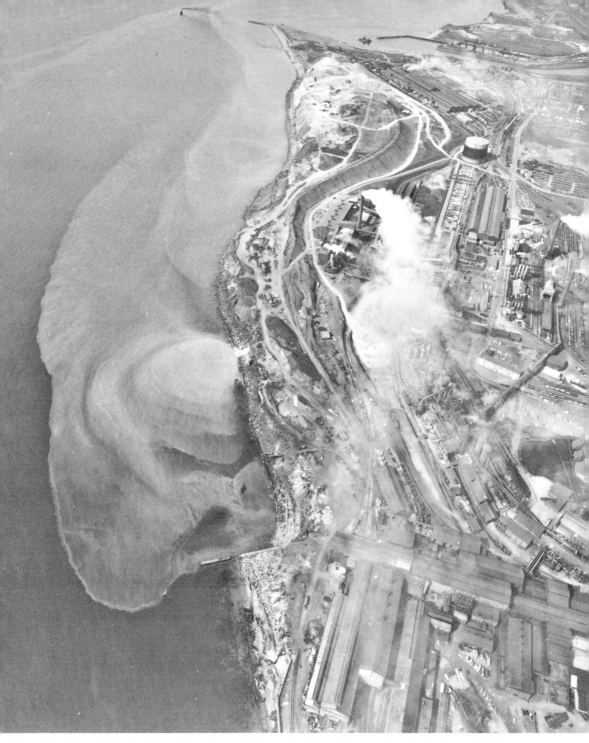

Plate 19 Industrial and urban areas gather together materials and hence dispose of the wastes in a concentrated form. This steel works at Workington, Cumberland, England, can be seen to be emitting wastes into both the sea and the atmosphere. *(Aerofilms Ltd, London)*

little compensation to the workers of the shut-down plant in an isolated part of Newfoundland. Cultural thresholds are very difficult to quantify, since man possesses the ability to adapt to changing external circumstances and little is known about the way in which levels of tolerance are felt.

Classification of wastes and pollutants

A division of the various types of wastes for purposes of discussion is attempted in this chapter, on the basis of the type of material and its ecological effect when it reaches a concentration sufficient for it to be called a pollutant. This method is chosen in preference

TABLE 11.1   Major waste products and their receiving environments

Wastes	Environments into which wastes are discharged: X / Environments into which wastes get transferred: O				
	Air	Fresh water	Oceans	Land	Clinical effects of residues on humans?
Gases and associated particulate matter (e.g. SO$_2$, CO$_2$, CO, smoke, soot)	X	O	O	O	Yes
Photochemical compounds of exhaust gases	X	O	?	O	Yes
Urban/industrial solid wastes			X	X	No
Persistent inorganic residues, e.g. lead (Pb), mercury (Hg)	X	O	OX	X	Pb—disputed Hg—definitely
Persistent organic compounds:					
Oil			X	O	No
Organochlorine residues	O	XO	X	X	Disputed
Pharmaceutical wastes		X	O		Unknown
Short-life wastes:					
Sewage		X	X		Possible bacteria carrier
Fertilizer residues with N$_2$, P		O	O	X	Yes, especially N$_2$
Detergent with P		X	O		No
Radioactivity	X	O	X	O	Yes
Land dereliction				X	No
Heat	X	X			No
Noise	X				Yes
Deliberate wasting—CBW, e.g. defoliation		O	O	X	Yes

to the alternative way of classification by type of environment (air, land, sea, etc.) since it involves less repetition. A summary chart of waste material by environment type is presented in Table 11.1.

Gaseous and particulate wastes emitted into the atmosphere

Fossil fuels and water vapour

The gaseous composition of the atmosphere is more or less constant except for the amount of water vapour. By-products of a gaseous and finely divided particulate nature are emitted into it: some are gases already present in the 'natural' air, others are foreign (Schaefer 1970), and some particles such as dust from exposed soils are also present in uncontaminated air. Notably, most of the emissions into the atmosphere are by-products of the combustion of fossil fuels for energy use. (Table 11.2 shows the relative values of common pollutants for one year in the USA. Radioactive wastes are also produced during power generation by nuclear fission, but are dealt with separately below.) The biggest product of such oxidation reactions is water, but this is not usually regarded as a contaminant, possibly since the atmospheric content is normally variable between 1–3 per cent by volume and emissions do not radically change this figure at ground level. At higher altitudes, it may be noted in passing, some writers have suggested that water emissions from turbojet engines may form coalescent condensation trails along busy airlanes. The actual evidence for this eventuality is scanty, but Bryson and Wendland (1970) calculate that if 300 supersonic transports (SSTs) were travelling at 2,400 kph, and 1 per cent make contrails with an average duration of 25 hrs and the average width is 1·6 km (figures all derived from military supersonic aircraft), then permanent gloom from a man-made cirrus cloud would cover the area of operation. The SCEP (1970) study is more cautious but suggests that water-vapour injection in areas of dense traffic may increase by 60 per cent and that greater cloudiness in the stratosphere will be likely, though no estimates of the magnitude are made.

TABLE 11.2   Emissions of air pollutants (USA 1969, in millions of tons p.a.; 1 million tons = 1·016 mt)

Source	CO	Particulates	SO_2	HC	NO_x	Total	% change 1968–9
Transportation	111·5	0·8	1·1	19·8	11·2	144·4	− 1·0
Fuel combustion in stationary sources	1·8	7·2	24·4	0·9	10·0	44·3	+ 2·5
Industrial processes	12·0	14·4	7·5	5·5	0·2	39·6	+ 7·3
Solid waste disposal	7·9	1·4	0·2	2·0	0·4	11·9	− 1·0
Miscellaneous	18·2	11·4	0·2	9·2	2·0	41·0	+ 18·5
Total	151·4	35·2	33·4	37·4	23·8	281·2	+ 3·2

Source: US President's Council on Environmental Quality 1971

CO, CO_2, SO_2 and H_2S

These four gases comprise the biggest volume of wastes emitted into the atmosphere (Landau 1968, Stern 1968). Carbon monoxide, mainly from the internal combustion engine, is the largest of the three and in the USA its volume equals the sum of all the other industrial contaminants (about 100 million tons/yr). In cities its concentration is usually between 1 and 55 ppm with an average 10 ppm, but detectable clinical symptoms appear at 100 ppm (a level often achieved in Oxford Circus, London) and humans are killed at 1,000 ppm. Los Angeles has established alert levels for CO at 100, 200 and 300 ppm. Its effect often spreads into buildings, especially during the heating season when it is drawn into apartment blocks and offices by upward currents of warm air: in one office building in New York, permissible CO levels were exceeded for 47 per cent of the time during which the block was being heated. Although deleterious to humans because of its affinity for haemoglobin, thus depriving body tissues of their oxygen supply, CO is not cumulative, and removal of the pollutant source allows a rapid return to a normal level. At high concentrations, however, its effect appears to be synergistic. Its major effect therefore is as a human poison, rather than a factor of ecological change.

Carbon dioxide is normally present at a concentration of about 310 ppm. Since, however, it does not affect people until the level reached is about 5,000 ppm, it is rarely regarded as a pollutant on a local scale except where carbonate-containing rocks are common building materials. Since the early nineteenth century, global emissions of CO_2, mostly from the combustion of fossil fuels, have risen rapidly to the point where some 14 per cent of the CO_2 in the atmosphere is produced by industry, and by AD 2000 an estimated 50 per cent will have been produced in this way, at current rates of increase. Oxidation of all the remaining fossil fuels present in the earth's crust would increase the amount of atmospheric CO_2 by seventeen times. Concern over CO_2 levels is therefore mostly at a global scale and is dealt with below.

Although produced in smaller quantities by resource use than the two previous gases, sulphur dioxide is much more toxic. It comes from the combustion of coal and fuel oils, at sulphuric acid plants, and in the processing of metal ores containing sulphur. In the atmosphere it lasts an average of 43 days, being converted to SO_3 and reacting with water to produce an aerosol form of sulphuric acid which is toxic to plants at 0·2 ppm and is highly corrosive of iron, steel, copper and nickel, while building materials containing carbonates find these compounds replaced by soluble sulphates. Sulphur dioxide is produced in very large quantities in urban-industrial areas: New York City emits nearly 2 million tons/yr (2·2 million mt) from coal, and Great Britain 5·8 million tons (5·9 million mt). A concentration of 1–5 ppm usually produces a detectable physiological response in man, and in London's great smog of December 1952, 1·34 ppm was recorded; elsewhere, urban concentrations yp to 3·2 ppm have been noted. Plants are injured at such levels, and animals including man suffer from inflammation of the upper respiratory tract. Like CO, therefore, SO_2 is particularly a pollutant of urban areas, although downwind transport of H_2SO_4 from industrial Britain is claimed to be acidifying the fresh-water bodies of Scandinavia. Some sulphates have been claimed to be damaging to health at concentrations 30–40 times lower than, for example, the SO_2 levels set for the USA by the Clean Air Act of 1970.

Hydrogen sulphide and its related organic compounds, mercaptans, are sometimes by-products of petroleum processing, coking, rayon manufacture and the Kraft process for making paper pulp. Hydrogen sulphide is also present when anaerobic bacteria are found in considerable quantity, as in inadequately treated sewage. Both these sources are nuisances rather than dangers, their odour being detectable at concentrations of 0·03 ppb (mercaptans) and 0·035–0·10 ppm (H_2S).

Smog

The combustion of coal, oil or natural gas in power plants and the internal combustion engine both result in the emission of nitrous oxides into the atmosphere (Haagen-Smit and Wayne 1968). Of these sources, the incomplete combustion of the auto engine is by far the most important contributor by a factor of about 6. Because of its motorized life-style and inversion frequency, Los Angeles provides many of the data on nitrous oxides and their atmospheric fate. LA County produces about 0·15 kg of nitrous oxides/cap/day and concentrations of 0·02–0·9 ppm are typical, with an alert level at 3·00 ppm. The major constituent is NO_2 (nitrogen dioxide), which is a respiratory irritant. It also absorbs sunlight, especially in the blue wavelengths, and so appears as a yellow-brown gas in which a concentration of 8–10 ppm reduces visibility to one mile. Since it absorbs sunlight, it can undergo photolysis, at a rate of 2 ppm/hr. The chemical reactions are complex (Fig. 11.2),

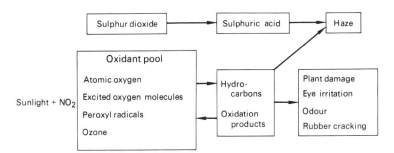

Fig. 11.2 A scheme of the reactions involved in photochemical air pollution.
Source: Landau 1968

but the products include ozone, formaldehyde and nitrous oxide (NO). This latter appears to be oxidized to NO_2, providing a further source of reactants. Numerous other substances are present in the ensuing 'photochemical smog' resulting either from atmospheric reactions or incomplete combustion in auto engines. They include other aldehydes, olefins, ethylene and peroxyacetyl nitrate (PAN) (Table 11.3). This somewhat heady brew bears little relation to laughing gas, and indeed lachrymation is one of the usual effects. Ozone concentrations of 1·25 ppm cause respiratory difficulties, and a series of smog-alert levels in Los Angeles and other North American and Japanese cities tell citizens, especially those with chronic respiratory ailments, of the potential dangers of smog levels. The effects of smog are not confined to people: damage to crops during the 1960s in California exceeded $8 million/yr, and on the eastern seaboard of the USA $18 million. The forests around the

Los Angeles basin, a vital reserve of recreation space, suffer from various forms of die-off due to atmospheric pollution and it is thought that ozone is probably the chief agent of biotic damage. Damage to materials is also prevalent, stretched rubber being one of the most vulnerable substances. Los Angeles, due to its geographical peculiarities, is the most quoted example of a smoggy city, and as such often used as a whipping-boy (whipping-girl would be more accurate, in view of its full name) by all opponents of the motor car. But practically all industrial cities suffer to some degree from photochemical smog, and any which are liable to air stagnation, usually in the form of inversions, are vulnerable to smog accumulation, like Toronto and New York in the summer of 1970; in large Japanese cities such as Kyoto and Tokyo, CO level readout panels are installed at some intersections and sometimes the traffic police wear masks as confirmation of the high levels of exhaust gases.

TABLE 11.3   Typical ranges of air contaminant levels in Los Angeles, smoggy and non-smoggy days

| Contaminant | Typical contaminant range, ppm | | Record maximum value, ppm |
	Smoggy day[1]	Non-smoggy day[2]	
Aldehydes	0·05–0·60	0·05–0·60	1·87
Carbon monoxide	8·00–60·00	5·00–50·00	72·00
Hydrocarbons	0·20–2·00	0·10–2·00	4·66
Oxides of nitrogen[3]	0·25–2·00	0·05–1·30	2·65
Oxidant	0·20–0·65	0·10–0·35	0·75
Ozone	0·20–0·65	0·05–0·30	0·90
Sulphur dioxide	0·15–0·70	0·15–0·70	2·49

[1] Defined as a day with severe eye irritation in central Los Angeles.
[2] Defined as a day with no eye irritation in central Los Angeles.
[3] $NO_x = (NO + NO_2)$.
Source: Stern 1968

Particulate matter

Industrial processes, auto exhausts, bare soil and backyard barbecues alike produce particulate matter, a conspicuous component of air pollution for many centuries. Dust comes from many sources including the gradual comminution of the debris which accumulates in cities and open spaces without vegetation. Soot consists of finely divided carbon and heavy hydrocarbons from combustion processes, and to this may be added finely particulate material from almost every urban-based resource process: ash, flour, rubber, glass, newspaper, lead and fluorides. The last-mentioned are produced in the manufacture of ceramics, bricks and phosphatic fertilizers and, especially in the form of hydrogen fluoride, can cause damage to plants, animals and man. Fluorosis, the mottling of teeth, occurs at concentrations of 20 ppm, but levels are usually less than 0·02 ppm except around poorly designed emission sites. Low levels of fluoride in drinking water are held to be beneficial to dental health and addition to the water supply is often practised, except where public opinion regards it as another unacceptable pollutant. Many other chemicals are present as particulates, but concentrations above 50 mg/1,000 m³ air seem to be unusual.

The particulate materials have well-known effects. The reduction of visibility is obvious in most cities, soiling of paintwork, buildings and Monday's wash is commonplace, metals are corroded, and immense social and economic costs are incurred because of the aggravation of bronchial illnesses which takes place. Some writers also attribute carcinogenesis in people to one or more of the substances of this class of wastes. Their order of magnitude can be gauged by the fallout: in Great Britain large cities experience depositions of 500–2,000 tons/mi²/yr (131·6–526·3 × 10⁶ kg/ha) whereas small towns and rural areas receive 10–100 tons/mi²/yr (2·6–26·0 × 10⁵ kg/ha).

Effects at the global scale

All the effects so far discussed have been at a local or regional scale and apparent in a short period of time. But the dynamic nature of the atmosphere, its ability to provide reactants for chemical change, and its exchange processes with land and sea all ensure that many of the emissions are translocated far from their source, sometimes in a chemically altered form. Of the substances enumerated, most appear to have no global implications, although since monitoring is so recent and so fragmentary this should be regarded as an interim conclusion. Most of the sulphur compounds end up in the oceans as soluble sulphates with no known effects, for example; photochemical pollutants stabilize either as nitrates or as $CO_2 + H_2O$; the global emission of 33,528 mt/day of nitrous oxides means a yearly atmospheric increase of 2×10^{-6} ppm.

TABLE 11.4   Carbon dioxide production and accumulation

Year	Amount added from fossil fuel (mt/yr)	Cumulative amount added over previous decade	Concentration by volume (ppm)	Total in atmosphere (mt)
1950	6,700	52,200	306	2.39×10^6
1960	10,800	82,400	313	2.44×10^6

Source: SCEP 1971

Carbon dioxide is the waste which has excited most interest. Table 11.4 shows recent figures for the amount added to the atmosphere, and the quantity remaining there, which is about 51 per cent of the emissions (SCEP 1971). Thus the oceans and terrestrial biomes appear to be absorbing 49 per cent of the carbon dioxide, but their ability to continue to take the same proportion is unknown and in any case must be impaired by a diminution in photosynthetic rates such as is caused by large-scale clearance of forests. More serious is the accumulation of CO_2 in the atmosphere. The hypothetical result is to produce a 'greenhouse' effect in which the additional CO_2 allows the absorption of more solar radiation and hence the rise of global temperatures with subsequent ice-cap melting and shifting of climatic belts. Interacting with the CO_2 is the increase in atmospheric turbidity resulting from particulate emissions. By scattering radiation this might reduce global temperatures. Since these latter have in fact fallen since 1940, it is tempting to suggest that the particles are 'beating' the CO_2. As Murray Mitchell (1970) points out, there are complications because natural particulate emissions from volcanoes have until recently far exceeded even the highest estimates of human-induced output. Mitchell considers that although CO_2 is more efficient than particulate matter in influencing planetary temperatures, by AD 2000 the continuation of present doubling times of these contaminants will make man-made particles the most important inadvertent modifier of climate.

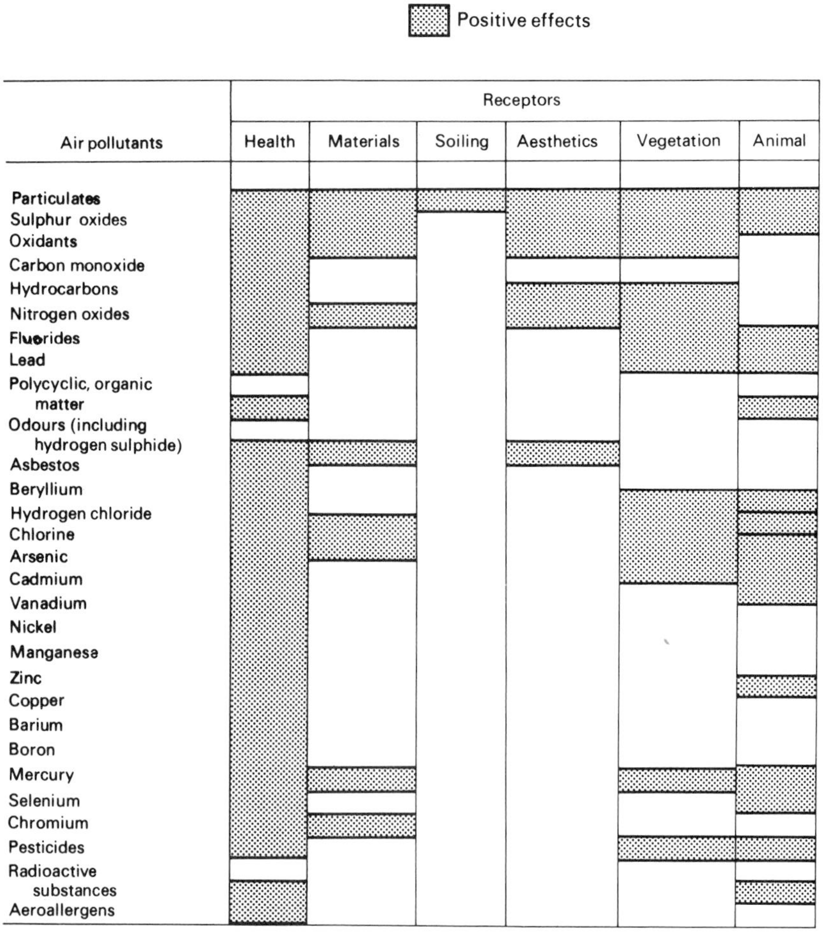

Positive effects

Air pollutants	Receptors					
	Health	Materials	Soiling	Aesthetics	Vegetation	Animal
Particulates						
Sulphur oxides						
Oxidants						
Carbon monoxide						
Hydrocarbons						
Nitrogen oxides						
Fluorides						
Lead						
Polycyclic, organic matter						
Odours (including hydrogen sulphide)						
Asbestos						
Beryllium						
Hydrogen chloride						
Chlorine						
Arsenic						
Cadmium						
Vanadium						
Nickel						
Manganese						
Zinc						
Copper						
Barium						
Boron						
Mercury						
Selenium						
Chromium						
Pesticides						
Radioactive substances						
Aeroallergens						

Fig. 11.3 The effects of air pollutants upon various receptors in the USA.
Source: US President's Council on Environmental Quality 1971

The deleterious effects to many people of this category of wastes are therefore seen at three scales. There is the point-source danger, as when a noxious gas is imperfectly controlled: an H_2S escape in Mexico in 1950 caused 22 deaths. Regionally, various pollutants doubtless exacerbate existing illnesses (especially respiratory troubles) and maybe induce them. In unusually severe episodes of smog or industrial pollution, premature death is caused. Many other substances are emitted in particulate form into the atmosphere, cause problems in terms of health, damage to materials and living matter, and are aesthetically unacceptable. A newspaper quoted a tentative estimate of the health costs of air pollution in the USA in 1968 as $6·1 \times 10^9$. A table showing which contaminants cause, in qualitative terms, these difficulties is reproduced as Fig. 11.3. Measures are now being adopted in most industrial nations to reduce air pollution in cities, but less attention is generally given to substances which do not directly affect the human population. At a global scale, problems become more nebulous. The probability of direct changes in climate resulting from CO_2 emissions seem small this century, but the longer-term possibilities are so serious that efforts to learn about trends of climatic change and the fate of industrially produced CO_2 must claim a high priority.

Economic poisons

The elimination of competitors

In the course of resource processes such as agriculture, many poisons are applied to ecosystems in order to eliminate or diminish the effect of man's competitors for the crop. We also apply poisons to ourselves in order to kill viruses and bacteria which are inimical to our health, to our immediate surroundings to kill the vectors of disease such as the malaria-carrying mosquito, or to kill competitors for stored food such as the rat. All the substances used as poisons interfere with the metabolism of organisms and are effective in small doses. Ideally, the toxic substance breaks down into biologically insignificant compounds as soon as it has performed its work, so that dead organisms contain no residue of poison to be passed to scavengers, and soils would contain no active toxin to be washed off into streams or be available to organisms other than the targets. Some substances used as poisons do not possess this quality, and some are converted to an even more toxic form when they remain in the environment: collectively they are known as persistent toxins (Rudd 1963, Mellanby 1967, N. W. Moore 1967). Both short-lived and persistent poisons are rarely totally effective or completely harmless: application to any population of plants or animals elicits a spectrum of response from the organisms. The toxity of some substances is dependent upon environmental factors, especially in an aqueous medium. Thus temperature, oxygen content, pH and calcium level may all affect the efficacy of a particular poison. All but the most extreme poisons leave a few resistant individuals and if their immunity is genetically transmissible, and poisoning continues at a constant level, then resistant populations may develop. Examples are the bacterium *Staphylococcus* which is often unaffected by penicillin, and the mosquito *Anopheles* (a vector of malaria), some strains of which are immune to the effects of DDT. The toxin is unlikely to affect all the species in a habitat, so that another species may experience a population surge and itself become a weed or pest. Most important of all the unwanted effects of economic poisons is that caused by persistent residues when they undergo ecological amplification. Typically their concentration increases as they pass from one trophic level to another through a food web. The concentrations in successive organisms are cumulative to the point where lethal or sub-lethal effects upon an organism, often far removed in time and space from the target, are sometimes observed: precautions against sheep warble fly end up preventing the reproduction of golden eagles, for example, or anti-gnat measures cause the death of grebes. The longer the food chain the higher the probability of physiologically significant concentrations in the highest predator levels.

What follows is an examination of some of the most commonly used toxic substances (about 9,000 are commercially available in the USA) which are applied mainly to terrestrial habitats, occasionally to fresh waters. Residues inevitably pass through the runoff phase of the hydrological cycle, and if sufficiently long-lived they accumulate in the oceans. Some of the indirect effects of these compounds form the basis for the discussion, but most of them are poisonous to humans if large quantities are inhaled, ingested or absorbed cutaneously as a consequence of escapes during application; few of the toxins discussed here have not been the direct cause of human death. However, it is with the unintentional effects of residues that we are mainly concerned.

Herbicides

Chemicals such as copper sulphate (as Bordeaux mixture) have been used for hundreds of years against pests in orchards. Sodium chlorate is a well-known weedkiller, highly explosive and moderately persistent; sulphuric acid is still used for the destruction of potato haulms. These simple substances have largely been replaced by complex organic compounds, of which DNOC is a much-used member. It is very poisonous (but not persistent) and protective clothing must be worn for its application, typically by spray at 10 lb/ac (1·8 kg/ha). Accidents from spray drift have had unpleasant results. More popular still have been the contact hormone weedkillers which affect broadleaved plants only (thus leaving cereals and grasses, for example) and are said not to affect man. Their effect is to stimulate growth hormones to the point where the plant grows so fast it virtually dies of exhaustion. Two popular examples are 2,4-D (non-persistent) and 2,4,5-T (highly persistent). Both have been criticized because spray drift is an indiscriminate killer of vegetation, and there is coming to light an uncomfortable amount of evidence suggesting that teratogenicity of human foetuses can result from certain levels of exposure to any 2,4,5-T which contains the contaminant dioxin. Two types of systemic total herbicides have also been developed. The first group, typified by Simazine and Monuron, are persistent and prevent regrowth for periods of up to one year; the second group are short-lived: the effect of Dalapon lasts for 6–8 weeks, Paraquat has a life of a few hours only once it reaches the soil. Dalapon is especially suitable for aquatic weeds since there is little apparent effect upon animal life.

Fungicides

Compounds of two metals dominate this group of toxins. Residues of copper-based substances are likely to be toxic to animals but are overshadowed in importance by the use of mercury. This is used as a seed dressing and, as discussed in the section on heavy metals (p. 306), the effects can be severe. The withdrawal of methyl mercury compounds in favour of phenylmercuric urea may have alleviating effects.

Insecticides

The success and adaptability of the insects has provoked a formidable battery of poisons. There are three main kinds: inorganic compounds, botanicals based on natural substances, and synthetic organic compounds of two major subtypes, the organophosphorus compounds and the chlorinated hydrocarbons. Outstanding among the inorganics is lead arsenite, deployed against caterpillars on fruit trees. Since the combination of lead and arsenic appears particularly frightening, it is comforting that in Britain the Food and Drugs Act 1955 lays down that no food may have > 1 ppm arsenic or > 2 ppm lead content. Lead arsenite is not applied later than 6 weeks before marketing. The botanicals are dominated by powders derived from two plants: rotenone, from the roots of *Derris elliptica*, is often called derris and is non-persistent, though deadly to fish if it drifts or is spilled into water-courses. The flowers of *Chrysanthemum cinerariaefolium* yield Pyrethrum, which paralyses insects but is non-persistent and non-toxic to most other groups. In some ways it is an ideal insecticide but is expensive, so that ways of synthesizing it cheaply by industrial methods are being sought, and by 1974 were showing signs of success.

Pesticides

From 1944 onwards organophosphorus pesticides, most of which are aimed at insects, became commonly used. Most of them are cholinesterase inhibitors which impede impulse transmission in the nervous system so that respiratory failure ensues. Two of the commonest are Parathion and TEPP, both of which are very toxic beyond the target group (1 oz (28·35 g) of TEPP will kill 500 people) but break down very rapidly. Both are suspected of having killed non-target organisms locally, but proof is difficult because of their rapid breakdown. Their close relative Malathion is safer, being much less toxic and having also a rapid disintegration rate into non-toxic substances. In many instances it could replace the persistent DDT but is much more costly to manufacture.

The most widespread and heavily used group of pesticides are the organochlorines. The most famous, DDT, was first synthesized in the nineteenth century but did not come into widespread use until the war of 1939–45, when its efficacy against malarial mosquitoes became known; after 1945 its role in agriculture quickly came to exceed that of medical applications. DDT shares some characteristics with several other commercially available organochlorines. It is highly toxic to insects, though resistant strains can breed, but is poisonous to many other groups as well, of which fresh-water fish are one of the most vulnerable. The whole group is long-lived, with lives of at least 10–15 years. Thus they

TABLE 11.5   Quantities (in metric quintals) of poisons used by sample countries 1

Country	DDT and related compounds	BHC and Lindane	Aldrin	Dieldrin	Organo-phosph(compou
USA	148,564	—	—	—	—
Canada	8,314	362	1,964	27	10,205
Sweden	2,430	1,050	—	—	1,900
UAR	46,010	—	2,240	—	13,690
Japan	9,783	28,416	—	61	22,623

These figures generally refer to the active ingredient of the commercial preparation.
Source: FAO *Production Yearbook 23*, 1969

persist in food chains, causing both sub-lethal and lethal effects at various trophic levels. A great deal of investigation has been done on the effects of DDT residues, usually meta-bolites such as DDE and DDD which share its characteristics, although DDE is con-siderably less toxic to most organisms. DDT and its metabolites appear to be distributed over the whole surface of the globe, including the far oceans and the lower layers of the atmosphere: for example, African pesticides appear in Caribbean winds (Wurster 1969). Analyses of DDT concentration in water are perhaps misleading, since it is scarcely soluble in water (1·2 g/litre) but highly soluble in organic substances (e.g. 100 g/litre in lipids) so that it will always 'flow' from the inorganic world to the organic (Woodwell 1967a). This may account for its presence in the fat and viscera of fish and penguins in Antarctica, along with other chlorinated hydrocarbons such as BHC, dieldrin and heptachlor epoxide (Tatton and Ruzicka 1967). Its ability to build up in food chains is well documented in an example from estuaries on the east coast of the USA, where a concentration in water of 0·0005 ppm is accompanied by concentrations of 0·33 ppm in *Spartina* grass, 0·4 ppm in zooplankton, 2·07 ppm in needlefish, 3·57 ppm in herons, 22·8 ppm in fish-eating mergansers, and 75·5 ppm in gulls (Woodwell *et al.* 1967). The DDT present (about 70 per cent as DDE) is all residual. At Clear Lake in California DDD was deliberately applied to kill gnat larvae. The application rate resulted in a concentration of 1 part DDD to 50 million parts water; in fish, concentrations of 40–2,500 ppm were found and in the predaceous grebes up to 1,600 ppm, which was lethal to a large number of birds (Hunt and Bischoff 1960). Sub-lethal effects are also common: DDT appears to inhibit calcium carbonate deposition in the oviducts of certain birds (e.g. pelicans and the peregrine falcon) and thin-shelled eggs which rarely come to term are the result. The Bermuda petrel, living at the top of a long marine food chain but out of contact with inhabited areas, has accumulated levels of 6–7 ppm of DDT in its eggs and chicks (Wurster 1969). Breeding success declined by 3·25 per cent p.a. during 1958–68, and an extrapolation of the trend would bring about complete failure to reproduce by 1978. It should be added that some recent work suggests that the levels of residual pesticides in organisms are due more to the ability of a particular species to excrete the compounds than to biological magnification; this does not alter the significant effects upon biota which have been detected.

ingle year (1968)

rsenicals	Botanicals	Copper fungicides	Mercury fungicides	Herbicides
—	1,527	168,699	—	1,833,841
,265	9	799	9,208	121,494
—	—	60	2,150	54,270
30	580	2,090	—	1,880
,194	994	28,628	182	265,424

Particularly because of its effects upon wildlife, notably avian raptors, DDT has attracted a great deal of attention. Less well known, therefore, are other chlorinated hydro-carbons which are equally or more toxic in residual form. The most potent of these is BHC, a mixture of several isomers of which the highly active γ-BHC (Lindane) is lethal to many forms of life but fortunately is unpalatable to vertebrates when applied as a seed dressing. Other members of this family are dieldrin, aldrin, endrin, endosulphan and heptachlor. At least two of these are transformed in the soil to more stable compounds, aldrin into dieldrin, with a life of at least 10 years, and heptachlor into heptachlor epoxide which is more persistent and more toxic. Death of wildlife in Britain led during the 1960s to voluntary bans on certain of these substances, e.g. dieldrin as a spring wheat dressing and as a component of sheep dip (Table 11.5). The replacement of cheap and at one time universally efficacious agents like DDT is likely to be gradual and expensive: gradual be-cause of the longer testing processes now considered essential before a biocide is introduced into the environment, and expensive because most substitutes are more costly to make. Metcalf (1972) quotes the costs of DDT in WHO anti-malaria campaigns as $0.185/lb ($0.084/kg) whereas Malathion cost $0.65/lb ($0.295/kg), Propoxur $1.60/lb ($0.725/kg) and Fenetrothion $0.73/lb ($0.331/kg); presumably the larger-scale production of third-generation pesticides found to be suitable might cause costs to fall.

The persistent organochlorines have attracted a good deal of opprobrium in recent years, though stoutly defended by those who point to the increased productivity and stability of agriculture gained by their use. Levels in human body fat are typically 12–16 ppm in DCs, so that in the USA most people are now legally unfit for human consumption. No adverse effects have as yet been noted, but since 1945 marks a zero datum line, no individual can yet have carried the current body burden through a normal life-span. Since newer and less persistent pesticides will be developed, together with non-chemical methods of biological control, it is to be hoped that heavy reliance upon persistent pesticides will soon cease, in view of their known dangers to man, animals and the general quality of the environment. In particular, synergistic effects may exert long-run changes in ecosystems which are impossible to predict (Sassi 1970).

Accidental contamination by organic substances

Oil

The dominant member of this category is crude oil. On one scale its loss during transport may be acutely dangerous to human life, the more so because of the inflammable nature of some of its constituents. More concern is generally expressed with its toxicity to plants and animals and with the aesthetic effects caused by spilt oil being washed up on beaches and shorelines (Zobell 1964). Fig. 11.4 sets out the toxicities of various fractions of crude oil over a broad spectrum of marine animals, from which it can be seen that the low-boiling aromatic hydrocarbons and non-hydrocarbons provide the greatest source of toxic materials: these are, however, the first to evaporate after a spill.

The scale of oil contamination of the biosphere is not accurately known. Most of it is found on the seas, in estuaries and large water bodies such as the Great Lakes, but oil-field spills along inland rivers are quite common. The total world oil production is of the order of 1.8×10^{15} g/yr; of this total 1.0×10^{15} g/yr is transported by sea, so that the marine emphasis in the list of sites of contamination is hardly surprising. (One quarter of the world's production passes through the English Channel.) The losses in transport through collisions, transfer leaks and explosions are estimated at 1×10^{12} g/yr, to which must be added tankwashing at sea, contrary to both law and shipowners' agreements, and the multitude of seepages from installations at transit points. These may together double the estimated total loss, and there is in addition a small background exudation from natural deposits (Hoult 1969). The refining processes of petrochemicals also produce wastes of the order of a Biological Oxygen Demand (BOD) of 100 lb/1,000 bbls (45.36 kg/1,000 bbls) processed. Hydrocarbon or oil wastes can be 3 per cent of the total treated, and in addition there are sulphur wastes like H_2S and mercaptans, alkalis, phenols, ammonia (some as basic

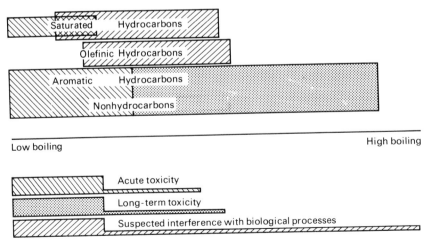

Fig. 11.4 A diagram of the toxicity to marine organisms with different fractions of crude oil. The low-boiling saturated hydrocarbons are the most poisonous but are the first to evaporate.
Source: Blumer 1969

nitrogenous compounds) and miscellaneous materials like chromate and phosphate corrosion inhibitors, tars and spent catalysts. Many of the compounds are not found in natural systems and in Kupchanko's (1970) words 'disposal is not always simple'.

Contamination by oil is largely a problem of marine ecosystems. Very little is known about the long-term cumulative effects of the fractions which have a long residence-time in the sea water, although some hydrocarbons can apparently be concentrated in food chains. The examples quoted are alkylated 4- and 5-ring aromatic hydrocarbons of the type which are known to induce carcinogenesis experimentally. They are likely to affect the flavour of sea food as well. Much more knowledge of the effects of oil on biota has accrued from large oil spills such as the wreck of the *Torrey Canyon* off Cornwall, England, in 1967 and the submarine seepage caused by drilling in the Santa Barbara Channel off California in 1969. Such incidents were treated very seriously and are well documented, but we may remember that incidents of the magnitude of the *Torrey Canyon* disaster (which carried 118,000 tons (119,888 mt) of oil) occur about once a week in the world as a whole. The seriousness of tanker incidents is exacerbated by the increasing size of vessels used: tankers of 210,000–250,000 tons are now used.

The effects of oil on marine biota vary considerably according to the initial composition of the oil, the rate of evaporation of various fractions, the species affected and, with littoral organisms, their place in the intertidal range. Emulsions of diesel oil at a concentration of 0·01–0·1 per cent cause the impairment of photosynthesis in kelp, and the more delicate red algae are very severely affected, probably because they often grow in pools where the oil can settle for long periods. The low-boiling saturated hydrocarbons are particularly toxic to invertebrates, but they often evaporate before reaching a shore (local wind and tide conditions are of course critical in such events), and this is thought to have happened at Santa Barbara, where the loss of mollusca, for example, was not particularly severe. The most obvious victims of large spills are seabirds, and many thousands usually perish. Birds which are rescued and cleaned often exhibit high mortality rates after release, but it is unknown whether this is due to pneumonia or a medium-term toxicity effect. In attempts to disperse the oil through the water rather than leaving it as a thick surface film, emulsifiers have sometimes been used as a clean-up agent. This has generally been disastrous for marine biota, especially mollusca. The detergents used are often more toxic to marine animals (Table 11.6) than is oil, but in any case the thinned oil can often penetrate the tightly closed valves of mollusca: thus limpets exhibit a mortality of 100 per cent if an emulsifier is used, but with oil alone they may survive. Emulsifier at a concentration of only 0·01 per cent caused 100 per cent mortality in cockles, and longer-term effects are hinted at by the reduction of photosynthesis in kelps at concentrations of 1–10 ppm. With both oil and emulsifier, separately or together, species at the ends of their littoral ranges exhibited greater losses. Partly this is caused by the long stay of oil in pools, partly because emulsifiers enable oil to penetrate deeper into pool water, and partly because the species are in any case under considerable stress at the extremes of their tolerances. Cleaning procedures using straw as at Santa Barbara, or chalk, appear to be more effective and less damaging to biota, and several techniques for physically dispersing or collecting the oil are now under development (Nelson-Smith 1970).

Apart from the concentrated oil spills which reach the public eye, there appears to be

TABLE 11.6   Toxicity of BP 1002 (detergent) to some sublittoral species at 12°C

Species	Common name	Concentration (ppm) needed to kill majority in 24 hrs	Notes
Coelenterata			
Calliactis parasitica	Sea anemone	25	Stay closed at 5 ppm
Crustacea			
Corystes cassivelaunus	Masked crab	10	
Portunus holsatus	Swimming crab	5	
Diogenes pugilator	Hermit crab	25	
Mollusca			
Nassarius reticulatus	Netted whelk	2·5	Some survived 2·5 ppm
Chlamys opercularis	Queen scallop	1	Affected at 0·5 ppm (tended to gape)
Laevicardium crassum	Smooth cockle	1	Affected at 0·5 ppm (tended to gape)
Spisula subtruncata	Smooth cockle	2	Affected at 1 ppm (tended to gape)
Ensis siliqua	Razor-shell	0·5	
Echinodermata			
Asterias rubens	Common starfish	25	Climbing stopped at 10 ppm
Ophiocomina nigra	Brittle-star	5	Affected at 2 ppm
Algae			
Delesseria sanguinea	Red seaweed	10	Took several days to change colour

Source: Ehrenfeld 1970

something of a universal distribution of small gobs of residual hydrocarbons. On his transatlantic voyage in the *Ra II*, Heyerdahl found lumps of oil residue throughout the voyage, while a survey ship in the Sargasso Sea reported that by volume they caught three times as much oil as Sargasso weed in their nets. Because oil is a valuable substance, and is getting costlier with time, the motivations to lose as little as possible are stronger than with unwanted residues of industrial or agricultural resource processes. But the costs are widely ramified, and include, besides the loss of natural resources, the loss of revenue to resort areas, and the costs of cleaning up by local government when the source of the spill cannot be traced. There are losses to the polluters if they are fined and even others incurred in investigating responsibility and in prosecution through the courts. The total of these can never be accurately assessed (Hawkes 1961). It will take a great deal of tough action by nation states along their shores to produce a noticeable decline in contaminated beaches (which although undesirable are probably in the long term the least important of the effects of oil pollution) and inshore pollution. The stopping of pollution on the open oceans requires international action of a scale not so far envisaged as practicable.

PCBs

Analogous to oil in some ways are a class of organic substances called polychlorinated biphenyls (PCBs) which are a by-product of the plastics, lubricants and rubber industries. These are long-lasting, insoluble in water but soluble in fat (N. W. Moore 1969). Their actual presence and their toxic effects are difficult to measure, but they appear to have been strongly implicated in the deaths of many seabirds and possibly of other biota too. They are also used in paper products and inks, and it has been feared that recycling paper may concentrate the PCBs which, being fat soluble, will migrate to foods packaged in the re-used materials. In some countries their chief manufacturer has seen fit either to withdraw these substances from the market or replace the most stable forms with more quickly biodegradable ones.

Derelict land

Creation of waste land

Many resource processes of an industrial kind produce land which is no longer valuable for any other purpose; the UK definition of derelict land, for example, is 'land so damaged by industrial or other development that it is incapable of beneficial use without treatment'. Mining of various kinds is the chief contributor of derelict land: open-pit mining produces a large hole together with dumped overburden and spoil, and the hole may fill with water. Machinery and buildings may with everything else be abandoned when extraction ceases after the average life of pits and quarries of 50 years. Shaft mining produces few holes, but tips of waste material are usual and subsidence may render unusable further areas of land. Surface mining is relatively cheap and over 50 minerals are produced in the USA by this means; costs are held down by the technological capacity now available to highly capitalized operators. Industrial processes such as smelting also create considerable quantities of waste, as do the armed forces, especially at war-training areas, and railways and waterways in periods of decline.

The actual amounts of derelict land in some industrial countries are very high. Measurement is difficult, since official definitions often include only land which is derelict and abandoned. Thus a tip heap still in use is not classified in the UK as derelict land, neither is land covered by any form of planning permission or restoration conditions, however impossible these may be to enforce. Thus in the West Riding of Yorkshire, England, there were officially 2,542 ha of derelict land in 1966, yet functionally derelict land was estimated from an aerial survey at 9,754 ha. Even using the official figures, England and Wales had 45,460 ha of derelict land in 1967, increasing at 1,417 ha/yr. The true amount is probably 101,250 ha; and most of it is a result of the extraction of some 406 million mt/yr of minerals which occurs in Great Britain: for instance, about one-fifth of the National Coal Board's land holdings are derelict land (Barr 1969). In the USA, an estimated 1,295 km^2 (5,000 mi^2) of land were disturbed by surface mining at January 1965, with an annual increment of 61,956 ha: an amount equivalent to a rectangle 16 × 40 km. An additional 129,600 ha were or had been in use for roads and exploration activities. Coal dominated the picture, being responsible for 41 per cent of the disturbance, with sand and gravel 26 per cent (US Department of the Interior 1967, US President's Council on Recreation and Natural Beauty 1968, Weisz 1970).

Effects of derelict land

The effects of dereliction extend beyond the immediate sterilization of tracts of land. Open mining may contribute dust to the local atmosphere, and waste material, especially if unvegetated, is a considerable source of silt. On 40 per cent of derelict sites in the USA, soil erosion was taking place on the tips, and strip-mined lands in Kentucky yielded 7.1×10^9 kg/ha of silt whereas undisturbed forest nearby yielded 6.5×10^6 kg/ha. Thus in the USA, 9,280 km of streams and 1,175 ha of impoundments are affected by the operations of open-cast mining of coal (US Department of the Interior 1967). Chemical effects may also occur when water leaches through waste materials with soluble elements in them: sulphur-bearing tailings may well yield streams contaminated with sulphuric acid.

Restoration

Treatment and reclamation of derelict land are not technically impossible but currently appear expensive. In Lancashire, England, 15·5 ha of derelict land cost the local authority £3,700 to buy, but reclamation and landscape cost £15,000, and the usual cost of reclamation is £32–£284/ha. Nevertheless, authorities in England like Lancashire and Durham County Councils have Treasury-aided reclamation programmes of an ambitious nature. Since 1965 Durham has launched 80 reclamation schemes on land made derelict by coal extraction and has treated 81 ha at a gross cost of £2·5 million; ongoing programmes plan to reclaim 200–250 ha/yr, but even this is not keeping pace with colliery closures. England and Wales have been reclaiming a total of 800 ha/yr in recent years and restoration conditions are usually placed on planning permission to extend mineral extraction, but these are often difficult to enforce (Baker 1970). The attitudes of the industrial revolution are clearly changing with regard to derelict land: where there's muck there's brass, but there is also dirt, dust, rats and even large-scale death as at Aberfan in south Wales. The psychological effects are also important: authorities of such areas which seek to attract new industry have great difficulty in persuading managers to locate amid mountains of waste or lunar landscapes of dust and water. The use of derelict land as a resource for filling in holes, for making new sites for housing and industry and for creating marinas and nature reserves is a necessity in small countries with large populations, and a desirable aim for others (Karsch 1970).

Organic wastes

Concentration in runoff

Most of the substances considered here are not persistent as are, for instance, chlorinated hydrocarbon pesticides, but contain certain elements present and important in the biosphere (of which nitrogen and phosphorus are the most studied), which are concentrated by man in the course of their use and are then released back into the biosphere. The effects are those of providing a large quantity of an element which may well have been limiting, and of accelerating the natural cycle of that substance in the biosphere.

Sewage

Contamination of fresh waters and shallow offshore seas by sewage is a common occurrence. Sewage is about 99·9 per cent water and 0·02–0·04 per cent solids of which proteins and carbohydrates each comprise 40–50 per cent and fats 5–10 per cent. Water carriage of sewage from urban areas dates only from the 1840s, before which the contamination of water supplies led to epidemics of cholera, typhoid and dysentery. Such outbreaks are still common in LDCs and in pockets of poverty in the DCs such as in migrant labour camps (e.g. in Florida early in 1973) and in regions of colonization with many native people (e.g. the Mackenzie Delta of Canada in October 1972). Treatment of sewage to kill the agents of these diseases is an important part of sewage processing where this exists: chlorine is generally used. The wastes of any human population will also contain bacteria and viruses from other ill people and from healthy carriers, which reinforces the need for treatment of the water component of sewage. Contamination of water by untreated sewage is denoted by the presence of the bacterium *Escherichia coli* which is not itself infectious but is an indicator of the presence of the agents of typhoid and dysentery.

Further sewage treatment consists of the separation of the organic matter from the water and its conversion to a biologically inactive and aesthetically inoffensive state. The end-product is sludge, a valuable fertilizer but one which is currently more expensive than factory-produced material. However, many large cities in the West do not treat their sewage at all: in metropolitan Canada, for instance, 100 per cent of the sewage of Toronto gets a two-stage treatment, whereas practically all the production of the population of Montreal and Quebec is poured untreated into the St Lawrence River. In Canada as a whole, less than 40 per cent of the households are connected to a sanitary sewer and only 60 per cent of sewage gets any treatment (MacNeill 1971). A well-fed human excretes 14 g N_2 and 1·5 g P per day, of which 20–50 per cent is removed by waste treatment. In the USA the mixture of treatment and non-treatment means that an estimated 450–680 million kg of nitrogen and 91–250 million kg of phosphorus (Bartsch 1970) reach the surface waters of the continent every year (Fig. 11.5). Even tertiary treatment of municipal sewage will not eliminate the eutrophication of fresh water. Algal blooms can occur at phosphorus concentrations of < 0·1 mg/l and nitrogen concentrations of 0·01 mg/l if other essential elements are present (Lawson and Brisbin 1970). Tertiary treatment is therefore different from nutrient removal, which calls for the even more expensive process of the removal of inorganic and organic compounds from a stabilized sewage effluent.

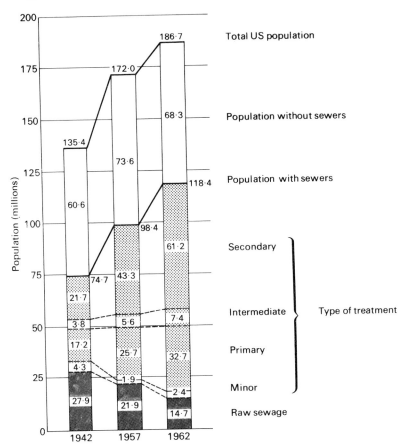

Fig. 11.5 Even in rich countries like the USA, sewerage may scarcely keep pace with the growth in population, although in 1957–62 it began to gain. Lack of sewers does not necessarily mean pollution if effective septic tanks and cesspools are used, but in the case of many large cities raw sewage is dumped into nearby water.
Source: A. Wolman 1965

Detergents

Phosphorus and nitrogen are the important elements in the contributions of fertilizer runoff to chemical changes in water bodies. More phosphorus is added from 'hard' synthetic detergents whose foaming reduces photosynthesis and inhibits oxygenation of the water. Concentrations of < 1 ppm may also inhibit oxygen uptake by organisms. 'Soft' or biodegradable detergents are now available and are replacing their forerunners, but both they and the organic cold-water detergents contain phosphorus: indeed 'enzyme' detergents are in fact phosphate pre-soaks (US Congress 1970).

Animal wastes

As a source of water contamination, the products of urban dwellers are globally less important than industry and agriculture. The volume of effluent from industry cannot even be estimated, but we may note that some 500,000 organic chemicals are synthesized, most of which are synthetically produced and whose effects on the biosphere are unknown. Agriculture produces the fertilizer runoffs already mentioned and also a great deal of solid residues. Crop residues in the USA amount to about 8 tons/family/yr and each year sees 58 million dead birds unfit for eating whose carcasses have to be dispersed. Intensive animal farming produces wastes analogous to a town: the volume of daily wastes from such operations are approximately 10 times those of humans. A poultry unit of 1 million chickens produces the same quantity of waste as 68,000 people, while each year the human population of the USA produces 153 million m³ of sludge and its domesticated animals 765 million m³ (Taiganides 1967). In New England dairy farms, each cow is responsible for a net loss to the environment of 119 kg/yr of nitrogen, 34 kg/yr of phosphorus and 53 kg/yr of potassium (Ashton 1970).

Eutrophication

The introduction of large quantities of nitrogen and phosphorus into water bodies is one of the major problems of wastes today (Sawyer 1966). Phosphorus is a scarce element in the

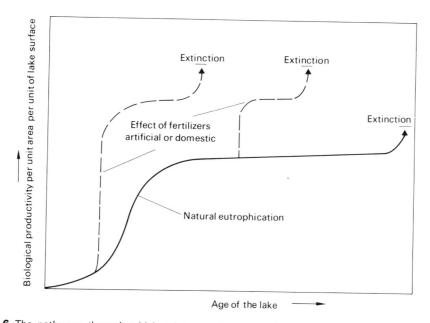

Fig. 11.6 The pathways through which a lake may become extinct. The solid line indicates the natural sequence, the pecked lines the effects of the addition of nutrients from fertilizers or sewage, i.e. eutrophication. The extinction of the lake then occurs far sooner than under natural conditions.
Source: Sawyer 1966

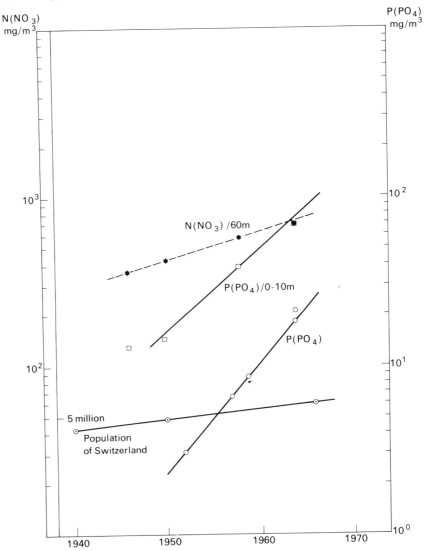

Fig. 11.7 Changes in nutrient concentrations as measured in the Zurichsee and Bodensee in Switzerland, compared with the rate of population growth. The cultural rather than metabolic reasons for eutrophication can be inferred.
Source: OECD 1970.

lithosphere and many ecosystems are adjusted to its scarcity: it is a limiting element in Liebig's sense (p. 42). The large quantities made available by human-induced concentrations lift such limits and 'blooms' result; nitrogen may then become the limiting factor and organisms such as blue-green algae take over from the plankton because they escape the nitrogen limits. 'Blooms' of such algae then follow. The additional nitrogen and phosphorus accelerate the ageing of lakes, themselves short-lived in geological terms, by nutrient enrichment or eutrophication (Fig. 11.6). Such a process happens naturally but is speeded up many times by human activities which result in large inputs of phosphorus and nitrogen (OECD 1970). Fig. 11.7 shows the build-up of nutrients in two European lakes which have undergone enrichment. Many other examples are known, of which the Great Lakes of North America are probably the best documented, especially Lakes Erie and Ontario (Charlier 1970, International Joint Commission 1970). The total dissolved solids in these two lakes have risen by 50 ppm in the last 50 years, for example, and the fish populations have changed almost completely (a situation complicated by the effects after 1945 of the parasitic sea-lamprey, which, however, cannot spawn in the tributaries of Lake Erie). The bottom fauna too has changed sweepingly, especially through increases in midge larvae and tubificid worms. In summer a serious depletion of dissolved oxygen occurs, *Cladophora* piles up in offensive heaps on the shores and blue-green algal scums are formed. The problem is complicated by the presence of pesticide residues: in 1969 a catch of 1,000 kg of coho salmon from Lake Michigan was destroyed because of the high concentration of DDT residues. Eutrophication is not confined to water: input–output studies of forested watersheds in New Hampshire showed that the aerially derived input of some mineral elements exceeded the loss by runoff. This suggests a gradual enrichment of this habitat, but the long-term effects are difficult to predict because of the considerable powers of nutrient absorption possessed by the forest flora.

One direct danger to humans has been detected. Nitrates can be converted in the digestive tract by certain bacteria to nitrites, and the same transition may occur in opened cans of food even if they are subsequently refrigerated. Nitrites react with haemoglobin, forming methemoglobin which will not take up oxygen. Laboured breathing and occasional suffocation results. The condition is most severe in human infants; in the central valley of California contamination of water supplies is such that only bottled water is often recommended for babies. Ehrlich and Ehrlich (1972) say that Elgin, Minnesota, was forced by nitrate pollution to find a new water supply. There is also the possibility that nitrites may react with creatinine (present in vertebrate muscles) to form nitrosarcosine, which can be carcinogenic.

The cessation of eutrophication of water bodies is clearly an immense task both technically and institutionally; but failure to achieve it will result in the loss not only of biologically significant elements of diversity but also in the diminution of an important element of environmental quality for humans.

Radioactive wastes

Effects of radiation (see Table 11.7 for a glossary of terms)

Natural radiation is emitted from a wide variety of sources such as X-rays and cosmic rays, but its level is such that a normal dose of 5 roentgens (5r) is accumulated over the first 30 years of life (a dental X-ray is 1r). In addition to this are certain man-made emissions which result from nuclear explosions in the atmosphere and underground and by the use of nuclear fission processes to generate energy. Nuclear testing in the atmosphere has been much reduced since the Test-Ban Treaty of 1967, although China and France have set off devices since then. Underground weapons testing has continued, especially by the USA and USSR, and there have been trials of nuclear explosions for non-military purposes as with the US Project Gasbuggy in 1967, when an attempt to improve natural gas yields was made by shattering a 'tight' reservoir rock beneath New Mexico. There has been a considerable rise since 1950 in the number of atomic power plants, and most writers foresee a much greater reliance upon atomic power in the future.

TABLE 11.7   Glossary of terms used in radiation studies

Roentgen (r)	The amount of X or gamma radiation produced in one cubic centimetre of standard dry air ionization equal to one electrostatic unit of charge. Describes the radiation field to which organisms may be exposed.
Curie (Ci)	One curie is the amount of any radioactive nuclide that undergoes 37 billion transformations per second.
Half-life	The average time required for half the atoms of an unstable nuclide to transform.
Dose	A measure of the energy actually absorbed in tissue by interactions with ionizing radiation.

Whenever energy is released by splitting atoms, so are potential contaminators of the ecosphere by the radioactive particles which are the products of the fission reaction. Atmospheric explosions yield numerous isotopes, some very short-lived, others like Sr-90 and Cs-137 having half-lives measured in decades. These are caught up in the atmospheric circulation and gradually come to the earth's surface as 'fallout'. Underground explosions release fewer particles but the chance of contaminating groundwater is always present, especially when the area used is highly faulted geologically.

The concern exhibited about radioactive wastes is caused by the deleterious effects of radiation upon people. Emissions are undetectable by human senses and ineradicable except by the processes of natural decay. A dose of 600r kills all exposed persons within 1 month, and 300r will kill 25 per cent of the exposed population and induce serious injury to 90 per cent of the remainder. Death from 300–600r doses may be from 'marrow death' as blood cells are not replaced, or from 'intestinal death' as the gut ceases to function; at 1,000r 'central nervous system death' occurs quite quickly: an employee at Los Alamos who received a multi-second exposure of 1,200r died within 36 hours. Irradiation of organs produces specific effects at lower doses: a dose of 50r will inhibit spermatogenesis for 1 week or will drop the lymphocyte count by 50 per cent for 1 week. 150r will cause retardation of bone growth in children (hence the 1950s concern about Sr-90 which is taken up by bone), and 250r will produce sterility in males for 1 year and defective genes thereafter, according to Schubert and Lapp (1957). There seems to be no threshold of radiation below which cancer, the shortening of life or genetic damage is not possible. At a dose of 1r per generation about 1 person in 8,000 will have severe genetic effects attributable to radiation, and the peaceful uses of atomic energy at the 1971 level make possible the production of about 5 mutations/100 million genes.

Radioactive material in food chains

Such concerns are exacerbated by the biological magnification of radioactive particles. Just as residues of persistent chemicals may accumulate in the biosphere far beyond the initial dose, so may long-lived isotopes. Clay minerals may selectively absorb and concentrate particles, for example, as with Sr-90, Cs-137, Co-60 and Ru-106. As might be expected, however, one of the most frequent processes is accumulation along food chains. Retention at the various stages depends upon many variables such as the differential uptake of various isotopes and their retention in different organs. In the total biomass, a major fraction of most of the radioactive isotopes is held in the primary production level, but this does not prevent large absolute amounts from reaching high trophic levels (Woodwell 1963, 1967b).

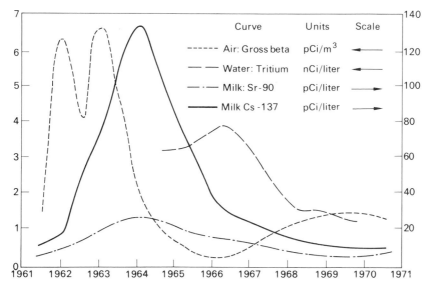

Fig. 11.8 Trends of selected radio-isotopes in the atmosphere, water and milk, as measured in the USA. The effects of the cessation of atmospheric nuclear weapons testing (except by France and China) is apparent.
Source: US President's Council on Environmental Quality 1971

Atmospheric nuclear testing produced very high rates of fallout in arctic regions, especially of Sr-90 and Cs-137. From the atmosphere the particles settle onto, and become incorporated in, the lichens of the tundra and taiga. Cs-137 is effectively retained in the upper parts of these organisms whereas Sr-90 is translocated through the whole plant, which grows very slowly, incorporating approximately 95 per cent of the fallout (half-lives 3–13 years) which settles on it. The lichens are important winter food for caribou which graze off them, especially the top parts, thus leading to high winter uptake levels of isotopes. Some native peoples depend largely upon caribou meat for food, though not usually in the winter, and adult males may eat 5–6 kg/week. Thus certain northern peoples of Alaska, Canada, Lapland and the USSR have body burdens of Cs-137 and Sr-90 which average 50–100 times higher than those of temperate-zone inhabitants (Hanson 1967a,

1967b). Cessation of atmospheric nuclear testing except by France and China has led to a diminution in fallout rates (Fig. 11.8).

Disposal of radionuclides

Caution has to be exercised over wastes from power plants because they may accumulate firstly in the fine silts and muds of estuaries and secondly in long marine food chains. Fluid wastes disposed of in solid rock may cause problems, as with the series of earthquakes triggered off around Denver, Colorado, by the pumping of liquid wastes into the rock beneath the Rocky Mountains arsenal of the US Army (Healy 1968). Radioactive particles were not present in this instance, but the events have served as a warning of the unsuitability of this method of disposal of wastes of any kind.

The generation of nuclear power creates large quantities of nuclear wastes. A 1 million KWe reactor will produce 72 million curies/yr of I-131, and 130,000 curies of tritium in its first year, somewhat less in subsequent years. No treatments yet proposed will remove these from the liquid or gaseous effluents of the reactors (Abrahamson 1972). At Windscale in Cumberland, England, the most significant radionuclide released into the sea is ruthenium-106 which is accumulated in marine algae. These include *Porphyra umbilicalis* which, as laver-bread, is eaten by Welshmen. Their appetite for laver-bread thus determines the level of radioactive waste discharged from the plant (Hedgpeth 1972). Most authorities connected with atomic power generation believe that their 'safe levels' are meaningful and that waste concentrations are held below these limits. More writers are now questioning this view, holding that since our knowledge of ecology is so thin, we cannot agree that it is safe to increase the radiation content of any part of the biosphere. There is also the question of accidents, against which considerable precautions are taken but against which insurance companies will not take a risk. In the USA, the Atomic Energy Commision described the possible effects of a major accident at a reactor which was small by today's standards; at worst, they thought that 3,400 deaths, 43,000 injuries, 7×10^9 property damage and crop damage over 150,000 mi² could occur (Abrahamson 1972).

The advent of very large-scale use of atomic energy by fission will produce 3×10^6 Ci/yr of tritium, along with other long-lived radionuclides (Table 11.8). Fusion of the high-level wastes, which are 1 per cent by volume but contain 90 per cent of the radio-activity, into ceramics and then burial in salt mines is the usual method advocated for disposition of these wastes. Weinberg and Hammond (1971) suggest that an installed capacity of 400,000 KW will require 78 km² of salt mine per year. Dangers are said to be low (Gordon 1970), though opponents of nuclear power are not slow to point out the various places where leakage could occur. Although some re-use of fissionable materials is possible (a plant in South Carolina is to be built to recycle spent fuels), the need to isolate such materials from the biosphere for about 250,000 years has led to the suggestion that containers of radioactive waste be placed every 10 km² on parts of the ice of Antarctica. They would sink under their own heat and weight, to rest at the rock-ice interface where they would be safe against all forms of natural disaster, and accidents would be impossible (Zeller *et al.* 1973). The Antarctic Treaty forbids the disposal of such wastes, but the signatories are among those likely to have to cope with perhaps a hundredfold increase in the quantity of high-level wastes in the period 1972–2000. Perhaps by the latter date nuclear fusion, which produces no radioactive wastes, will be a usable power source.

TABLE 11.8   Nuclear wastes as a function of power production, USA, 1970–2000

	1970	1980	2000
Installed nuclear capacity MW(e)	11,000	95,000	734,000
High-level liquid waste, annual production (gal/yr)	23,000	510,000	3,400,000
Accumulated volume (gal)	45,000	2,400,000	39,000,000
Accumulated fission products: megacuries			
Sr-90 (half-life 27·7 yrs)	15	750	10,800
Kr-85 (half-life 11·2 yrs)	1·2	90	1,160
H-3 (half-life 12·3 yrs)	0·04	3	36
Total for all fission products (gal)	1,200	44,000	860,000
Total for all fission products (tons)	16	388	5,350

1 US gallon = 3·785 litres; 1 ton = 1·016 mt
Source: SCEP 1970

Metals

Man's concentrations of natural elements

These elements are often essential to the metabolism of plants and animals but usually at very low concentrations. At high dosage levels they are frequently toxic to plants, animals and men and several of them are thought to be cumulative. They are of course part of the 'natural' environment but little is known about the development of tolerances, with the exception of the evolution of strains of certain plants, mainly grasses, able to withstand very high levels of, for example, lead and zinc, and thus grow on industrial waste tips formed at the sites of the smelting of these metals. But overall biological diversity is much reduced in such areas, and downstream from the tips at lead and copper mines, for example, their toxic effects are easily observable. The uses of metals are extremely widespread and, apart from the obvious and visible, include substances such as pesticides where 141 metals can be found in 112 compounds, and in additives like lead in petrol. Material concentrations in industrial areas are likely to be big pools of metals: sewage and urban solid wastes, for example, are high in their concentration of them. While in use, elements like lead, mercury, zinc, selenium, manganese, chromium, copper, cadmium and nickel are likely to be closely observed for toxicity, especially among workers handling them or consumers of products: hence the development of lead-free paints. However, their residual effects, as wastes and in unobservable forms like aerosols, are likely to escape notice until levels somewhere build up to a toxic concentration.

Lead

Among the toxic heavy metals, two which have come under the most scrutiny for possible pollutant effects from residues are lead and mercury. Lead is known to cause poisoning in most organisms, though tolerances vary. Some 180 kilotons (kt)/yr is estimated to be discharged into the oceans as a result of 'natural' processes, whereas about 2,000 kt/yr is mined (Lagerweff 1967). One of the newest (since 1923) and fastest-growing uses has been the addition of lead alkyls (commonly tetraethyl lead) to petrols as an 'anti-knock' additive (7,625 kt of leaded petrol sales in 1960, 14,010 in 1970). This results in an increase of lead in the atmosphere which eventually falls out, as the evidence collected by Murozumi *et al.* (1969) from cores of ice in Greenland shows (Fig. 11.9). Since the early 1970s, many countries have started to phase out the use of lead in this manner. Lead can enter drinking water from the atmosphere, from lead pipes if these are still used, and from the lead filler used in the joints of PVC pipes (Fig. 11.10).

Assessing the relationship between environmental (especially atmospheric) lead and lead levels in humans is a difficult matter (Bryce-Smith 1971, M. Williams 1971). Ingested and inhaled lead does not necessarily have a long residence time in the body as much of it is quickly excreted (Table 11.9). Tissue lead levels show, however, that there may be some accumulation in the body. Measurements in Manchester, England, revealed that a group of children had an average blood level of 0·309 ppm of lead, and that 4 per cent of them had

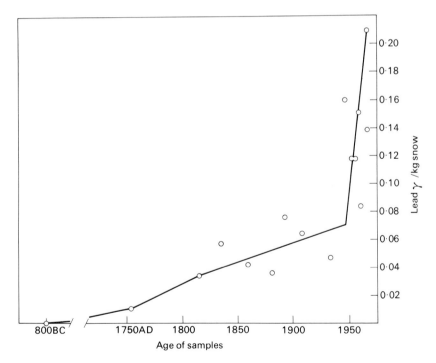

Fig. 11.9 The increase in the fallout of lead onto the snow of the Greenland ice-cap since 800 BC. Source: Murozumi *et al.* 1969

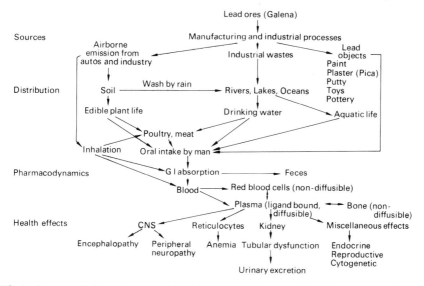

Fig. 11.10 A diagram of the pathways of lead in the biosphere and its effects on man. No mention is made of any natural flows of lead through the biosphere. GI = gastro-intestinal, CNS = central nervous system.
Source: Goyer and Chisholm 1972

levels above 0·8 ppm, a level which is associated with brain damage in children. The mean level in city-dwelling adults of the USA is 0·15–0·21 ppm, derived at least in part from an air level of 0·1–3·4 µg/m³. The USSR has tentatively set a maximum permissible level of 0·7 µg/m³ for the general atmosphere; in Britain the safety level for industrial workers in lead is 200 µg/m³ for a 40-hour week. Since air levels in cities are about 40 times less than this figure, there would seem to be little danger to humans, but the possibilities that

TABLE 11.9   Average daily intake of lead by a 'normal' person in the USA

Substance	Daily intake	Lead concentration in substance	Lead ingested per day (mg)	Fraction absorbed	Lead absorbed per day (mg)
Food	2 kg	0·17 ppm	330	0·05	17
Water	1 kg	0·01 ppm	10	0·1	1
Urban air	20 cubic metres (m³)	1·3 mg/m³*	26	0·4	10·4
Rural air	20 cubic metres (m³)	0·05 mg/m³*	1	0·4	0·4
Tobacco smoke	30 cigarettes	0·8 mg per cigarette	24	0·4	9·6

* Much of this is in the form of lead chloride and lead oxide.
Source: Walker 1971

the absorption rates of industrial lead and airborne lead are different, or that there might be synergistic results, should not be forgotten. Interestingly, imbibers of moonshine whiskey are at risk for lead poisoning, among other things (Goyer and Chisholm 1972).

Mercury

If there is some doubt about the status of lead as a toxic agent, then the case of mercury is much clearer. Mercury is used in industrial processes (its main use is in the production of chlorine and caustic soda in which there is a loss of 0·2 kg Hg per ton of the chlorine produced), and as an agricultural fungicide, so that it appears in industrial effluent and in runoff, both discharging frequently into lakes or at the coast (Table 11.10).

TABLE 11.10   Major uses of mercury in the USA, 1969

	kg
Electrolyte chlorine	71,300
Electrical apparatus	626,000
Paints	335,000
Agriculture	95,000
Pharmaceuticals	23,600
Paper industries	19,100

Source: Harriss 1971

The 'natural' level of mercury is of the order of a release of 5,000 mt/yr by chemical weathering, and human use adds about the same quantity (Harriss 1971). The pathways are shown in Fig. 11.11. Some is held in soils, but once in water it is rapidly absorbed by

TABLE 11.11   Mercury concentrations reported in environmental samples

Sample	Estimated natural levels	Concentrations measured in con- taminated samples
Air	2 µg/m³	2–20 µg/m³
Water:		
Sea water	0·00006–0·0003 ppm	0·0005–0·030 ppm
Fresh water	0·00006 ppm	0·0001–0·040 ppm
Soils[1]	0·04 ppm	0·08–40 ppm
Lake sediments[1]	0·06 ppm	0·08–1,800 ppm
Biological materials:		
Fish	0·02 ppm	0·5–17 ppm
Human blood	0·0008 ppm	0·001–0·013 ppm

[1] Mercury concentration is dependent on organic content.
Source: Harriss 1971

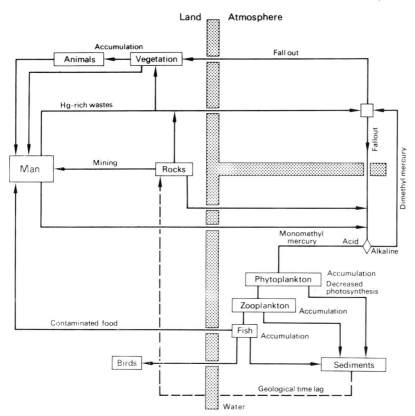

Fig. 11.11 A diagram of the pathways of mercury in the biosphere and man's position in them, both as a controller of some of the flows and the recipient of unwanted wastes.
After an original by Barbara Downey

particulate organic and inorganic material. Also, relatively innocuous inorganic or phenyl mercury is converted into toxic methyl or dimethyl compounds in sediments where bacteria are present. As with organochlorine pesticides, levels in organic matter are higher than in the surrounding water, and concentration in food chains is well established (Table 11.11). In organisms, mercury is concentrated in the liver, brain and kidneys, and alarm has been shown at the level of residues in foods such as tuna fish and swordfish, since the safe level suggested by the US Food and Drug Administration and WHO (0·5 ppm) has often been exceeded. Poisoning of humans from mercury-contaminated fish and shellfish has been established in Japan, where the symptoms of neural damage are known as Minamata disease after the town most strongly affected (Irukayama 1966). On the Manitoba–Ontario border in Canada, mercury levels in fish are 24 times the acceptable level in food of 0·5 ppm, and some of the Indians had body levels of 100–200 ppb (50 ppb is considered the safe upper limit). Eating of the fish is banned and no symptoms of mercury poisoning among the Ojibways have yet developed (Table 11.12).

TABLE 11.12	Concentration factors for mercury in some aquatic organisms
Algae	200–1,200
Large plants	4–2,400
Invertebrates	400–8,400
Fish (pike)	3,000

Source: Harris 1971

It has been shown that photosynthesis in some plants is inhibited by concentrations of 0·001 ppm of mercury, and that explosions of other populations and alterations in the structure of food webs are likely. Synergistic effects reported include an increased toxicity to crustacea of inorganic mercury and ethyl mercury chloride in the presence of low quantities of copper (US Geological Survey 1970). Public health standards in the USA and USSR of 0·005 ppm in drinking water have now been set and Japan will not permit > 0·01 ppm in industrial waste. Chlor-alkali plants in Canada may release no more than 0·005 lb of mercury per ton (2.54×10^{-4} kg/mt) of chlorine produced into rivers frequented by fish. These standards, however, ignore the long-term concentration and food-web effects and are perhaps insufficiently stringent, since at least 90 per cent of all mercury pollution in effluent can be eliminated without causing economic strain to the industries involved (Fimreite 1970). Agricultural residues are more difficult to deal with and withdrawal of mercuric pesticides, as happened in Sweden in 1966, seems the most logical step.

Solid wastes

Products of city metabolism

Urban areas concentrate materials greatly and there is a good deal of waste which has to be removed from the cities. Solid wastes are characterized by a great mixture of substances, including fine dust, cinder, metal and glass, paper and cardboard, textiles, putrescible vegetable material, and plastics. In addition, there is bulky waste such as old refrigerators, washing machines and autos (UK 1970, US President's Council 1971); in Britain these latter comprise 3–4 per cent of the total weight of refuse. The quantities of these materials are high: in the USA a year's solid wastes amount to 168 million mt (1965) or an average of 2 kg/cap/day or 907 kg/cap/yr. (The equivalent figure in 1920 was 1·25 kg/cap/day.) The high extremes of the distribution come from places like Los Angeles (2·59 kg/cap/day) and the San Francisco Bay area (3·62 kg/cap/day). Included in these totals are 48×10^9 cans (135/cap) bottles, together with 7 million junked autos. In the UK the number of discarded cars rose from 325,000 in 1967 to 600,000 in 1970 and is predicted to become 1,300,000 by 1980. The composition of the garbage is changing too: the last 10 years has seen a considerable rise in the proportion of plastics, paper and packaging materials, to the point

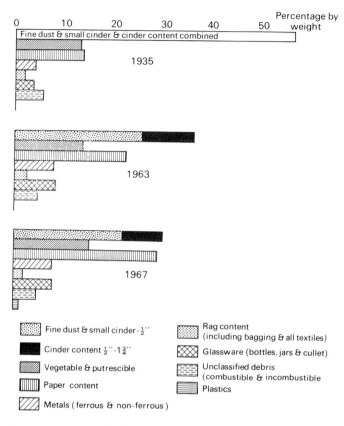

Fig. 11.12 The changing content of urban solid wastes in Britain 1935–67. The reduction of coal wastes, the late appearance of plastics and the increase in paper are the major features. Source: United Kingdom 1970

where Chicago refuse is about 56 per cent paper. The proportion of fuel wastes has, however, fallen: in Britain, the average weekly weight of garbage fell from 16·8 to 12·7 kg between 1935–67, reflecting a fall from 9·70 to 5·46 kg of dust and cinder (Fig. 11.12).

Under the carpet?

Such quantities of unwanted material can cause serious disposal problems. The simplest method is crude tipping or open dumping: in 1965 the USA had 17,000–22,000 such places, and in the UK (1963) 115 local authorities still used this method. More satisfactory is controlled tipping or the sanitary landfill. A layer of about 6 ft of refuse is covered by at least 9 in of earth, ash or other inert material, up to the level of the hole chosen. The surface can then be used for housing or sports fields, for example. Before such filling, the wastes can be pulverized by machines to a uniform particle size: by this means the volume is reduced and thus the life of the tip extended, and some of the refuse is more quickly biodegraded. Again, pulverized material can be subjected to fermentation before dumping: the heat generated (65 °C) helps to destroy bacteria and insect larvae. Incineration can be carried on inside cities, the residues used for civil engineering purposes, and power generated from combustible material, as at St Louis, where an electrical plant derives 15 per cent of its energy input from processed solid waste. Temperatures of 870–1,040 °C (1,600–1,900 °F) are commonly used, but unless electrostatic precipitators are used, air pollution is substituted for garbage problems; particulate matter from incinerators is estimated to constitute 10–15 per cent of New York City's airborne load. None of these methods is without its side-effects. Uncontrolled tipping contributes smells, windborne litter, dust, flies, rats and complete loss of amenity, and more seriously still, fire (used to consume the combustible components, it may smoulder inside the tip, breaking out sporadically), and contamination of ground water and streams by rainfall which has percolated through the tip. Controlled tipping is not immune to all these difficulties, and even wire fences will not control the airborne litter in a strong wind. Water percolation still occurs, and rats may find nesting places in hollow vessels or large objects which are not completely filled with the sealing material. Filler of earth or ash is often difficult to find, leading to delays in covering the tip or skimping of fill layers. Pulverization can create bad dust problems unless it is covered quickly; fermented material, like sewage sludge, could be sold, but it is expensive and is also very high in certain metals. One overall problem is the effect upon amenity, for although everybody wants their garbage taken away, nobody wants to live near the tip or the incinerator. There may also be a shortage of suitable sites within some jurisdictions and thus agreements with neighbours have to be made, or more often large cities have to exert pressures to gain space in outlying rural areas. Toronto, for example, in 1973 was prepared to pay $Can 6.50/ton to a railway company to haul and bury 400,000 tons/yr (out of a total solid waste production of 1·5 million tons) for at least 15 years. The residents of the intended receiving area were not thrilled by the prospect even when the company announced it would erect viewing platforms for the public to see the tipping and filling process. While the use of quarries and pits for such purposes is to some extent acceptable, the covering of wildlands such as mud flats and swamps is a much more serious loss in terms both of amenity and biological productivity.

Clearly, refuse is an immense potential source of raw materials, but steps towards re-use are very slow, with the exception of metals. Cars especially can now be virtually pelletized and the scrap sold to steel works. Paper can be recycled and many other materials re-used, but labour costs are very high and few people wish to do the work. Thus successful paper reclamation schemes like those of certain Canadian cities rely on subsidies from local taxes. In metropolitan Toronto, the borough of York spent $Can 687 to collect and ship 6 tons of waste paper for recycling which it sold for $Can 31. In 1970 the Greater London Council forecast that ferrous metal recovery was the only permanent salvage activity it could foresee in the future.

Solid wastes also include a variety of industrial materials, some of which are very toxic, like cyanide wastes. These can be neutralized, but unscrupulous industrialists pay truck drivers to dump the wastes by night onto open tips. A series of revelations of this practice in the English midlands in 1972 led to emergency legislation designed to prevent 'fly-tipping' of these materials. Probably only the tip of this particular iceberg has emerged (Dawe 1972).

Waste heat

Whenever energy performs work, heat is released which is radiated back into the atmosphere. Man concentrates this process spatially, and the resultant heating of air and water is called calefaction. In practical terms the commonest sources of concentrations of waste are power-generating plants. 1 KWH of energy generated from fossil fuels creates 6,000 BTU of heat; the same energy from nuclear fuels gives off 10,000 BTU. Nuclear plants in general produce about 50 per cent more heat than thermal plants. The demand for power has meant that in Canada, for example, waste heat from thermal power generation is predicted to rise 14 times in the period 1966–90, and by AD 2000 the amount of waste heat reaching Lake Ontario in January will be equivalent to 8 per cent of the solar energy input in that month (Cole 1969). Most of the heat is carried away as hot water and this produces distinct changes in biota. A body of water at 30–35 °C is essentially a biological desert and many game fish require temperatures of $< 10 °C$ for successful reproduction although they will survive above that temperature. A temperature rise of 10 °C will double the rate of many chemical reactions and so the decay of organic matter, the rusting of iron and the solution rate of salts are all accelerated by calefaction. Since the rate of exchange of salts and organisms increases, any toxins are liable to exert greater effects, and temperature fluctuations are also likely to affect organisms. Calefaction is therefore likely to exert a disruptive effect upon aquatic ecosystems, although some ways of putting the waste heat to beneficial use have been suggested. Where power plants are near deep ocean waters, the very cold water at depth could be brought up for efficient cooling and then pumped at its raised temperature into tanks used for raising fish or algae. Experiments in Hawaii and in St Croix in the Virgin Islands have suggested that a 100 MW plant could service a pond volume of 10^5 m^3 and produce 70 mt dry weight of carnivorous (third trophic level) fish/yr. Such a plan would also obviate the disturbance of the aquatic littoral community (Bienfang 1971). Such local developments do not countermand the fact that energy production and use all contribute heat to the atmosphere. The possible global effects are discussed in Chapter 10.

Noise

Noise is primarily a feature of cities, as exemplified by J. Caesar's action in banning chariots from the streets of Rome by day, thus producing insomnia by night. Defined as 'sound without value' or 'any noise that is undesired by the recipient', noise is still largely encountered in cities and so is not a major concern of this book. Noise levels in many urban-industrialized situations are known to be deleterious to human health and efficiency, with effects on the sense organs, cardiovascular system, glandular and nervous systems, while physical pain results at a level of 140 perceived noise decibels (pNdB) (Table 11.13; Molitor 1968, US Federal Council 1968).

TABLE 11.13   Noise levels (pNdB)

Silence	0	Rock band	100
Average residence	40–50	Compressors and hammers on	
Dishwasher	65	construction work at 10 ft	110
Auto at 20 ft	70–80	Four-engine jet at 500 ft	118
Light truck	75	Hydraulic press at 3 ft	130
Light truck accelerating	85	Threshold of pain	140
Subway train at 20 ft	95		

Source: US Federal Council 1968

Localized noise derived from sources such as traffic or pan-throwing neighbours may affect personal health but does not have any obvious ecological repercussions. Recreation areas may be affected by noise from motorboats, but environmental noise is particularly associated with aircraft, especially along flight-paths in the vicinity of airfields (Plate 20). Settlement location may need to be adjusted in such places with consequent ecological disruptions elsewhere. The sonic boom path associated with SST projects such as Concorde will produce noise of a very different order, in the form of sudden but repeated shock waves. These will cause disturbance to wild birds as well as domestic stock and buildings; if SSTs come into extensive use, subsonic flight over land seems to be a necessary condition.

Plate 20 The use of fossil fuel usually means noise. At this moment the Indian 'Palace in the Sky' is probably preferable to the Englishman's castle on the ground. *(Guardian, London)*

Chemical and biological warfare (CBW)

All effects so far discussed have been the unsought side-effects of resource processes, where ecosystems have been altered either unconsciously or because there were no apparent economic alternatives. With chemical and biological conflict (to which is added here the possibility of geophysical warfare), ecosystems are altered deliberately in order to produce military gain (R. Clarke 1968, Hersh 1968). Most CBW agents are aimed at people and thus ecological change would be indirect, but a few forms are aimed at ecological devastation.

With chemical warfare, for example, most of the potential agents are lethal to humans. From the use of arsenical smokes in the Sung Dynasty and sulphur fumes in the Peloponnesian Wars to the nerve gases like SE, GF, VE, and VX of which 70 mg inhaled or 1,250 mg cutaneously absorbed is fatal, the aim has been at other people; in addition the modern method of dispersal by aerosols would distribute such agents over wide areas. Modern nerve gases are cholinesterase inhibitors (thus the power to contract muscles is lost and death from asphixiation results quickly) and so are presumably effective against most animals. The chances therefore of eliminating a key animal in an ecosystem might be quite high. A misuse of biological resources occurs in the cultivation of disease organisms as a prelude to biological warfare. Numerous bacterial and viral diseases are suitable, especially those which have a high epidemicity. Anthrax, brucellosis, cholera, plague, tularemia, yellow fever and smallpox are all members of the gruesome list and several of them produce very high fatality rates. These again are aimed primarily at human populations, but several of them are diseases of wild and domesticated animals which might be expected thus to share in the general mortality accompanying any deliberate use, especially if the toxins were dispersed initially in aerosol form. Perhaps the most virulent of all these agents is the chemical toxin botulin, produced by the anaerobic bacterium *Clostridium botulinum*. A dose of 0·12 µg will produce 60–70 per cent mortality by inhalation or ingestion; treatment is difficult and there is no known antidote or vaccine. It decomposes after 12 hours in the air and so invaders could enter 24 hours after its use without danger. One ounce (28·35 g) of the 'A type' toxin is sufficient to kill 60 million people and 8 oz (226·8 g) should be enough for the entire population of the world. Dissemination by aerosols would be easy and the toxin is 1,000 times more effective when inhaled in spray droplets. It can be easily manufactured and stored indefinitely. Its use on a wide scale would undoubtedly produce respiratory paralysis of many animals other than those for which it was intended.

On a larger scale, man's planetary processes may be harnessable to harass an enemy. Several such activities are currently unpredictable in their effects or else not yet possible, but they do not appear to be far beyond the reach of technological developments (Calder 1968). Weather modification, for example, is usually employed to increase precipitation on a given area, as has been tried by the USA during the Vietnam War. If your enemy lives downwind he can be desiccated by the same method. Similarly the potential possibility of guiding a hurricane away from your own shores between guidelines of monomolecular films confers the equal possibility of guiding it onto an unfriendly shore. The upper layers of the atmosphere between 15–20 km altitude contain an ozone layer which absorbs most of the ultra-violet (UV) radiation from the sun; if a 'hole' could be created by chemical or physical action (e.g. UV radiation at 250 millimicrons wavelength decomposes O_3 atoms) then everything beneath would be burnt. At a crustal level, the strain energy present in large fault systems could be triggered off by underground nuclear explosions. At present the whereabouts of the resulting earthquakes cannot be foreseen (hence the worry over the large explosion under Amchitka Island in the Aleutians in November 1971), but improved knowledge of the behaviour of seismically unstable systems might tempt a dweller by the China Sea to have a jiggle at the San Andreas fault. On a larger scale altogether is the hypothetical possibility of setting off very large nuclear explosions at the base of ice-caps, especially in Antarctica, thus initiating outward sliding of the ice-sheet. The two results would be huge tsunamis that would wreck coastal developments even in the northern hemisphere, and greater ice accumulation owing to the changed albedo, thus bringing about a new 'glacial' period, with more temperate conditions in the tropics. Since only land-locked tropical states would benefit, the likelihood of an attempt seems as low as the likelihood that the sequence of geophysical events would actually follow the predicted path (MacDonald 1968).

The necessity of avoiding all the above eventualities has led to some measure of international agreement about the banning of CBW. As with large-scale nuclear warfare, or even intensive conventional bombing as in Vietnam (Westing and Pfeiffer 1972), the effects of widespread dispersal of the agents would affect not only people but the structure and functioning of many ecosystems, and many irreversible changes might be produced. In Vietnam, where aerial spraying of 2,4-D and 2,4,5-T has been used by the USA to defoliate forests and devastate crops (Table 11.14), Tschirley estimates that although mangroves may recover in about 20 years' time, some sprayed areas of forest may become vegetated with bamboo, retarding regeneration of forest considerably. By March 1969, 189,782 ha of crops had been destroyed and 1·67 million ha of 'jungle' defoliated. It is impossible to estimate the amount of accidental damage by spray drifts, and load dumping may deposit 1,000 gal (3,785 litres) in 30 seconds instead of 4 minutes, an unprecedented concentration (Tschirley 1969, Orians and Pfeiffer 1970, Whiteside 1970, Lewallen 1971). Even though dioxin, a contaminant of 2,4,5-T, appears to be associated with foetal teratogenicity, the USA has not regarded this activity as being chemical or biological warfare, although cessation of the practice has accompanied the USA withdrawal. Perhaps Tacitus best sums it up: 'Ubi solitudinem faciunt: pacem appellant'.

The invasion of the biosphere

As Table 11.1 has shown, the various components of the biosphere act as temporary or permanent resting places for man-induced wastes. Many contaminants pass through the atmosphere, for example, but gases such as CO_2 which remain there, and finely divided particulate matter, provide the most likely agents of widespread change. The chemical balance of gases in the atmosphere is apparently the product of biological processes and can be changed by man with possible effects upon the global climate. By contrast, contamination of moving fresh water is primarily a local or regional problem, and if the offending inputs

TABLE 11.14   Defoliating agents used in Vietnam

Code-name	Ingredient of mixture	lb/gal (114 g/litre) acid equivalent	Use
Agent Orange	2,4-D 50 2,4,5-T 50	4·2 3·7	General defoliation of forest, brush and broad-leaved crops.
Agent Blue	2,4-D 50 2,4,5-T 30 2,4,5-T 20	4·2 2·2 1·5	Used interchangeably
Agent White	2,4-D 50 Picloram	2·0 0·54	Forest defoliation—for long-term results
Agent Blue	Sodium cacodylate 27·7% Cacodylic acid 4·8% Water, NaCl to 100%		Rapid, short-term defoliation of grass and rice

Source: Orians and Pfeiffer 1970

cease, then the biological processes and the hydrological cycle restore the water to a purer condition (Wolman 1971). This may of course take some time, as in the case of the River Rhine, where *inter alia* a German factory discharges wastes with a daily BOD equivalent to the sewage of 4·7 million people, and Alsatian potash mines discharge enough salt to raise the chlorine content of the river from 150 to 350 mg/litre in 30 years. As Coleridge remarked, 'What power divine / Shall henceforth wash the river Rhine?' Relatively rapid cleansing is not possible in large lakes where poisoning and eutrophication can bring about apparently irreversible biological death if they proceed too far; small lakes at an early stage of enrichment can be saved. Soils also can accumulate nutrients with as yet unknown effects. Many residual poisons in soils form the greatest magnitude of contamination having the most measurable ecological effect. The oceans inevitably form the main repository for contaminants from land, fresh water and atmosphere, although they lose some volatile substances to the last of these. Even if accumulation ceased now, the great water bodies would harbour residual pesticides for many years to come, along with numerous long-lived industrial, chemical and pharmaceutical compounds and oil effluent. Apart from their role as a food provider, the oceans play a significant part in the CO_2/O_2 balance of the planet, and the inhibition of photosynthesis by contaminants may seriously affect both. It is difficult to estimate which environment suffers the most contamination, but probably that of the oceans is most significant (MacIntyre and Holmes 1971). In 1972 an international convention to reduce the dumping of waste materials into the sea was signed by 80 countries whose fleets account for about 90 per cent of ocean pollution. It prohibits the dumping of radioactive wastes, CBW agents, oils, cadmium and mercury, and organohalogen compounds. A special clause allows some of these to be dumped if they are immediately hazardous to human health. A second list contains substances which may only be offloaded in specific locations and quantities with prior permission from a secretariat: arsenic, lead, copper, cyanides and fluorides are included. The accord closely follows the terms of the Oslo Agreement for the North Sea (also of 1972) but includes large maritime nations such as the USA, USSR, Liberia, Japan and Greece. It is impossible so far to see what effect such conventions may have.

On the land, poisoning of animals and plants by various air- and water-borne effluents is a daily occurrence in industrialized countries and cumulative toxins build up steadily, although radioactive fallout has fortunately continued to decline. Mortality among predators at the tops of food chains has been accompanied by sub-lethal effects in these and other animals at lower trophic levels.

Inevitably the possible effects of all these wastes upon man has been the subject of most concern. Apart from direct poisoning during toxin application, mortality from waste products is not apparently very high, though deaths from contaminated drinking water or sewage-laden sea-water off resorts are doubtless not publicized by the communities in which they occur. Directly traceable incidents like Minamata disease are generally rare, and features like smog perhaps exacerbate existing ailments rather than induce new ones. But the increased volume and incidence of pollutants is so recent that no adult has yet gone through a life-span carrying for example the body-burden of DDT now common. Not until those born after 1950 have gone through a normal twentieth-century Western urban existence without showing significant damage can we say that the present levels of contamination are harmless.

More important than considerations of the personal health of individuals is the 'health' of the systems of the biosphere, for man is inextricably bound up in the webs of these systems and cannot exist apart from them. It is notable therefore that the effects of the various forms of pollution upon ecosystems can be generalized and indeed predicted. Putting together the evidence from ecological change caused by radioactivity, eutrophication, toxins, defoliation and deforestation, Woodwell (1970b) summarizes his findings that

> pollution operates on the time scale of succession, not of evolution, and we cannot look to evolution to cure this set of problems. The loss of structure involves a shift away from complex arrangements of specialized species toward the generalists; away from forest, toward hardy shrubs and herbs; away from those phytoplankton of the open ocean that Wurster proved so very sensitive to DDT, towards those algae of the sewage plants that are unaffected by almost everything including DDT and most fish; away from diversity in birds, plants and fish toward monotony; away from tight nutrient cycles toward very loose ones with terrestrial systems becoming overloaded; away from stability toward instability especially with regard to sizes of populations of small rapidly producing organisms such as insects and rodents that compete with man; away from a world that runs itself through a self-augmentive, slowly moving evolution, to one that requires constant tinkering to patch it up, a tinkering that is malignant in that each act of repair generates a need for further repairs to avert problems generated at compound interest.

To which may be added that all these shifts represent a movement away from systems which are highly valued in aesthetic and other non-economic terms to those of lower acceptability and value: in other words, a lowering of what we choose to call environmental quality.

The solution to the ecological downgrading caused by contamination can only be multi-dimensional. A suitable technology is an obvious starting place and may indeed be the easiest phase to achieve. Efficacious methods of material 'sieving' to prevent contamination of biospheric systems are available for many resource processes, although in some cases they merely transfer the site of the disposal problem. But nevertheless, sewage can be treated and smokes can be scrubbed, mine wastes can be reburied along with atomic wastes, and non-residual third-generation pesticides will replace the chlorinated hydrocarbons. But some contaminations are beyond the reach of technology: as long as industry persists, carbon dioxide and heat will be generated and led off into the atmosphere, and no technique for sieving out the DDT and related substances now in the oceans has been, or is likely to be, invented. So while recovery of many wastes is technically possible, there are some contaminant-caused problems to which no technological solution is at all likely. Movement towards greater sifting of the by-products of resource processes is likely to be accelerated by a shortage of the initial supply of the material. Current economic and social values dictate that the proper response to a materials shortage is to develop a new process which will render hitherto inaccessible sources usable or to achieve substitution by another material. The complexity of contemporary technology means however that long 'lead times' are inevitable for new processes, so that the time-scale of problem accumulation is much slower than the time-scale of finding solutions. Substitution may not always be possible because of scale factors: water is the obvious example here. Recycling of materials is, therefore, not popular in the DCs at present but is likely to become more applicable because of cost factors and because of public concern, for example over disposable but non-returnable articles like plastic bottles and paper products. This movement may gain impetus if ways of accounting are devised that include the full social costs of environmental contamination in its various forms; 'making the polluter pay' is unpopular in DCs because of the fear that industrial firms will become less competitive in world markets. But even though an estimated 287×10^9 must be spent in the USA on meeting air and water quality standards in the period 1971–80, this will only lower the rate of growth of GNP by 0.1 per cent; without such controls it would be 4.8 per cent p.a., with them, 4.7 per cent p.a. (Anon 1972). The loss of environmental quality due to insidious degradation is scarcely likely, however, to be susceptible to such analysis and will likely be ignored. Another institutional difficulty is the low status and satisfaction in working at materials recovery with present technology. A basic change in human values that puts healthy ecosystems before an unending supply of new materials would be ideal but seems destined to remain a low priority.

The atmosphere and the deep oceans are also a commons in Hardin's (1968) sense, and so international agreement is necessary for any of the clean-up processes to be effective. The scale and magnitude of the agreements necessary, for example to lower nitrogen and phosphorus levels in estuaries or to prevent untreated sewage reaching the seas, are immense and less capable of solution than the development of new technology. The guidelines issuing from the UN 1972 Stockholm conference make general references to pollution but offer no suggestions for implementing technological solutions on an international basis. 'The just struggle of the people of all countries against pollution should be supported' is not a blueprint for environmental cleanliness.

Finally, we must remember that pollution and contamination exist as the end-parts of resource processes and cannot sensibly be viewed outside this context; attempts to 'cure' pollution without considering the whole of the relevant resource process are as useful as trying to cure lung cancer with aspirins. Hence the primary importance of recycling wastes as sources of raw materials. The magnitude of the processes is inevitably linked to the ever-increasing rates of production of material goods and hence to population levels. People are not pollution, as some slogans aver, but there is little doubt that they are the cause of it, particularly the affluent ones; the example of China in reclaiming every possible material from every waste output is both a precept and a probable portent (Unger 1971). Pessimists tend to take as symbolic the story (only slightly embroidered from LaMore 1971) of the rich Texan who was buried in a king-size grave propped up in the front seat of a Cadillac convertible with the FM radio playing and the air-conditioning full on. One mourner was heard to say to another, 'Man, that's livin'.'

Further reading

CALDER, N. (ed.) 1968: *Unless peace comes.*
HODGES, L. 1973: *Environmental pollution.*
MARX, L. 1971: *Waste.*
MOORE, N. W. 1967: A synopsis of the pesticide problem.
MURDOCH, W. W. (ed.) 1971: *Environment,* 189–366.
SINGER, S. F. 1970: *Global effects of environmental pollution.*
STERN, A. C. (ed.) 1968: *Air pollution.*
STUDY OF CRITICAL ENVIRONMENTAL PROBLEMS (SCEP) 1970: *Man's impact on the global environment: assessment and recommendations for action.*
STUDY OF MAN'S IMPACT ON CLIMATE (SMIC) 1971: *Inadvertent climatic modification.*
WOODWELL, G. M. 1970: Effects of pollution on the structure and physiology of ecosystems.

Part III
The perception of limits

12

Resources and population

This section opens with a discussion of the growth of and future prospects for man's numbers. This leads into a consideration of some of the spatial and social consequences of the interaction of population and resources, and an evaluation of the developing concepts of resource and environmental management especially as enunciated in the DCs.

Population

Historical perspectives

Many general references have been made to population growth and its relationship to resource use. Since it is people who use materials and environments, both as metabolic requirements and cultural accessories, an examination of the past, present and probable future numbers of people and their distribution is considered at this point. There are numerous specialized works on demography and population geography (e.g. J. I. Clarke 1965, Zelinsky 1966, Bogue 1969, Petersen 1969, Trewartha 1969, Zelinsky, Kosinki and Prothero 1970), and only their general conclusions are presented here.

Estimates of the world's population before about AD 1650 are, as a UN publication sharply puts it, 'vague reconstructions', although perhaps the stage when the totals were one and two is reasonably well documented. Estimates for prehistoric times and for the first 1600 years AD are generally based on calculations of culture area by population density, where the latter is inferred from values for present-day examples of such economies as hunting and gathering or shifting agriculture. The taking of censuses began in 1655 and is now common, although many of them are probably not very reliable; on a world basis we may, however, expect a degree of cancellation of errors. The estimated numbers up to the present can be seen in Fig. 12.1, and Table 12.1 gives Deevey's (1960) estimates of population total and density for various periods.

Though the data are scanty before AD 1650 they give a consistent picture of a population with a very slow rate of growth (Fig. 12.1). High infant mortality rates and low longevity meant that rates of increase were small; in Roman times the average life expectation for men was about 30 years, and this was not altered significantly until the coming of scientific medicine in Europe. The replotting of the curve for total world population upon a logarithmic basis reveals a number of surges in population (Fig. 12.2), the first of which was coincident with the Neolithic revolution and the advent of agriculture, when population increased 25-fold due to increase in the means of subsistence. Once agriculture had become

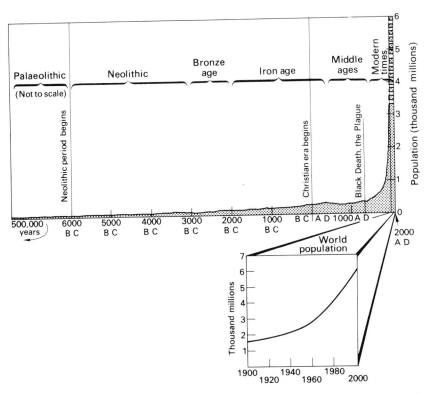

Fig. 12.1 The growth of the world's human population since the Palaeolithic, and projected at current rates of increase to AD 2000. Catastrophes like the Black Death had remarkably little long-term effect. Source: Trewartha 1969

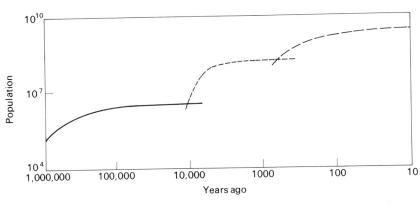

Fig. 12.2 A logarithmic plot of the population curve: surges in population are inferentially connected by Deevey (1960) with the invention of tool making (solid line), the agricultural revolution of the Neolithic (short dashes) and the scientific-industrial revolution (long dashes). Other writers (e.g. Durand 1967) interpret the latest surge as originating before the scientific-industrial revolution. Source: Deevey 1960

TABLE 12.1   Population growth

Years ago (base-date = 1960)	Cultural stage	Area populated	Assumed density per km²	Total population (millions)
1,000,000	Lower Palaeolithic (hunting–gathering)	Africa	0·00425	0·125
300,000	Middle Palaeolithic (hunting-gathering)	Africa and Eurasia	0·012	1·0
25,000	Upper Palaeolithic (hunting–gathering)	Africa and Eurasia	0·04	3·34
10,000	Mesolithic (hunting–gathering)	All continents	0·04	5·32
6,000	Village farming and early urban	Old World / New World	1·0 } / 0·04 }	86·5
2,000	Village farming and urban	All continents	1·0	133
310 (1650)	Farming and industrial	All continents	3·7	545
210 (1750)	Farming and industrial	All continents	4·9	728
160 (1800)	Farming and industrial	All continents	6·2	906
60 (1900)	Farming and industrial	All continents	11·0	1,610
10 (1950)	Farming and industrial	All continents	16·4	2,400

Source: Deevey 1960

firmly established (4000–3000 BC) three main zones of occupance existed: high-density areas of agriculture and gathering around the agricultural hearths and diffusion areas; areas with thinly spread gathering and hunting cultures; and unoccupied areas. By about 2000 BC the agricultural occupance of much of Eurasia and the northern half of Africa is postulated. Beyond this core lay the food gatherers and hunters, and the uninhabited areas were still considerable, though reduced in size. Within the agricultural areas densities were higher in favoured places and highest of all where cities had developed. At the time of the Classical world, 200 BC–AD 200, the populations of the world are dominated by empires. The Indian subcontinent held 100–140 million and mainland China 71 million; Imperial Rome under Augustus had some 54 million people who constituted a quarter to a fifth of the world's population. Between AD 1000–1600 a steady but slow growth is seen on most continents (Table 12.2) in spite of intermittent checks imposed by famine and plague. The exception is the Americas, where the colonists and conquistadors were responsible for reducing the aboriginal populations to fractional levels through warfare and disease, although it has been argued that a group like the Maya were on the verge of collapse, having outrun their resource base.

A population of 470–545 million in AD 1650 seems very large by comparison with the figures for BC/AD 0 or 4000 BC, but becomes small in the context of the accelerated growth after AD 1650. The magnitude of thē subsequent growth is widely agreed upon with some relatively minor variations according to the sources used (Table 12.3). The major components of the growth 1750–1950,-continent by continent, are shown in Table 12.4, using

TABLE 12.2   Approximate population (millions) of the world and its subdivisions, AD 1000–1600

Year	World	Europe	Asiatic Russia	South-east Asia	India	China Major[1]	Japan	South-east Asia, Oceania	Africa	The Americas
1000	275	42	5	32	48	70	4	11	50	13
1100	306	48	6	33	50	79	5	12	55	17
1200	348	61	7	34	51	89	8	14	61	23
1300	384	73	8	33	50	99	11	15	67	28
1400	373	45	9	27	46	112	14	16	74	30
1500	446	69	11	29	54	125	16	19	82	41
1600	486	89	13	30	68	140	20	21	90	15

[1] China proper, plus Manchuria and Korea, Outer Mongolia, Sinkiang and Formosa.
Source: Desmond 1965

TABLE 12.3   Estimates of world population (millions)

	1650	1750	1800	1850	1900
Wilcox	470	694	919	1,091	1,571
Carr-Saunders	545	728	906	1,171	1,608
Durand	not estimated	791	978	1,262	1,650

Source: Durand 1967

TABLE 12.4   Estimates of population growth 1750–1950 (millions)

Areas	1750	1800	1850	1900	1950
World	791	978	1,262	1,650	2,515
Asia (exc. USSR)	498	630	801	925	1,381
Africa	106	107	111	133	222
Europe (exc. USSR)	125	152	208	296	527
USSR	42	56	76	134	180
North America	2	7	26	82	166
South and Central America	16	24	38	74	162
Oceania	2	2	2	6	13

Figures in italics are those which lack a firm foundation.
Source: Durand 1967

Durand's (1967) work, to which reference should be made for discussion of the reasons for the growth in each individual continent. The major point of interest is the phase of accelerated population growth which has lasted to the present. Its inception varies from place to place and is prior to 1750 in Europe, Russia and America and probably before 1650 in China. The absolute numbers would of course rise quite steeply even with a constant rate of population growth, but as Table 12.5 shows, the actual rate itself has undergone acceleration, except in twentieth-century Europe and the USSR. The more accurate figures

TABLE 12.5   Annual rate of increase (per cent)

Areas	1750– 1800	1800– 1850	1850– 1900	1900– 1950
World	0·4	0·5	0·5	0·8
Asia (exc. USSR)	0·5	0·5	0·3	0·8
Africa	0·0	0·1	0·4	0·7
Europe (exc. USSR)	0·4	0·6	0·7	0·6
USSR	0·6	0·6	1·1	0·6
North America	—	2·7	2·3	1·4
South and Central America	0·8	0·9	1·3	1·6
Oceania	—	—	—	1·6

Figures in italics are those which lack a firm foundation.
Source: Durand 1967

TABLE 12.6   World annual rate of increase

Decade	%
1900–1920	0·6
1920–30	1·1
1930–40	1·0
1940–50	1·0
1950–60	1·8

Source: Durand 1967

of decadal rates for the twentieth century in Table 12.6 exhibit the same trend: the 1950–60 period shows an even greater jump in the rate. Close inspection of estimates of growth for individual nations has revealed little relationship between the development of industrialization and the expansion of population. Why there should then have been a simultaneous upturn in rates of growth in the eighteenth and early nineteenth centuries is not known. No simple explanation of causality is acceptable and Durand's (1967) hypothesis seems more plausible: he suggests that the stimulus of agricultural improvement in the sixteenth and seventeenth centuries provided the potential for considerable population expansion but that this was held back by the transmission of diseases which followed exploration and trade in the same period. By the eighteenth century sufficient resistance to imported infections had built up for the population potential to be realized. At the end of the nineteenth century the dichotomy of demographic process between industrial and less developed countries was apparent: the former had death control (giving lower rates of infant mortality and greater longevity) and a measure of birth control, but the latter had experienced only the initial impact of the death control techniques which are dominated by modern medical practices such as antisepsis, immunization, disease vector control and pharmaceutical improvements, together with a knowledge of nutrition science.

Present numbers, distribution and density

Estimates by the United Nations of the populations of the continents are given in Table 12.7, and the percentage contributions of the various areas shown in Table 12.8. These are summarized in the map of population density, Fig. 12.3. Such statements of distribution reveal that Europe and Asia together contain over three-quarters of mankind, and that Asia has more than half, whereas less than 10 per cent live in the southern hemisphere. Between 20°N–60°N in the Old World are found four-fifths of the population, in a zone which includes also most of the great deserts of the Old World, along with the Alpine and Himalayan mountain systems. Within this zone are two great concentrations of man: southeast Asia, where approximately one-half of the world's people live on one-tenth of the habitable area, and Europe (including European Russia) where one-fifth of the global population occupy less than one-twentieth of its ecumene. There are in addition secondary

TABLE 12.7   Estimated world population, mid-1973
(millions)

World	3,860	Latin America	308
Africa	374	Europe	472
Asia	2,204	USSR	250
North America	233	Oceania	21

Source: Population Reference Bureau 1973

TABLE 12.8   Continental percentages of world population, 1920–73

	1920	1960	1973
Africa	7·9	8·5	9·7
Asia	53·3	56·1	57·2
North America	6·5	6·6	6·0
Latin America	5·0	6·9	7·9
Europe	18·1	14·2	12·2
USSR	8·7	7·1	6·4
Oceania	0·5	0·5	0·5

Source: Population Reference Bureau 1969 and 1973

Fig. 12.3 World population density: only in regions of unfavourable climate are low densities found, but high densities are seen both in urban-industrial regions of the world and in rural-agricultural regions, especially in Asia.
Source: Trewartha 1969

Inhabitants per square

Mile	Km
Over 250	Over 100
125–250	50–100
25–125	10–50
2–25	1–10
Under 2	Under 1

concentrations in the eastern half of North America, California, coastal Brazil, the Plate estuary, the valley of the Nile, west Africa, south-east Africa and south-east Australia. Looked at politically, six states (China, India, Pakistan, Bangladesh, Japan and Indonesia) have nearly half the world's population and, contrarywise, some pocket populations like Gambia (0·4 million in 1972) and Iceland (0·2 million in 1972) continue to exist. Considerable variations in density are revealed by Fig. 12.3. The environmentally inhospitable parts of the globe are principally those too cold, too dry or too high for mass settlement and at concentrations of $< 1/km^2$ contrast with the favoured agricultural areas like the valley of the Ganges and maritime east Asia, and with intensely used industrial and agricultural zones, such as west and central Europe, both at $100/km^2$. The inner cores of Western cities have traditionally held the densest agglomerations of people, but migration to suburbs is lessening the populousness of such places.

Future growth and numbers

Interest in the growth rates of populations and the consequent future numbers centres around the avilability of resources for them and also their effects upon the biosphere, especially that of the wastes they produce. But just as the reasons for population growth in the past can never all be known, so future growth cannot be predicted without making certain assumptions about demographic variables and the way in which these are affected by social and economic conditions. Some projections therefore assume constant fertility while others may assume that a form of demographic transition to lower birth rates will occur as nations become industrial, as happened in nineteenth-century Europe. Both of these assumptions may turn out to be untrue.

The simplest measure of population growth is the annual percentage increase which relates easily to doubling times (Table 12.9). The best estimate of the present world rate (1973) is 2 per cent p.a., which gives a doubling time of about 35 years. This average rate is composed of a multitude of national rates of greater or lesser accuracy of estimation, most of which are within the range 1–2·5 per cent but with extreme variants (Table 12.10). By continents, Europe appears to have the lowest rate of growth and Latin America the

TABLE 12.9   Growth rates and doubling times

Increase % p.a.	Years to double population
0·1	693
0·5	139
1·0	70
1·5	47
2·0	35
2·5	28
3·0	23
3·5	20
4·0	18

Source: Hardin 1969

TABLE 12.10   Population growth rates 1969 and 1972 (per cent per annum)

	Mean 1969	1972	Highest 1969	Highest 1972	Lowest 1969	Individual countries 1972	
World	1·9	2·0					
Africa	2·4	2·6	3·6	3·4	0·9	0·8	
Asia	2·0	2·3	7·6[1]	8·2[1]	1·1	1·2	
North America	1·1	1·1	2·0	1·7	1·0	1·0	Canada and USA only
Latin America	2·9	2·8	3·8	3·4	0·9	0·8	
Europe	0·8	0·7	2·7	2·8	0·1	0·0	
USSR	1·0	0·9					
Oceania	1·8	2·0					Australia and New Zealand only are listed

[1] For Kuwait: exaggerated by immigration from a (1972) natural increase of 3·6 per cent p.a.
Source: Population Reference Bureau 1969 and 1972

highest; East Germany has the lowest national rate of growth and Kuwait the highest, largely because of immigration. (For the purposes of this discussion migration has been ignored; although significant nationally, as in Lebanon, it is not relevant at the global scale.) Demographically two main groups exist, those with a birth-rate (BR) over 35/1,000 and those whose BR is < 35. The first group comprises most of the LDCs and has two subgroups, the first of which has BR <35 and death rate (DR) >15/1,000. This is best represented in Africa and Asia, where DRs remain high at present but are falling under the impact of modern medicine. The second subgroup has DRs <15 and is responsible for the very high growth-rates of Latin America, since BR remains high but DRs have fallen substantially. A BR of <35 is characteristic of the DCs and a few LDCs which have low absolute populations. A subdivision can be made on the basis of BR = 20; above this level are a few DCs whose birth rates seem bound to fall and thus bring them into a typical DC position where BR <20. These countries have gone through a demographic transition to low birth rate and low death rate.

The different demographic types can be linked to variations in family characteristics, as detailed by Petersen (1969). These types are conceptualized in terms of the demographic transition in Europe but may have a relevance elsewhere to populations whose cultural characteristics are changing. In medieval times there was a traditional pre-industrial family where late marriage and non-marriage helped to depress birth rates. Guilds permitted marriage of their apprentices only when their service was complete, and younger children who would not inherit their father's farm, for example, might well enter the Church, whose clergy were supposed to be celibate. This family type was succeeded during the industrial revolution by the proletarian family in which early marriage was favoured by the availability of work within the factory system. There were few institutional barriers to sexual relations and illegitimacy was high, since in some countries the mother could force support from the putative father. Additionally, enough bastard children put out to work at an early age could ensure a comfortable living for the mother. The third type may be called the rational family and was coincident with the rise of a middle class. A sense of parental responsibility for limiting family size arose which was helped by the availability of contraceptive methods, and the age of marriage also began to rise.

All such generalizations are of course abstractions from a multitude of cultures, and as Zelinsky (1966) points out, it is easy to forget that all demographic characteristics are a result of cultural practices: the adoption of modern medicine is merely one of these. Any real understanding of population growth must therefore start with an assessment of the cultural variables involved, which naturally includes the peoples' perception of themselves and their physical and social environments.

Population projections

The pitfalls inherent in making forecasts of population levels beyond the immediate future are considerable (Dorn 1965). For example, it is often assumed that as the LDCs industrialize they will undergo the same type of demographic transition to low BR and low DR as did Europe in the nineteenth century. Yet there is no certainty of this since very different cultures are involved, apart from the assumption of the inevitability of industrialization in the poorer countries.

The assumptions underlying projections must therefore be clear if the estimates of future numbers are to have any usefulness. Two types of assumptions are most often used:

(1) constant fertility projections, in which the recent growth rate is projected into the future, i.e. a simple extrapolation of present trends; and

(2) changed fertility projections, in which assumptions are made about the socio-economic conditions affecting natural increase and migration, principally the former.

The uncertainties are so great that the UN projections, for example, employ three variants (high, medium and low) based on differing assumptions about the impact of medical and contraceptive programmes and of nutrition standards in various parts of the world. The high variant assumes that fertility will remain constant until 2000; the medium projection assumes that it will decline after 1975 at rates previously observed in some areas; the low variant posits an immediate decline in fertility which then remains continuously at low levels until 2000. Since the low variant is somewhat unlikely, the medium and high projections are most often quoted. Table 12.11 compares the 1969 figures with two of the projections for AD 2000. We can note two salient features of these projections: first, that the medium variant involves a virtual doubling of world population by 2000; second, that a large proportion of the additional people will be Asians: they above all others will be the most numerous. Frejka (1973) forecasts that the present ratio of 30 : 70 between the rich and the poor nations will inevitably become 20 : 80 and perhaps even 10 : 90, during the next few decades. Making certain assumptions about the coming of a demographic transition to the LDCs, he suggests that a virtually stable world population of 8,400 million is likely to be achieved by about AD 2100. This will probably be held in many quarters as a somewhat optimistic estimate.

TABLE 12.11   World and continental population projections (millions)

	World	Africa	Asia	North America	Latin America	Europe	Oceania	USSR
Mid-1969	3,551	344	1,990	225	276	456	19	241
2000—UN projection, constant fertility based on 1969	7,522	860	4,513	388	756	571	33	402
2000—UN projection, medium variant based on 1969	6,130	768	3,458	354	638	527	32	353
2000—UN projection, medium variant based on 1972	6,494	818	3,777	333	652	568	35	330

Source: Population Reference Bureau 1969 and 1972

The 2 per cent p.a. rise in world population does not seem particularly large unless the characteristics of an exponential curve with this increment are considered carefully. At present the doubling time for the population is 35 years, and at 2 per cent p.a. it will go on doubling at that interval no matter what the absolute level of population. The projection of this rate of growth unchanged into the future quickly brings very high absolute figures. A population of 3,000 million in 1960 rising at 2 per cent p.a. becomes 1×10^{15} in AD 2600. Each person will then have 5 ft² (approximately 0·5 m²) of room: this stage has thus been called SRO (Standing Room Only) day. Still at 2 per cent p.a., the year AD 4000 or thereabouts would see the earth as a mass of humanity expanding outwards at the speed of light. The types of life which such increased populations would enjoy (*sic*) have been explored by Fremlin (1964). In 890 years' time, for example, the present population, increasing at 2 per cent p.a., will be $60,000 \times 10^{12}$. To cope with such numbers the entire planet would be covered with a 2,000-storey building. Occupying 1,000 of these floors, each person would have 7·5 m² of floor space, while the rest of the building would be devoted to food-producing and refrigerating machinery. Life would be nearly sessile, but travel over a few hundred metres in any direction might be permissible so that each individual could then choose his friends out of some 10 million others. The limiting condition of this way of life would be the technological ability to radiate into space all the heat produced by the people and their machines, for the outer skin temperature of the 2,000-storey building would have to be at 1,000°C.

The possibility of shipping off excess population to other planets has been suggested from time to time. Even if the planets were hospitable environments, able to support human life, the economics are rather startling. At present the daily increment of people in the world is about 125,000. At present prices, to remove one day's increment to a hypothetical planet would cost $US369,000 million. If therefore the USA cut down its standard of living to 18 per cent of its present level, in one year it could set aside sufficient capital to finance the export of one day's additional people. As Hardin (1959) remarks,

'Such a philanthropic desire to share the wealth may be judged noble in intent but hardly in effect.'

These apparent fantasies of huge numbers and SF-type technologies have one serious purpose: to make us aware that absolute limits exist. If there were not the nutrition limit set by photosynthesis or even photosynthesis plus 'unconventional' foods, then there are the space limits and the heat limits. Therefore let nobody be persuaded that the earth has some infinite capacity for people.

Population control

Attempts to vary rates of increase have a long history (Benedict 1970). Most of our knowledge (and a great deal of folklore) has been concerned with efforts to increase fecundity, particularly in pre-industrial societies with high rates of infant mortality. Modern medicine is also a death-control mechanism, particularly as it affects longevity and infant mortality. Death control is usually more acceptable than birth control, although there is considerable evidence for the latter in pre-industrial groups, especially if we include abortion and infanticide as methods of reducing increase. Modern concern to limit birth stems from two types of motivation. The first is concern with the physical and economic health of an individual family, or a particular woman, where hardship occurs if too many children are born too quickly. However, the spacing of children does not necessarily mean a small number of births and medicine in many places enhances their chance of survival. A second reason for advocating birth control is the economic, social and ecological health of an entire community or nation, especially where resources are scarce or where the rate of growth is placing great strains on the ability of the community services to cope with it. Observation of the areas of fastest growth will often reveal a certain coincidence of rapid increase with poorly developed social infrastructures. The response to a desire for a slower growth rate comes in two phases. The first of these may be called the family planning phase, in which the efforts of government or private programmes are directed at individuals and families. Emphasis is placed on the advantages both to parents and to children of smaller or well-spaced families. Sterilization and contraceptive techniques are widely offered. However, abortion, usually illegal, is probably of more significance than any of the physical and hormonal contraceptives. Likewise, late marriage is a very effective factor in limiting births, as has been shown in China. The targets for family planning programmes usually aim at slowing a growth rate (e.g. by 1 per cent p.a.) in LDCs (Plate 21) or at eliminating 'unplanned' births in the DCs. The adoption of family planning programmes may, according to Davis (1967), have very limited results in terms of decelerating population expansion since, by offering only the means for couples to control fertility, such programmes neglect the means for society to do so. The very features that make family planning acceptable render it ineffective for the second phase, which is population control. This is linked to the circumstances of the community rather than the individual and envisages either a specific target population to be achieved by a slower rate of growth or a stabilization level with zero growth or even a diminution in absolute size. The persuaders aim at replacement level only, i.e. a maximum of two children per family (Fig. 12.4). Again, sterilization and contraception are the most widely offered

Plate 21 Jumbo-sized population increases need commensurate communications media. How many loops would an Air India Boeing 747 (see Plate 20) have bought? *(Camera Press Ltd, London)*

means, although the popularity of legal abortion is growing. No country has yet adopted a distinct control policy with announced targets in terms of absolute numbers, but some of the governments of the richer DCs are under strong pressure from neo-Malthusian pressure groups to do so. The US Commission on Population Growth and the American Future (1972) reported that no substantial benefits would appear to accrue from the continued growth of the nation's population, and recommended (with a few Commissioners dissenting) that the USA welcome the idea of and plan for a stabilized population; no positive steps to this end had emerged from the government by mid-1973. Opposition to both family planning and population control has often been strong, and the number of countries which have official and semi-official programmes is perhaps surprisingly high (IPPF 1972). An emphasis in Asian countries is noteworthy, especially where ethnic Chinese are concerned, and it is interesting that Singapore has announced its intention to cut social welfare programmes to people with more than two children.

A common theme of most opponents of population control is the right of the individual family to decide on its size: their procreative activities are no concern of the community. This is becoming less acceptable as it is more widely realized that every new individual requires resources which have significance to a wider group: the community, the nation or even the whole world. In hunting societies, where the limits of the environment are

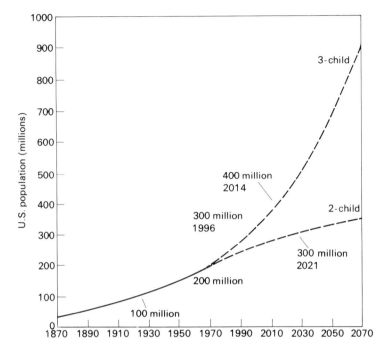

Fig. 12.4 The projected effects upon the US population of two-child and three-child families.
Source: US President's Council on Environmental Quality 1971

closely perceived, population control appeared to be adjusted to the needs of the community, but the coming of agriculture seems to have put the onus on the family. First agriculture and then industrialization have allowed environmental limits to be perceived as virtually infinite. The advent of modern ecology has brought back into focus the limits to the carrying capacity of the planet, and the realization of an upper limit to the number of people that the earth can support. In the face of this fact the options appear to be twofold. If the population exceeds the carrying capacity then the natural checks of famine, disease and war will probably operate: the latter can now produce some very large-scale oscillations indeed; or we can bring to bear all the knowledge of science, values and communication that we possess in an effort to level off the exponential curve. Very few countries in the Third World, according to Notestein (1970), would at present find the aim of zero population growth acceptable and so far only in a few of the faster-growing populations has family planning begun to reduce birth rates. Hong Kong, Japan, Taiwan, Korea, Singapore, Fiji, Mauritius, Seychelles and Reunion are the countries where the BR has declined owing to family planning programmes (Nortman 1971, IPPF 1972). On the other hand, some countries are actively concerned that their population is not high enough and give pro-natal financial inducements; notable among this group are the USSR and other Socialist republics of eastern Europe. Government inducements to breed in France, for example, having been less than successful, it may be wondered if this may not be the cheapest way to bring about declines in fertility.

A major problem is that although the problems caused by a rapidly increasing population can be identified on a world scale, their solution must inevitably be national. This produces a growing fear in the LDCs and among minority groups that 'they' are trying to subjugate 'us' by controlling 'our' numbers. As far as the LDCs are concerned, no power on earth can now stop them far exceeding the DCs numerically, but since concern over the global population–resources–environment balance comes mainly from the DCs it would seem prudent for them to practise what they preach in terms of population control.

Summary

The complex factors of demography boil down to one or two salient features as far as we are concerned here:

(1) Demographic history shows a rapid expansion of population after the seventeenth century, following thousands of years of very slow growth.

(2) The world population, currently (1971) at 3,600 million, has very uneven distribution, with a particular concentration in Asia.

(3) A world growth rate of approximately 2 per cent p.a. gives a doubling time of 35 years, irrespective of the absolute numbers.

(4) There is general discrepancy between the high rates of increase in the LDCs and a low rate (nearing stability in Sweden, for example) in the DCs.

(5) A rapid rate of urbanization prevails in both DCs and LDCs.

(6) Despite the widespread acceptance of family planning programmes, they have generally failed so far to reduce birth rates significantly outside the DCs, except perhaps in the highly urbanized or specially aided parts of Asia, together with mainland China.

Population–resource relationships

Growth

As populations have grown, so have the magnitudes of those resource processes which supply materials, so that the graph of population growth also describes in general terms the use of energy or the consumption of food. The important exception is that, worldwide, some resource processes are increasing in volume even faster than the population, i.e. per capita use is also going up: energy and water use are examples. This situation is most striking in the DCs, where access to technology creates a different kind of access to resources beyond those which are necessary to sustain life. In the LDCs, cultural consumption is by no means absent (particularly in those with a well-developed social stratification), but there is much greater emphasis on the provision of necessities such as food, shelter and employment. The contrast between the population–resource relationships of different types of countries allows the construction of a regional classification of the type put forward by Zelinsky (1966) and which appears as Fig. 12.5.

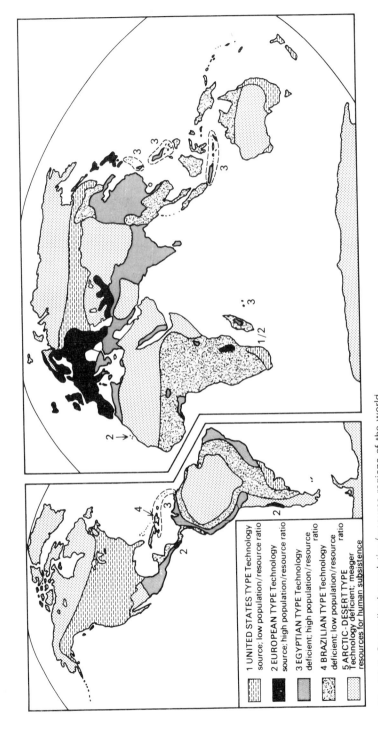

Fig. 12.5 Generalized population/resource regions of the world.
Source: Zelinsky 1966

1 UNITED STATES TYPE Technology
  source; low population/resource ratio

2 EUROPEAN TYPE Technology
  source; high population/resource ratio

3 EGYPTIAN TYPE Technology
  deficient; high population/resource
  ratio

4 BRAZILIAN TYPE Technology
  deficient; low population/resource
  ratio

5 ARCTIC-DESERT TYPE
  Technology deficient; meager
  resources for human subsistence

A diagnostic feature of these regions is the role of technology as part of the culture. The degree of application of mechanical and electronic technology, backed by expert knowledge, has been seen to alter the perception of available resources and hence lead to prosperity. Inherent in the role of technology as a creator of resources is its power to destroy them, either by misapplication or by means of the waste products which it creates; in addition it may have little to do with the long-term ecological stability of a resource process. Thus, while cognizant of the vital role of technology as a means of gaining access to environmental resources, we must not be so blinded as to fail to recognize its spin-off effects, not the least of which are its use for its own sake and the economic constraints created by the expensive machinery which is now widespread (Galbraith 1967). On the other hand, technology increases the chances of averting or minimizing economic and ecological disasters through the ingenuity it confers. Other factors must be considered when designating resource–population regions. The role of external enterprise and capital in creating resources (among which oil is the outstanding example) helps to emphasize that most of the regions are not self-contained in their resource processes: the way in which the DCs gather up resources from all over the world is an obvious example. Again, the use of money means that, outside subsistence economies, individuals do not gain their materials from their immediate surroundings.

Type A regions constitute technological source areas, where invention, research and development are at a high level. This is combined with a large land area which is well stocked with available and potential resources and has a low or moderately sized population relative to its size and to other nations. The high level of technology means that the people have access to the resources and also create the effective demand to ensure their use; prosperity allows the purchase from other countries of what they lack. The high levels of material wealth have been gained at the price of widespread environmental damage during phases of very rapid development and exploitation, and it is not surprising that the strongest public pressures for high-quality environments and 'environmentalist' crusading have come from the epitome of this group, the USA. In these countries, economic growth (i.e. the expansion of the magnitude of material-using resource processes) is in general a publicly espoused aim and its measures are seen as measures of the general welfare of the people. In the wealthiest, there may be some questioning of the purpose of such growth, particularly since the desired rates of expansion are very difficult to achieve in energy- and machine-intensive economies. This type of population–resource situation may be labelled 'the US type', but it also includes Canada, Australia, New Zealand, the USSR, part of Argentina and, with qualifications, Uruguay, south Brazil, South Africa and Rhodesia.

Type B may be categorized as 'the European type'. This is also a technology source area but differs from the US type because the population is high in both absolute numbers and density, the countries smaller and their heritage of resources less abundant and more fragmentary than those of larger nation-states. There is less room for trial and error than with type A and so a more 'conservative' attitude towards land and water resources has developed which is less profligate and damaging than the US type, although the number of people makes considerable environmental manipulation inevitable. Many of the man-made ecosystems, such as European agriculture, are essentially very stable, but the margin of stability is not very wide. Economically, an elaborate system of international exchange has to develop in order to ensure material supplies for the urban-industrial base. Thus trade with LDCs is widespread, partly as a historical result of colonialism, and international blocs (of which the EEC is the latest and largest) are commonplace. Again, economic growth is an explicitly stated goal of public policy, often being said to be necessary in order to clear up the legacy of a long history of industrial impact upon the environment and upon people. However, the value of growth is being questioned to some extent, as is shown by the

Plate 22 Immigration and natural increase, along with a small land base, produce squatter settlements like these in Hong Kong. Although its economy is perhaps closest to the European type, this colony's problems are exacerbated by its isolated location. *(World Council of Churches, Geneva)*

intention of Japan to develop an index of social welfare to replace GNP as an indicator of the performance of the economy. We may expect nations with a very slowly growing population and a culture capable of accepting changes in social aims, such as Sweden, to revise their attitudes towards growth in the near future. As would be expected, the European countries themselves provide type-specimens of this category, along with nations like Japan and Israel. In transit to this group are nations like Chile, together with Hong Kong (Plate 22) and the island of Puerto Rico; aspiring candidates who have passed some of the examinations would appear to be Mexico and Libya.

Type C envisages countries with large resource bases but which are deficient in technology. Their populations are relatively low, so that there is very little sense of pressure upon resources, except perhaps in the urban areas, but material standards are low as well. Their status is not permanent: increased technological development will allow them to move into the European category, but absence of such development if combined with rapid population growth may well depress them into type D countries. Such nations much desire economic growth and may even want population growth in order to try and achieve it faster. But they are hindered by economic factors such as the control of many of their exportable resources by outside interests or dependence upon world prices which may not move in their favour. This group may be labelled 'the Brazilian type' and is concentrated in three main areas: Indochina-Malaya (but excluding North Vietnam, Java and the north and central Philippines), tropical Africa, and South America. Standards of resource management vary widely and are critical in determining the movement of nations out of this category.

Type D is the most unfortunate group. Not only is there a deficiency of appropriate technology but the population presses hard upon the resources and is generally growing at 2 per cent p.a. or more. The capacity to deal with population–resource imbalances is frequently lacking, so that both the means of subsistence and the means of employment are deficient. Institutional factors may exacerbate the troubles of such nations. Small size of territory may impinge harshly upon a growing population, as may for example the activities of a landowning class who occupy all the productive land and grow cash crops for export upon it. This forces the peasants onto marginal lands which may erode quickly, depriving them of basic nutrition at the same time as their population levels far outrun any animal protein supply. Development programmes are most likely to misfire in such areas, not only because the limitations of the environment may be misunderstood and prediction of ecological side-effects inaccurate, but because of institutional factors centring around resistance to change on the part of the entrenched rich as well as the bewildered poor. This type can be labelled 'the Egyptian type' and includes part of southern Europe as well as classic LDCs in Africa like Ruanda-Burundi, Latin American and Caribbean areas like Haiti, Jamaica, Central America and the Andean highlands, India, Pakistan, Bangladesh, Sri Lanka, Syria and the islands of the Pacific and Indian Oceans. Escape from this category has been limited: Japan and probably China are outstanding examples.

Type E territories possess low resource bases because of the constraints of physical geography, and their populations are low, consisting either of people living on subsistence economies or those engaged in developing resources like minerals and oil. This 'arctic-desert' type also encompasses the oceans, only the fringes of which are subject to any form of inhabitation.

Controlling growth

The achievement of the economic growth espoused by most Western countries has usually been the result of private entrepreneurial ventures either aided or resisted by government. In centrally planned economies, the state has made all the running. But during the period since 1920 resource development has been increasingly subject to attempts to achieve an orderly, programmed rate of development, rather than submit to the irregular pyrotechnics of unfettered free enterprise. The first stage is usually termed *resource management*. Attempts are made to optimize yields from a particular resource process by exerting governmental control or influence upon part of the resource process. Such influence may be used to bring about regional development, as in the New Deal period of the USA, or to realize the maximum use of a potential resource, as with water-impoundment schemes which supply water for irrigation, urban-industrial purposes, recreation, and for the generation of hydro-electric power. A feature of resource-management philosophies in recent years has been to try to minimize the impact of economic development upon people and ecosystems not directly parts of the particular resource process. At a simple level this may mean building fish ladders alongside dams to enable migratory salmonids to reach their spawning grounds, or screening a new electricity-generating plant with mounds of earth and tree-plantings. More complex, and usually expensive, ameliorative measures include the whole battery of technological devices for removing toxic or harmful contaminants from industrial wastes, or the construction of new sewage-treatment schemes for large urban areas. The underlying values behind the abstraction labelled resource management are clear. They are devoted to development and change rather than preservation of the natural state, and to expansive growth of the scale of economic activity. Since exponential growth has for so long been the norm, it accepts the values of such a phase as correct, even when admitting that there may be deleterious side-effects. Above all, the concept acknowledges no upper asymptote to development, either because it cannot contemplate the reality of such a feature or because it believes that technological and social change will make the idea redundant. This set of values leads inevitably to problems in the balance of population and resources which have two dimensions, each with spatial implications. The first of these is the identification of problems, which can be viewed at a global scale, since certain manifestations are worldwide, as with the raising of expectations due to the ubiquity of electronic communications, and the global dispersal of certain by-products of technology such as carbon dioxide and pesticide residues like DDT. The second dimension is the solution of problems which at present can scarcely be contemplated other than in the framework of the national state. World government is scarcely a foreseeable reality, and even world gatherings for identification of problems (like the UN 1972 conference in Stockholm) ran into political difficulties.

The heightened awareness of the inter-relationships of biota and their inanimate surroundings has made possible the further step of identifying the wider concept of *environmental management*. It is recognized that it is the bioenvironmental systems of the planet which provide resources and that any resource process must be rationally managed in order to ensure a sustained yield—preferably one which is capable of due increase, but in which the existence of limits is recognized. In addition the deployment of an individual resource process must not be inimical to the operation of others with which it may share space or identical ecosystems. It is realized that the environment has simultaneously to be useful as a provider of materials, to be beautiful as a provider of recreation, wildlife and valued landscapes, and to be life-supporting as a provider of space, food and essential biological systems such as those which produce oxygen and carbon dioxide (O'Riordan 1971a). All things to all men, in fact, in which varying types of society exhibit different attitudes

(Table 12.12) and determine their own orders of priority. It would be unreal to pretend that environmental management is at present much more than a concept except in the relatively simple situation of Antarctica, but the formation of Ministries and Departments of the Environment in some countries may encourage integrative planning. If, however, we consider process-response situations such as the avoidance of flood hazard (O'Riordan 1971b) as environmental management, then the number of instances may be increased.

TABLE 12.12   Attitudes in environmental management

Purpose of environmental management	Resource-population type			
	USA	European	Brazilian	Egyptian
Useful, i.e. for materials	Dominant aim but decreasing emphasis	Dominant but decreasing; imports always significant	Dominant as industrialization proceeds	Basic development often for export to USA and European types
Life-supporting, i.e. food and ecological stability, gaseous exchange	Increasing realization of wider implications	Importance only recently realized; too densely populated to achieve 'natural' stability	Food important, otherwise environment not much valued, although knowledge of implications sometimes present	Struggle for food often dominant, knowledge of other processes discounted
Beauty	Strong motivation for preservation as reaction to over-use	Always a feature of culture; now getting stronger in face of increased impact	Residual or marginal land may thus be employed	Wildlife on residual land may hold interest, otherwise little valued

The purpose of environmental management is to produce resources but simultaneously to retain a sanative, life-supporting environment. There is, therefore, an attempt to reconcile the demands of socio-economic systems with the constraints of the biosphere. To this end, long-term strategies are essential and are based on two aims: the first is to reduce stress on ecosystems from contamination or over-use; the second is to pursue short-term strategies that are sufficiently flexible to preserve long-term options: no resource processes should be developed which bring about irreversible environmental changes. As a set of values, environmental management is ambivalent towards economic growth. It recognizes that there is an absolute limit to the materials and surface of the planet but sees no reason to prevent the use of the resources up to that limit provided that some ecological stability can be maintained, whether by preserving the natural systems or by increasing man-directed inputs of energy, matter and information.

Frameworks of resource management in developed countries

Within the United States and European types of resource–population relationships, the purposes of resource management differ between the free-market economies and the planned economies, i.e. between capitalist and socialist nations. In the free-market countries resource management comprises multiple aims: the provision of the material needs of the community by encouraging individuals to invest money and time and hence realize personal profits; the provision of environments for recreation and wildlife by protecting land from certain kinds of resource process; and the permitting of certain places to be used for waste disposal. Woven throughout the pattern are the roles of various levels of government: encouraging here, discouraging there and preventing everywhere. In principle, governments aim at maximizing the general good of the community, although they are often criticized for adopting the values of only one section of the population, and hence often will provide resources which individuals cannot profitably develop, such as nature conservation and countryside recreation. But the overall aim is economic growth, usually as measured by increases in GNP per capita. In this aim, there is little significant difference between free-market economies and Socialist centrally planned ones. In the latter, the government acts as sole entrepreneur and 'profits' are to be distributed over the entire population. Theoretically, integrated resource and even environmental management should occur, but the evidence seems to indicate that the USSR, for example, experiences problems of environmental contamination just as severely as the West (Gerasimov *et al.* 1971, Goldman 1971, Pryde 1972) and the writer's own experience of, for example, river pollution in Czechoslovakia bear out such reports. More thorough Communism, as practised in the People's Republic of China, may diminish contamination problems (Unger 1971), although we should note that large concentrations of heavy industry are not yet widespread in that country.

Along with citizen groups, most governments have tried to mitigate the impacts of resource development (especially industry) by a variety of measures, while retaining the general aim of an expanding economy. Such activities are often referred to as 'conservation', although they fall well short of the integrative approach to man–environmental relationships which perhaps better deserves that label. Another name for tidying-up activities is 'the search for environmental quality' and a general attention to the landscape effects of industrialization and transportation is often a key element. Thus highway signs are regulated or eliminated, factories landscaped, and auto junkyards screened with trees. A wider concern with the protection of valued landscapes and open space may also be part of the same movement, so that green belts around cities may be created, as around the major cities of Britain. Alternatively, urban growth may be directed along particular axes, with 'green wedges' in between them; ideally this brings undeveloped land close into the city centre. In many European countries, the motivation to set aside valued landscapes is part of the 'conservation' movement: the 'Naturparken' of Denmark and West Germany and the National Parks of England and Wales are examples. Along with such movements often goes the desire to provide more open space and access to resources for outdoor recreation, which can frequently be combined with landscape protection. Here again, the protagonists are often called 'conservationists'. Many of the State Parks of the USA, the

Provincial Parks of Canada, and local arrangements such as the East Bay Regional Park District in California or the parks of the Metropolitan Toronto and Region Conservation Authority, are part of the same resource process. Much of the current effort in nature protection is also carried on in order to save biota and habitats from encroachment because of their national or regional significance in aesthetic or educational terms, rather than for their part in the stability of the biosphere on a global scale. The encouragement of a rare predator or wader to breed successfully on the margins of its range will elicit devotion and money that no unspectacular alga suffering from biocide toxicity can hope to receive.

The strongest of all these drives in the DCs is for pollution control. Many environmental contaminants are not only aesthetically undesirable but can be shown to be directly damaging to humans, and so in the industrial nations considerable legislation is being passed (and sometimes enforced) to control wastes. Water Quality Acts, such as those of the USA, set standards for the concentration of various effluents of a toxic or unaesthetic character. In the UK a standing Royal Commission on Environmental Pollution has been set up and all the water authorities are expected to deal with offences against the pollution laws. Noise is another area in which attempts to control levels are being made, in particular from aircraft and heavy vehicles. Few would deny that anti-pollution moves bring about improvements in the environmental quality for many people. However, the clamour is directed against one phase only of the resource process (the last) and does not consider the magnitude of and necessity for the earlier parts of the process. To this extent pollution abatement, like the other operations discussed in this section, is truly cosmetic. It improves the surface, but if the ecology of the resource process is unstable then it will not be corrective. Indeed, it may hide the need for more radical re-orientations of resource processes and can thus be used as camouflage by entrepreneurs and politicians. An example of the cosmetic approach can be seen in the declaration by the European Conservation Conference, meeting in 1970 (Council of Europe 1971). The human rights proposed are those of having air and water 'reasonably free from pollution', freedom from noise, and access to coast and countryside. Member nations are urged to combat pollution and, somewhat vaguely, to ensure the conservation of the European environment. Individuals, states article 30, should be ready to pay the costs of conservation. The other provisions largely concern planning for 'rational' use of resources and the reduction of pollution, especially the unwanted effects of the internal combustion engine, jet aircraft and chemicals such as pesticides, fertilizers and detergents. The aims and desirability of population and industrial growth are nowhere mentioned and the whole document is clearly an acceptance of current trends, subject to some improvements in national and regional planning and cleaning up of the more serious pollutants.

The next step beyond cosmetic procedures is to try to assess the ecological impact of a proposed development before it is put into effect. If the percussive effect of the change is deemed unacceptable (by standards that are not usually defined objectively but emerge empirically from public quasi-judicial proceedings) then another site is sought. Indeed, any enquiry may be specifically directed to choose between limited possibilities, as was the Roskill Commission of 1971 on the site of London's third airport. Symbolically, however, this Commission was not allowed to investigate whether London ought to have another major airfield, merely where it should be, so that only one phase of the resource process was considered. In the USA the 1969 Environmental Protection Act sets forth environmental policies for the nation which go beyond the loosely formulated suggestions of the European Declaration quoted above. For example, one of the objectives for the USA is to 'achieve a balance between population and resource use which will permit high standards of living and a wide sharing of life's amenities'. As far as actions by the Federal Government are concerned, it must 'utilize a systematic, interdisciplinary approach which will insure the integrated use of the natural and social sciences and the environmental design acts in planning and decision-making which may have an effect upon man's environment'. Any legislation or other Federal action which affects the quality of the human environment has to be investigated for its environmental impact and any adverse effects pointed out, along with alternatives to the proposed action; the relations between local and short-term uses of the environment and the maintenance of long-term productivity must be stated too. This Act tries therefore to impose limitations on the magnitude of resource processes if there are environmentally detrimental effects (Caldwell 1971).

Nations with well-established Socialist governments such as those of the USSR and eastern Europe have theoretically an institutional structure which will enable them to avoid the environmentally stressful features of free-market economics. Yet in performance they rarely seem any better and sometimes manifestly worse. A variety of reasons seems to account for such a position. Firstly, although integrated control of a resource process should exist, *de facto* it often does not. Secondly, resource managers are as keen as any capitalist to dispose of their wastes as cheaply as possible and thus externalize the costs. Because there is an ideological attachment to industrial and general economic growth, this cannot be slowed down because of difficulties over aesthetics or contamination. Lastly, because Marxism is held to be so superior to capitalism, it is hard to admit that the end-product may be the same and that Marxist-Leninist fish are as dead as capitalist fish. Socialist governments may well outshine the Western nations at tasks like pollution control when they have decided to undertake the job; in fields like nature conservation their record is excellent. We may surmise nevertheless that Socialist nations will find it harder than most to deviate from goals of perpetual economic growth, particularly while they feel militarily threatened.

Resource management in Brazilian and Egyptian categories

The purposes of the development of resources in these two groups are twofold. Firstly, they are used for regional and national purposes in order to produce metabolic and cultural materials such as food, housing and roads, and also to provide jobs and create wealth to be used as capital for further development. Secondly, many bioenvironmental resources are developed for export to European and US type countries. Oil is an obvious instance, but many metal ores and crops like cocoa, coffee and rubber also enter this category. Such use brings income to the supplier, but it also brings dependence upon demand in the DCs; where the product is dispensable or subject to fashion or is overproduced, then the fortunes of the producers (as happens with cocoa and coffee) are fickle indeed; on the other hand where the product is so important, as with oil, that the industrial nations are virtually dependent upon the supplies, then the LDCs force up the price and nationalize expensive plants virtually with impunity.

The desire of the countries of the Third World to be masters of their own destinies leads them into the process of 'development', undertaken with substantial assistance from the richer nations. This is usually undertaken in response to particular exigencies such as under- or malnutrition or a chronic lack of employment or shelter, or to ensure the occupational survival of a political leader. As Caldwell (1971) points out, the process of development proceeds from a set of assumptions about the relationship of man and nature which were developed in the West during the phase of the industrial revolution and few if any of which (particularly those about the long-term effects on the stability of ecosystems of constantly increasing impacts of a technology based on fossil fuels) are verified by scientific evidence. Indeed, some writers aver that development is primarily for the benefit of the industrial nations and that this economic imperialism is mostly designed to secure large quantities of cheap raw materials at an immense profit for the industrialists, at the same time making the area safe for further penetrations by such entrepreneurial enterprise. Woodis (1971) says that in one of its operations in an African country, a rubber company takes home three times as much profit as the nation's entire revenue; that 28 per cent of UK overseas aid goes to pay back interest on former aid; and that the drop of 15 per cent in export prices of raw materials from tropical Africa in 1955–9 entailed a loss of twice the annual amount of foreign aid. Many large multi-national companies have annual economies many times the size of some small newly independent nations; it has even been rumoured that one corporation thought about buying one such country and running it as a tourist enterprise, having renamed it Tarzania.

Given that even the most exploitive resource-development programme will leave a residue of investment capital, or that disinterested aid from an international agency has been granted, development is not without hazard. The assumptions referred to above ensure the dominance of technical and economic factors in evaluating priorities at the expense of behavioural and ecological considerations. In the desire to transform simple agrarian societies into more complex industrially based economies, it may be forgotten that both traditional systems and natural ecosystems have passed the evolutionary tests of selection for survival but that the new ecosystems and new cultural values are not guaranteed to share such properties. The more interference with the old order, the greater the chance of unpredictable synergistic effects, and the success of a practice in one place may encourage unwarranted optimism about its potential in another. The hazards of the imposition of cultural complexes based on high-energy societies upon those accustomed to the flow of only solar energy, or for example the development on small islands of mining by techniques usually employed on large continents, may be disastrous: Taghi Farvar and Milton (1972) bring together a large number of unhappy case-histories; and in the same volume Caldwell considers that there are six barriers to success in 'development', only one of which is ecological, the others being derived from various parts of the cultural milieu, including the political. Development thus provides us with an example of a situation where, within the ecological envelope of facts, the cultural world of values is all-important and cannot in the least be ignored, a conclusion of significance when considering any alterations in the nineteenth-century assumptions which underlie so much of our thinking about man and nature. In the meantime many millions of individual people live far below their full potential as humans.

The area in which outside ideas can claim a little success is nature conservation, especially where this is a source of revenue from tourism. More wide-ranging environmental protection is virtually absent, with the possible exception of forest reserves established to prevent the denudation of steep hillsides or to safeguard a supply of wood for construction and fuel. Long-run ecological stability with no visible benefits is therefore, and understandably so, subordinate to economic growth in the short-term.

Growth and progress

It seems pertinent to remind ourselves that growth of economies and populations on the scale to which we are accustomed is a feature of the last 150 years only. But expansion rates of 5 per cent p.a. and above have come to be the normal situation for resource managers, their mentors, and of those who laid down the ground rules for both of them. Because growth has been a normal situation and because it appears to offer solutions to most problems, including those it has itself created, it has become almost everywhere a desirable goal and indeed equated to a large extent with the concept of 'progress'. Earlier in this century some questioning of the equivalence was heard, albeit faintly: one character in Aldous Huxley's *Point Counter Point* (1928) explodes, 'Progress! You politicians are always talking about it. As though it were going to last. Indefinitely. More motors, more babies, more food, more advertising, more everything, for ever. . . . What do you propose to do about phosphorus for example?' Although most of our present concern has shifted from the supply of that element to its disposal, the rest of Huxley's ideas have a contemporary air. Whether, where and how far the expansion of the magnitudes of resource processes can follow their present trajectories into the future is the subject of the last chapter of this book.

Further reading

ALLISON, A. (ed.) 1970: *Population control.*

BARR, H. M. *et. al.* (eds.) 1972: *Population, resources and the future: non-Malthusian perspectives.*

DAVIS, W. H. (ed.) 1971: *Readings in human population ecology.*

DURAND, J. D. 1967: The modern expansion of world population.

GORDEN, M. and GORDEN, M. (eds.) 1972: *Environmental management.*

HABAKKUK, H. J. 1972: *Population growth and economic development since 1750.*

HINRICHS, N. (ed.) 1971: *Population, environment and people.*

O'RIORDAN, T. 1971: *Perspectives on resource management.*

PEACH, W. N. and CONSTANTIN, J. A. 1972: *Zimmermann's World Resources and Industries.* 3rd edn.

PRYDE, P. R. 1972: *Conservation in the Soviet Union.*

RIDKER, R. G. 1972: Population and pollution in the United States.

TAGHI FARVAR, M. and MILTON, J. P. (eds.) 1972: *The careless technology: ecology and international development.*

US COMMISSION ON POPULATION GROWTH AND THE AMERICAN FUTURE 1972: *Population and the American future.*

ZELINSKY, W. 1966: *A prologue to population geography.*

13

An environmental revolution?

The last section of this book first examines the extension of the present patterns of resource processes, in particular the environmental and social problems which are created, and then moves to consider two main sets of reactions to the disharmonies which are evident. The first of these is the argument that technological development will eventually provide solutions; the second, by contrast, advocates a radically different approach to the relations of man and nature. The book ends with a consideration of alternative models of the future based largely upon these two types of reaction.

Impacts upon the environment

There is no doubt that an increasing disharmony between man and nature is becoming apparent, especially in phenomena such as malnutrition, soil erosion, gross pollution, and the attrition of the aesthetic qualities of parts of the environment which are valued in several cultures. One of the major concerns is that the increasing magnitude of resource processes is creating a set of environmental problems which in turn may impair not only the usefulness of the environment but also its life-supporting capability, its ability to absorb wastes and its beauty. The environmental problems created by more people using more materials can be divided into those with an environmental linkage, and those with a largely social linkage (Russell and Landsberg 1971). The former group in turn comprises regional problems such as sewage, sulphur dioxide fallout, the habitat requirements of migratory birds, or particular geographical entities such as the Rhine or the Nile and the uses made of them. Much stronger anxiety, however, has been expressed about global problems such as food supply and the consequences of agricultural intensification, residual pesticides, the effects of the contamination of the oceans by oil, and the alteration of atmospheric processes by increased loads of carbon dioxide and particulates. The most vivid statement of this view is Ehrlich's (1971) scenario for 'ecocatastrophe' in which poisoning of the oceans by organochlorine pesticides reduces food supplies to Asia at the same time as biocide-resistant strains of pest virtually eliminate the land-based food supplies. The demand for food of a very high and rapidly growing population is the trigger-factor of a worldwide nuclear war which he predicts will take place by 1979. A more penetrating analysis which emphasizes the role of population growth in creating environmental disharmony is given by Ehrlich and Holdren (1971). They suggest that the increases in human numbers have caused a totally disproportionate impact on environment. For example, the provision of minerals and fossil fuels to an expanding population even at fixed levels of consumption requires that as the nearest and richest ores are worked out, then the use of lower-grade ores, deeper drilling and extended supply networks all increase the per capita use of energy and hence the per capita impact on the environment (Table 13.1). Similarly, the environmental impact of supplying water needs rises dramatically when the local supply is outrun: ecological, aesthetic and economic costs are incurred in diverting

TABLE 13.1   World per capita use of selected resources per year

	Petroleum (bbls)	Natural gas (ft³)	Copper (lb)	Phosphate rock (lb)	Potash (lbK₂O)
1910	0·19	—	1·15	7·1	—
1930	0·70	1,060	1·70	12·8	2·48
1950	1·52	2,780	2·80	20·1	4·5
1960	2·62	5,700	3·76	30·2	7·1

1 bbl = 159 l; 1 ft³ = 0·0283 m³; 1 lb = 0·4536 kg
Source: McHale 1972

TABLE 13.2   World increases in agricultural activity 1955–65

Increase	%
Food production	34
Tractors used	63
Phosphates used	75
Nitrates	146
Pesticides	120

This table does not show the amounts of water and energy, for example, needed to manufacture the fertilizers and pesticides.
Source: SCEP 1970

supplies to the growing region. Increase of food production likewise requires energy uses disproportionate to the population fed because of the need to obtain and distribute water, fertilizer and pesticides (see pp. 219–20). Some indication of the environmental consequences may be inferred from Table 13.2.

The role of population density is also relevant, since some proponents of growth argue that countries with a low density can afford high rates of growth. Density is not necessarily a good criterion for the effect of populations upon the biosphere: industrial nations, for example, gather in resources from a very wide area. The Netherlands is often quoted as an example of a very dense but wealthy population, but it is the second largest importer of protein in the world and also imports the equivalent of 27 million mt/yr of coal. In addition, many environmental problems are independent of the distribution of population, especially those involving contamination of the oceans and atmosphere.

A cooler, more detailed view is taken by the authors of the SCEP (Study of Critical Environmental Problems) group (1970), who conclude that the current 'ecological demand' (i.e. the stress put upon planetary bioenvironmental systems by man's demands upon them) is not yet sufficiently great to cause a breakdown. Nevertheless, they point out the rapid rises in demands for materials, energy and space, some of which are set out in Table 13.3, and by considering Gross Domestic Product (GDP) minus services as an index of 'ecological demand', they calculate that it has been increasing at 5–6 per cent p.a., doubling in the 13·5 yrs after 1950, so that the next doubling of population (in 35 yrs at 2 per cent p.a.) will increase the environmental impact sixfold. These rates explain why environmental

TABLE 13.3   World average annual rates of increase in economic activity, 1951–66 (based on constant dollars)

Activity	% annual increase	Doubling time (yrs)
Agricultural production	3	23
Industry based on farm products	6	11
Mineral production	5	14
Industry based on mineral production	9	7
Construction and transport	6	11
Commerce	5	14

Source: SCEP 1970

problems appear to have erupted so suddenly and why many students fear that the future will bring more problems than exist at present to the point where a few more doublings of population will bring about the likelihood of the breakdown of the systems of the biosphere.

The differences between Ehrlich and SCEP, therefore, is only one of time: they agree that the planet cannot for much longer go on supplying the demands made on it for the supply of materials and the provision of valued environments, while absorbing the impact of the disposal of wastes, all within the framework of a human population doubling every 35 years.

The role of population growth in creating environmental problems has been closely examined by Commoner (1972a, 1972b), who suggests that the misapplication of technology is the most important factor in the growth of environmental disharmony. In the United States, for example, crop yield in Illinois increased 10–15 per cent in 1962–8 while the quantity of nitrogenous fertilizer doubled; similarly for detergents and non-returnable bottles Commoner calculates that it is the technology that creates the difficulties, not the rise in the numbers using it. While there is no doubt that 'ecologically faulty' technology exists, it seems that none of these arguments meet those of Ehrlich and Holdren (1971) quoted above, and they manifestly do not apply to those parts of the world where technology is distinctly lacking; to some extent Commoner appears to be lacking a wider perspective beyond the particular situation of the USA.

Thus while not every environmental ill can immediately be laid at the door of population growth, there emerges a strong suggestion that nowhere does the latter bring any benefits. To LDCs it brings medical and social problems; to DCs it may bring environmental problems beyond those of aesthetics; and in both groups, high densities of population add their own special difficulties.

Social values

The environmental disharmonies caused by rises in the scale of resource processes are paralleled by some negations of the social benefits which the growth has brought to most people. Economic growth expressed as GDP and Gross National Product (GNP) appears not to solve social problems, even of privileged areas. In the USA, evidence of primary malnutrition may be found among the poorer people; in less specific terms economic growth does little to narrow the gap between rich and poor in technologically based societies. If real net income rises by 10 per cent for the entire population, then the differences between the well-off and the deprived remain exactly the same as before; furthermore, the hard core of the poor do not share in economic growth and are dependent upon handouts from those whose benefit is direct. In DCs, economic growth is not really necessary to remove the very poor from their predicament: a minor redistribution of wealth (e.g. the reduction of the military budget by 25 per cent for the UK) would achieve the desired end (Mishan 1971). Indeed, some economic growth which goes into military expenditure might well be employed in a more useful fashion: one atomic submarine and its missiles would pay for $150 million in technical aid and one aircraft carrier could be replaced by 12,000 secondary schools (McHale 1972).

Another social argument advanced in favour of economic growth is that it produces more goods so that individuals and societies have more choice, which contributes to greater economic welfare. Such enhanced freedom tends to be illusory because there is constant replacement of models: one cannot choose a car from all the types ever made, only from those currently on the market, and the difference between alternative makes at the same price is more or less negligible. The proliferation of choice may bring forward harmful products which commercial interests have not properly evaluated, and much of it is not necessary: a choice between 50 makes of transistor radios at roughly the same cost is scarcely essential. Lastly, satisfaction with earnings may depend more upon an individual's place within the income structure than with his absolute level of wealth. This was exhibited during the miners' strikes of 1972 and 1974 in Britain, where one of the workers' chief sources of dissatisfaction was their fall in the 'league table' of industrial earnings.

The greatest externality of economic growth as measured now is its failure to take account of its environmental impact, largely because a money value can not be placed on environmental values lost. This book has chronicled numerous side-effects of economic growth, none of which will feature in the balance-sheets of those who caused them. Some measures of total goods and services such as GDP actually count deleterious impacts as components of the growth: if because of industrial emissions more people become ill, then the costs of extra hospital building and medical equipment adds to the GDP; if they die as a result of the same factor then presumably the undertaker's fees are added too. Such methods of accounting also omit the hidden costs of loss of earnings due to environmentally related illness, which can be no negligible sum as shown by Table 13.4. As was said in Part I, Boulding (1971) points out that GNP is simply a measure of decay (of food, clothing, gadgets and gasoline, as they are used), and the bigger the economic system the more it decays and the more that has to be produced simply to maintain it.

TABLE 13.4   Costs of diseases associated with air pollution, USA, 1958 ($ US million)

Respiratory cancer	680	
Chronic bronchitis	159·7	The categories of cost included
Acute bronchitis	6·2	are premature death, mor-
Common cold	331	bidity, treatment and preven-
Pneumonia	490	tion.
Emphysema	64	
Asthma	259	

Source: Newbould 1971b

Since economic growth depends upon the extension of the use of machines, many humanitarian writers have stressed that technology provides its own imperatives, some of which lead to attrition of the quality of human relations; electronic means of communication are probably the most sinister of these since, for example, 'the boss' can be isolated entirely from 'the worker' when audiovisual links are effected. Similarly the social worker may never have actually to see or to smell the derelict, and the doctor will be able to diagnose his patient from a safe distance. Paradoxically, the same media could bring about a sense of closeness on a world scale, the 'global village' to which McLuhan refers. The large size of organizations needed to control resource processes inevitably means impersonality and alienation, and the flexing of corporate power (of the 50 largest economic entities in the world 13 are corporations; in a recent year General Motors grossed more money than the total economy of Italy and of 73 other members of the UN) as in the case of a company which offered large rewards to anybody who could prevent the election of a particular politician in a LDC. More strictly relevant to our present theme is the rapid obsolescence which is associated with the products of machine technology. The social consequences are obvious since people will spend time and energy trying to possess the latest model, either willingly or at the behest of advertising. Probably more important is the heavy demand upon resources which such changes make, especially in an open-flow resource process without any recycling. Planned obsolescence is therefore a development which, although perhaps making sense (and a good deal of money for somebody) in terms of contemporary economics, is inimical to rational resource and environmental management.

Social consequences of size

Economic growth is very largely industrial growth, since advanced agriculture is an outgrowth of industry, dependent upon it for chemical inputs and for power supply, and industrial activity is largely carried on in cities and conurbations. The role of the city and its life-styles cannot therefore be overlooked in any consideration of the future of resource processes.

The major externality of industrial growth is its environmental effect, already discussed. But there are other effects which, assessed in social terms, are part of the unrest which causes the seeking of alternative ways of living. Behind the anxieties lies the thought that the transition to an urban-industrial life-style, after spending 90 per cent of his evolutionary history as a hunter, may set up psychic strains in man. Many of the traits which conferred a selective advantage in the hunting stage are now of distinctly less value, especially since population densities are so high in cities: aggressiveness is one such characteristic. Many of the biological mechanisms of adaptation to environmental struggles and stresses are now useless, and this is posing its own threat because there are insufficient challenges in bland surroundings which require little effort and thus provide few outlets for traits like aggression except in ritualized forms such as spectator sports. Personality structure breaks down if sensory stimuli are removed and indeed the intestinal tract fails to develop normally if conditions are totally germ-free (Dubos 1967). On the face of it, man appears to be a very adaptable species, for the overall health and survival rates of the inhabitants of Western cities are very good even though the people are isolated from nature. The price of such successful biological adaptability is, according to Dubos (1967), paid in social terms: people no longer mind ugliness, exhaust fumes and other contaminants, and even regard such conditions as normal. Since man could survive and reproduce in underground shelters or similarly confined conditions, the lower common denominators of existence become accepted for the sake of a grey and anonymous peace and tranquillity. Existence of these ideas suggests that because so many industrial and urban conditions do not immediately threaten biological survival, then we can give up perceiving the objective reality of their true effects, both in terms of environmental impact and in living conditions for man which are, to say the least, sub-optimal. Fortunately, our adaptability is cultural as well as biological and so it seeks to encompass the future as well as acknowledge the limits of the past. Thus arises the army of those engaged in trying to better the human condition.

Since the growth in economies and populations today leads inexorably to a rise in the size of cities, the observed behaviour of man in these agglomerations is now the subject of considerable concern, especially among US workers, whose cities seem to be experiencing forms of social change rather more rapidly than elsewhere in the West. As with much ethological study, experimental animals provide the first steps in research and the work of Calhoun (1962) is well known. His rats were provided with ample subsistence and adult mortality was so low that 5,000 adults might have been expected at the end of a 27-month period, yet the population had stabilized at 150 adults. Even 150 adults exerted considerable social stresses. Behavioural sinks developed in which a pathological 'togetherness' of 60–80 female rats tended to disrupt the sequences of activity necessary for mating, home-building and the rearing of young, and infant mortality ran as high as 96 per cent among

Plate 23 The negative qualities of city life can be exemplified by the famous *Oshiya* (pushing boys) of the Tokyo subway during rush-hours. *(Keystone Ltd, London)*

such disorientated females. Males also developed aberrant behaviour, among which pan-sexuality and total withdrawal were most noticeable, along with a group that was hyper-active, homosexual and cannibalistic, and which set upon females in oestrus. To extrapolate the results of such investigations to human populations in cities would be facile, but both Leyhausen (1965) and Calhoun (1971) have argued that the urban way of life exerts particular influences upon human behaviour patterns. They suggest that the size and population density of cities cause individuals to lose their place among the social-spatial order, thus developing psychic stress and other disorders. The possession of individual territory may serve as a secure, defensible base which enables the person to tolerate the socio-environmental insults, so that high-rise flats may be the antithesis of what is required for healthy living. Certainly, high rates of neurosis and delinquency are often associated with high-rise developments, although the evidence linking them is only circumstantial. More easily accepted perhaps is Milgram's (1970) analysis, largely con-cerned with a comparison of New York City with other metropolises and smaller settle-ments. He concludes that the modern city produces an overload in sensory input, so that social relations become superficial, anonymous and transitory, and low-priority inputs (such as other people in trouble) are disregarded. In transactions, boundaries are redrawn so as to offload responsibility, and individuals block themselves off by means of receptionists, hall porters and unlisted or disconnected telephones. Further screening devices and specialized institutions emphasize the anonymity of the individual, and thus reinforce the aggressiveness which is necessary in the competition for facilities as in rush-hour transport and lunch-hour ingestion (Plate 23). Some degree of anonymity is also a redeeming feature of the city. Minorities are much less stigmatized than in rural areas or small towns, and innovative behaviour can flourish instead of being smothered, as in the more normative situation of a group whose individuals are known to all the members. The role of absolute

TABLE 13.5   Crime in public housing in New York (felonies per thousand families, 1969)

	Three-floor walkups	Mid-rise (6–7 floors)	High-rise (13–30 floors)
Interior public spaces	5·3	16·5	37·3
Outside grounds	12·7	10·0	16·2
Inside apartments	12·0	14·5	14·5

Source: *Toronto Globe and Mail*, 30 October 1972

TABLE 13.6   US urban crime rates per 100,000 population, 1957

Crime		> 250,000	Size of city 50,000– 100,000	< 10,000
Criminal homicide	Murder, non-negligent Manslaughter, manslaughter by negligence	5·5	4·2	2·7
		4·4	3·7	1·3
Rape		23·7	9·3	7·0
Robbery		108·0	36·9	16·4
Aggravated assault		130·8	78·5	34·0

Source: Parsons 1971

size in providing the settings for certain types of behaviour is demonstrated by figures from the USA set out in Table 13.6. While individual differences between the categories of city size might not be statistically significant, the upward trends in crime rates are impressively similar—although once again it is essential to exercise caution about extrapolating such figures to other cultural contexts. The types of building are probably significant as components of the US situation: again, large buildings have higher crime rates (Table 13.5), possibly because of their lack of 'defensible space', in the large interior areas which belong to and are surveyed by no one, whereas in smaller apartment blocks the interior public space becomes an extension of the home.

One incontrovertible drawback of cities is their ecological instability, dependent as they are upon inputs of food, water and power, and upon having their wastes removed (Table 13.7). Weiner (1950) points out that disconnection of the water supply to New York City for six hours is reflected in the death rate, while power disconnections cause hypothermia among the old and enhanced pregnancy rates in the fertile. In such a sense cities appear parasitic, but many dwellers in rural areas are similarly dependent upon supplies bought by money: the farmers and smallholders who might survive a real famine would be over-run by urban hordes long before harvest time, whatever the crop, so that in reality the two are interdependent. The city is therefore ecologically difficult (and, on the whole, anathema to ecologists) because it masses demands for all types of resources, and generates others external to it, such as countryside recreation. It concentrates wastes, the disposal of which may create high levels of contamination of ecosystems (Table 13.7). But probably

TABLE 13.7   Magnitude of city metabolism (daily flows in tons ($=$ 1,016 kg) of a city of 1 million population, USA)

Input					Output		
Water			625,000		Sewage		500,000
Fuels	Coal	3,000			Refuse		2,000
	Oil	2,800					
			9,500	BECOMES	Air	CO	450
	Nat. gas	2,700			pollutants	SO_2	150
	Motor	1,000				Particulates	150
						NO_x	100
Food			2,000			Hydrocarbons	100

Source: McHale 1972

none of these problems is intractable, and a fruitful field for technological development exists in the neutralization of the deleterious processes. Socially the city is ambivalent, with some evidence that very large agglomerations may enhance socially undesirable be-haviour. The city is, however, a centre of innovative thought and hence is in the vanguard of the study of both its own deficiencies and those of the economic growth which caused it to arise; many of the new approaches to man-environment relations have their origins in the cultural and intellectual ferment of urban conglomerations.

The ethical infeed

A further aspect of the feedback from our social and environmental situation is the failure of man's use of the earth to measure up to certain ethical principles which have been principally formulated, in this context, in the West. The first of these may be summarized as the 'duty to posterity' argument. Its basis is the exhortation to pass on the inheritance of one generation in an unimpaired condition to the next. In terms of resource processes this means the avoidance of foreclosing options for the future by making irreversible changes in the present. Obedience to such a dictum would appear to be ecologically sound as well, since it would have the effect of retaining maximum biological diversity. The difficulty comes with acknowledgement of the effects of increasing technological capability, which often removes the closure imposed at an earlier time or, by creating substitutes, throws the whole resource process into irrelevance. So it has been argued that since we cannot know what the future will hold, we automatically do the best for future generations by maximizing present benefits since this will build up capital in terms of wealth and knowledge which will enable future problems to be tackled successfully. Both versions are perhaps rather too exclusively economic in their orientation to find much favour with either ecologists or the promoters of ethics, who tend to be rather puritan by nature (Boulding 1970).

A second ethical theme is the idea of each generation of men as stewards of the earth who hold it for only a limited period and who are obliged to account for their tenure. This is basically a theistic idea, although a demythologized version seems to have a fairly wide secular appeal. One of its statements is in Aldo Leopold's (1949) 'land ethic' in which men are adjured to respect the qualities of the earth and to gain their living from it without damaging the chances of fruitful yield in the future. Although the formulation of his exposition derives rather strongly from its origin in erosion and flooding problems in north-central North America, the general idea could be applied to resource processes as a whole, except that the criteria for what constitutes acceptable environmental manipulation as distinct from damage are left undefined. An elaboration of a similar theme is presented by Black (1970), who traces the notion of stewardship in those Judaic and Christian scriptures whose influence upon the contemporary world-view held by the West is acknowledged to be strong. He finds numerous examples of the concept of a man who is merely a temporary guardian of a resource and who is expected not merely to protect it against harm but to enhance its value. The earth must therefore be replenished as well as subdued. Since Black is a biologist, the way in which the ethical behaviour he advocates is seen to be consonant with sound scientific principles of environmental management is of considerable interest. Boulding (1971) also concludes that a shift in ethics towards man as a steward is a necessary part of the reconciliation between ecological and economic imperatives. A more specifically Christian formulation of similar principles is given by Montefiore (1970), who regards the totality of planetary systems as objects for the disinterested love which Christians are enjoined to profess. A similar view was taken by the Churches' Board of Social Responsibility document for European Conservation Year, 1970. Toynbee (1972) has even gone so far as to suggest that monotheistic religions encourage environmental exploitation and that only a reversion to pantheism and the religions of the East will suffice to alter present values. Unless instant conversions are made, we may harbour a suspicion that, even if efficacious, the time-span involved would be too long to alleviate some of the most pressing difficulties. In so far as the social costs of industrialization have been ignored in both capitalist and socialist countries, the so-called 'work ethic' has been a contributory factor, and as Bruhn (1972) suggests, it is time for ethics and science to unite to produce a guide to individual and collective behaviour which will stress the quality of life rather than the mere production of goods in the DCs; inevitably, the importance of 'work' (which many might suspect to have been strongly implanted by Protestant capitalism in the nineteenth century) would require radical re-evaluation.

Summary

The social difficulties created by continued expansion of present-day processes in the DCs are concisely summarized by Wagar (1970). In the first place we cannot be certain that present arrangements will go on, since neither free-market nor centrally planned economies have as yet developed systems capable of rapid effective response to environmental attrition; rather resource management by crisis has been the rule. Technological unemployment threatens domestic tranquility and there is a reliance upon defence industries for growth which might not be sustained. Again, the levels of organization are so complex that chain reactions of failure are very easy; and lastly growth can be sustained only by disproportionate inputs of energy and materials whose environmental impact has become clear.

Responses to the problems discussed so far in this section may be classified into two groups. The first allows that problems exist but predicates its answer upon continued economic growth; it is often divided about the role of population increase; the second requires a radical reorientation of material use and an immediate move towards stable population levels. The first approach will be called 'the technological fix'; the second the 'environmentalist' viewpoint.

The technological fix

This set of ideas admits that there are significant problems in the relations of population, resources and environment, but suggests that the difficulties are correctable by only relatively minor alterations in technology and institutions. Prognostications of ecological instability are discounted, and to Maddox (1972b), the state of mind of the catastrophists is more dangerous than what they predict.

The importance of population growth as a factor in problems of imbalance is subject to close scrutiny. An eventual levelling-off is regarded as desirable (and often as a by-product of other processes such as economic development), but the components of growth may be viewed differentially: for some regions a drastic retardation is required, for others no particular action seems necessary. Notably, the argument that the DCs should come quickly to zero growth because they dominate such a large proportion of the world's resource processes is not admitted as valid, since it is their growth which brings benefits for everybody else in its wake. In the DCs it is pointed out that many environmental problems are caused less by population growth than by the misapplication of technology by those in search of quick and high profits, such as the manufacturers of detergents, pesticides, chemical fertilizers, large overpowered automobiles, flip-top beer cans and electric carving knives. Commoner's (1972a) argument, that the ecologically unsound developments of the past two decades would have created severe trouble even if the population had been stable, is usually quoted, although it is apparent that, once launched, such developments can be fuelled by higher levels of population.

Reliance upon economic development to alleviate resource-related difficulties is especially strong in the LDCs, with obvious cause. Some also see higher populations as an eventual strength rather than a problem and may rely on political change to bring about better material conditions. In a wider perspective, they are not willing to be the environmental saviours of the DCs by acting as reservoirs of oxygen-producing plants or picturesquely backward tourist spots (Castro 1972). Many see reduced rates of population and economic growth in the DCs as deleterious (Wolfers 1971), since demand for their raw materials is thereby lessened; it seems, however, a curious world in which the rich must consume ever more to support the poor, and the implications of the political thralldom such linkages bring are not lost in many LDCs.

Economists who are also optimists point out that scarcity of any material resource will enforce substitution for it, but they note too that alleviation of shortages may be slow, and the ability of the price mechanism to give adequate forewarnings of the need for the development of substitutes in the face of the rapidity and magnitude of the doublings of demand now taking place has not yet been tested. Once a shortage is evident and there is an expectation that prices will rise faster than the rate of interest, then it pays a resource manager to stop production altogether, bringing about an unstable situation. Another improvement which can be made possible by economics is the internalizing of costs, particularly in the case of pollution control, and free-market economists incline to the view that if the costs are fully accounted then pollution becomes uneconomic; more intervention-minded writers (Brubaker 1972) ask if the contaminator can then purchase an unbounded right to pollute, and thus end up in favour of the concurrent imposition of governmental regulations.

Improvement of institutions is a hardy perennial in this field and nobody can deny its need; in particular, the closing of the commons is seen as a useful step: presumably nations might bid for the oceans, but the atmosphere is more difficult to apportion in view of its restless nature. Redistribution of food might help, along with an international larder to help the Mother Hubbard states over hard times in the short run; and no doubt the channelling of capital to the LDCs is not without its turbulent stretches.

Most important of all to those who advocate increased development, albeit directed to different places and sometimes to new ends, is the faith that technology will eventually provide answers. At a simple level of appeal, an energy-resource supplier will say at his annual shareholders' meeting, 'Why can't the environmentalists go away and leave us alone: something will turn up'; in a much more elaborate version, Eastlund and Gough (1969) envision the day when an ultra-high-temperature plasma acts as a fusion torch to reduce any material to its elements for separation so that on a large scale urban sewage could be processed, all solid waste recycled, electricity produced through fuel cells, and water desalted, all using only heavy hydrogen from sea water as a basic material and producing as a 'waste' only helium which will itself be quite valuable. (Waste heat will of course be produced too.) As always, science is a two-edged weapon, and believers in technology share with environmentalists a concern over what criteria would be used to decide what was to be produced from such a horn of plenty, and who would decide which buttons to press.

Another kind of world

As a reaction both to those who foresee imminent and inevitable doom and to those who see solutions mainly in terms of continued technological development, a set of views which emphasize the biological and physical limitations of the planet as a home for man have been put forward. Their answer lies in the adoption of a totally different strategy of man–environment relations, which is characterized largely by steady states of everything pertaining to man, be it population levels or economic activity.

The envelope of the alternative is clear. This is the objective knowledge about the ecosphere and its functioning which modern science is beginning to provide. As ecology, for example, becomes more sophisticated, its level of contribution will increase: Boulding (1966a) did not get into much trouble when he described ecologists as 'a lot of bird-watchers'. Indeed, ecology's major contribution so far has been to provide a holistic conceptual framework for thinking about the ecosphere rather than detailed, accurate and predicative data about the way it will behave in any given circumstances, although improvements will no doubt be brought about as a result of current research. One major general contribution of ecology has been the knowledge of limits. Since ecosystems function within the wider limits of finite solar radiation and finite cycling times of scarce mineral elements, we become aware of a set of finite limits to food production and of a finite boundary even to a population supported by continuously recycled materials. Terrestrial space is clearly finite and cannot be created, give or take a polder or two. Wastes may also produce limits, especially heat where there are probably not only safe limits beyond which atmospheric systems may be unpredictably altered, but absolute limits beyond which the transport out into space cannot take place at a sufficiently fast rate. The thresholds at which these limits might be expected to operate, other than at local scales, and the rates of activity which might bring them down upon us are uncertain, but no amount of technology or wishful thinking can make them go away, since they are inescapable parts of the physical constitution of the planet. An additional set of limits may be produced by the breakdown of the behaviour patterns of humans under conditions of high density. The evidence, as discussed above, is not conclusive, but since there is clearly a cultural dimension to tolerance of crowding, then expressions of aversion to particular conditions are probably significant. Thus if people feel that Britain, for example, is overcrowded, then perhaps it is overcrowded and action needs to be taken to stabilize and possibly reduce the population.

Within the envelope of the limits just discussed, a conception of an alternative man–environment relationship has grown up. Although deriving its fundamental thesis from the observations of biology, it has been given added impetus by inputs such as the NASA pictures of this fragile but fertile planet spinning alone in an infinity of hostile space. Thus the outstanding articulator of the idea, K. E. Boulding (1966c), has called it the 'spaceship earth economy'. He contrasts it with our present economy, which he calls the 'cowboy economy', being characterized by flamboyance, waste and a taste for burning candles at both ends; if we book a passage on the *Titanic*, there is no point in going steerage.

Basic principles of the 'spaceship earth' concept

The purpose of this alternative model is to establish a dynamic equilibrium. Populations are stable, or oscillate with only a small amplitude around a constant level. All materials are conserved by undergoing recycling. There is thus an end to exponential growth on a world scale, although individual parts may exhibit growth within the overall limits. The idea is thus analogous to preferred limits of population in hunting societies, as distinct from populations which necessitate the use of all the food resources of the group's territory.

Although the basic concept is simple, the specific conditions for its possible success need more detailed examination, and we must begin with the search for ecological understanding. At the traditional scales of ecological research, work is still essential to secure the fundamental understanding of how ecosystems work and, indeed, whether the ecological model of the functioning of nature is a correct one. In particular, more knowledge of the predictability of ecosystem response to various natural and anthropogenic stimuli is required, as is a deeper understanding of the nature of ecological stability and the conditions under which it can be expected (Woodwell and Smith 1969). Knowledge of the complete system of 'man and his total environment' is required, as Egler (1970) has stressed. Although the working of component parts of this ecosphere need to be better understood, a feeling for the whole is essential, especially for the repercussions of unwanted changes in unexpected places. In general, a determination to regard the phenomena of both physical and cultural systems holistically is necessary, unpopular though this is with 'pure' scientists who see an invasion of their carefully guarded swimming pools by the unwashed hordes from across the tracks. The integrated view is characteristic of geography as an intellectual discipline, and geography deals with the cultural dimension as well as the ecological, but geographers have shown few signs of wishing to put their feet into the turbulent waters of environmental debate, with certain honourable exceptions (Burton and Kates 1964, Zelinsky 1970, Eyre 1971). The development of schools of study, let alone administrative structures, at the integrative level of man and his total environment is slow in coming and subject to considerable opposition and general inertia.

In practical terms, the 'spaceship' economy is predicated upon the attainment of a stable population at a world scale. Growth of world population must clearly stop at some time, and the equilibrium approach prefers an all-out effort to bring this about by cultural and technical means rather than leave it to the alternatives. These latter are likely to be either psychological, with stress causing spontaneous abortion, inadequate parental care of infants or possibly enhanced rates of foetal re-absorption, or directly Malthusian, through famine, war and disease. Even if measures such as those of Fremlin were adopted there is still a limit to the number of people supportable on this planet. In bringing about population stability, priority needs to be given to the DCs and the Egyptian type of LDC. The importance of the European-US-type nations is twofold. Firstly, they are the dominant users of resources and producers of contaminants. Statistics for almost any part of a global resource process will show the USA itself in the lead for per capita use, followed closely by other nations of the US type, and hotly pursued by the European-type countries. A further reduction of the already slow rate of increase of population would help to remove the fundamental cause of their need for resources, although cultural demands would doubtless keep consumption levels high and the actual reduction of usage rates would have to be a cultural decision of a different kind from agreeing to attempt to stabilize population. Secondly, Western material culture is the object of aspirations in many LDCs who think that population control is basically an imperialist gambit to keep the Third World in its 'proper' place. It is essential therefore to practise what is preached, and to make it clear that population stabilization by the rich ought ultimately to be for the greater benefit of the poor.

The need for population control in resource-poor and technology-poor nations is self-evident. It is probably their only way of moving away from the precarious balance between adequacy and insufficiency, whether of food or employment. Intensified and more productive agriculture may improve living standards, but it inevitably causes a wholesale drift to the cities, where industrialization rarely proceeds fast enough to provide jobs for the influx, partly because capital accumulation per capita is low at times of rapid population growth. Furthermore, the basic resources for the industrial development of many of the populous LDCs are lacking: cheap energy, in particular, is likely to be difficult to acquire. Additionally, their rapid rates of population growth (often in excess of 2 per cent p.a.) impose strains upon their social structures, especially in the cases of newly independent nations lacking political stability. Not the least problem is the high proportion of young people in a rapidly growing population, many of whom will have material and educational aspirations on a scale undreamed of by their parents. Urgency is less marked in nations of the Brazilian character, since they can for a time contain their people by developing hitherto unattractive areas, witness the Brazilian plans for the Amazon Basin. But there can be no question of their freedom from eventual limits, and prudence would seem to dictate a halt to growth before their population-resources imbalances become national rather than local or regional. The fragility of many of the biomes in these countries, especially those in the tropics, serves to underline the virtues of leaving a wide margin of safety which is not dependent upon technology, an implement which is still generally lacking in such places and sometimes unwisely used where present.

Apart from cultural change, a large investment of money is needed to bring about population stabilization, and since fertility control is the most acceptable method, we may reflect that it is probably money better spent than on prestigious projects like a national airline or on developments which merely postpone decision-making, like some large dams. But one major difficulty is the time factor: another doubling of the world's population seems inevitable following the passage through the demographic structure of those already born. Thereafter, present campaigns for fertility control may show some effect on absolute numbers if they have been successful. To judge by present declines in fertility in LDCs, the highly urbanized societies and those with numerous ethnic Chinese people are showing the greatest response, as in Hong Kong, Taiwan and Singapore; there is also the example of Japan in the post-1945 period: it looks as if urbanization in the Third World may be a useful trend as far as reducing birth rates is concerned; however, there are indications that some techniques for 'selling' contraception are meeting with resistance, and the attachment of family planning to medicine and consequent association with illness may reduce acceptability.

But an equilibrium economy requires not only the attainment of a stable population but also its maintenance. If this is to be achieved, it will fundamentally require the acceptance of the notion that the maximum size of an individual's family is for society to decide, and not for the parents alone. In effect the situation will have been brought back to the condition of 'primitive' hunting groups which limited their populations to the number sustainable on a preferred food source rather than let it expand to the boundary of the entire supply of nutrition. A fairly drastic social adjustment consisting of the yielding up of an individual choice is therefore indicated. Those who argue the unacceptability of such a change must be asked to consider the other choices which will become unavailable in a condition of a serious imbalance of population, resources and environment. Even if the theses of Parsons (1971) are not all accepted, few of the developments of technology which some believe will avert any 'environmental crisis' seem to propose increased personal liberty and choice as their concomitants, let alone their immediate purposes.

The cycling of materials

This necessary condition is based on the premise that some materials, e.g. metals, will be in short supply because of the demands of increased populations wishing to share in the benefits of an industrial way of life. In addition, the environmental alterations inevitably associated with the extraction of lower qualities of materials will be diminished if supplies can be re-used. Relatively few materials are actually destroyed in the course of their use, so that given the appropriate technology and cost structure, recycling becomes a feasibility for many items: those containing metals and wood products (Plate 24) are obvious examples, but the idea can be applied to many diverse materials, including water, sewage and textiles. Some losses are unavoidable, as for example the escape of metals through friction; new sources would be used only to make up such losses, but additions to the total stock would presumably be made only after satisfaction of the strictest criteria. Probably the critical feature of the recycling economy would be the availability of energy to power the recycling processes, and in view of present attitudes towards the future costs of energy, Berry (1972) has suggested that the production and recycling of goods be evaluated from the point of view of energy economies. Using as measures the loss of thermodynamic potential involved in the manufacture of a new car and its subsequent recycling, he observes that, given increased demand for cars and present technology, recycling is a questionable process compared with extending the life of the machine, which would diminish by two to three times the energy used, since fewer new cars would be needed. Even bigger savings could be achieved by improvements in the technology of the basic recovery and fabrication processes of metals, where thermodynamic savings of five to ten times the present expenditure could be made. So, economies of energy use brought out by recycling are small compared with extended lifetimes of goods and smaller still compared with a technology which loses less energy; yet since recycling is more economically feasible it would be a useful start (a saving of 1,000 KWH/vehicle in the USA is equivalent to eight to ten generating stations) towards a policy of thrift. Industrialization of the LDCs, adds Berry, may only be achievable if policies of thermodynamic thrift are brought into effect.

Re-use has the further advantage that all wastes become important sources of raw materials and thus environmental contamination is reduced, except for the non-re-usable

Plate 24 Things to come? A recycling centre run by voluntary labour in Berkeley, California. Here, bottles are sorted into various kinds and the truck behind serves as a temporary repository for old newspapers. *(I. G. Simmons)*

substances, to which pollution-control measures will have to be applied. Pollution control *per se*, although useful and necessary at an early stage of moving to a closed-cycle economy, now becomes only a last-ditch treatment of intractable wastes.

Moving towards a recycling of materials will be difficult economically. Theoretically the price of recycled materials should make them more attractive as supplies from fresh sources become more expensive; but because of the nature of exponential curves, the limits of supply may be suddenly upon us before the price mechanism has had time to react so as to show the need for research and development into recycling technology and the accompanying changes in social patterns. Additionally, the external costs of pollution are not now levied upon the producer but upon society at large (Crocker and Rogers 1971, Davis and Kamien 1972). Effective legislation and taxation to internalize pollution costs and governmental inputs into recycling technology to prime the pump are therefore urgent priorities now.

Ecosystem balance

The ideas of overall economic and ecological stability embodied in the spaceship earth economy have to be translated into quantities of various types of ecosystem. Because the world cannot return to a pre-agricultural economy, the ecosystems of man's creation must also be included. A valuable start on the analysis needed to provide the criteria for balance between different types of ecosystems has been provided by E. P. Odum (1969). He emphasizes that nature is a mosaic of ecosystems at different levels of succession, some of them 'young' with low inherent stability and diversity but high productivity; by contrast, mature ecosystems have high stability and diversity but their productivity may be lower. Globally, the major ecosystems of the natural world exhibit a developed state of internal symbiosis, good nutrient conservation, high resistance to external perturbation, and low entropy. On the other hand, as Odum puts it,

> Man has generally been preoccupied with obtaining as much 'production' from the land as possible, by developing and maintaining early successional types of ecosystems, usually monocultures. But, of course, man does not live by food and fibre alone; he also needs a balanced CO_2–O_2 atmosphere, the climatic buffer provided by oceans and masses of vegetation, and clean (that is, unproductive) water for cultural and industrial uses. Many essential life-cycle resources, not to mention recreational and esthetic needs, are best provided man by the less 'productive' landscapes.

Different types of ecosystems must therefore form a balanced pattern. As in nature there is a mix of mature, stable systems with immature, unstable ones, so in the man-manipulated world there must be an intercalation of man-dominated simple systems alongside complex natural ecosystems. Four types of ecosystems may be distinguished:

(1) Non-vital systems, or the 'built environment' of urban and industrial areas. These are in fact dependent upon imports from outside, e.g. of oxygen and water, for their continued existence; in the natural state the nearest analogy is probably a volcano, for it too emits sulphur dioxide, carbon dioxide and particulate matter into the atmosphere. Other non-vital systems of the natural world might include ice-caps (which, however, act as reservoirs of water and affect climate) and the most barren deserts, to which cities are not infrequently compared by writers with bucolic yearnings, although perhaps cities are morphologically more akin to karst terrain.

(2) Intensively used biotic systems with high productivity and capacity for high yield to man. Like natural systems at an early stage of succession, man-directed systems such as agriculture have a low diversity of species and are unstable. However, they are easily exploitable and hence highly valued in economic terms. As in comparable natural situations, the growth qualities of the plants and animals selected for rapidity, and quantity of production is valued above quality.

(3) Compromise areas, such as those devoted to multiple-use management of forests, or intermixtures of forest, agriculture and grazing or other wild land, are analogous to natural ecosystems approaching, but not yet at, maturity. They are characterized by higher diversity than the earlier stages of succession and by the development of complex

webs of interdependence between organisms, in contradistinction to the linear chains, dominated by grazing, of earlier stages.

(4) The mature wild systems, i.e. areas of 'climax' vegetation which are basically unaltered by man. In addition to being important reservoirs of biotic diversity, they are vital agents in gaseous interchange, and provide a source of recreational and aesthetic pleasure. Their metabolism is diametrically different from that of early successional phases since it is a highly bound network of food webs with high internal conservation of nutrients by cycling, and has very high resistance to external perturbation. The characteristics of such ecosystems, compared with those in early stages of succession, are set out in Table 13.8. These natural systems play a role far beyond the value which conventional economics accords them. They are the 'anchormen' of total global stability, and perform a function

TABLE 13.8   Trends in the development of ecosystems

Ecosystem attributes	Developmental stages	Mature stages
Food chains	Linear, predominantly grazing	Weblike, predominantly detritus
Biomass supported/unit energy flow	Low	High
Total organic matter	Small	Large
Species diversity-variety component	Low	High
Size of organism	Small	Large
Life cycles	Short, simple	Long, complex
Mineral cycles	Open	Closed
Nutrient exchange rate between organisms and environment	Rapid	Slow
Internal symbiosis	Undeveloped	Developed
Nutrient conservation	Poor	Good
Stability	Poor	Good
Entropy	High	Low

Source: E. P. Odum 1969

which is 'protective' rather than 'productive' but no less vital. If the oceans are included as mature systems, we may note the suggestions quoted by Odum that the oceans are the governor (in the mechanical sense) of the biosphere, slowing down and controlling the rate of decomposition and nutrient regeneration, thereby creating and maintaining the highly aerobic terrestrial atmosphere to which the higher forms of life, ourselves included, are adapted.

Nature has a mosaic of these four types: so must man, if long-term stability of the biosphere is to be attained. The model elaborated is capable of simulation by computer to work out national limits for the size and capacity of each type of system, and the flows between it and the others. The next task seems to be to translate this functional-dynamic model into spatial terms, and using a per capita approach at US levels of consumption, Odum and Odum (1972) conclude that about 5 ac/cap (2·025 ha/cap) is needed by men for all purposes, of which two-fifths should be devoted to natural environments. Whether this proportion should be different in, for example, more fragile environments, what is the particular role of the oceans, and what effect cultural difference might have, are not discussed. The minimum scale at which the ratios become effective needs also to be explored by simulation. The strategy for balance between different kinds of ecosystem confirms yet again the importance of limits, for it is implicit that the now vital and highly productive ecosystems can only expand to certain limits, beyond which the protective systems cannot balance them.

Social and economic adjustments

The primary and ineluctable requirement for the implementation of the closed-cycle economy is population control, which must be aimed at producing a stable world population, with the initial priorities of achieving stable or even declining populations in the US and European types of resource–population situation, and stability in the UAR group. The Brazilian type can possibly be allowed to grow a little more, but not for long.

The basis of value of environmental resources will also undergo change in a recycling economy. Whereas present economic systems value throughput and high turnover allows low prices, the opposite is likely to occur in a revised system. Because of the need to conserve materials, articles which have a long life, preferably free of losses through wear, are likely to be relatively less expensive than those requiring frequent trips through the recycling process. Thus the Chippendale chair ought to cost less than the cardboard one, and the tough dress that lasts their whole adult lives will be easier on the ladies' fashion budget than the frilly number lasting only a few parties. (Such an equation ought to bring home the truly revolutionary nature of the spaceship earth concept.) The same argument, *mutatis mutandis*, will apply to more costly material possessions like vehicles, and the current idea of building disposable towns will be seen as an evanescent efflorescence of an age that denied its own limitations. The final disappearance of the goal of unlimited growth may also be a signal for a major redistribution of incomes. The gap between rich and poor should diminish, partly because less growth will provide fewer opportunities for rapidly gained entrepreneurial profits, and partly because a more coherently planned economy may well value more highly the present poor. A lessened emphasis on the quantity of industrial production will reverse the present trend to energy-intensive production in favour of labour-intensive outputs. This should encourage production of quality goods and services and perhaps restore to the manual workers some of the dignity and job-satisfaction which mass-production has taken away from them. Since labour is likely to be in shorter supply in a stable population, unemployment might reasonably be expected to diminish, and re-evaluation of those currently rejected as too old (rather than incapable) for particular tasks is likely to occur.

The role of industry must change. Nobody advocates a return to some pastoral condition where factories are unheard of and the cross-stitching on the shepherds' smocks is sullied only by the spots of blood from their inevitable tuberculosis, but certain shifts in industrial policy are advocated. Most important is the abandonment of the 'technological fix' as an article of faith, acknowledging that in many respects natural systems are much more efficient than those which are man-made. Next in priority is a realization that for some of the difficult problems caused by population growth, there are no simple (or even complex) technological panaceas worth having (Ehrlich and Holdren 1969). The disparate time-scales upon which population growth and technological development operate, and the complexity of man–environment relations outside the narrowly conceived context of food production, are all taken to suggest that present technology will not suffice to maintain the expected populations of the world, even given optimistic assumptions. Rather is it the case that technology will only become effective and life-enhancing in a stable economy, when the possibility of applying several technological schemes along a broad front (instead of the current piecemeal approach which usually creates several difficulties for each one it removes) becomes more feasible.

Given the abandonment of the ideology of growth, the redirection of technological effort becomes possible and its contribution to a harmonious relation of man and nature immense. New criteria of success will be essential, especially with regard to the environmental consequences and in the discarding of those material uses which are totally ephemeral and add nothing to the quality of anybody's life. Beyond such a stage it is possible that the kind of 'de-development' proposed by Ehrlich and Harriman (1971) may be essential in the European and US groups of nations. Here the control of 'needs' induced by advertising, the freeing of industrial policy from the hands of a few individuals unaccountable to the society which supports them, the enhancement of private affluence at the expense of public squalor, and all the excrescences of the 'disposable society' will have to be firmly controlled without undue delay, as requisites of the closed-cycle economy. Adaptation to a new type of economy, together with the many unsolved problems of the LDCs, will ensure a series of challenges to industry of an unprecedented nature. There is no desire to abandon technology, but neither should there be any intention to allow the big corporations (and their Socialist equivalents) to dominate the resource processes of the biosphere; control of the harmful technology described by Commoner (1972a, b) is necessary but is only a first step.

Brief, if insufficient, mention must be made of some of the institutional adjustments which would be necessary to the success of an equilibrium economy. At a global scale, international agreement on certain movements towards stability will be necessary, especially where the prohibition of poisoning or over-use of commons like the oceans is concerned. Moves towards lessening nuclear testing underground and towards the elimination of nuclear weapons altogether would also be a useful adjunct. Co-ordination of the programmes of nation states and economic groups like the EEC as they alter their goals would be a function of the UN, but a tighter global control is probably an unrealistic prognosis. The main effort would have to come from independent states and the blocs to which they have given over some of their sovereignty: it is they who would lead their people through the difficult task of reorientating their way of life.

It is of course possible that a different type of process might occur: that the changed consciousness of individuals may itself work towards a life-style which is consonant with long-term ecological stability. Thus whole populations may become 'greened', as Reich (1971) has postulated of American youth. Whether or not the contradictions of that book render its main thesis invalid, the revolution of outlook which he describes appears to be confined to the young, and to only a proportion of them. Whether we then have time to wait and see if their world-view persists into middle age, whether it is adopted by their children, and whether they are sufficiently numerous to infect the whole population with their different values, is a luxury we may not be permitted. Like it or not, the political process will have to be the lane down which change is pursued, albeit one lined with thorn hedges. We may parenthetically note that a stable population will have a higher proportion of elderly people in it than a growing one, so that a state of gerontocracy will presumably be even more likely than in the days of the simultaneous reigns of de Gaulle, Adenauer and Macmillan. Some conflict with the aspirations of the young may confidently be predicted.

A journey of a thousand miles

At the time of writing, the negative inputs to the search for new attitudes to the relationship of population, resources and environment have been dominant, whether in the form of 'doom-mongering' or in the more muted form of eloquent writers such as Dubos and Mumford. Positive responses like the setting-out of the spaceship earth concept have attracted less attention because they can spell out the future in less detail than can the forecasters of gloom who merely have to assume the continuation of present trends. More elaborate plans for a stabilized economy have appeared, which not only set out the conceptual framework in more detail but also formulate plans for the introduction of certain transitional stages at appropriate times, i.e. the 'orchestration' of change. The most pioneering of such documents is the 'Blueprint for Survival' (Goldsmith, Allen et al. 1972), produced in semi-popular form. After an analysis of the present trends in the growth of population and economies, and their impact upon the environment, it turns to specific remedies of the kind discussed above, and the co-ordination of their introduction. Its core is the assertion that exponential growth is unsustainable for long periods and that conscious measures to bring about an upper asymptote are better than the free operation of the market and Malthusian checks. It can be criticized in detail, as can all such syntheses, but its basic propositions are consonant with the concept of an equilibrium economy.

The type of measures needed to forestall collapse of ecological and economic systems are also set out by Meadows et al. (1972). Here, complex modelling by computer of several variables in the planetary system (population, industrial output, food production, level of pollution, resources) is used to predict the outcome both of continuing present trends and of altering singly or in concert the variables (Fig. 13.1). Needless to say, continued exponential growth leads to breakdown, and alternatives are explored. The authors conclude that at present very little can be said about the practical day-to-day steps that can be taken to realize the goal of equilibrium, since the models are too lacking in detail to enable all the implications of the transition from growth to equilibrium to be understood. They emphasize, however, that the greatest possible impediment to any sort of stability, or to a more just utilization of the world's resources, is population growth. If stability is the only alternative to the difficulties caused by growth, it also offers numerous advantages, as they argue

equilibrium would require trading certain human freedoms, such as producing unlimited numbers of children, or consuming uncontrolled amounts of resources, for other

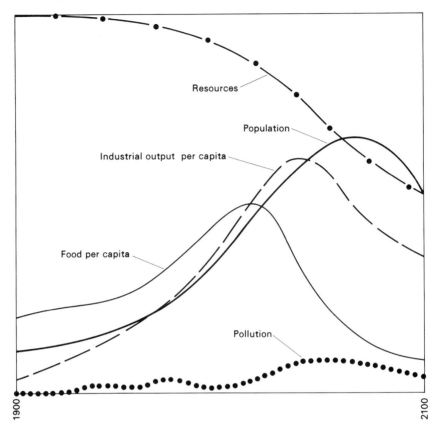

Fig. 13.1 A world model with 'unlimited' resources and pollution controls. Pollution generation per unit of output is reduced to 25 per cent of its 1970 value, but resource availability is doubled by cheap nuclear power, which also makes extensive recycling possible. Population and industry then grow until the limit of arable land is reached; food per capita declines and industrial growth is slowed as capital is devoted to food production.
Source: Meadows *et al.* 1972

freedoms, such as relief from pollution and crowding, and the threat of collapse of the world system.

It is possible that new freedoms might also arise—universal and unlimited education, leisure for creativity and inventiveness, and, most important of all, the freedom from hunger and poverty enjoyed by such a small fraction of the world's people today.

This work and that of Forrester (1971) have been subject to considerable criticism, principally by economists who argued that the assumptions are too simplistic. Others argue that because of the multiplier effects in the model, the alteration of one or two rates by 1 per cent may produce totally different conclusions from those reached in the study quoted. These antagonisms are not particularly relevant, for the importance of the complex modelling is in its demonstration of a technique which can be further refined as our knowledge of natural and social processes becomes more accurate.

Adjudication: limits of all kinds

If the human species is to continue to depend upon the natural systems of the biosphere for life-support, for materials, for valued surroundings and for waste disposal, then it must acknowledge the existence of limits.

The most obvious of these are the ecological limits of which numerous examples have been given in this work, outstanding among which is the SCEP (1970) calculation that every doubling of population increases the 'ecological demand' by six times. Within these limits, a new linkage is needed in which the socio-economic systems realize the importance of the protective systems and reflect this value in their economies. This will contrast with the present situation where wild-lands are usually regarded as raw materials which acquire value only if transformed to something else.

Politicians must also realize that these limits prevent them from promising unlimited 'growth' to their constituents. More realistically, those leaders might well work towards a condition in which all people had a 'right' to life-support from the planet. A fundamental flaw in the world's legal systems allows individuals to appropriate portions of the complex cycles upon which we all depend. They may contaminate part of the water cycle or the air, or may clear protective forest in order to enhance short-term gain from exploitive agriculture. The ownership of land and water must not therefore confer the right to remove it from the life-support systems, and those who wilfully release wastes which disorder those systems must be made to desist: a process which is beginning to take effect.

If limits are to be culturally accepted, then the poor have to be reassured that the rich are not merely pulling up the ladder behind them, having achieved their desired level of material prosperity. This applies both to rich and poor in industrial nations, and to rich and poor countries collectively. In industrial countries with clearly differentiated social strata most of the pressures both for cosmetic conservation and 'environmentalism' come from the 'middle class' and are often denounced on that account. There is often truth in the idea that cosmetic acts merely impose middle-class values upon the whole of the society and use up wealth which might be better spent upon necessities for the poor. Wider concepts of the closed-cycle equilibrium type, however, are basically advantageous to the less privileged groups in society. At present, the poor have a smaller share in the proceeds of economic growth, for example; the industrial workers suffer most from pollution both at work and in their homes, for the better-off can always move house to the cleaner suburbs and handle nothing more contaminating than the latest issue of *Playboy*. The much vaunted example of London's clearer air following smoke abatement programmes has merely transferred the pollution from London to the areas around the coking plants, and to Scandinavia. Some LDCs may forgo the energy-intensive economies of the West and opt for intermediate technology aimed at improving rural life, but those where industry has been made the basis of economic development will wish to attract more capital. Such LDCs can scarcely be expected to stabilize their economies at the present stage, but many will presumably follow the examples of the DCs as they have over the benefits of industrialization; the relationship between the two groups at a time when DCs were stabilizing economies but LDCs still expanding is a difficult and complex issue which needs a great deal of study.

Admission of limits to the carrying capacity of the planet need not carry with it the automatic connotation of doom if all expansion of flows through resource processes is not stopped immediately. It is possible that the choice of chaos or survival currently postulated is a false one. There may be two kinds of limits in the capacity of the earth. The first of

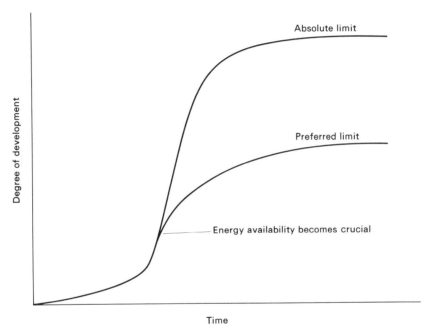

Fig. 13.2 A scheme of two alternative limits to world development: the absolute limit involves replacement of natural life-support systems by man-made processes, the preferred limit does not. The availability of cheap and safe energy is crucial to the pursuit of the absolute limit.

these is the *absolute limit* in which a man-made stability replaces that of natural systems. A first stage might be the conversion of the earth largely to a food–man monoculture, but later the immense technological contribution of the type envisaged by Fremlin (1964) would be mandatory. The human populations that could be supported would be huge, but there would be little room for other than technological life-support systems. The alternative might be a *preferred limit*, in which the natural systems continue to be crucial for our survival and in which they are valued accordingly. A diversity of habitat and culture would remain (unlikely to happen in the absolute-limit alternative) but the supportable population would be lower than in the technology-dependent world; this latter alternative is of course identical with Boulding's spaceship earth concept. The two limits are depicted in Fig. 13.2. There may be a third alternative in which the intensive use of cheap energy means that all man's needs can be produced in industrial plant which is as much as possible isolated from the biosphere. Man's material needs would be supplied by an economic system parallel to but in minimal interaction with natural systems. Plans for underground and offshore nuclear power stations could presumably be extended to all kinds of manufacturing and processing installations so that, given adequate technology and favourable geology, even food could be produced from atomic and molecular building blocks in underground and submersible factories, or even in space, leaving the biosphere relatively free of human impact, although many people would still want to live on the earth's surface. In spite of its apparent reasonableness, this alternative has an air of science fiction about it. But both it and the system which depends upon the supersession of natural systems depend upon the provision of a cheap, clean and ubiquitous energy supply whose waste heat can be safely radiated into space without a major disturbance of atmospheric patterns. And so attention to developments such as controlled fusion reactions, alternative methods of energy conversion, more locally autonomous power sources of a non-fossil and non-nuclear type, more efficient technology which will effectively utilize energy inputs (few steam plants today operate beyond an efficiency of 45 per cent), and energy-conservative buildings, domestic heating systems and transport networks, are all vital and pressing needs. Without them only the environmentalist model offers hope of any quality of life.

If there is a choice between these alternatives, what criteria are to be used in making decisions? There is no doubt that the preferred limit is safer: it gives much wider margins for error, and forecloses fewer options than the absolute limit. It also offers a greater diversity of all kinds to individual people: of different employments, different places to visit and different cultures to exist alongside. But it is a world in which growth is no longer equated with progress; it is analogous to the condition of men in hunting societies who limited their populations to those who could be fed by a preferred food supply such as meat, rather than an absolute food supply which included rodents and roots.

The outlook of those who wish to advocate the preferred limit is essentially optimistic. Those who propose totally technological solutions are seeking to avoid dangers, but the spaceship earth proponents see a different kind of world. They do not wish to return to some forgotten Eden without machines (indeed they want more technology, not less, but applied in a different manner), but to create a world of stability in which the resources are used equitably by an adequately nourished population which does not poison its own habitat with the wastes. They see it as the most hopeful way of coming to grips with what Caldwell (1971) views as man's most fearsome problems: the containment of population growth, the management of energy flows, the development of stable ecological and political orders, and the formulation of a coherent political and ethical doctrine for human behaviour in relation to natural systems, and furthermore one which neither attempts the unforeseeable nor commits the irrevocable. Bringing this about is a task of immense difficulty, because it can only be made meaningful to diverse groups of men in terms of the lineaments of their own culture: success is unlikely if new ways are imposed internationally or by foreign-educated governors. But because of the accelerating rush to instability brought about by the exponential growth of numbers of people, consuming materials and energy, and subsequently discharging waste, all men should recognize that ecological instability is their common enemy, one which will not distinguish between rich and poor, black, white or brown, PhDs and peasant farmers. The alternatives are clear: to try to develop to an absolute limit in one of its forms, to aim for a preferred limit, or to adopt no overall strategy and allow present-day institutions to respond to individual problems as they arise. As was said at the beginning of this book, man is a material-using animal. He must also make moral choices.

Further reading

BECKERMANN, W. 1973: Growthmania revisited.

BLACK, J. 1970: *The dominion of man.*

BOYD, R. 1972: World dynamics: a note.

BOULDING, K. E. 1966: The economics of the coming spaceship earth.

CALDWELL, L. K. 1971: *Environment: a challenge to modern society.*

COLE, H. S. D. *et al.* (eds.) 1973: *Thinking about the future.*

COMMONER, B. 1972: *The closing circle.*

DETWYLER, T. R. and MARCUS, M. G. 1972: *Urbanization and environment.*

EHRLICH, P. R. and HOLDREN, J. P. 1969: Population and panaceas: a technological perspective.

— 1971: Impact of population growth.

ELLUL, J. 1964: *The technological society.*

GOLDSMITH, E. *et al.* 1972: Blueprint for survival.

HARDIN, G. 1973: *Exploring new ethics for survival. The voyage of the spaceship Beagle.*

MCHALE, J. 1969: *The future of the future.*

MADDOX, J. 1972: *The doomsday syndrome.*

MEADOWS, D. L. *et al.* 1973: *The limits to growth.*

MISHAN, E. J. 1967: *The costs of economic growth.*

MONTEFIORE, H. 1970: *Can man survive?*

MONCRIEF, L. W. 1970: The cultural basis for our environmental crisis.

ODUM, E. P. 1969: The strategy of ecosystem development.

STUDY OF CRITICAL ENVIRONMENTAL PROBLEMS (SCEP) 1970: *Man's impact on the global environment: assessment and recommendations for action.*

SPILHAUS, A. 1972: Ecolibrium.

WAGAR, J. A. 1970: Growth versus the quality of life.

WARD, B. and DUBOS, R. 1972: *Only one earth.*

Appendix

The slow pace of the production of a book (mostly the fault of the author) contrasts with the fast pace of events in the field of resources. These last remarks are therefore intended to update some of the trends described in the main chapters of the book, where recent developments have made them look unduly aged. Not all the numerous happenings can be considered, so emphasis will be put upon developments in attitudes towards resources and environment.

Energy

A 'crisis'

The Arab-Israeli war of October 1973 precipitated a situation which had been looming for some time, namely that oil production would be held at current rates or even reduced, and at the same time its price raised substantially. The shortages hit hardest at Europe, Japan and, although not nearly so dependent upon Arab oil, the USA. Oil landings in Europe and Japan fell to some 80 per cent of the previous year's totals and provoked numerous effects, some of which are described in the next section. The difficult question posed is whether that particular situation is the first taste of a real shortage caused by the depletion of the crude oil resource, or whether it is largely political and economic. Placed against Hubbert King's estimates in Chapter 10, the latter answer seems the more convincing. The key element, it would seem, is price. The sudden cessation of the supply of a cheap fuel will no doubt induce many kinds of short-term adjustments in industrial countries, but the high price on world markets may well lead eventually to an increased rate of recovery, so that the middle 80 per cent will probably be extracted on schedule. Indeed the 'conspiracy' theory of the oil crisis has the international oil companies withholding supplies in order to create shortages so that governments can be panicked into allowing oil prices, and hence company profits, to rise markedly. Some US Congress hearings on the oil industry held early in 1974 provided a few embarrassing moments for senior oil company executives.

Effects

Most noticeable to the average citizen has been the extra cost of oil and petroleum products for all uses, including domestic heating and motoring as well as industry. Shortages have also been evident in queues for gasoline in the USA and Britain, in restrictions on pleasure motoring in most of Europe, and reductions on deliveries of heating oil. At the time of writing, the extra costs of energy had not worked their way through the industrial system and so were not adding greatly to the inflation rampant in the West. The penetration of energy use into all facets of the industrial way of life has, however, been brought home to most people and even some governments. The rush for solutions has meant a re-evaluation of some fuels and grades of fuel which were becoming unpopular because of their pollutant qualities (high sulphur content coal and oil, for example); the introduction of emission standards for various parts of the USA was put back by the Environmental Protection Agency, and some existing controls were relaxed: the influence of environmental consciousness in government seems to have been rather easily eradicated.

Medium-term solutions

Immediate responses from industrial nations have been to accelerate the discovery and extraction of oil and natural gas, particularly where the sources are under the control of the consuming nation. Thus the years of controversy over the Alaska pipeline were speedily ended by the US Congress with only the most token of oppositions from environmentalist groups. The offshore oil recovery programme of Britain was accelerated by all possible means, and until the dissolution of Parliament in February 1974 a Bill to nationalize land needed for the oil industry's operations was proceeding through legislative process. Its effect would have been to bypass most of the cumbersome democracy whereby people who opposed such changes were allowed to argue their case publicly and at length. Another move was the re-evaluation of coal. The large reserves in the USA, for example, and the discovery of thick seams in Yorkshire, England, raised hopes that this source might again be the major underpinner of industrial economies. Token gestures in the direction of the problems of the environmental impact of surface mining and of pollution from combustion of low-grade coals were often made, but more promising were the technologically based suggestions that the processing of coal might make its use more flexible. The most promising of these products seems to be methanol, whose emission characteristics are superior to gasoline, which can be produced by the gasification of coal (Reed and Lerner 1973, Valéry 1974), and which could possibly be done underground. Inevitably, there are difficulties such as the lower kilometres per litre achieved, but it seems superior to hydrogen, for example, where storage-weight factors are prohibitive for small plant and moving vehicles: the equivalent of a 10-gallon (45-litre) petrol tank would be 16 gas cylinders weighing 1·25 tons (1,270 kg).

The consumption side of the balance sheet has also been under consideration and strong pleas made against unnecessary use of energy. One area where the use of energy is particularly excessive is packaging, especially where plastics are used. The energy costs of extra packaging, transporting the weight, and collecting and disposing of the resulting garbage have not been detailed but must be enormous. Domestic premises designed to be heated with cheap oil, with thin walls and large areas of glass, are probably due for review too. The realization of the high energy costs of the 'consumer society', together with shortages of some materials, have put new life into the recycling idea, although actual practice is lagging behind both the technology and the ideas. The conservatism of industries which might recycle waste, and of the collecting agencies in towns and cities, may yet be changed by the rapidly altering economics of materials supply, and intervention by governments ought theoretically to speed up the transition to a waste-using economy. Yet more conservative of energy might be the stipulation that most durable goods must last longer.

Longer-term solutions

The introduction of greater reliance upon nuclear power seems a virtual certainty in industrial nations, using atomic fission immediately and atomic fusion in the more distant future. The expansion of nuclear fission plants has been marked by considerable controversy over the safety of the present choice of the atomic energy authorities of the USA and, because they wish to purchase American reactors of that particular type, the UK. The highly technical arguments centre on the probabilities of certain classes of accident and on the disposal of large quantities of highly dangerous waste. Although these reactors are stoutly defended by their manufacturers and by government agencies already committed to them, there remains the thought that safety is too important to be left to the experts, and notably the 1972 Pugwash Conference thought it was unwise to embark on nuclear fission programmes as a major energy source. Such developments are being seen as Faustian compacts with society, in particular the next generation of breeder reactors whose production of plutonium raises the spectre of its promiscuous use for hostile acts. Opinion varies about whether it can inexpensively be rendered unsuitable for such use.

Beyond lies nuclear fusion, still in its infancy, although the major engineering problems seem along the road to solution, especially in the USSR. The use of lasers in a combined fusion-fission reaction (in which a deuterium-tritium fusion would then split boron nuclei) is also under development. Estimates suggest a commercial introduction of fusion power in 30–40 years' time, but few argue that the energy will be cheap.

Increased interest is also being shown in other energy sources, such as solar power, wind power, geothermal power, and the heat of the earth's core. Large-scale development seems a long way off (with the possible exception of solar-heated buildings), but they are all equilibrium sources, i.e. they do not impose an additional heat burden upon the atmosphere, and so may avoid the heat-limit problems associated with fossil fuel and nuclear power. By contrast, energy is now seen to be so intertwined with the Western way of life that proposals for 'democratizing' its use are emerging from radical thinkers such as Ivan D. Illich (1974).

Other shortages

Materials

Imbalance between supply and demand of some materials has developed, most noticeably in paper and metals, with resulting increases in price. In the case of the former, the explosive rises in demand caused by higher standards of living in terms of literacy and, above all, packaging, have outstripped the growth of the trees. Re-use is often practicable, but substitution seems a more likely development. With metals the picture is less clear since financial speculation in metals' futures has raised their price and kept them off the market. Nevertheless an upsurge of consortia aiming at exploiting the sea-bed has been seen, with recovery of manganese, copper, nickel and cobalt as the prime targets.

Food

Famine has again been widespread, especially in drought-prone regions like the Sahel and Ethiopia, and in other places the growth of population seems to be about to engulf even the achievements of the green revolution. Late in 1973, for example, FAO predicted a 9 million mt shortfall in wheat, Thailand banned rice sales abroad, the Philippines put all cereals under military control, and floods in Pakistan caused widespread destruction of crops. An international grain reserve has been called for several times, but the potential donor nations are having difficulties with, for example, fertilizer supplies: one estimate suggested that the US production of feed grains would drop by 20 million tons in 1973–4. An unknown factor is the consequence of the higher price of fossil fuels. Blaxter (1974) calculates that in the UK the energy input-output ratio for potatoes is 0·87, so that the input of fossil fuels is greater than the solar energy trapped; for wheat the same ratio is 2·2, milk 0·3 and eggs 0·16, these last two presumably being acceptable because of their protein content. Given such relationships, the ability of Western farmers to contribute to a world food larder may be considerably diminished.

Resources and environment

The MIT computer-based studies supported by the Club of Rome and published by Meadows *et al.* (1972) attracted more attention than the treatment in this book would indicate. Numerous arguments reached the pages of most journals and newspapers, the anti-limits critics producing evidence that the parameters were too aggregated, that the outcomes were especially sensitive to very small alterations in the rates of certain variables, and that important cultural feedback mechanisms were omitted. Defenders, on the other hand, pointed to the use of 'the intricate defensive' and thought that none of the detailed criticisms invalidated the main conclusion, which was that material-based economic growth could not go on for ever. True to the Anglo-Saxon mind, various compromises have been put forward, most of which hinge on the question of economic development in the LDCs. Almost all the developments cited so far in this Appendix are likely to prove inimical to the improvement of their lot, unless a two-tier price structure for oil were to be promulgated. At $8/bbl (a conservative estimate) the oil bill for the LDCs of Asia, Africa and South America will rise from $5,200 \times 10^6$ in 1973 to $27,000 \times 10^6$ by 1980. Such direct effects, which cancel out, for example, India's hope of self-sufficiency in foreign exchange by 1979, and turn Kenya's forecast growth rate of 7·4 per cent into a negative figure within 18 months, are paralleled by backlash effects from the DCs who may wish or be forced to cut back production which involves primary materials from the Third World. Especially vulnerable will be countries which rely on industries based on semi-manufactured products like plastics and synthetic fibres, such as Singapore, Hong Kong, Korea and even, perhaps, China. One response may be to follow the Arabs' example and exercise monopoly power: copper, tin, bauxite and cocoa are possible cases for OPEC-type treatment. But in the face of falling demand they might not achieve more than stabilization of incomes.

A small but growing body of opinion in the LDCs may wish to abandon the industrial path to sufficiency and opt for an intermediate-technology, low-energy-using route, which concentrates on rural improvements first. If successful such an economy might have much to teach the West, but it is difficult to see how it might succeed in the face of populations growing at 2–3 per cent per annum. So 1974, being World Population Year, is clearly a time for renewed efforts to reduce fertility in the LDCs (countered by news of India's large cuts in government finance of family planning), even if not yet to the barely replacement levels of parts of Europe and of the USA.

No changes of any significance in the balance and attitudes of cornucopians and environmentalists seem to have taken place, although new champions of both seem to be emerging. Perhaps 1972 was the high-water mark of intense public concern over population, resources and environment: now it is time for cooler appraisals, long-term strategies and fundamental questions of purpose.

Bibliography

ABERG, B. and HUNGATE, F. P. (eds.) 1967: *Radioecological concentration processes.* New York and London: Academic Press.

ABRAHAMSON, D. E. 1972: Ecological hazards from nuclear power plants. In M. Taghi Farvar and J. P. Milton (eds.), 795–811.

ADAMS, A. B. (ed.) 1964: *First World Conference on National Parks.* Washington, DC: US Government Printing Office.

ADAMS, W. P. and HELLEINER, F. M. (eds.) 1972: *International geography.* Toronto: University of Toronto Press.

AITKEN, P. L. 1963: Hydroelectric power generation. In Institute of Civil Engineers, 34–42.

ALLISON, A. (ed.) 1970: *Population control.* Harmondsworth: Pelican.

ALTSCHUL, A. M. and ROSENFELD, D. 1970: Protein supplementation: satisfying man's food needs. *Progress* **54**, 76–84.

ALVERSON, D. L., LONGHURST, A. R. and GULLAND, J. A. 1970: How much food from the sea? *Science* **168**, 503–5.

AMERICAN SOCIETY OF RANGE MANAGEMENT 1964: *A glossary of terms used in range management.* Portland, Oregon: American Society of Range Management.

AMIDON, E. and GOULD, E. M. 1962: *The possible impact of recreation development on timber production in three California National Forests.* Berkeley: US Forest Service Pacific SW Experimental Station Technical Paper **68**.

ANDREWARTHA, H. A. and BIRCH, L. C. 1954: *The distribution and abundance of animals.* Chicago: University of Chicago Press.

ANON 1972: Environmental cleanup—a $287 billion project. *Pollution Abstr.* **3** (6), 4–9.

ARBEJDSMINISTERIET DANMARKS 1968: *Arbejdstid og Ferie.* Copenhagen: Labour Ministry of Denmark.

ARKCOLL, D. B. 1971: Agronomic aspects of leaf protein production. In N. W. Pirie (ed.), 9–18.

ASHTON, M. D. 1970: *The relationship of agriculture to soil and water pollution.* Report on the 1970 Cornell Agricultural Waste Management Conference. Washington, DC: Reports of the UK Scientific Mission in North America, UKSM **70/12**.

BADGLEY, P. C. and VEST, W. L. 1966: Orbital remote sensing and natural resources. *Photogram. Engineering* **32**, 780–90.

BAKER, F. C. 1970: *Derelict land.* 'The Countryside in 1970', 3rd Conference, Report **18**. London: HMSO.

BAKUZIS, E. V. 1969: Forestry viewed in an ecosystem concept. In G. M. Van Dyne (ed.), 189–258.

BALIKCI, A. 1968: The Netsilik Eskimos: adaptive processes. In R. B. Lee and I. De Vore (eds.), 1968a, 78–82.

BARNARD, C. (ed.) 1964: *Grasses and grasslands.* London and Melbourne: Macmillan.

BARNARD, C. and FRANKEL, O. H. 1964: Grass, grazing animals and man in historic perspective. In C. Barnard (ed.), 1–12.

BARNETT, H. J. 1967: The myth of our vanishing natural resources. *TRANS-action* **4** (7), 6–10; text reprinted in R. Revelle *et al.* (eds.), 180–86; and in W. H. Davis (ed.), 201–4, with the original photographs.

BARNETT, H. J. and MORSE, C. 1963: *Scarcity and growth.* Baltimore: Johns Hopkins Press for RFF.

BARR, H. M., CHADWICK, B. A. and THOMAS, D. L. (eds.) 1972: *Population resources and the future: non-Malthusian perspectives.* Provo, Utah: Brigham Young University Press.

BARR, J. 1969: *Derelict Britain.* Harmondsworth: Pelican.

—— (ed.) 1971: *The environmental handbook.* New York: Ballantine/London: Friends of the Earth.

BARRY, R. G. 1969: The world hydrological cycle. In R. J. Chorley (ed.), 11–29.

BARTSCH, A. F. 1970: Accelerated eutrophication of lakes in the United States: ecological response to human activities. *Environmental Pollution* **1**, 133–40.

BAUMHOFF, M. A. 1963: *Ecological determinants of aboriginal California populations.* University of California Publications in Archaeology and Ethnology **49** (2). Berkeley and Los Angeles: University of California Press.

BAYFIELD, N. 1971. Some effects of walking and skiing on vegetation at Cairngorm. In E. Duffey and A. S. Watt (eds.), 469–84.

BEAUMONT, P. 1968: Quanats on the Varamin Plain, Iran. *Trans. Inst. Brit. Geogr.* **45**, 169–79.

BECKERMANN, W. 1973: Growthmania revisited. *New Statesman* (19 October), 550–52.

BECKINSALE, R. P. 1969a: Human use of open channels. In R. J. Chorley (ed.), 331–43.

—— 1969b: Human responses to river regimes. In R. J. Chorley (ed.), 487–509.

BENEDICT, B. 1970: Population control in primitive societies. In A. Allison (ed.), 165–80.

BERKOWITZ, D. A. and SQUIRES, A. M. (eds.) 1971: *Power generation and environmental change.* Cambridge, Mass.: MIT Press.

BERRY, R. 1972: Recycling, thermodynamics and environmental thrift. *Bull. Atom. Sci.* **28** (5), 8–15.

BIENFANG, P. 1971: Taking the pollution out of waste heat. *New Sci.* **51**, 456–7.

BIRDSELL, J. B. 1968: Some predictions for the Pleistocene based upon equilibrium systems among recent hunter-gatherers. In R. B. Lee and I. De Vore (eds.), 1968a, 229–40.

BJERKE, S. 1967: Landscape planning and nature parks. Copenhagen: Naturfrednings-foringen (mimeo).

BLACK, J. 1970: *The dominion of man.* Edinburgh: Edinburgh University Press.

BLAXTER, K. 1974: Power and agricultural revolution. *New Sci.* **61**, 400–403.

BLUMER, M. 1969: Oil pollution of the ocean. In D. P. Hoult (ed.), 5–13.

BOARD, C., CHORLEY, R. J., HAGGETT, P. and STODDART, D. R. (eds.) 1971: *Progress in geography* **3**. London: Edward Arnold.

BOGUE, D. J. 1969: *Principles of demography.* New York: Wiley.

BORGSTROM, G. 1965: *The hungry planet.* New York: Macmillan.

BORMANN, F. H. and LIKENS, G. E. 1969: The watershed-ecosystem concept and studies of nutrient cycles. In G. M. Van Dyne (ed.), 49–76.

BORMANN, F. H., LIKENS, G. E. and EATON, J. S. 1969: Biotic regulation of particulate and solution losses from a forest ecosystem. *Bioscience* **19**, 600–610.

BORMANN, F. H., LIKENS, G. E., FISHER, D. W. and PIERCE, R. S. 1968: Nutrient loss accelerated by clear-cutting of a forest ecosystem. *Science* **159**, 882–4.

BOUGHEY, A. S. 1968: *Ecology of populations.* New York: Macmillan.

BOULDING, K. E. 1962: *A reconstruction of economics.* New York: Science Edition.

— 1966a: Discussions in: F. Fraser Darling and J. P. Milton (eds.), 291–2.

— 1966b: Ecology and economics. In F. Fraser Darling and J. P. Milton (eds.), 225–34.

— 1966c: The economics of the coming spaceship earth. In H. Jarrett (ed.), 3–14.

— 1970: Fun and games with the Gross National Product: the role of misleading indicators in social policy. In H. W. Helfrich (ed.), 157–70.

— 1971: Environment and economics. In W. W. Murdoch (ed.), 359–67.

BOURNE, H. K. 1970: Preservation versus use of the American National Parks and other scenic and recreation areas. Washington, DC: Reports of the UK Scientific Mission in North America, UKSM **70/1**.

BOX, T. W. and PERRY, R. A. 1971: Rangeland management in Australia. *J. Range Management* **24**, 167–71.

BOYD, R. 1972: World dynamics: a note. *Science* **177**, 516–19.

BRACEY, H. C. 1970: *People and the countryside.* London: Routledge and Kegan Paul.

BRADY, N. C. (ed.) 1967: *Agriculture and the quality of our environment.* Washington, DC: Publication **85**, AAAS.

BRAIDWOOD, R. 1970: The agricultural revolution. In J. Janick (ed.), 4–12.

BRITISH TRAVEL ASSOCIATION-KEELE UNIVERSITY 1967: *The pilot national recreation survey, Report* **1**. London: BTA.

BROWN, H. 1954: *The challenge of man's future.* New York: Viking Press.

— 1970: Human materials production as a process in the biosphere. In *Scientific American* (ed.), 115–24.

BROWN, H., BONNER, J. and WEIR, J. 1963: *The next hundred years.* New York: Viking Press.

BROWN, L. H. 1971: The biology of pastoral man as a factor in conservation. *Biol. Cons.* **3**, 93–100.

BROWN, L. R. 1970: Human food production as a process in the biosphere. In *Scientific American* (ed.), 95–103.

BROWN, L. R. and FINSTERBUSCH, G. 1971: Man, food and environment. In W. W. Murdoch (ed.), 53–69.

—1972: *Food.* London and New York: Harper and Row.

BRUBAKER, S. 1972: *To live on earth.* Baltimore: Johns Hopkins Press for RFF/New York: Mentor Books.

BRUHN, J. G. 1972: The ecological crisis and the work ethic. *Int. J. Environ. Studs.* **3**, 43–7.

BRYAN, R. 1973: *Much is taken, much remains.* Belmont, Calif.: Wadsworth.

BRYCE-SMITH, D. 1971: Lead pollution and mental health. *Biologist* **18**, 52–8.

BRYSON, R. A. and WENDLAND, W. M. 1970: Climatic effects of atmospheric pollution. In S. F. Singer (ed.), 1970a, 130–38.

BURTON, I. and KATES, R. W. 1964: Slaying the Malthusian dragon: a review. *Econ. Geogr.* **40**, 82–9.

— (eds.) 1965: *Readings in resource management and conservation.* Chicago: University of Chicago Press.

BURTON, I., KATES, R. W. and SNEAD, R. E. 1969: *The human ecology of coastal flood hazard in Megalopolis.* Chicago: University of Chicago, Department of Geography Research Paper **115**.

BUSH, R. 1973: *The National Parks of England and Wales.* London: Dent.

BUTZER, K. 1964: *Environment and archaeology: an introduction to Pleistocene geography.* Chicago: Aldine Press.

CAHN, R. 1968: *Will success spoil the National Parks?* Boston: Christian Science Monitor Reprints.

CALDER, N. 1967: *The environment game.* London: Secker and Warburg.

— (ed.) 1968: *Unless peace comes.* Harmondsworth: Pelican.

CALDWELL, L. K. 1971: *Environment: a challenge to modern society.* New York: Doubleday Anchor Books.

— 1972: An ecological approach to international development: problems of policy and administration. In M. Taghi Farvar and J. P. Milton (eds.), 927–47.

CALDWELL, M. 1971: World resources and the limits of man. In P. H. G. Hettena and G. N. Syer (eds.), 15–37.

CALHOUN, J. B. 1962: Population density and social pathology. *Sci. Amer.* **206** (2), 139–48.

— 1971: Psycho-ecological aspects of population. In P. Shepard and D. McKinley (eds.), 111–33.

CANTLON, J. E. 1969: The stability of natural populations and their sensitivity to technology. In G. M. Woodwell and H. H. Smith (eds.), 197–205.

CARPENTER, K. J. 1969: Man's dietary needs. In J. Hutchinson (ed.), 61–74.

CARSON, R. 1963: *Silent spring.* Boston: Houghton Mifflin.

CASSIDY, N. G. and PAHALAD, S. D. 1953: The maintenance of soil fertility in Fiji. *Fiji Agric. J.* **24**, 82–6.

CASTRO, J. A. DE A. 1972: Environment and development: the case of the developing countries. In D. A. Kay and E. B. Skolnikoff (eds.), 237–52.

CHAMPAGNAT, A. 1965: Protein from petroleum. *Sci. Amer.* **213** (4), 13–17.

CHAPMAN, P. F. 1970: Energy production—a world limit? *New Sci.* **47**, 634–6.

CHARLIER, R. H. 1970: Crisis year for the Great Lakes. *New Sci.* **44**, 593–6.

CHORLEY, R. J. (ed.) 1969: *Water, earth and man.* London: Methuen.

CHRISTY, F. T. and SCOTT, A. 1967: *The common wealth in ocean fisheries.* Baltimore: Johns Hopkins Press.

CIRIACY WANTRUP, S. V. 1938: Soil conservation in European farm management. *J. Farm Econ.* **20**, 86–101.

CIRIACY WANTRUP, S. V. and PARSONS, J. J. (eds.) 1967: *Natural resources: quality and quantity.* Berkeley and Los Angeles: University of California Press.

CIVIC TRUST, 1964: *A Lee Valley Regional Park.* London: The Civic Trust.

CLARK, J. G. D. 1954: *Excavations at Starr Carr.* Cambridge: Cambridge University Press.

CLARKE, C. 1967: *Land use and population growth.* London: Macmillan.

CLARKE, J. I. 1965: *Population geography.* Oxford: Pergamon Press.

CLARKE, R. 1968: *We all fall down*. Harmondsworth: Pelican.

CLAWSON, M. 1963: *Land and water for recreation*. Chicago: Rand McNally.

CLAWSON, M. and KNETSCH, J. L. 1966: *Economics of outdoor recreation*. Baltimore: Johns Hopkins Press for RFF.

CLAWSON, M., LANDSBERG, H. H. and ALEXANDER, L. T. 1969: Desalted water for agriculture: is it economic? *Science* **164**, 1141–8.

CLOUD, P. 1968: Realities of mineral distribution. *Texas Quarterly* **11**, 103–26.

— 1969: Minerals from the sea. In NAS/NRC, 135–55.

COLE, H. S. D., FREEMAN, C., JAHODA, M. and PAVITT, K. L. R. (eds.) 1973: *Thinking about the future*. London: Chatto and Windus for Sussex University Press/New York: Universe Books (as *Models of Doom*).

COLE, L. C. 1969: Thermal pollution. *Bioscience* **19**, 989–92.

COLES, J. M. and HIGGS, E. S. 1969: *The archaeology of early man*. London: Faber and Faber.

COLWELL, R. N. 1968: Remote sensing of natural resources. *Sci. Amer.* **218** (1), 54–69.

COMMONER, B. 1972a: *The closing circle*. London: Cape.

— 1972b: The environmental costs of economic growth. In R. Dorfman and N. S. Dorfman (eds.), 261–83.

CONKLIN, H. 1954: An ethnoecological approach to shifting agriculture. *Trans. N.Y. Acad. Sci.*, Ser. II, **17**, 133–42.

— 1957: *Hanunoo agriculture in the Philippines*. Rome: FAO Forestry Development Paper **12**.

COOK, E. 1971: The flow of energy in an industrial society. *Sci. Amer.* **224** (3), 135–44.

COSTIN, A. B. 1964: Grasses and grasslands in relation to soil conservation. In C. Barnard (ed.), 236–58.

— 1971: Water. In A. B. Costin and H. J. Frith (eds.), 71–103.

COSTIN, A. B. and FRITH, H. J. (eds.) 1971: *Conservation*. Ringwood, Victoria: Penguin.

COSTIN, L. N. 1970: Range management in the developing countries. *J. Range Management* **23**, 322–4.

COULSON, J. C. 1972: Grey seals on the Farnes: kindness kills. *New Sci.* **54**, 142–5.

COUNCIL OF EUROPE 1971: *The management of the environment in tomorrow's Europe*. Strasbourg: European Information Centre for Nature Conservation.

COUNTER INFORMATION SERVICES, n.d.: *The Rio Tinto-Zinc Corporation Limited Anti-Report*. London: CIS.

COUNTRYSIDE COMMISSION: *Annual reports*. London: HMSO.

COX, G. W. (ed.) 1969: *Readings in conservation ecology*. New York: Appleton-Century-Crofts.

CRISP, D. J. (ed.) 1964: *Grazing in terrestrial and marine environments*. Oxford: Blackwell.

CRISP, D. T. 1966: Input and output of minerals for an area of Pennine moorland: the importance of precipitation, drainage, peat erosion and animals. *J. Appl. Ecol.* **3**, 327–48.

CROCKER, T. D. and ROGERS, A. J. 1971: *Environmental economics*. Hinsdale, Illinois: Dryden Press.

CROSLAND, C. A. R. 1971: *A Social Democratic Britain*. London: Fabian Society Tract **404**.

CRUTCHFIELD, J. A. (ed.) 1965: *The fisheries: problems in resource management*. Seattle: University of Washington Press.

DARBY, H. C. 1963: Britain's National Parks. *Advmt. Sci.* **20**, 307–18.

DARMSTADTER, J. (with TEITELBAUM, P. D. and POLACH, J. G.) 1971: *Energy in the world economy.* Baltimore: Johns Hopkins for RFF.

DASMANN, R. F. 1964a: *African game ranching.* Oxford: Pergamon Press.

— 1964b: *Wildlife biology.* New York: Wiley.

— 1968: *A different kind of country.* London: Macmillan.

— 1972: *Environmental conservation.* 3rd edn. New York and London: Wiley.

DASMANN, R. F., MILTON, J. P. and FREEMAN, P. H. 1973: *Ecological principles for economic development.* London: Wiley.

DAVIS, K. 1967: Population policy: will current programs succeed? *Science* **158**, 730–39.

— 1968: Review of C. Clark, 1967. *Sci. Amer.* **217** (4), 133–8.

DAVIS, O. A. and KAMIEN, M, I. 1972: Externalities, information and alternative collective action. In R. Dorfman and N. S. Dorfman (eds.), 69–87.

DAVIS, W. H. (ed.) 1971: *Readings in human population ecology.* Englewood Cliffs, NJ: Prentice-Hall.

DAWE, Q. 1972: Chaos that leads to killer dumps. London: *Sunday Times*, 16 January 1972.

DEEVEY, E. S. 1960: The human population. *Sci. Amer.* **203** (9), 195–204.

— 1968: Pleistocene family planning. In R. B. Lee and I. De Vore (eds.), 1968a, 248–9.

— 1970: Mineral cycles. In *Scientific American* (ed.), 83–92.

— 1971: The chemistry of wealth. *Bull. Ecol. Soc. America* **52**, 3–8.

DELWICHE, C. C. 1970: The nitrogen cycle. In *Scientific American* (ed.), 71–80.

DESHLER, W. W. 1965: Native cattle keeping in eastern Africa. In A. Leeds and A. P. Vayda (eds.), 153–68.

DESMOND, A. 1965: How many people ever lived on earth? In L. K. Y. Ng and S. Mudd (eds.), 20–38.

DETWYLER, T. R. (ed.) 1971: *Man's impact on environment.* New York: McGraw-Hill.

DIMBLEBY, G. W. 1962: *The development of British heathlands and their soils.* Oxford Forestry Memoir **23**.

DORFMAN, R. and DORFMAN, N. S. (eds.) 1972: *Economics of the environment.* New York: Norton.

DORN, H. F. 1965: Pitfalls in population forecasts and projections. In I. Burton and R. W. Kates (eds.), 21–37.

DORST, J. 1970: *Before nature dies.* London: Collins.

DOWNS, J. F. and EKVALL, R. B. 1965: Animals and social types in the exploitation of the Tibetan plateau. In A. Leeds and A. P. Vayda (eds.), 169–84.

DUBOS, R. 1967: *Man adapting.* New Haven and London: Yale University Press.

DUCKHAM, A. N. and MASEFIELD, G. B. 1970: *Farming systems of the world.* London: Chatto and Windus.

DUFFEY, E. (ed.) 1967: *The biotic effects of public pressure on the environment.* Monk's Wood Experimental Station Symposium 3. Great Britain: The Nature Conservancy.

DUFFEY, E. and WATT, A. S. (eds.) 1971: *The scientific management of animal and plant communities for conservation.* Oxford: Blackwell.

DUNN, F. L. 1968: Epidemiological factors: health and disease in hunter-gatherers. In R. B. Lee and I. De Vore (eds.), 1968a, 221–8.

DURAND, J. D. 1967: The modern expansion of world population. *Proc. Amer. Philos. Soc.* **111**, 136–59.

DUVIGNÉAUD, P. (ed.) 1971: *Productivity of forest ecosystems.* Paris: UNESCO.

DUVIGNÉAUD, P. and DENAEYER-DE SMET, S. 1970: Biological cycling of minerals in temperate deciduous forests. In D. Reichle (ed.), 199–229.

DWYER, D. J. 1958: Utilization of the Irish peat bogs. *Geogr. Rev.* **48**, 572–3.

EASTLUND, B. J. and GOUGH, W. C. 1969: *The fusion torch. Closing the cycle from use to re-use.* Washington, DC: US Atomic Energy Commission.

EGGELING, W. J. 1964: A nature reserve management plan for the island of Rhum, Inner Hebrides. *J. Appl. Ecol.* **1**, 405–19.

EGLER, F. E. 1970: *The way of science: a philosophy of ecology for the layman.* New York: Hafner.

EHRENFELD, D. W. 1970: *Biological conservation.* New York: Holt, Rinehart and Winston.

EHRLICH, P. 1968: *The population bomb.* New York: Ballantine.

— 1971: Ecocatastrophe! In J. Barr (ed.), 205–13.

EHRLICH, P. and EHRLICH, A. 1970: *Population resources environment. Issues in human ecology.* 2nd edn. San Francisco: Freeman.

EHRLICH, P. and HARRIMAN, R. L. 1971: *How to be a survivor.* New York: Ballantine/Friends of the Earth.

EHRLICH, P. and HOLDREN, J. P. 1969: Population and panaceas: a technological perspective. *Bioscience* **19**, 1065–71.

— 1971: Impact of population growth. *Science* **171**, 1212–17.

EHRLICH, P., HOLDREN, J. P. and HOLM, R. W. (eds.) 1971: *Man and the ecosphere.* San Francisco: Freeman.

ELLUL, J. 1964: *The technological society.* New York: Vintage Books.

ELTON, C. S. 1958: *The ecology of invasions by animals and plants.* London: Methuen.

— 1966: *The pattern of animal communities.* London: Methuen.

ENGLAND, R. E. and DE VOS, A. 1969: Influence of animals on pristine conditions in the Canadian grasslands. *J. Range Management* **22**, 87–93.

EYRE, S. R. 1971: Population, production and pessimism. In *Presidential addresses delivered at the Swansea meeting, 1971,* British Association for the Advancement of Science.

FAIR, G. M. 1961: Pollution abatement in the Ruhr district. In H. Jarrett (ed.), 171–89.

FARIS, G. T. M. A. 1966: *A contribution to the economic geography of present day forestry and forest products in the Sudan.* University of Durham, MA thesis.

FARMER, B. H. 1969: Available food supplies. In J. Hutchinson (ed.). 75–95.

FIMREITE, N. 1970: Mercury uses in Canada and their possible hazardous sources of mercury contamination. *Env. Polln.* **1**, 119–31.

FIREY, W. J. 1960: *Man, mind and land.* Glencoe, Illinois: Free Press.

FISHER, J., SIMON, N. and VINCENT, J. 1969: *Wildlife in danger.* London: Collins.

FITTER, R. S. R. 1963: *Wildlife in Britain.* Harmondsworth: Pelican.

FLAWN, P. 1966: *Mineral resources.* Chicago: Rand McNally.

FOOD AND AGRICULTURE ORGANIZATION (annually): *Yearbook of fishery statistics.* Rome: FAO.

— (annually): *Yearbook of forest products.* Rome: FAO.

— (annually): *Production Yearbook.* Rome: FAO.

— 1953: *Grazing and forest economy.* Rome: FAO.

— 1963: *World forest inventory.* Rome: FAO.

— 1967: *Wood: world trends and prospects.* Rome: FAO.

— 1970: *Indicative world plan for agriculture,* 2 vols. Rome: FAO.

FORD, E. D. 1971: The potential production of forest crops. In P. F. Wareing and J. P. Cooper (eds.). 172–85.

FORRESTER, J. 1971: *World dynamics.* Cambridge: Wright-Allen Press.

FRANKEL, O. 1969: Genetic dangers in the green revolution. *Ceres* **2** (5), 35–7.

FRASER DARLING, F. 1955: Pastoralism in relation to the populations of men and animals. In N. Pirie and J. B. Cragg (eds.), 121–8.

— 1956: Man's ecological dominance through domesticated animals on wild lands. In W. L. Thomas (ed.), 778–87.

— 1960: Wildlife husbandry in Africa. *Sci. Amer.* **203** (5), 123–34.

— 1963: The unity of ecology. *Advmt. Sci.* **20**, 297–306.

FRASER DARLING, F. and EICHORN, N. 1967: *Man and nature in the National Parks: reflections on policy.* Washington, DC: Double Dot Press for the Conservation Foundation.

FRASER DARLING, F. and FARVAR, M. A. 1972: Ecological consequences of sedentarization of nomads. In M. Taghi Farvar and J. P. Milton (eds.), 671–82.

FRASER DARLING, F. and MILTON, J. P. (eds.) 1966: *Future environments of North America.* New York: Natural History Press.

FREJKA, T. 1973: The prospects for a stationary world population. *Sci. Amer.* **228** (3), 15–23.

FREMLIN, J. H. 1964: How many people can the world support? *New Sci.* **24**, 285–7.

FROME, M. 1962: *Whose woods these are.* New York: Natural History Press.

FULLER, W. A. and KEVAN, P. G. 1970: *Productivity and conservation in northern circumpolar lands.* IUCN Pubs. New Series **16**. Morges: IUCN.

GABOR, D. 1963: *Inventing the future.* Harmondsworth: Pelican.

GALBRAITH, J. K. 1967: *The new industrial state.* Boston: Houghton Mifflin.

GALSTON, A. 1971: Crops without chemicals. *New Sci.* **50**, 577–9.

GAMBELL, R. 1972: Why all the fuss about whales? *New Sci.* **54**, 674–6.

GARVEY, G. 1972: *Energy, ecology, economy.* New York: Norton.

GATES, D. M. 1971: The flow of energy in the biosphere. *Sci. Amer.* **224** (3), 88–100.

GEERTZ, C. 1963: *Agricultural involution: the processes of ecological change in Indonesia.* Berkeley and Los Angeles: University of California Press.

GEORGE, C. J. 1972: The role of the Aswan High Dam in changing the fisheries of the southeastern Mediterranean. In M. Taghi Farvar and J. P. Milton (eds.), 159–78.

GERASIMOV, I. P., ARMAND, D. L. and YEFRON, K. M. (eds) 1971: *Natural resources of the Soviet Union: their use and renewal.* San Francisco: Freeman.

GIBBENS, R. P. and HEADY, H. F. 1964: *The influence of modern man on the vegetation of Yosemite Valley.* Berkeley: University of California Agricultural Experiment Station Manual **36**.

GLACKEN, C. J. 1967: *Traces on the Rhodian shore.* Berkeley and Los Angeles: University of California Press.

GOLDMAN, M. I. 1971: Environmental disruption in the Soviet Union. In T. R. Detwyler (ed.), 61–75.

GOLDSMITH, E., ALLEN, D. *et al.* 1972: Blueprint for survival. *The Ecologist* **2** (1), 2–43. Reprinted 1973, Harmondsworth: Pelican.

GORDEN, M. and GORDEN, M. (eds.) 1972: *Environmental management*. Boston: Allyn and Bacon.

GORDON, J. 1970: Nuclear power production and problems in the disposal of atomic wastes. In A. J. Van Tassel (ed.), 135–64.

GOUROU, P. 1966: *The tropical world*. 4th edn. London: Wiley.

GOYER, R. A. and CHISHOLM, J. J. 1972: Lead. In D. H. K. Lee (ed.), 57–95.

GREENWOOD, N. and EDWARDS, J. M. B. 1973: *Human environments and natural systems*. North Scituate, Mass.: Duxbury Press.

GREGORY, D. P. 1973: The hydrogen economy. *Sci. Amer.* **228** (1), 13–21.

GREGORY, R. 1971: *The price of amenity*. London: Macmillan.

GRIGG, J. 1970: *The harsh lands*. London: Macmillan

GULLAND, J. A. 1970: The development of the resources of the Antarctic seas. In M. W. Holdgate (ed.), Vol. 1, 217–23.

GWYNNE, P. 1972: Nuclear power goes to sea. *New Sci.* **55**, 474–6.

HAAGEN-SMIT, A. J. and WAYNE, L. G. 1968: Atmospheric reactions and scavenging processes. In A. C. Stern (ed.), Vol. 1, 149–86.

HABAKKUK, H. J. 1972: *Population growth and economic development since 1750*. Leicester: Leicester University Press.

HADEN-GUEST, S. (ed.) 1956: *A world geography of forest resources*. American Geographical Society Special Pub. **33**. New York: Ronald Press.

HAMMOND, A. L., METZ, W. D. and MAUGH, T. H. 1973: *Energy and the future*. Washington, DC: AAAS.

HANSON, W. C. 1967a: Radioecological concentration processes characterizing Arctic ecosystems. In B. Aberg and F. P. Hungate (eds.), 183–91.

— 1967b: Caesium-137 in Alaskan lichens, caribou and eskimos. *Health Physics* **13**, 383–9.

HARDIN, G. 1959: Interstellar migration and the population problem. *J. Hered.* **50**, 68–70.

— 1968: The tragedy of the commons. *Science* **162**, 1243–8.

— (ed.) 1969: *Population, evolution and birth control*. 2nd edn. San Francisco: Freeman.

— 1973: *Exploring: new ethics for survival. The voyage of the spaceship Beagle*. Harmondsworth: Penguin.

HARRAR, J. G. and WORTMAN, S. 1969: Expanding food production in hungry nations: the promise, the problems. In C. M. Hardin (ed.), *Overcoming world hunger*. The American Assembly, 1969. New York: Prentice-Hall, 89–135.

HARRISS, R. C. 1971: Ecological implications of mercury pollution in aquatic systems. *Biol. Cons.* **3**, 279–83.

HARTE, J. A. and SOCOLOW, R. H. (eds.) 1971a: *The patient earth*. New York: Holt, Rinehart and Winston.

HARTE, J. A. and SOCOLOW, R. H. 1971b: The Everglades: wilderness versus rampant land development in south Florida. In J. A. Harte and R. H. Socolow (eds.), 181–202.

HAUSLE, E. A. 1972: Potential economic values of weather modification on Great Plains grasslands. *J. Range Management* **25**, 92–5.

HAWKES, A. L. 1961: A review of the nature and extent of damage caused by oil pollution at sea. *Trans 26th North American Wildlife Conference*, 343–55.

HEADY, H. F. 1972: Ecological consequences of Bedouin settlement in Saudi Arabia. In M. Taghi Farvar and J. P. Milton (eds.), 683–93.

HEALY, J. H. 1968: The Denver earthquakes. *Science* **161**, 1301–8.

HEATHERTON, T. (ed.) 1965: *Antarctica*. London: Methuen for the New Zealand Antarctic Society.

HEDGPETH, J. W. 1972: Atomic waste disposal in the sea: an ecological dilemma? In M. Taghi Farvar and J. P. Milton (eds.), 812–28.

HELFRICH, H. W. (ed.) 1970: *The environmental crisis*. New Haven and London: Yale University Press.

HENDRICKS, S. B. 1969: Food from the land. In NAS/NRC, 65–85.

HERSH, S. M. 1968: *Chemical and biological warfare*. New York: Doubleday Anchor Books.

HETTENA, P. H. G. and SYER, G. N. (eds.) 1971: *Decade of decision*. London: Academic Press for the Conservation Society.

HICKLING, C. F. 1970: Estuarine fish farming. *Adv. Marine Biol.* **8**, 119–213.

HIJSZELER, C. C. W. J. 1957: Late-glacial human cultures in the Netherlands. *Geol. en Mijnbouw* **19**, 288–302.

HILL, A. R. 1972: Ecosystem stability and man: a research focus in biogeography. In W. P. Adams and F. M. Helleiner (eds.), 255–7.

HINRICHS, N. (ed.) 1971: *Population, environment and people*. New York: McGraw-Hill.

HODGES, L. 1973: *Environmental pollution*. New York: Holt, Rhinehart and Winston.

HOLDGATE, M. W. (ed.) 1970: *Antarctic ecology*. 2 vols. London and New York: Academic Press.

HOLDRIDGE, L. R. 1959: Ecological indications of the need for a new approach to tropical land use. *Econ. Bot.* **13**, 271–80.

HOLLING, C. S. 1969: Stability in ecological and social systems. In G. M. Woodwell and H. H. Smith (eds.), 128–41.

HOLM, L. G., WELDON, L. W. and BLACKBURN, R. D. 1969: Aquatic weeds. *Science* **166**, 699–709.

HOLT, S. J. 1971: The food resources of the ocean. In P. Ehrlich, J. P. Holdren and R. W. Holm (eds.), 84–96.

HOLZ, R. (ed.) 1973: *The surveillant science*. Boston: Houghton Mifflin.

HOOD, D. W. (ed.) 1971: *Impingement of man on the oceans*. New York: Wiley.

HOPKINS, W. H. and SINCLAIR, J. D. 1960: Watershed management in action in the Pacific southwest. *Proc. Soc. Amer. For.*, 184–6.

HORSFALL, J. G. 1970: The green revolution: agriculture in the face of the population explosion. In H. W. Helfrich (ed.)., 85–98.

HOULT, D. P. (ed.) 1969: *Oil on the sea*. New York and London: Plenum Press.

HOWARD, N. J. 1964: Introduced browsing animals and habitat stability in New Zealand. *J. Wildlife Management* **28**, 421–9.

HUBBERT, M. KING 1962: *Energy resources: a report to the NAS/NRC*. Washington, DC: NAS/NRC Pubn. **1000D**.

—— 1969: Energy resources. In NAS/NRC, 157–242.

HUBBERT, M. KING 1971: The energy resources of the earth. *Sci. Amer.* **224** (3), 61–70.

HUNT, E. G. and BISCHOFF, A. I. 1960: Inimical effects on wildlife of periodic DDD applications to Clear Lake. *California Fish and Game* **46**, 91–106.

HUNT, G. M. 1956: The forest products industries of the world. In S. Haden-Guest (ed.), 83–111.

HUNTER, J. M. 1966: Ascertaining population carrying capacity under traditional systems of agriculture in developing countries: notes on a method employed in Ghana. *Prof. Geogr.* **18**, 151–4.

HURD, L. E., MELLINGER, M. V., WOLF, L. L. and McNAUGHTON, S. J. 1972: Stability and diversity at three trophic levels in terrestrial successional ecosystems. *Science* **173**, 1134–6.

HUTCHINSON, G. E. 1970: The biosphere. In *Scientific American* (ed.), 1–11.

HUTCHINSON, J. (ed.) 1969: *Population and food supply.* Cambridge: Cambridge University Press.

HUXLEY, J. S. 1961: *The conservation of wildlife and natural habitats in central and east Africa.* Paris: UNESCO.

ILLICH, I. D. 1974: *Energy and equity.* London: Calder and Boyars.

INSTITUTE OF CIVIL ENGINEERS 1963: *Conservation of water resources in the United Kingdom.* London: ICE.

INSTITUTE OF ECOLOGY 1972: *Man in his living environment.* Madison: University of Wisconsin Press.

INTERNATIONAL JOINT COMMISSION, CANADA AND THE USA 1970: *Pollution of Lake Erie, Lake Ontario and the international section of the St Lawrence River.* Ottawa: Information Canada.

INTERNATIONAL PLANNED PARENTHOOD FEDERATION (annually): *Family planning in five continents.* London: IPPF.

IRUKAYAMA, K. 1966: The pollution of Minamata Bay and Minamata disease. *Adv. Wat. Polln. Res.* **3**, 153–80.

IUCN 1969: *Red data book.* 2 vols. Morges: IUCN.

— 1970: *United Nations list of National Parks and equivalent reserves.* Brussels: Hayez.

JACOBSEN, T. and ADAMS, R. M. 1958: Salt and silt in ancient Mesopotamian agriculture. *Science* **128**, 1251–8.

JANICK, J. (ed.) 1970: *Plant Agriculture.* San Francisco: Freeman/*Scientific American.*

JARRETT, H. (ed.) 1961: *Comparisons in resource management.* Lincoln, Nebraska: Bison Books.

— 1966: *Environmental quality in a growing economy.* Baltimore: Johns Hopkins Press for RFF.

JENNY, H. 1961: Derivation of state factor equations of soils and ecosystems. *Soil Sci. Am. Proc.* **25**, 385–8.

JEWELL, P. A. 1969: Wild mammals and their potential for new domestications. In P. J. Ucko and G. W. Dimbleby (eds.), 101–9.

JOHNSON, P. L. 1971: Remote sensing as a tool for study and management of ecosystems. In E. P. Odum, 468–83.

KALININ G. P. and BYKOV, V. D. 1969: The world's water resources, present and future. *Impact of Science on Society* **19** (2), 135–50.

KARSCH, R. F. 1970: The social costs of surface mined coal. In A. J. Van Tassel (ed.), 269–90.

KASSAS, M. 1972: Impact of river control schemes on the shoreline of the Nile delta. In M. Taghi Farvar and J. P. Milton (eds.), 179–88.

KATES, R. W. 1962: *Hazard and choice perception in flood plain management.* Chicago: University of Chicago, Department of Geography Research Paper **78**.

KAY, D. A. and SKOLNIKOFF, E. B. 1972: *World eco-crisis: international organizations in response.* Madison: University of Wisconsin Press.

KEMP, W. B. 1970: The flow of energy in a hunting society. *Sci. Amer.* **224** (3), 104–15.

KLAPP, E. 1964: Features of a grassland theory. *J. Range Management* **17**, 309–22.

KLEIN, D. R. 1970: Tundra ranges north of the boreal forest. *J. Range Management* **23**, 8–14.

KNETSCH, J. and CLAWSON, M. 1967: *Economics of outdoor recreation.* Baltimore: Johns Hopkins Press for RFF.

KOK, L. T. 1972: Toxicity of insecticides used for Asiatic rice borer control to tropical fish in rice paddies. In M. Taghi Farvar and J. P. Milton (eds.), 489–98.

KOVDA, V. 1970: Contemporary scientific concepts relating to the biosphere. In UNESCO, 13–29.

KRUTILLA, J. V. (ed.) 1972: *Natural environments.* Baltimore: Johns Hopkins Press for RFF.

KUCERA, C. L., DAHLMANN, R. C. and KRELLING, M. R. 1967: Total net productivity and turnover on an energy basis for tall grass prairie. *Ecology* **48**, 536–41.

KUPCHANKO, E. E. 1970: Petrochemical waste disposal. In M. A. Ward (ed.), 53–65.

LACK, D. 1966: *Population studies of birds.* Oxford: Clarendon Press.

LADEJINSKY, W. 1970: Ironies of India's green revolution. *Foreign Affairs* **48**, 758–68.

LAGERWEFF, J. V. 1967: Heavy metal contamination of soils. In N. C. Brady (ed.), 343–364.

LAGLER, K. F. 1971: Ecological effects of hydroelectric dams. In D. A. Berkowitz and A. M. Squires (eds.), 133–57.

LAMBRECHT, F. L. 1972: The tsetse fly: a blessing or a curse? In M. Taghi Farvar and J. P. Milton (eds.), 726–41.

LAMORE, G. E. 1971: At last—a revolution that unites. In M. A. Strobbe (ed.), 126–32.

LANDAU, R. (ed.) 1968: *Air conservation.* Washington, DC: AAAS Publication **50**.

LANDSBERG, H. H. 1971: Energy consumption and optimum population. In S. F. Singer (ed.), 1971, 62–71.

LAUT, P. 1968: *Agricultural geography.* 2 vols. Sydney: Nelson.

LAWSON, P. D. and BRISBIN, K. J. 1970: Pollution from municipal sources. In M. A. Ward (ed.), 67–76.

LEE, D. H. K. (ed.) 1972: *Metallic contaminants and human health.* London and New York: Academic Press.

LEE, R. B. 1968: What hunters do for a living, or how to make out on scarce resources. In R. B. Lee and I. De Vore (eds.), 1968a, 30–43.

— 1969: !Kung Bushman subsistence: an input:output analysis. In A. P. Vayda (ed.), 47–49.

LEE, R. B. and DE VORE, I. (eds.) 1968a: *Man the hunter.* Chicago: Aldine Press.

— 1968b: Problems in the study of hunters and gatherers. In R. B. Lee and I. De Vore (eds.), 1968a, 3–12.

LEEDS, A. and VAYDA, A. P. (eds.) 1965: *Man, culture and animals.* Washington, DC: AAAS Publication **78**.

LEITH, H. 1965: Versuch einer kartographischen Darstellung der Productivitat der Pflanzendecke auf die Erde. *Geographisches Taschenbuch 1964/5*, 72–80.

— 1972: Modelling the primary productivity of the world. *Nature and Resources* **8** (2), 5–10.

LEOPOLD, A. 1949: *Sand County almanac.* New York: Oxford University Press.

LEOPOLD, A. S. 1963: Study of wildlife problems in National Parks. *Trans. 28th North American Wildlife Conference*, 28–45.

LEWALLEN, J. 1971: *Ecology of devastation: Indochina.* Baltimore: Penguin.

LEWIS, G. M. 1969: Range management viewed in the ecosystem framework. In G. M. Van Dyne (ed.), 97–187.

LEWIS, R. S. and SPINRAD, B. I. (eds.) 1972: *The energy crisis.* Chicago: Educational Foundation for Nuclear Science.

LEYHAUSEN, P. 1965: The sane community—a density problem? *Discovery* **26**, 27–33, 51.

LIKENS, G. E. and BORMANN, F. H. 1971: Mineral cycling in ecosystems. In J. A. Wiens (ed.), 25–67.

LINDEMANN, R. L. 1942: The trophic-dynamic aspect of ecology. *Ecology* **23**, 399–418.

LOFTAS, T. 1972: *The last resource.* Harmondsworth: Penguin.

LONGHURST, A., COLEBROOK, M., GULLAND, J., LE BRASSEUR, R., LORENZEN, C. and SMITH, P. 1972: The instability of ocean populations. *New Sci.* **54**, 500–502.

LOVERING, T. S. 1968: Non-fuel mineral resources in the next century. *Texas Quarterly* **11**, 127–47.

— 1969: Mineral resources from the land. In NAS/NRC, 109–34.

LOWE, V. P. W. 1971: Some effects of a change in estate management on a deer population. In E. Duffey and A. S. Watt (eds.), 437–56.

LUCAS, R. C. 1964: Wilderness perception and use: the example of the boundary waters canoe area. *Nat. Res. J.* **3**, 384–411.

— 1965: Recreational capacity of the Quetico-Superior area. St Paul, Minn.: US Forest Service Lakes States Research Paper **LS–15**.

LUTEN, D. B. 1971: The economic geography of energy. *Sci. Amer.* **224** (3), 165–75.

MACARTHUR, R. H. 1955: Fluctuations of animal populations, and a measure of community stability. *Ecology* **36**, 533–6.

MACDONALD, G. J. F. 1968: How to wreck the environment. In N. Calder (ed.), 191–213.

MACFADYEN, A. 1964: Energy flow in ecosystems and its exploitation by grazing. In D. J. Crisp (ed.), 3–20.

McGAUHEY, P. 1968: Earth's tolerance for wastes. *Texas Quarterly* **11**, 36–42.

McHALE, J. 1969: *The future of the future.* New York: Ballantine.

— 1972: *World facts and trends.* 2nd edn. New York: Macmillan.

MACINTOSH, N. A. 1970: Whales and krill in the twentieth century. In M. W. Holdgate (ed.), Vol. 1, 195–212.

MACINTYRE, F. and HOLMES, R. W. 1971: Ocean pollution. In W. W. Murdoch (ed.), 230–53.

MACNEILL, J. W. 1971: *Environmental management*. Ottawa: Information Canada.

MCVEAN, D. N. and LOCKIE, J. D. 1969: *Ecology and land use in upland Scotland*. Edinburgh: Edinburgh University Press.

MADDOX, J. 1972a: The case against hysteria. *Nature* **235**, 63–5.

— 1972b: *The doomsday syndrome*. London: Macmillan.

MARGALEF, R. 1968: *Perspectives in ecological theory*. Chicago: University of Chicago Press.

MARKS, P. L. and BORMANN, F. H. 1972: Revegetation following forest cutting: mechanisms for return to steady-state nutrient cycling. *Science* **176**, 914–15.

MARSH, G. P. 1864: *Man and nature, or Physical geography as modified by human action*. Reprinted 1965, Harvard: Belknap Press (D. Lowenthal, ed.).

MARTINELLI, W. 1964: *Watershed management in the Rocky Mountain alpine and subalpine zones*. Fort Collins, Colo.: US Forest Service Rocky Mountain Research Station Research Note **RM-36**.

MARX, W. 1967: *The frail ocean*. New York: Sierra Club/Ballantine.

— 1971: *Waste*. New York and London: Harper and Row.

MATELES, R. I., BARUAH, J. N. and TANNENBAUM, S. R. 1967: Growth of microbial cells on hydrocarbons: a new source of single cell protein. *Science* **157**, 1322–3.

MATELES, R. I. and TANNENBAUM, S. R. (eds.) 1968: *Single cell protein*. Cambridge, Mass.: MIT Press.

MEADOWS, D. H., MEADOWS, D. L., RANDERS, J. and BEHRENS, W. W. 1972: *The limits to growth*. London: Earth Island Press.

MEGGERS, B. J., AYENSU, E. S. and DUCKWORTH, W. D. (eds.) 1973: *Tropical forest ecosystems in Africa and South America: a comparative review*. Washington, DC: Smithsonian Institution Press.

MEIER, R. L. 1969: The social impact of a nuplex. *Bull. Atom. Sci.* **26**, 16–21.

MELLANBY, K. 1967: *Pesticides and pollution*. London: Collins.

METCALF, R. L. 1972: DDT substitutes. *CRC Critical Reviews in Environmental Control* **3** (1), 25–59.

MICKLIN, P. P. 1969: Soviet plans to reverse the flow of rivers: the Kama-Vychegda-Pechora project. *Canad. Geogr.* **13**, 199–215.

MIKOLA, P. 1970: Forests and forestry in subarctic regions. In UNESCO, *Ecology of the subarctic regions*. Paris: UNESCO, 295–302.

MILGRAM, S. 1970: The experience of living in cities. *Science* **167**, 1461–8.

MISHAN, E. J. 1967: *The costs of economic growth*. London: Staples Press.

— 1971: *Twenty-one popular economic fallacies*. Harmondsworth: Pelican.

MITCHELL, J. M. 1970: A preliminary evaluation of atmospheric pollution as a cause of the global temperature fluctuation of the past century. In S. F. Singer (ed.), 1970a, 139–55.

MOISEEV, P. A. 1970: Some aspects of the commercial use of the krill resources of the antarctic seas. In M. W. Holdgate (ed.), Vol. 1, 213–16.

MOLITOR, L. 1968: *Effects of noise on health*. Council of Europe Public Health Committee Report **CESP (68)**. Strasbourg: Council of Europe.

MONCRIEF, L. W. 1970: The cultural basis for our environmental crisis. *Science* **170**, 508–12.

'MONITOR' 1972: Power to the people from leaves of grass. *New Sci.* **55**, 228.

MONTAGUE, A. (ed.) 1962: *Culture and the evolution of man.* New York: Oxford University Press.

MONTEFIORE, H. 1970: *Can man survive?* London: Fontana.

MOORE, C. W. E. 1964: Distribution of grasslands. In C. Barnard (ed.), 185–205.

MOORE, N. W. 1967: A synopsis of the pesticide problem. *Adv. Ecol. Res.* **4**, 75–129.

— 1969: The significance of the persistent organochlorine insecticides and the polychlorinated biphenyls. *Biologist* **16**, 157–62.

MOORE, R. M. and BUDDISCOMBE, E. F. 1964: The effects of grazing on grasslands. In C. Barnard (ed.), 221–35.

MORE, R. J. 1969: The basin hydrological cycle. In R. J. Chorley (ed.), 65–76.

MORGAN, W. T. W. (ed.) 1972: *East Africa: its peoples and resources.* 2nd edn. Nairobi: Oxford University Press.

MORLEY, S. G. 1956: *The ancient Maya.* Stanford: Stanford University Press.

MURDOCH, W. W. (ed.) 1971: *Environment.* Stamford, Conn.: Sinauer.

MURDOCK, G. P. 1968: The current status of the world's hunting and gathering peoples. In R. B. Lee and I. De Vore (eds.), 1968a, 13–20.

MUROZUMI, M., CHOW, T. J. and PATTERSON, C. 1969: Chemical concentrations of pollutant lead aerosols, terrestrial dusts and sea salts in Greenland and Antarctic snow strata. *Geochimica et Cosmochimica Acta* **33**, 1247–94.

MURRA, J. V. 1965: Herds and herders in the Inca state. In A. Leeds and A. P. Vayda (eds.), 185–215.

MUSGROVE, P. J. and WILSON, A. D. 1970: Power without pollution. *New Sci.* **45**, 457–9.

NACE, R. L. 1969: Human use of ground water. In R. J. Chorley (ed.), 285–94.

NASH, C. E. 1970a: Marine fish farming. Part 1. *Marine Pollution Bull.* **1**, 5–6.

— 1970b: Marine fish farming. Part 2. *Marine Pollution Bull.* **1**, 28–30.

NASH, R. 1967: *Wilderness and the American mind.* New Haven: Yale University Press.

NAS/NRC 1969: *Resources and man.* London and San Francisco: Freeman.

NELSON, J. G. and SCACE, R. C. (eds.) 1969: *The Canadian National Parks: today and tomorrow.* Calgary: University of Calgary Studies in Land Use History and Landscape Change National Park Series **3**. 2 vols.

NELSON-SMITH, A. 1970: The problem of oil pollution of the sea. *Adv. Mar. Biol.* **8**, 215–306.

NEWBOULD, P. J. 1971a: Comparative production of ecosystems. In P. F. Wareing and J. P. Cooper (eds.), 228–38.

— 1971b: The cost of a good environment. In P. H. G. Hettena and G. N. Syer (eds.), 91–103.

NEW ZEALAND FOREST SERVICE 1970: *Conservation policy and practice.* Wellington: New Zealand Forest Service.

NG, L. K. Y. and MUDD, S. (eds.) 1965: *The population crisis.* Bloomington: Indiana University Press.

NGUYEN-VAN-HIEP, 1971: Rapport sur la situation de la conservation au Vietnam en 1969. In *The National Park Situation in S. Asia*, IUCN 11th Technical Meeting (New Delhi, 1969), IUCN Publications New Ser. **19**, Vol. 3. Morges: IUCN, 54–62.

NORTMAN, D. 1971: *Programmes de population et de planning familial: un tour d'horizon.* 2nd edn. New York: Population Council Bulletins de démographie et de planning familial **2**.

NOTESTEIN, F. W. 1970: Zero population growth: what is it? *Family Planning Perspectives* **2** (3), 20–24; reprinted in W. H. Davis (ed.), 1971, 107–11.

OBERLE, M. 1969: Forest fires: suppression policy has its drawbacks. *Science* **165**, 568–71.

O'CONNOR, F. B. 1964: Energy flow and population metabolism. *Sci. Progr.* **52**, 406–14.

ODUM, E. P. 1959: *Fundamentals of ecology*. 2nd edn. Philadelphia: Saunders.

— 1969: The strategy of ecosystem development. *Science* **164**, 262–70.

— 1971: *Fundamentals of ecology*. 3rd edn. Philadelphia: Saunders.

ODUM, E. P. and ODUM, H. T. 1972: Natural areas as necessary components of man's total environment. *Trans. 37th North American Wildlife and Natural Resources Conference*, 178–89.

ODUM, H. T. 1957: Trophic structure and productivity of Silver Springs, Florida. *Ecol. Monog.* **27**, 55–112.

— 1971: *Environment, power and society*. London and New York: Wiley.

OECD 1970: *Scientific fundamentals of the eutrophication of lakes and flowing waters, with particular reference to nitrogen and phosphorus as factors in eutrophication.* Prepared by A. Vollenweider. Paris: OECD.

OORT, A. H. 1970: The energy cycle of the earth. In *Scientific American* (ed.), 13–23.

OPENSHAW, K. 1974: Wood fuels the developing world. *New Sci.* **61**, 271–2.

ORIANS, G. H. and PFEIFFER, E. W. 1970: Ecological effects of the war in Vietnam. *Science* **168**, 544–54.

O'RIORDAN, T. 1971a: Environmental management. In C. Board *et al.* (eds.), 173–231.

— 1971b: *Perspectives on resource management*. London: Pion Press.

O'RIORDAN, T. and MORE, R. J. 1969: Choice in water use. In R. J. Chorley (ed.), 547–73.

ORRRC 1962a: *Recreation for America*. Washington, DC: US Government Printing Office.

— 1962b: *Report 23, Projections to the Years 1976 and 2000*. Washington DC: US Government Printing Office.

OTHMER, D. F. and ROELS, O. A. 1973: Power, fresh water, and food from cold, deep sea water. *Science* **182**, 121–5.

OVINGTON, J. D. 1957: Dry matter production by *Pinus sylvestris* L. *Ann. Bot.* **21**, 287–314.

— 1962: Quantitative ecology and the woodland ecosystem concept. *Adv. Ecol. Res.* **1**, 103–92.

— 1965: *Woodlands*. London: English Universities Press.

OVINGTON, J. D., HEITKAMP, D. and LAWRENCE, D. B. 1963: Plant biomass and productivity of prairie grassland, savanna, oakwood and maize field ecosystems in central Minnesota. *Ecology* **44**, 52–63.

PADDOCK, W. C. 1971: Agriculture as a force in determining the United States' optimum population size. In S. F. Singer (ed.), 1971, 89–95.

PADDOCK, W. C. and PADDOCK, M. 1967: *Famine 1975!* Boston: Little, Brown.

PAINE, R. T. 1969: A note on trophic complexity and community stability. *Amer. Nat.* **103**, 91–3.

PARKER, B. C. (ed.) 1972: *Conservation problems in Antarctica*. Blacksburg, Va.: Virginia Polytechnic.

PARKER, I. S. C. and GRAHAM, A. D. 1971: The ecological and economic basis for game ranching in Africa. In E. Duffey and A. S. Watt (eds.), 393–404.

PARSONS, J. 1971: *Population versus liberty*. London: Pemberton Books.

PATMORE, J. A. 1971: *Land and leisure in England and Wales*. Newton Abbott: David and Charles.

PAYNE, P. and WHEELER, E. 1971: What protein gap? *New Sci.* **50**, 148–50.

PEACH, W. N. and CONSTANTIN, J. A. 1972: *Zimmermann's World Resources and Industries*. 3rd edn. London: Harper and Row.

PEARSALL, W. H. 1957: *Report on an ecological survey of the Serengeti National Park, Tanganyika, November and December 1956*. London: Fauna Preservation Society.

PEARSON, F. A. and HARPER, F. A. 1945: *The world's hunger*. Cornell: Cornell University Press.

PETERSON, W. 1969: *Population*. 2nd edn. London: Macmillan.

PIGOTT, C. D. 1956: The vegetation of Upper Teesdale in the North Pennines. *J. Ecol.* **44**, 545–86.

PIPER, A. M. 1965: *Has the US enough water?* US Geological Survey Water Supply Paper **1797**. Washington, DC: US Government Printing Office.

PIRIE, N. and CRAGG, J. B. (eds.) 1955: *The numbers of men and animals*. Inst. Biol. Symp. **4**. Edinburgh and London: Oliver and Boyd.

PIRIE, N. W. 1969: *Food resources: conventional and novel*. Harmondsworth: Penguin.

— 1970: Orthodox and unorthodox methods of meeting world food needs. In J. Janick (ed.), 223–31.

— (ed.) 1971: Leaf protein: its agronomy, preparation, quality and use. *IBP Handbook* **20**. Oxford: Blackwell.

POLSTER, H. 1961: *Neuere Ergebnisse auf dem Gebiet der Standortsokologischen Assimilations- und Transpirations Forschung an Forstgewechse*. Berlin: Sitzber. Deut. Akad. Landwirtschaftwiss. **10**, 1.

POMEROY, L. R. 1970: The strategy of mineral cycling. *Ann. Rev. Ecology and Systematics* **1**, 171–90.

POPULATION REFERENCE BUREAU (annually): *World population data sheet*. New York: PRB.

PRICKETT, C. N. 1963: Use of water in agriculture. In Institute of Civil Engineers, 15–29.

PRIESTLEY, J. B. and HAWKES, J. 1955: *Journey down a rainbow*. London: Cressett Press.

PROVINCE OF ALBERTA 1968: *Water diversion proposals of North America*. Edmonton: Department of Agriculture Water Resources Division.

— 1969: *Prime: Alberta's blueprint for water development*. Edmonton: Department of Agriculture Water Resources Division.

PRYDE, P. R. 1972: *Conservation in the Soviet Union*. Cambridge: Cambridge University Press.

PUGH, N. J. 1963: Water supply. In Institute of Civil Engineers, 9–14.

PYKE, M. 1970a: *Man and food*. London: Weidenfeld and Nicolson.

— 1970b: *Synthetic food*. London: Murray.

— 1971: Novel sources of energy and protein. In P. F. Wareing and J. P. Cooper (eds.), 202–12.

RANDERSON, P. F. and BURDEN, R. F. 1972: Quantitative studies of the effect of human trampling on vegetation as an aid to the management of semi-natural areas. *J. Appl. Ecol.* **9**, 439–57.

RAPPAPORT, R. A. 1971: The flow of energy in an agricultural society. *Sci. Amer.* **224** (3), 116–32.

READER'S DIGEST PUBLICATIONS 1970: *The living world of animals.* London: Reader's Digest Assn.

REED, C. A. 1969: The pattern of animal domestication in the prehistoric Near East. In P. J. Ucko and G. W. Dimbleby (eds.), 361–80.

REED, T. B. and LERNER, R. M. 1973: Methanol: a versatile fuel for immediate use. *Science* **182**, 1299–1304.

REICH, C. 1971: *The greening of America.* Harmondsworth: Penguin.

REICHLE, D. (ed.) 1970: *Analysis of temperate forest ecosystems.* London: Chapman and Hall.

RENNIE, P. J. 1955: The uptake of nutrients by mature forest growth. *Plant and Soil* **7**, 49–95.

REVELLE, R. 1967: Outdoor recreation in a hyper-productive society. *Daedalus* **96**, 1172–91.

REVELLE, R., KHOSLA, A. and VINOVSKIS, M. (eds.) 1971: *The survival equation: man, resources and his environment.* Boston: Houghton Mifflin.

REX, R. W. 1971: Geothermal energy—the neglected energy option. *Bull. Atom. Sci.* **27** (8), 52–6.

RICHARDS, P. 1952: *The tropical rain forest.* Cambridge: Cambridge University Press.

RICHARDSON, S. D. 1971: The end of forestry in Great Britain. *Advmt Sci.* **27**, 153–63.

RICKER, W. 1969: Food from the sea. In NAS/NRC, 87–108.

RIDKER, R. G. 1972: Population and pollution in the United States. *Science* **176**, 1085–90.

— 1973: To grow or not to grow: that's not the relevant question. *Science* **182**, 1315–18.

ROBERTS, B. 1965: Wildlife conservation in the Antarctic. *Oryx* **8**, 237–44.

RODIN, L. E. and BAZILEVIC, N. I. 1966: The biological production of the main vegetation types in the northern hemisphere of the old world. *For. Abstr.* **27**, 369–72.

ROGERS, F. C. 1971: Underground power plants. *Bull. Atom. Sci.* **27** (8), 38–41, 51.

ROHMER, R. 1973: *The arctic imperative.* Toronto: McClelland and Stewart.

ROTHE, J. P. 1968: Fill a dam, start an earthquake. *New Sci.* **39**, 75–8.

RUBINOFF, I. 1968: Central American sea-level canal: possible biological effects. *Science* **161**, 857–61.

RUDD, R. L. 1963: *Pesticides and the living landscape.* Madison: University of Wisconsin Press.

RUSSELL, C. S. and LANDSBERG, H. H. 1971: International environmental problems—a taxonomy. *Science* **172**, 1307–14.

RYTHER, J. 1969: Photosynthesis and fish production in the sea. *Science* **166**, 72–6.

SAARINEN, T. F. 1966: *Perception of the drought hazard on the Great Plains.* Chicago: University of Chicago Department of Geography Research Papers **106**.

— 1969: *Perception of environment.* Washington, DC: AAG Resource Paper **5**.

SABLOFF, J. A. 1971: The collapse of classic Maya civilization. In J. A. Harte and R. H. Socolow (eds.), 16–27.

SAGE, B. L. 1970: Oil and Alaskan ecology. *New Sci.* **46**, 175–7.

SAN PIETRO, A., GREER, F. and ARMY, T. J. (eds.) 1967: *Harvesting the sun*. London and New York: Academic Press.

SARGENT, F. 1969: A dangerous game: taming the weather. In G. W. Cox (ed.), 569–82.

SASKATCHEWAN-NELSON BASIN BOARD 1972: *Water supply for the Saskatchewan-Nelson Basin: a summary report*. Ottawa: Information Canada.

SASSI, T. 1970: The harmful side effects of pesticide use. In A. J. Van Tassel (ed.), 361–95.

SATER, J. E., RONHOVE, A. G. and VAN ALLEN, L. C. 1972: *Arctic environments and resources*. Washington, DC: Arctic Institute of North America.

SAUER, C. O. 1952: *Agricultural origins and dispersals*. New York: American Geographical Society (reprinted 1969, MIT Press).

— 1961: Fire and early man. *Paideuma* 7, 399–407; reprinted in J. Leighley (ed.), 1963, *Land and life*. Berkeley and Los Angeles: University of California Press, 288–99.

SAWYER, C. N. 1966: Basic concepts of eutrophication. *J. Wat. Polln. Control Fedn.* **38**, 737–44.

SCHAEFER, V. J. 1970: The inadvertent modification of the atmosphere by air pollution. In S. F. Singer (ED.), 1970a, 158–74.

SCHEIDER, E. V. 1962: The meaning of leisure in an industrial society. In *Recreation in wildland management*, University of California Extra-mural Forestry Field School report. Berkeley: University of California School of Forestry.

SCHUBERT, J. and LAPP, R. E. 1957: *Radiation*. New York: Viking Press.

SCHULTZ, A. M. 1964: The nutrient-recovery hypothesis for arctic microtine cycles. 2: Ecosystem variables in relation to arctic microtine cycles. In D. J. Crisp (ed.), 57–68.

— 1967: The ecosystem as a conceptual tool in the management of natural resources. In S. V. Ciriacy Wantrup and J. J. Parsons (eds.), 139–61.

SCHURR, S. H. (ed.) 1972: *Energy, economic growth and the environment*. Baltimore: Johns Hopkins Press for RFF.

'SCIENTIFIC AMERICAN' (ed.) 1970: *The biosphere*. San Francisco and London: Freeman.

SCOTTER, G. W. 1970: Reindeer husbandry as a land use in northern Canada. In W. A. Fuller and P. G. Kevan (eds.), 159–69.

SCRIMSHAW, N. 1970: Food. In J. Janick (ed.), 206–14.

SEARS, P. B. 1956: The importance of forests to man. In S. Haden-Guest (ed.), 3–12.

SEHLIN, H. 1966: The importance of open-air recreation. In *First International Congress on Leisure and Tourism*, Theme **1**, Report **1**. Rotterdam: Alliance Internationale de Tourisme.

SEMPLE, A. T. 1971: Grassland improvement in Africa. *Biol. Cons.* **3**, 173–80.

SENGE, T. 1969: The planning of national parks in Japan and other parts of Asia. In J. G. Nelson and R. C. Scace (eds.), 706–21.

SEWELL, W. R. D. and BURTON, I. 1971: *Perceptions and attitudes in resource management*. Canadian Department of Energy, Mines and Resources Resource Paper **2**. Ottawa: Information Canada.

SHACKLADY, C. A. 1969: The production and evaluation of protein derived from organisms grown on hydrocarbon residues. *Proc. Nutrition Soc.* **28**, 91–7.

SHAPLEY, D. 1973: Sorghum: 'miracle' grain for the world protein shortage. *Science* **182**, 147–8.

SHELL OIL COMPANY 1972: *The national energy position.* (?) Houston: Shell Oil Co.

SHEPARD, P. and MCKINLEY, D. 1971: *Environ/mental: essays on the planet as a home.* Boston: Houghton Mifflin.

SIMMONS, I. G. 1966: Wilderness in the mid-20th century USA. *Town Planning Rev.* **36**, 249–56.

— 1967: How do we plan for change? *Landscape* **17**, 22–4.

— 1971: *Sequoia sempervirens*: conflicts over conservation. *Advmt. Sci.* **27**, 301–3.

— 1973: The protection of ecosystems and landscapes in Hokkaido, Japan. *Biol. Cons.* **5**, 281–9.

SIMONS, M. 1969: Long term trends in water use. In R. J. Chorley (ed.), 535–44.

SINDEN, J. A. and SINDEN, L. B. 1964: A forest recreation survey: implications for future development. *Scottish Forestry* **18**, 120–27.

SINGER, S. F. (ed.) 1970a: *Global effects of environmental pollution.* Dordrecht: Reidel.

— 1970b: Human energy production as a process in the biosphere. In Scientific American (ed.), 105–13.

— (ed.) 1971: *Is there an optimum level of population?* New York: McGraw-Hill.

SMITH, K. 1972: *Water in Britain.* London: Macmillan.

SOLOMON, M. E. 1969: *Population dynamics.* London: Edward Arnold.

SONNENFELD, J. 1966: Variable values in space landscape: an enquiry into the nature of environmental necessity. *J. Social Issues* **22**, 71–82.

SPENCER, J. E. 1966: *Shifting cultivation in SE Asia.* Berkeley and Los Angeles: University of California Press.

SPILHAUS, A. 1972: Ecolibrium. *Science* **175**, 711–15.

STAATSBOSBEHEER (NETHERLANDS) 1966: *The task of the State Forest Service in the Netherlands.* Utrecht: SBB.

STAMP, L. D. 1969: *Nature conservation in Britain.* London: Collins.

STARK, N. 1972: Nutrient cycling pathways and litter fungi. *Bioscience* **22**, 355–60.

STATHAM, D. C. 1971: Development of the Yorkshire potash industry. *Town Planning Rev.* **42**, 361–76.

STERN, A. C. (ed.) 1968: *Air pollution.* 2 vols. 2nd edn. London and New York: Academic Press.

STEWART, C. M. 1970: Family limitation programmes in various countries. In A. Allison (ed.), 204–21.

STODDART, D. R. 1968: The Aldabra affair. *Biol. Cons.* **1**, 63–70.

STODDART, D. R. and WRIGHT, C. A. 1967: Ecology of Aldabra atoll. *Nature, Lond.* **213**, 1173–7.

STOTT, D. H. 1962: Checks on population growth. In A. Montague (ed.), 355–76.

STREETER, D. C. 1971: The effects of public pressure on the vegetation of chalk downland at Box Hill, Surrey. In E. Duffey and A. S. Watt (eds.), 459–68.

STROBBE, M. A. (ed.) 1971: *Understanding environmental pollution.* St Louis: Mosby.

STUDY OF CRITICAL ENVIRONMENTAL PROBLEMS 1970: *Man's impact on the global environment: assessment and recommendation for action.* Cambridge, Mass.: MIT Press.

STUDY OF MAN'S IMPACT ON CLIMATE 1971: *Inadvertent climate modification.* Cambridge, Mass.: MIT Press.

SUMMERS, C. 1971: The conversion of energy. *Sci. Amer.* **224** (3), 149–60.

SWANK, W. G. 1972: Wildlife management in Masailand, east Africa. *Trans. 37th North American Wildlife and Natural Resources Conference*, 278–87.

SWEET, L. E. 1965: Camel pastoralism in N. Arabia and the minimal camping unit. In A. Leeds and A. P. Vayda (eds.), 129–52.

TAGHI FARVAR, M. and MILTON, J. P. (eds.) 1972: *The careless technology: ecology and international development.* New York: Natural History Press.

TAIGANIDES, E. P. 1967: The animal waste disposal problem. In N. C. Brady (ed.), 385–394.

TALBOT, L. M. 1966: *Wild animals as a source of food.* US Department of the Interior Bureau of Sport, Fisheries and Wildlife Special Scientific Report—Wildlife **98**. Washington, DC.

— 1972: Ecological consequences of rangeland development in Masailand, east Africa. In M. Taghi Farvar and J. P. Milton (eds.), 694–711.

TALBOT, L. M. and TALBOT, M. H. 1963: The high biomass of wild ungulates on east African savanna. *Trans. 28th North Amer. Wildlife Conf.*, 465–76.

— (eds.) 1968: *Conservation in tropical south east Asia.* IUCN Publications New Series **10**. Morges: IUCN.

TANSLEY, A. G. 1935: The use and abuse of vegetational concepts and terms. *Ecology* **16**, 284–307.

TATTON, J. O'G. and RUZICKA, J. H. A. 1967: Organochlorine pesticides in Antarctica. *Nature, Lond.* **215**, 346–8.

THOMAS, T. M. 1973: World energy sources: survey and review. *Geogr. Rev.* **63**, 246–58.

THOMAS, W. L. (ed.) 1956: *Man's role in changing the face of the earth.* Chicago: University of Chicago Press.

THORSTEINSSON, I., OLAFSSON, G. and VAN DYNE, G. M. 1971: Range resources of Iceland. *J. Range Management* **24**, 86–93.

TOYNBEE, A. 1972: The religious background of the present environmental crisis. *Int. J. Environ. Studs.* **3**, 141–6.

TREWARTHA, G. T. 1969: *A geography of population: world patterns.* London: Wiley.

TSCHIRLEY, F. H. 1969: Defoliation in Vietnam. *Science* **163**, 779–86.

TUAN, YI FU 1968: Discrepancies between environmental attitude and behaviour: examples from Europe and China. *Canad. Geogr.* **13**, 176–91.

TURNER, J. 1962: The *Tilia* decline: an anthropogenic interpretation. *New Phytol.* **61**, 328–41.

UCKO, P. J. and DIMBLEBY, G. W. (eds.) 1969: *The domestication and exploitation of plants and animals.* London: Duckworth.

UNESCO 1970: *Use and conservation of the biosphere.* Paris: UNESCO Natural Resources Research **X**.

UNGER, J. 1971: Profits from waste. *Far Eastern Economic Review* **73**, 51–2.

UNITED KINGDOM 1970: 'The Countryside in 1970', 3rd Conference, Report **4**: *Refuse disposal.* London: HMSO.

UNITED NATIONS (annually): *Demographic yearbook.* New York: UNO.

— (annually): *Statistical yearbook.* New York: UNO.

DEPARTMENT OF SOCIAL AFFAIRS 1953: *The determinants and consequences of population trends*. New York: UN Population Study **17**.

DEPARTMENT OF ECONOMIC AND SOCIAL AFFAIRS 1958: *The future growth of world population*. New York: UN Population Study **28**.

— 1964: *World population prospects as assessed in 1963*. New York: UN Population Study **41**.

US COMMISSION ON POPULATION GROWTH AND THE AMERICAN FUTURE 1972: *Population and the American future*. Washington, DC: US Government Printing Office/New York: New American Library.

US CONGRESS 1970: *Phosphates in detergents and the eutrophication of America's waters*. Washington, DC: House of Representatives Report **91–1004**.

US DEPARTMENT OF AGRICULTURE 1955: *Water*. Yearbook of agriculture 1955. Washington, DC: US Government Printing Office.

US DEPARTMENT OF THE INTERIOR 1967: *Surface mining and our environment*. Report of the Strip and Surface Mine Study Policy Committee. Washington, DC: US Government Printing Office.

US FEDERAL COUNCIL FOR SCIENCE AND TECHNOLOGY, COMMITTEE ON ENVIRONMENTAL QUALITY 1968: *Noise-sound without value*. Washington, DC: US Government Printing Office.

US GEOLOGICAL SURVEY 1970: *Mercury in the environment*. Washington, DC: USGS Professional Paper **713**.

US NATIONAL PARKS SERVICE 1967: *Administrative policies for natural areas of the National Park system*. Washington, DC: US Government Printing Office.

US PRESIDENT'S COUNCIL ON ENVIRONMENTAL QUALITY 1971: *Environmental quality 1971*. Washington, DC: US Government Printing Office.

US PRESIDENT'S COUNCIL ON RECREATION AND NATURAL BEAUTY 1968: *From sea to shining sea*. Washington, DC: US Government Printing Office.

US PRESIDENT'S SCIENCE ADVISORY COMMITTEE 1967a: Losses and protection of food. In *The world food problem*. Washington, DC: US Government Printing Office; abridged version reprinted in R. Revelle *et al.* (eds.), 257–72.

— 1967b: Agricultural-technical and resource opportunities. In *The world food problem*. Washington, DC: US Government Printing Office; abridged version reprinted in R. Revelle *et al.* (eds.), 242–9.

VALÉRY, N. 1974: The best substitute for petrol may be petrol. *New Sci.* **61**, 203–5.

VAN DER SCHALIE, H. 1972: WHO project Egypt 10: a case history of a schistosomiasis control project. In M. Taghi Farvar and J. P. Milton (eds.), 116–36.

VAN DYNE, G. M. (ed.) 1969: *The ecosystem concept in resource management*. London and New York: Academic Press.

VAN HYLCKAMA, T. E. A. 1971: Water resources. In W. W. Murdoch (ed.), 148–52.

VAN RENSBURG, H. J. 1969: *Management and utilization of pastures in east Africa (Kenya, Tanzania, Uganda)*. FAO Pasture and Fodder Crop Series **3**. Rome: FAO.

VAN TASSEL, A. J. (ed.) 1970: *Environmental side effects of rising industrial output*. Lexington, Mass.: Heath Lexington.

VAYDA, A. P. (ed.) 1969: *Environment and cultural behavior*. New York: Natural History Press.

VERNEY, R. B. 1972: *Sinews for survival: a report on the management of natural resources.* London: HMSO for the Department of the Environment.

VICKERY, P. J. 1972: Grazing and net primary production of a temperate grassland. *J. Appl. Ecol.* **9**, 307–14.

WADE, N. 1973: World food situation: pessimism comes back into vogue. *Science* **181**, 634–8.

WAGAR, J. A. 1970: Growth versus the quality of life. *Science* **168**, 1179–84.

WALFORD, L. A. 1958: *Living resources of the sea.* New York: Ronald Press.

WALKER, C. 1971: *Environmental pollution by chemicals.* London: Hutchinson.

WARD, B. and DUBOS, R. 1972: *Only one earth.* Harmondsworth: Penguin.

WARD, M. A. (ed.) 1970: *Man and his environment.* Part 1. Oxford: Pergamon Press.

WAREING, P. F. and COOPER, J. P. (eds.) 1971: *Potential crop production.* London: Heinemann.

WATER RESOURCES BOARD 1966: *Water supplies in SE England.* London: HMSO.

— 1969: *Planning our future water supply.* London: HMSO.

— 1970: *Water resources in the north.* London: HMSO.

WATT, K. E. F. 1965: Community stability and the strategy of biological control. *Canad. Entomol.* **97**, 887–95.

— 1968: *Ecology and resource management: a quantitative approach.* New York: McGraw-Hill.

— 1973: *Principles of environmental science.* New York: McGraw-Hill.

WATTERS, R. F. 1960: The nature of shifting cultivation: a review of recent research. *Pacific Viewpoint* **1**, 59–99.

WATTS, D. 1971: *Principles of biogeography.* London: McGraw-Hill.

WECK, J. and WIEBECKE, C. 1961: *Weltwirtschaft und Deutschlands Forst- und Holzwirtschaft.* Munich: Bayerischer Landwirtschaftsverlag.

WEINBERG, A. M. 1968: Raw materials unlimited. *Texas Quarterly* **11**, 92–102.

WEINBERG, A. M. and HAMMOND, R. P. 1971: Limits to the use of energy. In S. F. Singer (ed.), 42–56.

WEINER, N. 1950: *The human use of human beings.* Boston: Houghton Mifflin.

WEISZ, J. A. 1970: The environmental effects of surface mining and mineral waste generation. In A. J. Van Tassel (ed.), 291–312.

WEST, O. 1972: The ecological impact of the introduction of domestic cattle into wild life and tsetse areas of Rhodesia. In M. Taghi Farvar and J. P. Milton (eds.), 712–25.

WESTHOFF, V. 1970: New criteria for nature reserves. *New Sci.* **46**, 108–13.

WESTING, A. H. and PFEIFFER, E. W. 1972: The cratering of Indochina. *Sci. Amer.* **226** (5), 21–9.

WESTOBY, J. C. 1963: The role of forest industries in the attack on economic underdevelopment. *Unasylva* **16**, 168–201.

WHARTON, C. R. 1969: The green revolution: cornucopia or Pandora's box? *Foreign Affairs* (April), 464–76.

WHITE, G. F. (ed.) 1964: *Choice of adjustment to floods.* Chicago: University of Chicago Department of Geography Research Paper **93**.

— 1966: *Alternatives in water management.* Washington, DC: NAS/NRC Publication 1408.

WHITESIDE, T. 1970: *Defoliation.* New York: Ballantine/Friends of the Earth.

WIENS, J. A. (ed.) 1971: *Ecosystem structure and function*. Corvallis: Oregon State UP.

WILLARD, B. E. and MARR, J. W. 1970: Effects of human activities on alpine tundra ecosystems in Rocky Mountain National Park, Colorado. *Biol. Cons.* **2**, 257–65.

WILLIAMS, M. 1971: Lead pollution on trial. *New Sci.* **51**, 578–80.

WILLIAMS, W. A. 1966: Range improvement as related to net productivity, energy flow and foliage configuration. *J. Range Management* **19**, 29–34.

WOLFERS, D. 1971: The case against zero growth. *Intern. J. Env. Studs.* **1**, 227–32.

WOLLMAN, N. 1960: *A preliminary report on the supply of and demand for water in the US as estimated for 1980 and 2000*. Washington, DC: US Senate Select Committee on Water Resources 86th Congress 2nd Session, Committee Report **32**.

WOLMAN, A. 1965: The metabolism of cities. *Sci. Amer.* **218** (9), 179–90.

WOLMAN, M. G. 1971: The nation's rivers. *Science* **174**, 905–18.

WOODBURN, J. 1968: An introduction to Hadza ecology. In R. B. Lee and I. De Vore (eds.), 1968a, 49–55.

WOODIS, J. 1971: An introduction to neo-colonialism. In R. Revelle *et al.* (eds.), 303–12.

WOODWELL, G. M. 1963: The ecological effects of radiation. *Sci. Amer.* **208** (6), 2–11.

— 1967a: Toxic substances and ecological cycles. *Sci. Amer.* **216** (3), 24–31.

— 1967b: Radiation and the pattern of nature. *Science* **156**, 461–70.

— 1970a: The energy cycle of the biosphere. In *Scientific American* (ed.), 25–35.

— 1970b: Effects of pollution on the structure and physiology of ecosystems. *Science* **168**, 429–33.

WOODWELL, G. M., CRAIG, P. P. and JOHNSON, H. A. 1971: DDT in the biosphere: where does it go? *Science* **174**, 1101–7.

WOODWELL, G. M. and SMITH, H. H. (eds.) 1969: *Diversity and stability in ecological systems*. Upton, NY: Brookhaven Symp. Biol. **22**.

WOODWELL, G. M., WURSTER, C. F. and ISAACSON, P. A. 1967: DDT residues in an east coast estuary. *Science* **156**, 821–4.

WURSTER, C. F. 1968: DDT reduces photosynthesis by marine phytoplankton. *Science* **159**, 1474–5.

— 1969: Chlorinated hydrocarbon insecticides and the world ecosystem. *Biol. Cons.* **1**, 123–9.

WYNNE-EDWARDS, V. C. 1962: *Animal dispersal in relation to social behavior*. New York: Hafner.

YOUNG, G. 1973: *Tourism: blessing or blight?* Harmondsworth: Penguin.

ZELINSKY, W. 1966: *A prologue to population geography*. New York: Prentice-Hall.

— 1970: Beyond the exponentials: the role of geography in the great transition. *Econ. Geogr.* **46**, 498–535.

ZELINSKY, W., KOSINSKI, L. A. and PROTHERO, R. M. (eds.) 1970: *Geography and a crowding world*. New York: Oxford University Press.

ZELLER, E. J., SAUNDERS, D. F. and ANGINO, E. E. 1973: Putting radioactive wastes on ice: a proposal for an international radionuclide depository in Antarctica. *Bull. Atom. Sci.* **29** (1), 4–9, 50–52.

ZEUNER, F. E. 1964: *A history of domesticated animals*. London: Methuen.

ZOBELL, C. E. 1964: The occurrence, effects and fate of oil polluting the sea. *Adv. Water Polln. Res.* **3**, 85–109.

ZU LOWENSTEIN, H. 1969: The story of a sophisticated breed. *Ceres* **2** (1), 44–6.

Index

Prepared by Brenda Hall, MA, Registered Indexer of the Society of Indexers